One Priest's Wondering Beliefs

One Priest's Wondering Beliefs

*Progressive Christianity: A Critical
Review of Christian Doctrines*

John E. Bowers

RESOURCE *Publications* • Eugene, Oregon

ONE PRIEST'S WONDERING BELIEFS
Progressive Christianity: A Critical Review of Christian Doctrines

Copyright © 2016 John E. Bowers. All rights reserved. Except for brief quotations in critical publications or reviews, no part of this book may be reproduced in any manner without prior written permission from the publisher. Write: Permissions, Wipf and Stock Publishers, 199 W. 8th Ave., Suite 3, Eugene, OR 97401.

Resource Publications
An Imprint of Wipf and Stock Publishers
199 W. 8th Ave., Suite 3
Eugene, OR 97401

www.wipfandstock.com

PAPERBACK ISBN: 978-1-62032-265-9
HARDCOVER ISBN: 978-1-62032-929-0
EBOOK ISBN: 978-1-62032-271-0

Manufactured in the U.S.A.

This book is dedicated *in memoriam* of Dr. Fred Karaffa and of Nancy Burdick who were members of the group but died before this printing. And to the late Sr. Cintra Pemberton who caught me in my spiritual desert and showed me the beginnings of my pilgrimage.

Contents

Acknowledgments | ix

Introduction: How in the world did I get here? | xi

Part One

Chapter 1: The Foundation Stones of My Faith | 3
Chapter 2: The Stepstones of my Pilgrimage | 21
Chapter 3: My Circle of Standing Stones | 32

Part Two

Chapter 4: Sin Again, for One Last Time | 69
Chapter 5: Tell us about the God | 124
Chapter 6: What Think Ye of Jesus? | 160
Chapter 7: Thoughts about the Institutional Church | 178
Chapter 8: All Religion is Metaphor | 212
Chapter 9: Faith and Spirituality | 230
Chapter 10: Four Other Doctrinal Matters | 238
        The Authority of Scripture | 238
        Resurrection | 248
        Atonement Theology | 256
        Prayer | 261
Chapter 11: Where I Net Out | 269

Part Three

Chapter 12: Failed Values | 281
Chapter 13: The Vision: Communitarianism | 303

Bibliography | 337

Acknowledgments

FIRST THANKS ARE TO my Nancy for her understanding, forbearance, patience, endurance, and copy editting while I wrote these pages; my silence and absence were no fun for her. And then to the Rev. Susan Lehman, my friend across many decades, the first soul I found who could tolerate hearing what I was thinking and was so gracious as to share her own thoughts and help me begin sorting through mine. To Professor Ron Santoni PhD, who encouraged me to write this volume, and hung in thoughout the process; his corrections and skill were crucial for me. And then to Marilyn Boldon who has given not only support, but often acted nearly as an administrative assistant as I have produced initial materials. And finally to the Beyond Orthodoxy group of similarly searching members of St. Luke's Church in Granville, Ohio among whom I shared, and learned and discovered: Dr. Doug Boldon, M. D., Richard Warren, the Rev. Ed Burdick, Russ Potter, Susan Potter, Jo Helen De Pue, Margo Santoni, Jane Karaffa, Sue Black, Sara Jean Wilhelm, Sarah Schaff and Bob Karaffa (Dr. Santoni and Marilyn Boldon are also in this group). Finally, my thanks to the Rev. Canon James Hanisian, a friend who chatted with me over the last months, fine-lining each chapter, pointing to problems in the text, and giving approval even while disagreeing in some places. And to the Very Rev. Richard Ullman who advised and also confirmed that I am not the only retired priest whose beliefs are wandering. And to the Rev. Barry Cotter who helped shape the final form.

And my thanks to our rector, the Rev. Dr. Stephen Applegate, who puts up with us.

Introduction: How in the world did I get here?

4:47am on a Sunday morning in May, 2007: I awake in the dark hours of this morning from a particularly vivid dream. I've been sorting files in my office. It seemed only days before the moment of my retirement, and I was cleaning out, going through boxes and boxes of saved stuff (I'm a packrat of ideas). In one box, two bundles of paper napkins, neatly stacked together and bound up: notes of important things to remember from luncheons and conversations, from ruminations, from studies. But they are old, have not even been looked at for years, and really are not worth examining; they probably were not worth keeping. I tossed them. Ted Blumenstein, several years dead, came walking through the office, marveling at some of the stuff I was throwing away. Pictures, short articles, longer ones, chapters out of books, conversations, all sorts of stuff. Susan Lehman was there too, and other old, unidentified friends. Sometimes they were surprised at what all I kept and what I decided to throw away. In my daytime world I have this habit of making booklets of what I choose to garner and keep. And part of what I was doing in my dream was sorting through old collections and deciding what to keep, what was worth gluing together into a makeshift book to be put on my shelf as a referent.

And that is what these pages are about too, sorting through, and deciding what to keep, what is worth binding into my reference books (a relatively small collection), and what is worthy only of the dustbin.

This book is about where this retired and aging Episcopal priest finds himself wandering spiritually today. When I packed it in over sixteen years ago from being a professional churchman, an advocate of orthodox doctrine, within a few years I found myself wandering, theologically, spiritually, exploring. In my younger years I'd heard of priests who'd *lost their faith*. Now I was acting like one of those but, oddly enough, I didn't feel I was losing anything. I was questioning, challenging, looking in different directions. But I wasn't losing anything. Instead I seemed to be wandering into new places, thinking about things in new ways. My fields had broadened. And I felt I was gaining, growing. But I was also pretty sure my fellow clergy could not appreciate where I was wandering. This was not something I thought they'd want to hear from me. So mostly I kept my mouth shut about these things. I tried to broach the subject at lunch one day with my closest clergy friend, also retired. He remained stoically quiet, listened, but said not a word back. I did not venture the subject again. Nor did he. We let it lay right where it had plopped. But now is the time to raise the subject again.

INTRODUCTION: HOW IN THE WORLD DID I GET HERE?

I must lay out one disclaimer: I expect this volume to be ripped to shreds by theologians, philosophers, and professional churchmen as unscholarly and in many ways inaccurate, perhaps even sloppy thinking. But I'm not writing to them. I'm very clear with myself, and with you, that I am no scholar. You will see in these pages brief flourishes of what appear to be scholarly stuff. They are not. They are the remnants of the preacher's tools I'd accumulated over thirty years, bits and pieces of scholarly stuff I'd captured and stored away. They are useful pitons, but my work is not that of a scholar, but of a spiritual pilgrim. These pages will probably elicit a fair amount of wrath from fundamentalist and evangelical Christians, maybe even some mainline Christians. I am goring many oxen here. So if these pages anger you, just put the book away, I'm not writing to you either. The audience I am trying to reach is those Christians whose beliefs have started to grow beyond the orthodox hedge, who have begun to wonder and question and disagree, who have begun to think, "Hey, wait a minute . . . " But who feel alone or unfaithful in doing that.

To give you a context for these chapters I'll tell you how I got to this spiritual place. I did not set out to come here. It just happened. Naturally. No traumatic precipitant. Just a slow wandering, a searching, a groping for what might make sense where the old sense-making was unraveling. A seeking. Until I found myself here. If there were any goads I would identify two, both on the same day. On December 31, 1998 I retired from thirty-four years of active ministry in the Episcopal Church. At the modest retirement party the suffragan bishop made me a present of a book, Jack Miles's **God: a biography** which immediately found a resting place on my bookshelf and stayed there untouched for several years. Retired, I was no longer professionally required to stay within the bounds of conventional orthodox doctrine, and as I listened to preachers, I began to wonder (or, perhaps, wander). Several years later I finally picked Miles's book off my shelf. His conclusion was a bit startling, but sound. At St. Luke's Church I offered to teach Miles' book at the Sunday morning adult sessions. To teach something one must become fairly intimate with it, and I came away from those sessions quite shaken by Miles' book.

In hindsight, I actually had begun this pilgrim wandering many years before. Not quite a decade before retirement I was stumbling across increasingly frequent references to "Celtic Spirituality" and the "Celtic Christian Church," and had become curious. A few light books roused my anger that the first 800 Celtic years of my Anglican heritage had been suppressed and withheld from me. I explored, learning that the Western version I'd received as gospel was not the sole evolution of Christianity. Meanwhile my understandings of the Christianity I had been preaching were becoming less convincing to me. I reached out to those Celtic roots of the Anglican experience. I found Sr. Cintra Pemberton leading pilgrimages into Celtic lands (Wales, Scotland and Ireland) and eventually went on five different pilgrimages with her, learning about those different understandings and expressions of the Christian experience. And now

Introduction: How in the World did I get Here?

knowing there are other ways to be a Christian, I began to wander theologically, searching for understandings more sensible than those that had been fed to me. So by retirement time I was ready to wander even farther afield. It took several years to get started, but then, wander I did.

To tell the whole story would be long and cumbersome. There were several paths I wandered, and several pilgrims with whom I wandered. In Part One of this volume you can catch the flavor of those spiritual wanderings, and a few of the people and places. Those chapters are not terribly germane to the central effort of this volume, but the evolution of my faith is an important part of the pilgrimage, so I start by sharing some of that. Eventually I found a small group of pilgrims wandering their own similar paths and we have shared for three years now. That group has been helpful and comforting, a coterie of fellow pilgrims to walk strange new paths with. Our discussions have not only informed me, but clarified my thinking.

For the moment I have arrived at a resting place in this pilgrimage, a place where I can reflect, and sort through, and begin to piece together. I've done some of that now, so the time has come for me to share more widely. I tell out these thoughts, not because they are so wonderful that others ought to know about them, but because I suspect that many unknown others are also wanderers and wonderers who are no longer adequately filled up by what the church doles out as spiritual fodder. I unveil these thoughts in the hope that other wanderers will be encouraged in their wanderings and wonderings, and perhaps even be willing to risk sharing with a few others whatever wonders they see and hear and feel and think and wonder as they search out the God's way in the God's world.

I need to mention one piece that was perhaps most critically useful for me in my pilgrimage. Our associate pastor, a trained spiritual director, perhaps catching a whiff of some distress in me, offered to talk with me one day. I unburdened onto him where I was in my pilgrimage, and he loaned me a book I didn't really want, James Fowler's **Stages of Faith**. While the other books I've read prodded me along my pilgrimage, Fowler's book actually showed me the path I was on, and that I was not lost, merely growing, getting on. The best piece of soul medicine I've had as a pilgrim.

What I have to share at this moment is not a complete, well-organized systematic theology, merely a collection of thirteen chapters. I have written them each to be free-standing, but since I have written them in a clutch, they are inevitably somewhat intertwined. I begin with those three chapters which will give some idea whence my pilgrimage began, and what were my *club-haulers* along the way, and some journaling which shows the course my pilgrimage has taken and gives some taste of just how that happens. Then follow in Part Two eight chapters. The first is on **Sin**, which I consider the very linchpin of Augustine's theological system, and therefore of Western Christianity's thinking. I believe **sin** a deplorable, and very dysfunctional organizing principle for holding a theological system together, so I have sought to jerk it clean out

xiii

of the structure to see where the other pieces might fall. The next three chapters then follow in course: about the God, Jesus, and the institutional church. Those four discussions together will feel like *tearing things down*. The next three chapters cover other doctrines I think pertinent to and supportive of my pilgrimage. And then I attempt to sum up with a piece on *where I net out*, intended not as a final and earth-shaking revelation, but simply what I see as I look around at this resting place. My pilgrimage will probably continue onward. In Part Three I attempt some rebuilding *(which is the core of my faith, though it may not be yours)*. I offer my critical thoughts about our current American scene, and conclude with my own vision of where the Christ might want us to go, i.e., my vision for our future.

If all this gives a little support and courage for your own spiritual pilgrimage, then I will be satisfied. And if it does not, then I simply did not intend this volume for you.

Part I

The Pilgrimage from There to Here

Chapter 1: Foundation Stones

When I first realized I had begun to wander theologically, away from the orthodox compound, I did have the wits to take a quick look around and make note of the spiritual foundations that had carried me thus far, to this place I seemed to be now leaving. It may be useful to point out to you as we begin, the spiritual foundation stones that sustained me through thirty-four years of ministry, and then when I retired, launched me into this spiritual pilgrimage.

Theological Foundations

I can still remember, though not with absolute clarity any more, the days of my seminary years, especially the middler year. The church, particularly the Episcopal Church, had been important in my life from the age of eight. I became as active as a child and teen could be in a very small, struggling congregation all those years. My dad had been an acolyte in his tender years, so I was one now. I was carefully building up my understandings, what it was about, how it worked (the *it* here is sedulously undefined). I was a lector long before we had lectors, a watcher of priests, and rarely even a preacher. It was equally observed and concluded by all that I was headed for the ministry. So it came about that in that horribly dark and painful middler year of seminary all of my tenderly laid, childish foundations were being carefully and methodically demolished, torn down, block by block. Not maliciously, but lovingly and very deliberately, with what felt like sledge hammer blows. It had to be if I was to become a theological priest who really thought and cared about Christian and spiritual foundations.

That was an incredibly painful year. I went to seminary expecting to fill in small gaps and round off unshaped edges; instead the center was being ripped out of me and carefully reconstructed, but this time with sound, mature and intellectually competent, well crafted, state-of-the-art foundation stones. And that foundation was sound enough to sustain me in building my spiritual life alongside others through my thirty-four years of active ministry. Good foundation stones. Stones well-jointed together into a solid reliable, and very functional, quite orthodox *(though some might suggest "flaming-liberal")* foundation for a serviceably theological and spiritual dwelling. It has served me quite well through my ministry. But as I neared, and have now lived into retirement, when orthodoxy is no longer more important (as a professional and sworn orthodox priest of the church) to me than understanding the spiritual world in which I have found myself, I have noticed, underneath the moss that's grown on the north side of those foundation stones *(and on and other sides as well)* that the weather has finally gotten to them. Spiritual winds have etched and eroded them. Like old sandstone they're getting a little soft and crumbly, at least around the edges. I've studied hard through my thirty-four years of ministering to keep them well tuck-pointed, sturdy, soundly jointed. And to keep them current, consistent with the latest and best discoveries and understandings of the Scriptures. And then, some cumbersome spiritual experiences have accumulated too. And as I've lived into my retirement life, taken time to look around, to ponder how these unexpected and fairly extra-orthodox spiritual experiences that have tumbled into my life without my asking, and occasionally on request, how these might fit in, I've noticed that the old, carefully constructed and fairly orthodox foundation no longer contains or underpins what I discover is now building up in me. So I find myself re-examining those old stones, and how they are put together, and what stands atop them as my spiritual dwelling place. I find myself quietly, reflectively wondering. What I am gradually coming to discern across the decades of study, and the decades of the spiritual experiences I have accumulated, or which have tumbled in on me unrequested, is that the spiritual house I now live in, whose dimensions and shapes I can see only dimly, all that no longer fits the old, carefully laid foundations. It is all much broader, and airier, and far less clearly defined. I suppose some will fretfully, perhaps fearfully, suggest that I have "lost my faith" *(whatever that means)*; but I will respond, "No, not lost. Simply grown spiritually beyond the old foundations." Though I must confess that those old foundation stones, seeming to have been heaving slowly out of the earth beneath my feet with all the freezes and thaws of my life, are now fairly vague and shapeless. I feel them with my toes rather than see them. So I will now lay before your view as many of the older ones as I can find, so that you may comprehend the shape of this evolving structure within which I find myself.

Giving Myself to Christ

I cannot recall the details any more. It probably was in my fifteenth year that I went off to my first and only Senior High Conference. We wrestled with Martin Buber's latest work and with some other classroom kinds of issues. And I befriended Karl, a fellow pipe smoker; I was probably much readier to associate with like-minded males at that age than girls with funny shaped skins, though both Karl and I were rather taken *(I should say "smitten")* with "Peaches," as she chose to be called *(but in all likelihood we were no more smitten with her than all the rest of the testosterone-drenched teenage males in that week)*. "Peaches" in a swim suit was a sight to behold! The conference was filled with all the usual activities, but one impacted me more than all the rest put together. On Friday evening we had a guest speaker, an evangelist who had just returned from missionary work in South American. He told us about his experiences, and somewhere in the course of the evening he launched into his evangelist mode.

Chapter 1: Foundation Stones

Billy Graham could have done no better. I have no recollection of what he said to us. But I can clearly see the picture he evoked in my head. Over the altar in the tiny mission church where I was growing up was a copy of the very famous painting of Christ standing outside the door (to the heart, of course), lantern raised, knocking and seeking entrance. I can't say whether he referred to that picture specifically, or whether whatever he was saying called that picture to my consciousness. But I clearly remember seeing that picture in my mind's eye. And he called upon us to give our Selves, our lives to Christ. And I did that night. We were instructed to spend the rest of the night in silence. And I can recall going back to my room with my three roommates, myself in tears. I'd never been to an old-fashioned revival, but I now suspect I had just experienced a not-so-Episcopal version of that. I had given myself to Christ, and although I suspect that my choice to reach for the ministry had preceded that evening, that evening certainly sealed the decision. I can look back and realize now that I was far too young to soundly make that decision, but it was made, nonetheless, and quite irrevocably, as it turned out.

Caldey Abbey

I jump far ahead. I did my first and only sabbatical in 1996, the thirty-first year of my ministry. I had already been digging my way into understanding the ancient Celtic church and its spirituality for four years, and I was hoping for a sabbatical to spend some weeks living in a community that was trying to live out a Celtic spirituality. After a global search I concluded there was no such community. Early in my search a friend who knew my sabbatical hopes handed me an article about a Cistercian monastery in Wales with the comment that I might spend part of my sabbatical there. I read the article; the community was uncompromisingly Cistercian, which is to say, very Roman Catholic, not in the least *Celtic*. No, I was looking for Celtic and was not interested. But for some unfathomable reason I filed that article in an obscure folder. I was at the same time involved with a handful of people working to weave a network of people interested in "Celtic Christian spirituality" (I put that in quotes because that phrase was, and still is, very ill-defined.) We called it *Anamchairde* (ah-Nam-CAR-dja), Gaelic for "soul-friends." We developed a newsletter. And then one day I got a letter from a fellow named Gildas. He had been handed a copy of our newsletter by a friend of his, one Nona Rees, and was very interested in what we were trying to do. He was a monastic, had taken a vow of poverty, and so was limited in what he could contribute or ways he might help our effort. But he wanted to help. Something about the way he worded that letter made his offer of help sound very personal, as though aimed directly to me, and very immediate. Though he was responding to the newsletter (my name was on its masthead along with seven others), his response and his offer of help seemed as though it was written to me personally, and warmly. I noticed the return address. Could it be? I dug into my files and found that buried article. Not only was this the same monastery, but the face staring at me from the cover page was Gildas himself. Now that was damned spooky. I felt triangulated, hit by the same message from two different and unrelated directions, and I had by then in my life concluded to pay attention when I was triangulated. So I responded to Gildas's letter. We exchanged letters until I began to discern that perhaps I was intended to spend some sabbatical time in that monastery, Caldey Abbey on a tiny island off Tenby on the south coast of Wales. It seemed that Gildas was very into the study of Celtic stuff himself, and that Caldey Island had its own Celtic heritage, had been home to a Celtic monastic community and to several important Celtic saints, notably Illtyd and Samson of Dol. The pieces of my sabbatical felt like they were coming together, and Caldey was at the center. I did go there and lived among the monks for five weeks. That sounds like a short time, but living amongst austere Cistercians it is not. I was beginning to write my own small book on Celtic spirituality, and intended to use those five weeks to complete the work. It turned out to be exactly the right place to do that work.

The Cistercians were a reform movement within the Benedictine monks in the twelfth century. Some monks thought the Benedictines were becoming too worldly, and felt the need to purify and intensify their monastic life, to get back to the basics. They still worship seven times a day in chapel, beginning the day with the hour-long psalm vigil at 3:30am and ending the day with compline at 7:30pm. And they cram Bible-study, *lectio divina*[1] and a couple of community exercises into each day, along with an afternoon of physical labor assigned by the abbot. It is a disciplined, demanding, and **very** austere life. I remember during one conversation with Gildas in my room, as we talked, how he looked longingly at the face-bowl in my room; it was a luxury forbidden to him. His cell contained a bed, a desk, a chair, and a hook to hang his wardrobe on. Nothing else! This is austerity. I was assigned a room in the guest quarters inside the monastery walls; mine was the only room in the monastery with a single electrical outlet so I could plug in my computer, or alternatively, the small electric heater they offered me. The monastery is unheated, and the Atlantic winds can be pretty chill in mid-spring. That day Gildas told me that the most terrifying moment of his whole life happened in the moments after he'd taken his final, life-long vows and went back to his cell, and as he stood there and looked around, he'd said to himself, "This is it. This is the rest of my life!" He had been told that his cell would teach him everything he needed to know, and over the years he had learned that was right.

Gildas was the cook for the monastery while I was there, and the food was as austere as his cell. I was never hungry in those five weeks, but the wildest menu item I had was on the Feast of Pentecost when we had a dessert (a rare occurrence) of a thin

---

1. *Lectio Divina* (translate "Divine Reading") is a traditional Benedictine practice of scriptural reading, meditation and prayer intended to promote communion with God and to increase the knowledge of God's Word. It does not treat Scripture as texts to be studied, but as the Living Word. *Lectio Divina* has four separate steps: read; meditate; pray; contemplate.

Chapter 1: Foundation Stones

slice of fruit cake and a bottle of ale. Theirs is not a vegetarian diet, but meat or fish usually happened only once a week.

Within the discipline of this kind of austerity interesting things began to happen for me spiritually. I was fascinated that I was able to get into their worship routine in only three days. I missed the vigil very rarely, though after the vigil when the monks went back to their cells and began their day with Bible study and *lectio divina*. I had to roll back into the sack for another hour's sleep; but then I was writing until 10:00 at night. At first the frequent worship was an intrusion into my writing schedule, and I sometimes resented it. But I intuited that this worship discipline was essential to the writing I was doing, giving support and meaning to my writing. Within a week and a half I realized that the worship was no longer an intrusion, but instead had become the structure for my day and my writing effort. Without it I would have been floundering. And I was enjoying the worship, mainly the singing of the psalms. As Gildas walked me down to the boat to the mainland on the day I was leaving he told me that the monks had commented that I had fit into their life better than any other guest they'd had. For myself I had learned that I could probably be content living that monastic life. But while it might have been beneficial to me spiritually, I don't think it would have been healthy for me over all. Yet I am quite aware that those five weeks, living on a tiny island on the south coast of Wales with fifteen monks, became one of the most important foundation stones in the spiritual house I am building right now. I learned that there is much more to spiritual life than I had been taught, and that it is not bounded by what can be found in the Scriptures, which I had also been taught.

In one conversation with Gildas (we had only three in the whole five weeks. Cistercians do not take a vow of silence, but their rule is of no **unnecessary** conversation, and that makes for a whole lot of silence) he told me that he had learned that one of the best times of the day for prayer was at dusk, just before dawn and just afer sunset, and that the chapel in the old fifteenth-century Benedictine ruins up the hill, kept barely usable with a still-consecrated altar, was one of the best places to pray, particularly just before dawn. So one morning when I was fairly awake, after the vigil I betook myself up the hill to the old ruins. It had been raining lightly, and the wind was still brisk. It was well before dawn so the cloudy sky was quite dark, and I had no flashlight with me. In the near blackness, the wind blowing globs of water off the tree limbs onto me, I made my way up the hill, around the mill pond and into the old courtyard, searching out the door into the choir where the Benedictines had sung their psalms five hundred years before. There was barely enough light inside to make things out, but my eyes gradually became accustomed to the blackness. I sat in the choir to pray: prayers of silence, of listening. I had become stalled in my writing, having nearly completed my articles on Celtic spirituality, but stuck trying to compose several prayers in the Celtic style for which I had no copy in **Carmina Gaedelica**. I was somewhat frustrated because time was running out for me on Caldey; but I was not praying that night about those prayers, or anything else. This was listening-prayer time. After a while I became aware of a strange sound in the choir. It took me a moment to identify it. The sound of the monks's robes as they processed into chapel for Compline! (For all the other hours the monks straggled into the chapel individually, but at Compline they were coming from their daily chapter meeting and processed silently in order of seniority into the chapel; their robes made a very identifiable swishing sound as they came in together.) I actually looked around to see if the Cistercians were coming! They were not. But now there was a presence in the room with me, a warm and friendly presence. Perhaps the fifteenth-century Benedictines? As that sound diminished I realized that it was raining lightly outside, and what I was hearing was the sound of the rain on the slate room. And yet there was still a presence in the choir with me, as though the medieval monks were praying with me; not a spooky feeling, but the warm and friendly presence of monks appreciating my joining their silent choir. I sat for some moments wondering when suddenly I had to fish a frantic pencil stub out of my pocket and a scrap of paper, as words came tumbling out. It was one of the prayers that had stumped me for days, and it poured out into notes that were almost in finished form. I marveled! That prayer had been **given** to me; it came through my hand but not out of me. (Oh, I can appreciate hearing the sound of lightly falling rain as monks processing in coupled in the workings of the writer's unconscious mind, but this plainly felt like something other than those. And who says that anything in life must have only a single cause?) I wondered for a few minutes, as the sense of that presence gradually evaporated and I was again alone in the chapel. I decided to move a dozen feet into the sanctuary. That was a spookier space: on the left side was a large door, overhung with a black curtain, leading into the ruined dormitory where it was rumored that the black monk still wandered, searching for the silver and gold altar vessels secreted during a Viking raid and never recovered. But it was starting to lighten just a bit, and through the window over the altar I could see the tree limbs outside shaken by the blustering winds. I sat in the silent sanctuary a few minutes, reaching again for that listening prayer, when suddenly I once more had to grab my pencil stub and paper and again the words of a second prayer came tumbling out, again nearly polished. And again it felt like a gift given. By now the space once again felt empty except for me, but comfortable, no longer spooky. I went down to join the monks for Prime in chapel.

    I was fairly exhausted in my work toward the end of my stay in the monastery, and my work was far enough along that I could give myself the luxury of a day off. I pocketed some fresh fruit at breakfast and begged from Gildas a small hunk of cheese and a bottle of water, and told him I was going off alone to Sandtop Bay and would not be back for noonday meal or chapel until supper or Compline. So after mass I bundled up and made my way up the hill and across the top of the island, a mile or less, to Sandtop Bay on the west end of Caldey. It had been blowing a gale the day before so there were still high winds and the seas were up. Sandtop is fairly exposed to the Atlantic winds so I had to search a while to find the spot protected enough from the winds and blowing spray. The bay is protected on two sides with seventy or so foot cliffs, and on the backside with high, steep sand dunes which in a high wind can be difficult to negotiate. And this day the wind was coming in from just about due west, the unprotected direction. I searched for twenty or more minutes before I chanced upon a small location just barely protected, and fortunately furnished with the only grass-tufted hummock that provided a comfortable seat. And there I besat myself for four or five hours. What happened to me there is not very describable. I watched and I listened and I smelled. What I sensed was God-at-play.

The combers rolled in by the minute, through the hours, steadily, breaking into foam a hundred yards out, drawing lines across the narrow bay, swiftly marching row after row onto the beach, one upon another upon another endlessly, relentlessly, each rushing up the beach and hissing into the sand, disappearing as it began its retreat and the next took its place, rushing and hissing. It was marvelous. A show, as if staged just for me, as though I were not there to see it at all; only God. The edges of each wave on either side of the beach crashed against the cliffs, throwing spray high into the air where the winds caught and tossed it up, over the tops of the cliffs high above the hissing sands. The wind was strong enough that when standing I had to lean into it, and then it would gust, teasing me, trying to throw me off-balance and onto the ground. And the winds carried mists of salt spray onto my lips and my eyebrows and my hair. I had tasted salt spray years before, deep at sea, riding a Navy destroyer; it is not an unpleasant taste and sensation: refreshing, cool—gritty and cleansing. Wet. The sky was a marvelously deep blue, the color of the skies in Edinburgh when the breeze is refreshingly cool but the winds high aloft are crisply cold, and the clouds are white puffs of cotton scudding across. Gulls and other birds I did not know relished the winds, took delight in riding them, soaring higher and higher and then swooping down across the beach, laughing to each other as they coasted up over the sand dunes and then turned back seaward to take the ride again; a play-day for them, searching if by chance there might come an edible tidbit to be snatched from one of the waves.

I could write pages to describe that day, but by now you may have the notion of it. It was refreshing. Cleansing. Enervating. A taste of the very essence of life. A pleasure for the ears and eyes and nose and skin, and even the tongue. Of course it had come just when I needed it in my work. But I think it would have been the same even if I'd not needed it so badly, if I could have just paid attention. God was playing, and letting me watch. Perhaps taking delight in my pleasure. I knew of a certainty that I was in Her presence that day, and there was nothing needing to be said or heard, by me or by Her. Eventually the chill of the wind crept into my bones and I had to move. I made my way to the other side of the beach, to the cliffs where there were several small caves and the waves crashed at my feet. But the magic was ebbing away. (John O'Donohue tells us that the soul is a shy presence that can not be aggressively hunted. It does not want to be seen with too much clarity, but rather seems much more at home in a candle-like kind of light that has a hospitality for shadows and wonderful openings in the darkness.) I think when I crossed that beach looking for more, I became the hunter-too-aggressive, and whatever opening I had been cosseting that day turned shy, and closed gradually away. I made my way back up the sand dunes collapsing underneath each footfall, and across the top of the island, and back down to the abbey. What a glorious day. It still remains crystal clear in my memory. It taught me how to find God.

The legends are very clear that Celtic saints (not martyrs but holy men and women) almost always lived part of their lives within the monastic community, within the circle of the monastery, but also had a place away, a *dysert* a desert place to which they retreated for hours or days or weeks or months after the model of the Egyptian Desert Fathers. They lived both in community amongst their fellow monastics with all the interpersonal stresses that necessarily entails, and away, in isolation, in the extreme austerity of a crude hermitage embraced by and embracing the natural world where God can whisper quietly and be heard. I understood why they did that, and how rewarding that would be.

Early in my stay I became aware that at the vigil in the abbey there was usually one other sitting near me in the nave of the chapel where we non-monks resided during the hours. A woman! Almost always there before me, she left very quickly after the last "Amen." She was there only for vigil, very rarely for mass, no other hours. It was dusky in the chapel at the vigil hour, barely light enough to softly sing the psalms, so I could not make her out well. But she headed quickly out the nave door into the dark night, while I always went the other direction through the cloister and on into the guest quarters and my room to toss off a few more knots of sleep in the before-morning-cold. I had been there more than three weeks when one morning as I came in and made my way past the choir toward my accustomed place, she moved toward me and extended a note into my hand, retreating to her accustomed place. The abbot rapped; we began the vigil. I surreptitiously read my note. She was inviting me to tea! I scratched out a note of acceptance and as we passed in leaving I gave it to her. Not a word spoken. I cornered Gildas and asked about her. He was delighted that she had invited me; she had asked him about me, and was curious about my work. He gave me directions to her place. Turned out that Sr. Dolores was a *solitary,* had been a nun, an educator, for many years head administrator of a large school, but during her sabbatical had discerned that she was being called to become a solitary who lives alone, in minimal contact with others. She had had to leave her order, requiring a papal release, to live out this calling, and had been accorded this small cottage to live in by the abbot. Her story is too involved to tell you now; I only want you to understand that within an hour's conversation I knew she was a person with whom I could safely confide my soul. I told her of that experience in the chapel of the ruins; and she confided to me that she had experienced presences on this island as well, in a specific place, on the path behind her cottage near the pathway to the chapel door. Gildas told me that he too sometimes experienced presences, on the path to the top of the hill, above the old

Chapter 1: Foundation Stones

ruins and near the top; and also where Sr. Dolores experienced them, and occasionally in other places. My experience was not crazy. It was not even odd!

I spoke of that night in the chapel of the ruins when I felt the presence(s), and shortly was given one, then a second prayer for my book. That happened to me twice more. After I had completed my stay at Caldey Abbey I crossed over to Ireland to deliberately seek out holy places there. (Ireland reputedly has more ruins per square inch than anywhere else in the world; a few of them HAVE to be holy.). My first stop was at Glendalough, the site of an ancient monastic city south of Dublin in the Wicklow Mountains, a particularly lovely area in the particularly lovely island of Ireland. Glendalough was founded by St. Kevin *(Coemgen)* in the sixth century and quickly became one of the more important schools and monastic cities in Ireland. Today it is one of the best preserved of the old monastic cities. But today it is badly infested with annoying clouds of tourists by the busload. Glendalough ("Glen of the two lakes") is renowned as a holy place, but, infested with tourists, holy it is not. You have to be out **early** in the morning in order to have enough time **before** the busses arrive, or else late in the afternoon, after the busses have left. It took me the first of my two days there to learn that. So on the second day, out early but with my soul **anticipating** the horde of tourists, I found no *thin places* in the monastic city ruins that morning. Late morning, with a little food in my backpack for lunch, I made my way a mile and a half or so up the hill where I hoped the bussed-in tourists would not have time to come. I came to a small circle of stones on the hillside, supposedly the foundation of a hermit's cell, traditionally thought of as the hermitage cell of St. Kevin himself. An almost complete circle of stones sunken into the ground. Perhaps a monk's hermitage cell. Possibly even Kevin's. It was on a lovely wooded hillside fairly high above the upper of the two loughs. The view was exquisite, almost breathtaking. If I'd been Kevin, I'd have chosen just this site. I mused a while, admiring the views in several directions. And then I carefully selected a stone to perch upon where I could gaze at the lough and slip into my listening-prayer, the very thing Kevin might have done. I was not too long in silence when suddenly once again I was compelled to dig into my backpack for a pencil stub and paper scrap and scribble out the words that came, not from my head but through my fingers. There on the paper was another prayer I'd needed, though I hadn't been particularly troubling over it. As I was scribbling a young man came climbing by. He paused and glanced at me, then climbed unspeaking on up the hill. As he came back down a little later he said hello but passed on. When I went down the hill I discovered him and his wife and baby picnicking at the bottom. I stopped and introduced myself; he was a just-published writer who had recognized what I was doing and did not want to interrupt. They shared their lunch with me, and I mine with them. A delightful time. Another gift of a prayer.

There was only one more time this happened to me, though I had offered myself to the opportunity many times. I was nearing the end of my sabbatical time. The moment when Nancy would join me for our reunion and vacation was looming, and my excitement with it. I was in the Burren, a unique area of limestone mountain-desert in County Clare, the west of Ireland. Nancy and I had been here on our honeymoon a decade before. Two places I was seeking, the small fishing village of Doolin, a hangout for local folk musicians, and Corcomroe Abbey. I cannot tell you much about that abbey. We had sought it out simply because it was in the Burren, and on the map. But it had turned out to have a particular draw for Nancy. It is an interesting ruin, particularly for the carvings of heads on every corbel and every other offered place (while the Celts had not been head-hunters, they did believe that the head was the seat of courage, and so usually a warrior kept the heads of brave enemies he'd taken, in hope that the courage would pass onto him), but Corcomroe had not spoken to me with any power. This day I sought it out anyhow, reason unknown. Maybe just filling time until . . . Maybe because it was Nancy's place and I was drawing back toward her. Whatever! I was there. I walked about, trying to feel the place, but getting nothing in particular. The cemetery is still active. Eventually I sought out a cool place, sitting on the ground against the cemetery wall, just watching as the tombstones ruminated their cud. And suddenly, once again the pencil stub, the scrap of paper, the words tumbling out, and another prayer. Maybe it was just my unconscious mind. But by now I had grown leary of that too-easy rationalization. I felt that God had caught me once again, this time when I was not needing it, or seeking it. Just trying to show me She could do it at will, without my help.

I have tried many times in the years since then to open myself to that kind of experience again, but it has not happened. Maybe I just haven't found the right thin places. But somehow I think that it was the spiritual discipline of a place and community like Caldey Abbey that put me in the right frame to be open to those experiences, and that without that discipline I cannot be so radically open to God. I'm just guessing. I only know that it doesn't happen these days, or at least, hasn't.

Loughcrew

I need to tell you about one more holy place. As I was making my way westward across Ireland near the end of my sabbatical time I stayed a couple of days at a B&B outside of Navan, northwest of Dublin. The operator was very friendly (as I found most Irish). She was curious what I was about, and after five weeks in a Cisterian monastery I'd talk to anybody about anything they'd listen to, so I told her, in some detail. *(She had a curious practice of punctuating sentences with a sudden, sharp intake of air, almost a gasp. At first I thought she was surprised or shocked by something I'd said, or by something she'd seen over my shoulder. Eventually I realized it was just her habit of punctuation.)* She was quite interested and said she might be able to help. It just happened *(gasp)* that she had been entrusted with the key to one of the locked chamber tombs at Loughcrew and I really should visit there. I looked it up on the map and it was doable, so I added it to the agenda. I drove out there next day, arriving at late morning, entrusted

Chapter 1: Foundation Stones

key in pocket and unprepared for what I found. Loughcrew is a cluster of chamber tombs very like the renowned Newgrange, only much, much smaller. There must have been a dozen or more of them, each one surrounded by its own cluster of five to a dozen small chamber tombs. Every hilltop as far as I could see with my binoculars seemed to be home to a chamber tomb with its cluster of smaller ones. When I found the one for which I had the key it was already populated with a busload of school kids. I bided my time, checking out other tombs, hoping they would leave before another bus arrived. They did. And no one else had come yet! I had that site to myself. This particular tomb was the largest in this complex, and its central burial chamber had not yet been completely studied by the archeologists, so was kept locked to protect it behind a barred door such that you could see in, but could not get in. But! I *had* the key! Furtive glances around, no one in sight. Unlock door, creep in, lock door behind me, sneak down the passageway, right into the central burial chamber. No bones or anything, a few candles; some others have been here before with motives as subversive as mine. Some modest but ancient spirals and cupped circles on the stones, nothing spectacular, but certainly authentic. Probably three to five thousand years old. I settled down to experience this space. Here I was alone, in an ancient burial site which certainly had been used, sitting in the very place where the body, probably many bodies had been interred sequentially. Considered a holy place by the pagans who'd made it. Maybe a portal to the spiritual world? I settled in to stay a while, not particularly in prayer; just being there, listening, feeling, sensing, wondering. One family came and explored and left without detecting me. Alone again. Very quiet. There was enough light from the entrance and a hole in the center of the otherwise intact roof to keep it from feeling spooky. Did it feel holy? Sacred? I could not be sure whether the very vague sense I had was of **this** place, or merely my feeling of *oddness* for being in it. I came away unsure. But it was certainly a unique experience. I thanked my hostess for her generosity. I knew not what to make of it. I still don't.

Standing Stone Circles

In Chapter 2 I talk a little about a circle of stones named *Gors Fawr*. It was not my first circle of stones, but it was my introduction. Nancy and I have sought out a number of circles over the years, even made that search one of the foci of a vacation in Scotland after the end of my sabbatical. I will not offer a discourse on them; you can search that out for yourself. I only need to say that they may be very important. Perhaps holy sites. Not Christian, but holy nonetheless. We do not, after all, have a monopoly on holiness.

My first circle had been the most famous, Stone Henge. Suzy and I encountered it on my first trip to the British Isles the year before she died. Unfortunately we got there only a day or two before the summer solstice, and the surrounding grounds were a solid encampment of self-proclaimed *druids* and new-agers, and people pretending to be white witches and such. There was nothing holy about that site on that day. Someone *(in deep reverence I would suppose)* had spray-painted some graffiti on the stones, so they were now well fenced off and unapproachable. A tourist attraction to pass by as quickly as possible.

I may have encountered another circle of stones before *Gors Fawr*, I can't recall. I do remember a few standing stones (not circles), while on Celtic pilgrimages that seemed to have some unnameable, faint power about them; or maybe it was my imagination. Or my hope. My next circle after Stone Henge was likely the Ring of Brodgar on Mainland in the Orkneys, a circle three hundred and forty feet in diameter with stones that stand as high as fifteen feet. Nancy and I were introduced to it during a small local tour, and then returned to walk among the stones and experience them for ourselves. I don't remember experiencing anything of power among them, though they are very impressive.

Clearest in my mind are several circles Nancy and I sought out the summer of 1996, at the conclusion of my sabbatical, these on Lewis in the Outer Hebrides. The first, *Ceann Hulavig* was off the beaten track, lost in a field you could only get to by walking blindly over a hilltop. We had to get directions from two farmers chatting at a gate; they looked at us and at each other in barely disguised amusement. It was not a huge circle (actually an ellipse forty-three by thirty-one feet) with only five stones still standing, though the stones ranged up to eight and a half feet tall. We spent a while there, in amongst the stones, comparing what we were experiencing, sensing *something* but with such a vague intensity that we were not the least sure it wasn't simply our imagination, or wishful thinking. Then two younger folks came over the hilltop from a different direction. They were carrying dowsing rods and dowsing every now and then. When they got close to the circle they started dowsing seriously. We watched a while, doing our own exploring. After they'd covered the area I asked, "Finding anything?" "Yes," was the reply, "the intersection of two ley lines. (One theory of the placement of standing stone circles is that they mark the intersection of ley lines, lines of power that run along the earth's surface). Actually, several ley lines." I sensed something from one of the stones.

We went on to the "The Men of Callanish," a most impressive circle (again, an ellipse forty-three by thirty-nine feet with a central pillar, thirteen stones, and an avenue of nineteen stones), considered second only to Stone Henge. Called "The Men of Callanish" because the swirls in the graining of the Lewissean gneiss (the oldest stone in the world) create in some of the stones the impression of faces. The stones, while much smaller than Stone Henge, are much more beautiful, and the site is more inspiring, overlooking Loch Roags. But by now it has become the major tourist attraction of Lewis, with a tourist center and all, and signs directing people to stay on the paths outside the circle itself. Too busy to emit any holiness or power for an average observer such as myself.

Chapter 1: Foundation Stones

But only three-quarters of a mile away we found *Cnoc Fillibhir* within full view of Callanish. Within sight of the highway, it is bypassed by folks headed for Callanish, and so is left alone. We spent over an hour there and no one else came! Two concentric ellipses (the outer forty-five by forty-three feet with thirteen stones, five of them fallen, and the inner thirty-four by twenty-one feet of now only four stones, but taller than the outer ring) made of the same stone as Callanish, so with the same beautiful graining. We had the time and aloneness to explore this circle and felt with some certainty some power emanating from at least one of the stones. Three hundred yards down the hill toward the loch was still another circle, *Cnoc Cneann*.

I confess that I do not know what to make of these circles of standing stones. I am somewhat repulsed by their attraction for new-agers and self-styled druids. But on the other hand, something about them draws me too, and what my guide in Wales said makes some peace in me about them. I suppose their age, and some unexamined supposition in me that the ancients who sited and built them were working from some ancient wisdom now lost to us, piques my curiosity. Probably pure fantasy, wishful thinking. But the mystery of them is still one of my foundation stones. I cannot bring myself to dig it up and roll it off the slope. I am stuck with it.

The Smell of Dirt

I remember from my tender years the smell of the dirt in the woods, on a hot August day when the temperature was almost unbearable up at the top, but down here, in the quiet, stillness of the shadowed woods it was dimmer and cooler and dank, and as I sat beside that tiny creek, watching the water trickle by, hoping to see a crawdad, the sweet, smell of the cool damp earth was luscious! I did not recognize it then, but God was there, watching me, comforting me in the hollow of Her hand.

The Voice of God

The prophets heard God speaking ("The LORD said . . . "). Some preachers of the evangelical bent claim to hear God speaking. I am a doubter. Only liars and crazy men claim they hear God speaking to them audibly. There are far too many Elmer Gantrys in this world for me to trust any of them. But I have heard the voice of God, once. I was in chapel, in seminary, in that rough middler year when everything theological I'd brought to seminary was being ripped out of me and new understandings put into their places. The pain was intense. I had only one question, "Did I belong here? Was I intended for ministry in the church?" And the answer coming out of my pain was, "No, bail out now." But I had a wife and two small children, no occupation, no way to make a living, not the slightest notion what else in life I might want to do, or be able to do. Suzy pointed out that I didn't even have a suit to wear to a job interview. And so I was praying furiously, Tell me, God, do I belong here? Do you want me now? God, give me some sign. But the more furiously I prayed, the deeper the silence I was hearing back. There was no answer for me. So I prayed even more furiously. Until finally one evening in chapel as I knelt and intensely prayed I heard a voice behind me, to my right, two pews back, "Be quiet and do your studies." Or I think it might have said, "**Shut up**, and do your studies." I looked back. The voice had been loud and clear and firm. But there was no one in that pew. There was no one even near that pew. The voice was not one I recognized. Not a student. Not a faculty member. I had clearly heard it. But no one else in the chapel looked like he had heard it. And it was not the answer I'd wanted. I went home from chapel befuddled. What had I heard? Had I hallucinated? Had I needed an answer so desperately that I'd unconsciously manufactured one? But if I had, this was not an answer I would have wanted. I did not trust people who said that God talked to them, they were crazy, hallucinating. But I had heard it. It took several days to accept that I had in fact heard it. That the answer had been directed at me. That, even though it was not an answer I'd wanted, my prayer had been answered. But it had not taken away the pain, had not relieved the anguish, had not stopped the tearing out of everything that had brought me here. The answer was there, clear as a bell; but so was the pain.

That event got me through a few more weeks, but the pain was still winning. I needed to get the hell out. I needed to leave, to quit. Suzy (my first wife, long dead of cancer) reasoned, pleaded, cried, and finally suggested one thing I could grab hold of, "Go talk to Al Dalton first." Al had been my chaplain that summer in the Clinical Pastoral Training program, he had opened doors for me, and I had come to trust him. So I drove that night in complete desperation to talk to Al. He sat me down and he listened, long into the night, and quietly, gently suggested to me the same thing that voice had, do my studies. That was a course financially feasible, it was not fatally final, and if when I completed the course, I could still choose not to go on. Al was considerably gentler and kinder to me than that voice had been, and he suggested to me just about the same thing that it had. But he had taken the time to help me understand the wisdom of that option. I went back to Bexley and finished the course. I consented to ordination and ministered for many years, not without rough places, but to the end, with no regrets.

I've never heard that voice again. Nor have I ever sought it that furiously. I have no doubt that it was God I heard. But I did learn from that event to listen for God in other ways, in the sound of others's voices. And I've heard His answers many times. But never again in that voice. At least, not yet.

Karl Barth

I remember hearing about an interview of Karl Barth, the premier conservative theologian of the last century. He was asked to summarize what he believed as simply as possible. After a long pause he quoted the children's song, "Jesus loves me, this I know. . . ." The interviewer asked back, but why would you believe that? And Barth answered, "My mother told me." I guess for me that's getting down to the bedrock fundamentals. We believe because sometime in our history someone whom we trusted implicitly said, "Believe this." It may be as simple as that.

My Relationship with Jee-zuz

In retrospect I realize that, despite having given myself to Christ at that summer youth conference, I have nowhere identified as one of my foundation stones a close, personal relationship with the Christ (or JEE-zuz, as some would prefer). That is an important curiosity for me. There is, has always been, so much talk in the church of one's relationship with Christ, of the warmth and strength and power of that relationship. It clearly is the cornerstone of faith for very many Christians, if not most. In some corners it is promulgated as the ***only*** sure foundation of a **true** Christian faith. But just as clearly it is not for me! William James has observed that some can pray while others cannot; and I have similarly concluded that is true of the Christward relationship as well; it is for some people and for others it is not.

    I remember one summer afternoon when I arrived at the Cincinnati airport for an impromptu interview arranged by a seminary classmate with his bishop. I was out of work and desperate for a parish. I should have been willing to say anything needed to get the job. The interview progressed quickly to the fateful question, "Tell me about your relationship with Christ." As I heard the words come out of my mouth I knew there was no job for me with this bishop. To my detriment I told him the truth, that I really felt no strong relationship with Christ, that my relationship was primarily with the godhead. I supposed aloud that as I had no brothers, only sisters, a brotherly relationship with Christ was less natural to me than one with God the Father himself, that it was He to whom I regularly prayed. The interview proceeded, but there was no fire left in it, and I heard no more from that bishop. Obviously my lack of a close, intimate relationship with Christ was a liability, not an asset.

    I have aggressively sought a Christward relationship at several points in my life, but Christ seems never to have chosen to befriend me *(or perhaps God knows that would not be appropriate for Jack Bowers)*. I remember kneeling at the altar rail at St. John's in Cambridge and fervently praying for, pleading for that relationship. The small parish was in trouble, slowly dwindling in the heart of a slowly declining small city. I was flailing about, grasping for any tool that would lift us out of our survival mode and make us strong. We had a small prayer group meeting weekly to sing and share and offer intercessory prayers together (a "Prayer and Praise" group). A few of that circle were zealous advocates of the charismatic route, and a few others, while not so zealous, were passively compliant and willing. And I was silently asking myself whether I could, if it were beneficial to the parish, go that route. So after going with them to a charismatic workshop at the Mecca of charismania in Ohio led by the national star Chuck Irish himself *(in whose voice I still could hear the same anger-fulled cynicism I'd heard when I taught him Greek in seminary)* and after wrestling with myself about that charismatic possibility, I concluded that while it ran counter to my fiber, I could. So I knelt at the altar rail several days in a row and prayed, pled, really. I asked for Jee-zuz to come into my life *(in the newly devised tradition of charismania the pronunciation "Jee-zuz" seems to be preferred, along with the very frequent use of " . . . I jess wanna . . . " in every spontaneous prayer)*. With some reluctance and trepidation I even prayed for the gift of *speaking in tongues* (i.e., glossilalia), which is (in that tradition) the absolutely surest proof that one has received Christ into his/her life. I may have prayed nearly as furiously as I had that middler year in seminary, but this time no voice. No consoling *warmth* of "the Baptism in the Spirit." And no tumbling words of an unknown tongue (I tried, and only a few poorly contrived scraps of oral garbage came out.) I had to conclude that this salvific solution was not for the people of St. John's or for me.

But throughout most of my life I have been content relating only to the one God. The Trinity, described as an unsolvable mystery, has always been a problem for me. I have preached it, have proclaimed it; but I have always stumbled some over it. I am too damned logical; the math of the Trinity just doesn't work for me. And that, coupled with my non-relationship with the Christ, (and at seminary I was accustomed to refer to the third person of the Trinity, the Holy Spirit, as "the Blue Blur," which was as close as I could come to defining it), has urged me to see this lack as an important foundation stone, perhaps, to follow my metaphor, a *limen* through which an alternative understanding (or better yet "opportunity") might enter, or be sought. It may be, in some odd, inverse kind of way, that this lack of an intimate relationship with Christ is one of my most important foundation stones, perhaps the cornerstone.

John O'Donohue

Sr. Cintra Pemberton's pilgrimages were life-giving during a decade of spiritual famine in my life. She was a monastic, of the Episcopal Order of St. Helena, who made a ministry and a specialty of putting together and leading pilgrimages in Celtic areas, and she was exceedingly good at it. She understood the need to see something ancient and holy but new to us, and also to have time and space to stop and reflect, to ponder what that ancient, new holiness is pointing toward in one's life. This was her way of helping fund her order, but also do a very specialized ministry. I have gone with her to Wales, both north and south, to west Scotland and to Orkney, and finally to west Ireland. It was on that last one that I met John O'Donohue. We were in Connemara, and someone who was scheduled to lecture the pilgrim group on Celtic spirituality had to cancel at the last minute and Cintra quickly arranged a backup. But he had to cancel as well, and recommended O'Donohue, whom Cintra knew not a whit about.

Chapter 1: Foundation Stones

He arrived, a few minutes late, fairly breathless, had been caught up in a pre-marital counseling session, and sat down to talk to us.

O'Donohue was a priest in the Roman Church (or at least was then; he was on the outs with his bishop as well as others, and eventually did not finish in orders), a native of Connemara, a poet, philosopher (his doctorate was about the mystic Meister Eckhart), theologian, teacher, and Celt. As he began to talk to our pilgrim group I shortly realized that he was not so much talking **about** Celtic spirituality as **being** it. I soon realized that there was little linearity to his lecture, he seemed to be talking in circles and ellipses and spirals. He was obviously well educated and grounded, but his thinking, or at least his lecture, was much more associative than linear. To some he seemed to be rambling. But my sense was that instead of lecturing us about Celtic spirituality he was simply immersing us, dipping us in it. I was completely fascinated and utterly captivated.

I came away determined to lay hand on his only publication at that time, a set of six audio tapes entitled **Anamchara** (Gaelic for "soul-friend"). They have since been transposed into written form and published as a book, but much was lost in that process. The words are the same, but the melody and lilt of his voice is probably as important as the words themselves. I recommend the tapes in preference. From a vast knowledge of western philosophers and Christian mystics he simply talks on the tapes, wandering from topic to topic, never exhausting one before he moves on, but frequently returning to revisit topics, moving in a circular or spiral pattern, all about the spiritual life. That is obviously his first love, teaching about the spiritual life. He does it well. And he takes me places, points out to me things that no one else has ever mentioned to me. He introduced me to the interior life, and to my soul which lives at the back of the interior landscape behind my eyes. And he invited me to spend some of myself exploring that interior landscape and getting acquainted with my soul.

Over my years I have gradually come to conclude that there are basically two poles to the spiritual life. The external thrust is to spend oneself delivering God's love (that is, mercy AND justice) to the world, to those around me. Feeding the poor, lobbying on behalf of the oppressed, being God's active agent in the world. This is the social action effort of the church and of Christian people, really of all godly people. The other pole, the inward thrust is the exploration of the interior landscape, the befriending of one's own soul, becoming close to the God who is the ground of our being and who is found through the soul. I learned some about that during my stay with the Cistercians; they did not teach me directly, I simply observed them, and heard squibs about their doing of it. Brother Gildas was taught his "cell would teach him everything he needed to know." It took me a while to get myself around that idea. But when I heard O'Donohue talking about the interior landscape, and getting acquainted with one's soul, I think I began to understand how the solitude and silence of the monk's cell would teach one everything he needed to know.

Part I: The Pilgrimage from There to Here

My ministries have always been focused on institutional issues, social system dynamics and such; and I have pushed gently toward social action, perhaps too gently. And I have ever so gradually tried to offer more and more around the inward journey, about the spiritual life, about the feeding of the soul. But I have been struck that very few are interested in that kind of stuff. Maybe it is food for only a few. Maybe the inward journey, like psychoanalysis, is only for a very few. Maybe the population of monasteries is about at the right level for the total population of our era. But as I age, I am more and more inclined to think that is what it's really all about. That spiritual stuff is the real cornerstone. Both poles must be there for a healthy spirituality; but all the social action in the world is worthless to the doer without at least a bit of the inward thrust. Some of us are better at one than the other; but we all need some of both.

****

There are probably some other foundation stones which I have not yet thought to describe, or which may be so deeply buried that I am not even aware of them. If you poke and prod a bit in me we may together discover some more of them. This spiritual structure of mine is definitely a *work in progress*. But I suspect that these are the more important of those stones.

Chapter 2: The Stepstones of My Pilgrimage

–or–

How I Got from Preaching the Good News of Jesus Christ to This Place in a Spiritual Desert

THERE HAVE BEEN A few stepping stones as I wandered in this spiritual wilderness, stones that have given me a firm footing for at least one step, that have guided me, or even directed my wandering. I will tell you about them.

But before I start I must first state a few axioms about my spiritual wanderings. The first I learned from my homiletics teacher. One day after class he corralled me, "Jack, you have an absolutely puritanical sense of honesty." That comment followed on my refusal to preach what I did not myself believe *(I had refused to parrot an obvious but obnoxious theological point)*. My puritanical honesty seemed a strange notion to him. I mulled over that notion of my puritanical honesty only a few instants and then agreed. As you read you need to be aware that I do have a puritanical sense of honesty. It is one of my drivers.

The second of my axioms is that St. Luke's is my chosen *circle of standing stones*. American Protestant Episcopalianism is the DNA of my spiritual bones, it is the flowing blood that gives me life. I was born into it; I chose it; it shaped me, my mind, my spirit. I could choose no other, even if I wanted to. And St. Luke's is the flesh and spirit and community of American Protestant spirituality which I have chosen. I may be still somewhat new to most members, but St. Luke's is today parent and forebear to me. So wherever my spiritual pilgrimage might lead me, St. Luke's is a given, is axiomatic. That is not as simple as a conscious choice; it is home, and in my bones. It matters not what I think, what I believe, what direction my soul wanders, St. Luke's is my circle of standing stones. It is where I live, even on days when I seem not part of it.

My other axiom is this: as a servant of the church I have always been more of a *searcher* than I ought to have been. I was employed to tend to the institution; my drivenness was to relentlessly search for truth. Those two motivators are in conflict. Those who tend the institution serve best docilely and parrot-wise. My sense was always that we (church professionals) spent far too much energy and investment on very dumb institution matters, and far too little on helping people develop their spirituality and spiritual lives. But that latter impulse dumbfounded me because I, for one, did NOT know how to enable people's spiritual lives, nor did I know anyone who could teach me how to do that. That seems to have been a lost art in the church. So I struggled **very** hard trying to keep peace within me toward the orthodox teachings of the church, mainly through my studies, particularly studies of the Scriptures, all the while stumbling along to keep the institution from bumbling into some roadside ditch. And finally I retired! I was no longer required by my professional responsibilities to stay within the boundaries of orthodoxy. I was free to wander! And so I have. Far and wide. Searching.

For the next step of this narrative I borrow an image from my readings of sea-stories, particularly of the Jack Aubrey and Horatio Hornblower series: there was once upon a time a naval battle maneuver called "club-hauling." When a sailing ship in battle (a smaller warship, e.g., a frigate) was in immanent peril of being taken by broadside or boarding, one extreme means to escape was to turn the ship so sharply that the pursuer could not turn simultaneously and therefore lost tactical advantage, so that the pursued could then re-engage from a more advantageous position, or else flee to escape. Club-hauling was perhaps the only way to execute such a radical turn of a ship, and it could only be done in waters shallow enough that an anchor could reach and grab the bottom. While at full speed the captain dropped the anchor on that side of the bow to which he needed to turn. As the anchor grabbed the bottom it was stopped off and would then jerk the head of the ship toward that side wrenching the ship into that direction so quickly that the engaging enemy could not react fast enough to keep his advantage. The one disadvantage of this maneuver was the loss of the anchor; the cable had to be cut the very instant the ship was turned, and before the anchor slowed the forward motion of the ship; under those conditions there was no opportunity to retrieve the anchor; a best bower was expensive equipment. But to rescue the ship in battle, or better yet, to turn the tide of the battle was worth that cost. Club-hauling.

In my spiritual pilgrimage since retirement I have experienced several club-haulings, books that have so violently jerked my head around as to send me spiritually off in an entirely other direction, escaping the muddle I was in, wondering whether to re-engage or to flee. While not as spiritually painful as my middler year of seminary when my childish theological foundations were necessarily ripped up and a more solid set of theological foundation stones set into place, while less painful, these have been equally traumatic and have sent my spirit wandering off in equally new and different directions.

The first of these club-haulers was William James's lectures of 1902, **The Varieties of Religious Experiences**. I probably should have read this book while still in seminary, but I cannot recall that anyone suggested it to me then. James might have helped me start to build a much sounder theological[1] foundation and framework. To read James's book had occurred to me a few times previously, but I may have been

---

1. Read "spiritual," since as an INTP (Myers-Briggs Personality Inventory) my primary method of doing spiritual work is quite intellectual; Thomas Aquinas is my model.

Chapter 2: The Stepstones of My Pilgrimage

shied off by an early experience of a flaky parishioner who was into paranormal stuff and engaged in automatic writing; her correspondent was William James. So **after** I retired I finally picked up *Varieties* to read. It was not an easy read; it forced me to re-sort some of my theological thinking. In these twenty-four lectures James tackled the psychology of religious experiences. A hundred years later, there is nothing radically striking to us in this work, but reading it set me to the task of organizing anew much of my thinking about religious experiences, the spiritual life, and my own spiritual development, not just from a *faith* point of view, but from the vantage of early psychology as well. James did not challenge or attack religious belief and experiences, but rather examined them from a nonjudgmental outsider's vantage (though I think he was a Christian believer himself.) I came away from his lectures with a deeper and clearer understanding that there are two fundamentally different religious orientations. He called the one "healthy-mindedness," a dedicatedly positive and affirming orientation toward the good. The other he called "the sick soul," an unshakeable orientation to dwell on the evil aspects. The first sees man and the world as fundamentally good, the other sees man and life as irretrievably bad. This second type of soul is the one inclined toward the *conversion* experience, understanding that the only available salvific force from unrelenting evil is God; the "healthy-minded" soul is inclined not to conversion, but to grow gradually in his faith. Through James's eyes I could understand why the two are so irreconcilably different in their makeups and outlooks, and unable even to comprehend or be at peace each other. In passing, James also pointed my attention briefly toward the mystical experience.

This book alone was not earth-shaking for me. But James's analysis did set me to re-think and draw some new conclusions from my observations about spirituality and religiosity, and about my own spiritual experiences and yearnings. In essence I suppose it urged me onward in the spiritual pilgrimage which I had already begun after my retirement (that is, when my profession no longer seemed to prohibit my exploring far beyond the boundaries of orthodoxy). This, my first club-hauler.

At my retirement party Bishop Ken Price had given me my second club-hauler, a book he liked and thought I might find interesting. It was Jack Miles's ***God: A Biography***. The title alone is jarring, as was intended; how can one presume to write a biography of God? The book had lain on my shelf untouched and outside of my curiosity for several years when for some unfathomable reason I picked it up. I read with fascination. It was definitely inside my ballpark, i.e., it accepts the Hebrew Scriptures unquestioningly. Miles begins by stipulating his premise that the order of the books as presented in the Hebrew (the Masoretic text a.k.a. the *Tanach*) Scriptures is not mere happenstance (certainly **not** chronological), but is itself the editor's statement about God as profoundly theological as the words of the texts themselves. Miles then guides us through each of the books in Masoretic order, focusing solely on the nature of the god therein presented: "What does God say? "What does God do?" and "How is God described?" This approach began to make order for me out of what had formerly been a chaos, God appearing so radically differently in various parts of the Scriptures. I read with interest and fascination. Then a year or so later I volunteered to teach Miles's book in a short adult series at St.Luke's Church; that effort forced me to really internalize Miles's book, not simply read it while nodding yes. I was profoundly shaken. I understood now a pattern in God's various behaviors, and even more, I very much disliked and disapproved of the God I found there. These Scriptures, which I adore, taught me a god whom I would **not** choose to worship, adore, or be obedient to.

I summarize the course, and therein a god very much in flux. We first encounter God in the two creation stories. In the first God is remote, majestic, solitary and absolutely omnipotent; in the second God is little more than a bumbling incompetent, and is vengeful to boot. While I prefer the second, I do not like or trust that God. After the first eleven chapters of **Genesis** God becomes little more than a family friend to Abraham's lineage, and a not terribly helpful friend at that. In the second book, **Exodus** we encounter a quite different, ferociously militant God, brutal and unrelenting in organizing, leading and flogging this people whom God had chosen for himself, but who had not really chosen God for themselves. In the third, **Deuteronomy** God is at his absolute zenith, militarily competent but a harsh and very demanding lord. But thereafter God appears to be in decline *(in my eyes, not Miles's appraisal)* In the four books about the kings God tinkers and complains, [so-and-so] ". . . did evil in the eyes of YHWH" is the drumbeat in these stories. And then in the books of the prophets God seems to have a mental breakdown, alternately and vehemently berating, cajoling and bemoaning *(sounds bipolar!)* And from that point God seems to diminish and wane through the story, appearing less powerful, less present, and less a part of the story until at last in **Esther** God is neither present nor even mentioned!

Now I had to take a deep, deep breath, and begin to ponder. This is not the God I had thought it was. Nor is this an attractive God. Not a god I want. The God of the Christian writings is somewhat more desirable (though not in John's **Revelation**). But still not the God I had thought I was worshiping. Gradually my mind and my spirit began to watch my swirl of spiritual notions from a different vantage point. What if the God who is portrayed in our Scriptures is not so much *the God* but is more *the god whom the people need* at that moment in their history? That makes some sense of the changing-ness of the God of Hebrew Scriptures, and allows an even different God during the time of early Christian formations. So God, or at least the god we worship, perhaps is relative, a perception shaped by the needs of our era and culture.

The next club-hauler that came to my hand was Karen Armstrong's **A History of God**. Armstrong's purview is broader yet. She is primarily interested in the God of Scriptures, which takes in Jewish, and Muslim understandings as well as Christian (and she takes some sidelong glances at Buddhism as well), and she looks at the whole scope of writings, not just the Holy Scriptures of each. Her task is to trace how the concept of god changes and evolves through the course of the history of each religion. She presents a breathtaking vista. Tracing the history of each of these three religions in turn, she shows how they develop separately (though not without contact and mutual influence), but in parallel. Their patterns come out similarly. And I began to understand through her eyes that the god we know at any point in history is the god whom we need at that particular point in our history. Obversely, the Holy Scriptures are not so much the story of our relationship with the god as the history of the evolution of our perceptions of God, perceptions founded not so much on observations of the god in action as on what we need from God at that moment in our history. The god who stands behind all that is really not very visible at all in those writings. And what we do get is very much an acculturalized version of the God; for Christians a Trinity, for Jews a YHWH, for Muslims an 'Allah, versions that evolve as the cultures evolve.

A new book came on the scene, Robert Wright's ***The Evolution of God*** and I picked it up. Wright is a journalist, a writer, a cultural evolutionist and a devotee of games theory who is widely read with a prodigious grasp. Wright[2] begins by looking at god as witnessed in the most primitive societies we can reconstruct, the hunter-gatherer groups of early humans. And he traces the concept of god through the evolution of societies, and finally to monotheism. He then takes on the Hebrew Scriptures through the eyes of historical criticism which begins to date the several threads of those Scriptures (J, E D and P, et al.) glancing at how the political situation at those dates shapes the separate stories which are then woven together into one as though it were a single text, creating a near-chaotic jumble (e.g., Does Noah invite two of each species into the ark, or seven? Both lines are in the final copy of his story). He looks at the several threads in the early Christian writings and their several emphases. And then he looks at Islam in its two phases of Mohammad's life. Much of his understanding about how religion evolves is built around his understanding of game theory, of zero-sum games vs. non-zero sum games. And the way he puts it together makes sense to me. In the end Wright allows that his own conclusion is to be, not atheistic, but agnostic. Does he believe in God? Probably not in the traditional sense, he allows; but as one who sees culture as evolving, he thinks he detects in that evolution a *moral axis* built into the created universe. And if we want to call that "God," that is as close as he can come to believing.

I came away from Wright's book with an appreciation of his *shredding* of the Holy Scriptures, a high respect for his notions, and a skepticism about his conclusions. But also to discover with a wide open field who might be the God behind all this.

If the God behind all this can not really be discerned by looking through the several so-very-culturally-defined windows in the several collections of holy writings, then how can the god be discerned, I pondered? Can one find that god for himself? Each of the great religions of the world has had its mystics. Is mysticism the better, the more direct way to god than the holy writings? I have always looked askance at the mystics. Now I opined that with a better look at mysticism perhaps I can learn my way into my own contemplative, mystical experiences, and thereby

---

2. For my fuller discussion of Wright's book, see Chapter 3 (54–57)

know god for myself. A copy of Evelyn Underhill's 1911 book ***Mysticism: a study in the nature and development of man's spiritual consciousness*** had lain on my bookshelf virtually untouched for over two decades. I had several times tried to read from the writings of Julian of Norwich and a very few other Christian mystics, but those attempts had fairly baffled me, and I had always come away with a sticky-sweet *(or better, a "sickeningly-sweet")* slightly nauseated feeling, very unenlightened, always disappointed. Those writings are simply incomprehensible to me. So on leaving for a three-week cruise on the coast of Norway, I packed Underhill's book along with two other unfinished volumes to fill in my idle travel time. After finishing the other two volumes, I began to force my way through Underhill's book; tough reading. Very understandable, but very difficult reading.

    Underhill was of the same era as William James. And her task was similar to his. Underhill would appear to have been a mystic herself, but the task of this book was to codify the mystical experience. Ranging through the history of (primarily) the Christian church, Underhill fretted out the pattern of a mystic's development. She discerned very specific steps and stages in the evolution of the mystic's experiences of *the divine* and laid them out in fair detail with examples of each step from different mystics across the ages. She was very clear from the outset of her book (whether accurately or not) that one does not choose to be or to not be a mystic. You either are, or you are not. That much is immutable, a given, she claims. Some, perhaps only a few, are fated to have deeply mystical experiences, but most of us are not, and cannot. *(That revelation belayed my desire to experience the mystical for myself; I have never been a mystic, and therefore, in Underhill's world and word, I can never become one. No good to pine for it.)* Then as I forced my way through her description of the nine successive stages in the development of the mystic's life I realized that I would not have wanted that life anyhow. It is painful, disorienting, solitary, and indescriptable. I would not have been healthy as a mystic. While a deep introvert who enjoys and very much needs his time alone, I also need some intellectual interaction with others *(which is why I seek your company)* to keep me on even keel; as a solitary mystic I would easily be tipped toward insanity (i.e., living in my world of pure fantasy). So I am thankful in one sense that the mystical experience is not available to me.

    Several conclusions I drew from Underhill's work are unsettling for me. It seems abundantly clear from her point of view that many, if not most, of the great innovators and motivators of the church have been mystics. The church owes much to them out of their experiences. It seems equally clear that the experiences of the mystics are outside of the rational realm, and are beyond any comprehendible description. The writings and art produced by mystics simply do not make sense to those of us who have not had such experiences ourselves; their verbal or artistic representations are bizarre, and defy any rationality or understanding. So why should we credit them at all? Why not discard them as uninformative and useless? Because those mystics have themselves proved to be very valuable in the life of the church, as inspirers, as motivators and innovators. Through their mystical experiences they become highly energized persons with direction and purpose which spills over onto others around them. Underhill is also clear that mystics's attempts to communicate the content of their experiences are always shaped by their own (religious) culture; so Christians tend to have experiences around the Trinity and around the life (past and present) of Jesus. Jewish and Islamic mystics likewise tend to have experiences consistent with their religious worlds. So while the content of their experiences might appear to be different, the pattern of their experiences and evolution are surprisingly similar. And in addition Underhill is clear that while the mystical experiences themselves are supra-rational and almost entirely incommunicable, they are very self-authenticating. They cannot be authenticated by rational processes or by any form of outside observation; but they are so very powerful, and so impactful on the life of the mystic her/himself as to be self-authenticating (this is very problematic for me: a schizophrenic's auditory hallucinations are likewise completely authentic and impactful for that schizophrenic). Lastly, Underhill seems clear that the mystics appear to have two different kinds of experiences of the divine which sound very similar to James's two kinds of basic religious orientation, the "healthy-mindedness" and the "sick-soul." While all mystics experience some of both types, some of them are more oriented toward experiences of overwhelming love and inclusion (union), and others sound more oriented toward experiences of emptiness, lostness, and unworthiness (transcendence).

Underhill's analysis of the mystic's experience and evolution is a hundred years old now. Nor am I aware of any other analyses that would come to different conclusions about mysticism (though I have not yet actively tried to search those out). But I am still curious. I have asked around, but not yet pursued, whether there are any contemporary, unbiased (not written out of a pro- or anti-religious bias) psychological or psychiatric appraisals of the mystical experience. Are we dealing with a psychiatric abnormality? Or are mystics normal (i.e., psychologically, mentally, spiritually healthy) persons with very abnormal experiences? I have pondered so deeply as to wonder whether the person who has mystical experiences is simply someone blessed (or cursed) with a capacity of memory so powerful that s/he can recall (in contemplation) memories of *in utero* experiences, memories from before there were sufficient stimuli to create describable memories. That might explain the shape the mystic's experiences seem invariably to take.

In my frustration with the limits and frailties of Christian thinking, I have taken a couple of very cursory glances at Buddhist writings. Most of those come out to me as a sort of gibberish, utilizing English language to try *(but fail)* to express ideas very foreign to Western thought and language. The result for me has always been incomprehension and a vague notion that "this guy *may* be saying something intelligible, but I can't make it out, and he might just as plausibly be deliberately writing gibberish and pawning it off as wisdom in order to make some money." But one book by a Roman Catholic theologian Paul Knitter, **Without Buddha I Could not be a Christian** made sense to me, comparing and contrasting, and enlightening Christian thinking by squinting through Buddhist eyes; but he did not go far enough for me. A friend loaned me three books on Buddhism, and one of those, written by the Dalai Lama himself, makes profound sense to me. No gibberish. Just three simple concepts: interwovenness, ignorance, and compassion. And then I had an opportunity to hear the Dalai Lama in person. I went to see him with some anticipation. I came away from an hour and a half assured that I had been in the presence of a true mystic, that his vision is both understandable and made sense of my world, and, that it came from beyond himself. And further, that I had been with the warmest, most personable, most charming presence I had every experienced (that while sitting at the extreme fringe of a crowd of ten thousand gathered in that stadium!) I am far too old, far too far along in my life, far too imbued in the Western, Protestant-Anglican, Celtic-Christian milieu to ever become a Tibetan Buddhist, but he certainly did tempt me. And his notions greatly encouraged my wonderings.

I started writing about these stepping stones in 2011. Since then several more books have fallen into my life with some impact. One was Jim Holt's book, **Why Does the World Exist?** in which he surveys philosophers, theologians, physicists and mathematicians across the ages. No new insights for me in those pages, but a confirmation of where I was already headed, that there is no clear (or even vague) reason why humankind or the world or universe should exist, no purposefulness; and in the process he stumbles across the issues of whether the God exists, likewise to no conclusion.

A most impactful book was **Psychiatry & Mysticism**,[3] a collection of twenty-five professional papers. Since reading Evelyn Underhill's study of mysticism I had been searching for some even-handed psychiatric appraisal of mysticism: were mystics some kind of kook, or normal persons with some abnormal ability? Were their reports credible in the everyday world or just religious flotsam? After several blunted searches I finally stumbled into Dean's book, and found four of those papers[4] quite informative to my question, and in particular the very last by Julian Silverman, **On the Sensory Bases of Transcendental States of Consciousness**. This was a real club-hauler!

For long I had puzzled over the place and authority of mysticism and mystical experiences. I gathered, along with William James and with Evelyn Underhill, that mystical experiences are at the core of the foundational experiences of many (perhaps most) great religious leaders and movers. I take Jesus himself to have been a profound mystic whose forty days in the wilderness produced insights that drove him into the prophetic ministry that has stretched into this day. Paul gives evidence on the

---

3. Dean, **Psychiatry & Mysticism**
4. The four papers of greatest interest in **Psychiatry & Mysticism**
Adams, Paul L. "*Metapsychiatry and Quaker Meditation*" 185-193
Benson, Herbert, Beary, John F., Carol, Mark P., "*Meditation and the Relaxation Response*" 207-222
Girof, Stanislov, "*Varieties of Transpersonal Experiences: Observations from LSD Pychotherapy*" 311-345
Silverman, Julian, "*On the Sensory Bases of Transcendental States of Consciousness*" 365-398

Chapter 2: The Stepstones of My Pilgrimage

Damascus road that he too was a mystic, and while his experience did not markedly change his personality, it did absolutely reverse his mission, and may have continued to energize his ministry throughout the rest of his life. The insights of the mystics who have been of significant importance in the life of the Christian church were not merely new, but also profoundly realistic and change-making. Our legends are rife with such stories that changed and motivated and energized and directed religious heroes.

They engaged in a certain kind of prayer in which, through the practice of a variety of disciplines, they thought themselves to enter the very presence of the God, sometimes returning with deep and exhilarating insights, which they attributed to being in God's presence. But I can not cite evidence, other than their convictions, that those insights were from God. Their reports of those experiences are incomprehensible to my scientifically inclined mind. I have gone so far as to wonder whether those visions/experiences are a sort of psychotic episode? They seem unlike anything *normal* I can see clearly how potent they were for the persons experiencing them, but to me their descriptions of those experiences seem gibberish. I do not doubt that the authors actually experienced them. But I do question the source, the origin, the genesis of those experiences. Other than the fact that those experiences are almost universally reported in *god-talk* language, I find no convincing evidence that they are in fact from, or about, some deity. So I was left wondering about the source, the meaning and therefore the value of those mystical experiences. And I was left questioning how the experiences might validate the usefulness of the subjects's wisdom, teaching, leading.

In this light Silverman's paper made profound sense to me. He sets a **scientific framework**[5] for examining the **sensory** and **attention patterns** of those *mystical*

---

5. Detail of Silverman's *schema*: When, by whatever cause, a person's perceptions (i.e., interpretations of stimuli) and response patterns are altered (i.e., non-normal) his *consciousness* (i.e., awareness) is altered, and his normal psychological structures for interpreting and responding to stimuli are interrupted (i.e., disorganized), so that the usual boundaries which structure his thought and perceptions become fluid. The key understanding is that perceptual and conceptual structures (i.e., the ways [processes, screens, filters, patterns] my brain has developed to perceive and understand the world in which I find myself) require the constant *nutrient* of their **accustomed** stimuli; conversely, prolonged minimal scanning and minimal differentiation weaken and disrupt these psychological structures, their functioning is no longer stabilized by constancies and their *reality* breaks down; new and awesome meanings may abound. Silverman discovered in his study that such altered perceptions and resultant disruption of psychological structures within the mystical experience have a high correlation with the sensory and attention patterns of persons (1) in the incipient or acute stages of a schizophrenic episode, (2) undergoing LSD psychotherapy, and (3) in conditions of extreme sensory deprivation. All four (mystics, schizophrenics, psychedelics, and sensory deprived) of these sets of persons experience (idiosyncratically) cosmic consciousness, oneness with the universe, ultra consciousness (i.e., one defying description), exhilaration, ecstasy, serenity, strong positive affect, oceanic engulfment, transcendence of time/space, ancestral and collective unconsciousnesses, new and startling insights, knowledge and understanding, heaven and hell, a diabolical mysticism.

The Bowers paraphrase of this process is that when perceptions are significantly changed, then the psychological structures we need to receive and process incoming data and our response to it begin to break down, and those psychological structures in turn begin to search for a new reality which makes sense of this new data set, which in turn potentially opens the door to new insights, new experiences. From Silverman's and the other three papers I deduce that the mystic, the person reacting to LSD or mescaline, the incipient or acute schizophrenic and the sensory deprived person are all experiencing similarly altered states of consciousness/awareness with similar interpretations/understandings of those. (Most mystics achieve their mystical experiences through several forms of sensory deprivation, i.e., attention narrowing.) I come away from Silverman's paper concluding that the mystic is momentarily experiencing a quite different *reality* than I am in my normal state of consciousness, and that because of temporarily altered psychological structures may actually arrive at new and different knowledge or understandings of reality.

In other words, their insights *may* be beneficial, but not reliably so. In such transcendental (*altered*) states of consciousness (i.e., awareness) persons can acquire genuinely new insights, though those insights are not necessarily valid in an *ordinary* state of awareness (i.e., consciousness); which is to say, such insights are not self-authenticating (as Evelyn Underhill claimed in her study), and must be adjudged with the light of others's *normal* state of consciousness. To say those are of God is to step out of a scientific or logical metaphor and make a statement that cannot be verified. For myself I am not willing to assert that the insights of schizophrenics, druggies and sensory deprived persons are necessarily from God; nor, therefore, can I be confident that the insights of mystics are necessarily from or about God. I conclude that I need not be necessarily accepting of, or trusting of mystical experiences, or accepting that they are of God. Nor am I myself any longer drawn to them.

For me Julian Silverman's study demystified the whole *corpus* of mysticism. I no longer wrestle with the *authority* of mystical experiences. The insights that arise out of some are profound, life-changing, even history-changing. The insights of others seem little but bits of gibberish. The real test for me is that some *work* i.e., are successful in coping with this **ordinary** reality and bringing about extraordinary change while others do not. For me the authority of those insights comes not from their source, but that they work in this reality. Whether the experiences themselves are of the God or about the God or caused by the God is indeterminate. I accept from catalogers like Underhill and Williams, and from the reports of the mystics themselves that the mystical experiences are exquisitely gizzard-tickling; but for my money they are *throw-aways* unless the insights they yield are useful and beneficial.

Suffice it to say I came away from his study convinced that the mystical experience is as simple as an altered state of awareness, and that the experiences and insights of mystics (whether about the God or anything else) are no more self-authenticating, reliable or verifiable than the insights of schizophrenics and psychedelics to which they are akin and need to be scrutinized just as closely and objectively as those others.

---

comprehensions of reality. My conclusion out of this (perhaps too simplistically) is that the insights of mystics are of roughly the same ilk as those of schizophrenics, drug-trippers, or sensorily deprived persons, and are no more to be automatically trusted than these. All such insights should be taken seriously, but scrutinized in light of **this** reality in which we daily live, and not from within such perception-altered experiences.

Chapter 2: The Stepstones of My Pilgrimage

Since arriving at that conclusion I have felt somewhat like I'm wandering spiritually without a guide, but fortunately with a small coterie of similarly wandering friends.

One other book has factored exceedingly important in my wanderings, the book which gave me real permission. I had been wandering some time, knew I had wandered beyond the hedges of orthodox doctrine, and while not feeling *lost*, was uncomfortable, unsure of where I was wandering. I sat down one afternoon with the Lutheran associate pastor at St. Luke's who is trained in spiritual direction and he helped me walk through and sort out what was going on for me. At the end of our session John loaned me a copy of James Fowler's book, **Stages of Faith**. Nothing else has been so affirming and assuring. Out of his research Fowler described six stages of faith development.[6] I learned that I was not lost, simply wandering my way beyond the conventional faith where I'd labored for all of my career, and out into the next stage. Known territory, unfamiliar to me but known to others. I was freed to wander.

---

6. a.) Intuitive-Projective Faith [3-7 years],
   b.) Mythic-Literal Faith [ca. 10 yrs, though some never grow beyond this stage],
   c.) Conventional (i.e., fits general beliefs) Faith [adolescence, sometimes permanent in adults],
   d.) Individuative-Reflective Faith,
   e.) Conjunctive Faith [no simple definition], and
   f.) Universalizing Faith [only a few, e.g., Gandhi and Mother Theresa].

Chapter 3: My Circle of Standing Stones

I HAVE NEVER BEEN able to sustain a discipline of journaling for more than a few days at a time. But at this Christmas Eve service I found my mind wandering. Not intentionally. Not even absent-mindedly, nor out of boredom. And the thoughts seemed substantive, worthwhile. So I paid attention. I suppose these bits may have been the beginning of my spiritual wandering. You might want to watch for that as we proceed.

St. Luke's in Granville is my circle of standing stones. What I mean by that will become apparent as you read.

December 24, 2007, Christmas Eve—11:20pm

I sit and listen. I sit and luxuriate, I wallow in the atmosphere. I sit and wonder. I suppose the midnight Christmas service has always been my favorite. As Susan Lehman suggested in my theological infancy, the Jews had it right, the Christians got it wrong when we switched from Friday evening to Sunday morning. I know the historical and theological rationales for the change. But they are *ex post facto*. And whatever rationalizations they scream in my ear, they still got it wrong. The reality is that evening times, midnight and pre-dawn are the magical times for worship. So the Christmas Eve midnight service has everything going for it, as does the Easter Eve Vigil. The hour and the colors and the smells and the cold, crisp breezes (maybe even snow!) outside, but inside the warm, friendly faces and bodies crowded together, enjoying being together, and surrounding, embracing, enfolding it all the dark and candlelit, mysterious night.

I cannot really remember my first Christmas Eve church service, but it was certainly in my pre-teen years. That and New Year's Eve were the only times I was allowed to stay up that late. It was a rare privilege, a special occasion. The very dark, small, old, clapboard church, candlelit (long before fire marshals thought to shut down such operations), one of the rare times when it was very filled with people, with two lighted balsam trees perfuming the air with Christmas aromas jammed inside the tiny sanctuary, so it was nearly impossible for the priest and acolyte to maneuver inside the altar rail, swatches of pines hanging from the window sconces and pew ends, red bows everywhere, and wonderful music, the organ and the singing choir, familiar but special Christmas carols. It all worked together to make that dark hour magical, and filled with mysteries intended to be savored, not solved. Warm, very tender memories. Powerful, healing memories. Binding, life-giving memories.

So tonight, an old man now, I sit and watch, and listen, and sense, and wonder: what's it all about? Oh, I know the theological content, the rational and supra-rational content. It's been my profession for over forty years. But tonight I sit and wonder what it's all about. Stephen preaches, thinner stuff tonight than his usual (but that's alright, because the preaching of the word does not carry the message this night; the darkness and every other wonderful thing inside this building convey the complex of messages), so I sit and hear the words, but my listening is more inward, a wondering: what's it about? What is wanting to be said to me? To be heard by me? The secular Christmas has become such an impossibly heavy, jangling and jarring noise (an annoying, no, a disorienting cacophonous racket I want to creep away from, really). What's the real message here in the dark quietness?

And here, in the dimming years of my life, I wonder what it's really all about, this Christian stuff? I've learned it and recited it and preached it and taught it for six decades now, but more and more in recent years I quietly wonder, what's it **really** been about? As I age, and the experiences of my spirit wander outside the boundaries of accepted and promulgated Christian orthodoxy, I wonder. And that's what these pages are about, my wonderings. Call it "speculative theology."

So as I sit in church on this Christmas Eve and wonder these days, I say to myself, "Now, Bowers, this is your chosen standing stone circle. So, what's it about? What is going on here, at the describable level, or at the unknowable?" The answer comes quietly, muttered deep inside myself in mumblings incomprehensible and unrepeatable, but significant. I can almost hear the words, the ancient truths, but not quite. Not yet. But I keep listening And anticipating.

****

Palm Sunday, 2008—Sitting in Church

Palm Sunday has never been satisfying to me, as a liturgist or as a participant. It is such an **odd** perversion of the regular Sunday liturgy. We begin with that curious little blessing of palm branches which are then given to all without instruction what to do with them (the kids's notion of sticking them in each others's eyes might be the best suggestion). And then we sing a hymn, sometimes processing about inside, or outside, or from outside to inside *(Stephen's favorite)* or watching others (the choir and crucifer, for instance) process around, all very messy and poorly organized. My sense and experience is that congregations don't like this falderal. But then, that's what I (as liturgist) have always intended, that they should be *very* discomforted by it. After all, it intends to capture just a smidgeon of what the disciples and bystanders might have felt, doesn't it?

Back in our usual (translate "accustomed") places, we go through some regular prayers and readings and such, standing and sitting (perhaps even kneeling), until we find ourselves sitting(!) in the middle of the Gospel reading, listening to the priest read (or having the Gospel read as a dramatic reading by members of the congregation) with all of us shouting "Crucify him, crucify him!" the **whole** Passion Story (and t-t-t-that, folks, is why we are wont to call this Passion Sunday, because we read the **whole** passion story in case some here won't make it back before Easter morn). The preacher preaches, trying to make sense of this and linking all of Holy Week together. And from there on out it's a regular Sunday Eucharist.

I've never felt it worked. But then in seminary and ever afterward no one taught us how to make it work, or what "work" might mean even in this context. What **should** this Palm Sunday liturgy do for us, or to us? We know that probably it's all most will see of Holy Week until Easter morning (although this week is the *very* core of what it's all about, not just Easter morning, but all of this week [yet few will participate on Maundy Thursday or Good Friday. And gawdforbid they might do anything about it on Monday or Tuesday or Wednesday or Saturday], and then they'll wonder why Easter turned out to be a let-down, not the whoop-tee-doo we want it to be.)

Holy Week tells the center and depth of the story, what Christianity is all about, how in Jesus' self-sacrifice God's redeeming of His people was worked out. This week is really the only liturgical work of the Christian year, and everything else is build-up or follow-up (or towards the end of Pentecost *let-down*). So this is it! How do we make it spiritually richer for people (assuming that they, like me, want it richer)?

And then I muse, "When you (Bowers, or anyone else still listening) have mastered all this (the Passion story, and the liturgy, and the Scriptures, and standard Christian theology, and all the exercises and stuff that goes with it), then do not give up, do not stop to rest a while. Do not think, 'This is it, this is all I need.' Because this is only a beginning place, one foundation stone, one among several possibilities, on which to build our spiritual lives." There are other foundation stones too: Judaism, Islam, Buddhism, Hinduism, naturalism. They all are reaching toward the same, toward the Eternal. And while we proclaim that ours is the best way, maybe even the only way, I'm not so sure there are not other ways, equally good, perhaps better ways, to discover the *Eternal* in our lives. But I am thinking that this stuff, by itself, will not do it!

****

Gors Fawr

Near the beginning of my pilgrimage sabbatical in Wales I hired a guide to carry me from St. David's at land's end down to Tenby on the southern coast, and enroute to show me some of the more powerful ancient ruins strewn along the way. I was on my way to the Cistercian monastery on Caldey Island to write my second book, daily prayers written in the Celtic tradition (i.e., of Alexander Carmichael's **Carmina Gadelica**) with a brief, opening exposition of Celtic Christian spirituality to buttress and inform the readers of my daily prayers. Terry John was my guide that day, a native of the region, well-educated, who had taught in London most of his years, but was now retired back homeward. And being a native he had the credentials to ask questions of his native elders and peers, questions about ancient lore and beliefs and traditions. So he carried within him ancient lore that is nowhere in the books. He took me past a single standing stone that on a certain night each spring is painted white. No one in the community seemed to know, or, more likely, was willing to admit, who did that. Nor had anyone any idea (or was willing to admit) why that was done. It had always been. I asked him to take me to a circle of standing-stones among other things. I wanted to *experience* it more than see it. I'd seen others, but always when I'd been in groups. I wanted to have quiet time alone in a circle, to feel whatever might be felt there, to sense whatever might be sensed. He took me to Gors Fawr. It is a modest circle of seventy-three feet with sixteen local stones, none being more than thirty inches tall. I wandered among the stones. He told me facts about the stones and the circle. After some time I asked him, "What was this about? I know some people claim these circles were astrological observatories, others that they were the site of religious ceremonies. What do you think they were?" He was quiet for a few moments (as though considering whether I could be trusted with his answer), and then shared that he thought the circles were multi-purpose. That they served as a community gathering place, and certainly were constructed with astrological dimensions for agricultural purposes, and were possibly also market places, might have been used for ceremonials and religious rites, perhaps for political and civic and governance gatherings. He found it significant that the circles were often within sight of other circles, so they must have had some larger-than-community purposes as well. And that all made sense to me. I did *feel* something at that circle, particularly at one of the stones, but I'd be hard pressed to tell you what I felt, certainly not something I'm aware of feeling in everyday happenings and places.

So these days when I find myself in church I usually am asking myself, "Bowers, this is the circle of standing-stones you have chosen, and that seems to have chosen you. What's it about? What's going on here today? Why are these people and I gathered here? If this is our metaphor, our circle of standing stones, what is it saying? What is it pointing toward? To what unknowable and inexpressible reality is it trying to give voice? What am I listening for here?"

****

The Liminal

I need to wonder aloud for a few minutes about the liminal. A Latin word, *limen* which we translate "threshold," that member of the doorway which we step over as we go in and out the house, or maybe we linger on it as we briefly contemplate the day ahead. The ancient Celts considered thresholds to be sacred places, places where we are most likely to encounter the holy, the sacred, the spirit world, the LORD. Not just doorway thresholds, but all kinds of thresholds, places of transition, when we step from one place, one time, one life into another. All primitives who live close to nature know about limens and liminality. Where the water of a spring which has spent eons underground unseen in blinded blackness, suddenly gushes forth cool, clear, fresh into the light and air for drinking and giving life. Where the river courses along the bank carrying flotsam and boats. Where the mountain top touches the sky. When the day meets the night, and night the day. Where the forest touches the open plain. At equinox when the dark of night becomes longer than daylight. Where the wilderness meets civilization, or one country warily touches another. When drowsiness slips into sleep. Where death overtakes life, and when new life is born. Thresholds, transitions, boundaries, crossings, moments when all creation seems to pause and breathe deeply, silently, watching to see.

I have learned that dusk and pre-dawn are the best times to pray; God is most willing to be present, or perhaps we are most open to Her presence. The instant when I discovered my wife dead, God held me back from tumbling down into the black abyss of chaos. When Nancy and I stood before our gathered family and friends and said "I do" to each other and to the gathered community. I have sat on the boulders at Govan's Chapel tucked into the gap in a cliff side as a gale blew sea foam around me and over the cliff top and knew I was with God. All places and times of transition are limens, moments when, for an instant, we are *in between*. My dad used to talk about "Hobble-de-hoy, neither man nor boy," in between being a child and becoming an adult. Limens are everywhere once we begin to recognize them and watch for them. And they can be very important moments in our spiritual lives, moments when we are vulnerable, and can be very present to God.

I have been in lots of liminal places. Sometimes Nancy and I make that an element, a goal of our travels, to discover and collect a few more liminal experiences. In-between places, in-between times. Places where time seems to slow and pause for a little before moving on to tomorrow. Places where the land ends, and I creep as close as I can *(I'm acrophobic)* to the edge of a cliff and look down eight hundred feet at the waves crashing on the rocks, and ask . . . *(there are no words)*. Caldey Island is a liminal place where time itself doesn't quite stop, but becomes unimportant, where the ancient and the present collapse together, and I could stand in one place and ask all the questions that had never been answered, no matter that there was no one, and nothing to answer. But there came an answer, not in words, not even in ideas or forms or images. Locked in a burial chamber in Loughcrew. Spaces for wondering. Sitting on the rocks at land's end and watching the waves crashing for hours, and hearing non-voices uttering, perhaps in my imagination, or in the rhythms of the seas and the pounding of the waves. Places to listen—and to hear the sound of the great nothing that lies beyond it all.

Chapter 3: My Circle of Standing Stones

The illustrating example of the liminal commonly given is of the tribal initiation rites for boys-becoming-men. The boys, about to become un-children are taken from their families and villages to a remote ritual site and subjected there to various ordeals or humiliations (sounds much like hazing rituals), trained by older men. The dark is often an integral part, as in a darkened hut, at night, in a cave. Sometimes mutilations such as tattoos or scarification or circumcision. This may go on for a few days or months or even years. There is often some encounter with the gods or the ancestors. They may be taught skills. At the end, a highly ritualistic reunion. The boys have died and are now reborn as men, sometimes with new names, sometimes needing to be taught to recognize relatives and friends. The liminal is a "betwixt and between" time, no longer boys, but not yet men. All old is stripped away, and the new is received, like recruits in miliary barracks stripped of "civies," dressed in ill-fitting uniforms, given rifles, and forced to live in an unnatural community. For a period the boys have no family or friends, just each other and a few older men as guides, so new relations must be built, without status or class. This is an in-between time when you give up the old and prepare to take on the new, get ready to become something, someone you have not been before. It is a time given to begin the processional from the known to the unknown. And it is a time to consider what it will be like to be a man. A honeymoon is a very palpable liminal time in which we stop being an individual and become a mini-community.

There are liminal **places** (boundaries, no-man's-lands, crossroads, land's ends, mountain tops, seashores, river banks, artesian springs, sacred worship places, cemeteries), and liminal **spaces** (two-dimensional plots of land, one-dimensional pathways and ley-lines, zero-dimensional omphalos *[translate: navel]* and axis mundi *[translate: axis of the earth]* the dream time (i.e., of Australian aboriginals), and liminal **times** (the New Year, equinoxes and solstices, birthdays and anniversaries, dusk and dawn, initiations, waking from sleep, "Once-upon-a-time" [of faerie tales]), and liminal **events** (births, marriages, deaths, life-changing happenings), and liminal **journeys** (pilgrimages, retreats, dyserts, sabbaticals), and even liminal **living** (persons of lameness or disabilities, babies born with cauls, hermits, tramps, priests and monastics and such, contrarians, fools). *Liminal* is stepping from the known to whatever lies beyond.

God is very close, very present, very accessible in liminals. Or perhaps, inversely, it is we who are, can be, more open to God in liminals. When I came down the stairs and discovered Suzy cold and dead, God clasped me tightly in Her embrace.

****

Maundy Thursday, 2008—Thoughts

We stand, we kneel, we sit, we sing together, we listen to the priest and to the choir, we recite in unison memorized ancient pieces, we read others aloud together, we speak responsively back to a reader. Liturgy is multi-sensual: splotches of colors, beautiful brocades, the sight and smell of candles (and in some other churches, the luscious, choking smell of incense rolling up in clouds), the sounds of the organ and piano and on occasion other instruments played with deep devotion, of voices singing, speaking, chanting, the taste of fish food wafers and wine, the warmth and smells and sensuousness of gathered bodies. And in the midst of all that we imagine we are speaking to God.

What does it mean tonight? This Maundy Thursday? We commemorate and symbolically enact the last meal Jesus had with his disciples. Tomorrow on our liturgical clock he will die! But this is tonight. And we try to live it out by commemorating the eating of that last meal, a Passover meal, the betrayer fleeing the room, the ragtag procession to Gethsemane, their sleeping vigil, his pleading "Take away this cup from me!" with gobs of bloody sweat, the clanging and chinking noises of steel weapons as the soldiers work into the park to take him, his surrender, him led away to trial, the faithful followers's stark terror of flight, scared shitless, running for their very lives. We commemorate. Tonight.

So tonight we gather as it is darkening, to go through the regular, familiar liturgy with only minor variations. The music is darker this night, heavier, to try to capture the mood of that last supper. Or perhaps to capture our own moods as we think forward to the gruesome execution tomorrow morning, as though we might be there. The rest of the liturgy is not so very unlike the way we celebrate it every other day. Until we get to the end. And then, in silence, they strip the altar. Take away every piece of color, every bit of shiny metal, every candle and bit of light. They veil the cross. They remove every moveable thing that makes this space look and feel liturgically lived in. While we watch, in silence, listening to the awkward noises. Noting the slight disorganizedness. And finally we leave in silence, sombered, as the place is darkened and some one lonely person prepares to spend hours here in this darkened, empty, spooky space, vigilling. In some places there is an unnerving variation, we wash each others's feet! Because he did it. In other places there is one additional piece; after they have stripped the altar, and everything else they can, they wash the altar, as we silently watch, not with soapy water to make it clean, but with wine and water to ritually purify it, to make it ready for the sacrifice. And what does all that mean?

This is the circle of standing stones that I have chosen for myself and which seems to have chosen me as well. So tonight I have to ask, "What does it mean? What is it about? What, beyond the obvious and the stated, is going on here? Why do we bother to do it? What is its power, for us? What are **we** here to commemorate? To **do**? Does it make ANY difference whatsoever?"

Eucharist (*making thanks*) is always about *community* about this community of the faithful (whoever they happen to be). In this **very** symbolic, very **stylized** meal we celebrate our community, we enact our chosen community, we reinforce and solidify this community we each have chosen for ourselves and for each other, this community that is for us the living body of the risen Christ. And as this community gathers we imagine that the Christ is present in every person who joins the circle, and in the gathered circle itself. Christ is here. Now. At this very moment! Or so we imagine.

But what is different about this night is that tonight we celebrate not just the community, but the community disassembled, torn apart, shredded, scared witless and running for our very lives. Community shattered. Obliterated! And what would it be like without community? That is the metaphor this evening. And what does the metaphor point toward? What truth, what reality beyond the *limen* does it open out for us?

****

The Imaginal

Several months ago I stumbled across the notion of the *imaginal* I recall not where. I Googled it and came up with three articles, which, I must confess, is all I've read on the topic. But I must also confess that the notion fascinates me, and I suspect it is one, if not the primary, gateway into the world of mysticism. Briefly the notion is this: that the faculty of the imagination enables us to enter, be in relation to, communicate with, be educated by non-physical cosmologies which are every bit as real as the physical/material world in which we live this material life. The articles I read, one by Dr. Gerald Epstein, a psychiatrist who uses the imaginal in his practice, and two by Henri Corbin, an interpreter of Arabic and Persian texts (perhaps an authority on Shi'a, Islamic mysticism, certainly conversant with it) introduced me to a strange new world.

The imaginal is very difficult for me; I am very much dedicated, both by psychological make-up and by ingrained training, to the left-brain, rational, linear kind of mental life. My personality type (INTP in Myers-Briggs) is such that if something is not logical, then it is nonsense. But the imaginal is the mental life of the right-brain. And I think I may have missed something potentially very significant for my life. I will not pretend that I understand this term "imaginal." I only know it **seems** to make sense to me.

Evidently we of the western world have been trapped and held captive by René Descartes (1596-1650) when he proclaimed, "I think, therefore I am!" *(though I was taught in Philosophy 101* "**Dubito**, *ergo cogito, ergo sum"*). And ever since we have locked ourselves into a thought system in which the linear, the logical, the left-brain is dominant, and right-brain processes are largely discarded as dealing with unrealities. In the West it is thinking alone that is important and worthy of being worked with (and it must be logical, linear thinking, dealing with the empirical, the hard-data stuff of this material life). "Imagining" and "imaging" are considered illogical, irrational, non-linear and therefore fictitious, unreal, and not useful. We bear this burden of logicality, perhaps to our souls's detriment and ill-health, and maybe even death. In consequence we have carefully learned that our imagination is the gateway to fantasy, fiction, the unreal, "made-up stuff," but not possibly to anything in any sense real or worthy of serious consideration, certainly nothing that should influence our lives.

I'm told that most of the peopled world do not feel so limited. In Eastern cultures they proclaim existence by saying simply, "I am," *(i.e., not compelled to prefix it with a condition of rationality)*. That includes the imaginal as well as the logical. And that, in turn, opens worlds hidden from us Westerners by our insistence of logicality. In particular the Chinese, Tibetan Buddhist and Islamic (Shi'a) cultures are open to and make much use of the imaginal. Epstein suggests that linear (left-hemisphere) thought processes deal primarily with factuality and the past, and cannot effectively cope with the future, whereas right-hemisphere (*gestalt*) processes, can deal effectively with the present and future, and are therefore much more potent and realistic for dealing with some kinds of psychological issues. Corbin is quite clear that imaginal processes open to us vast universes, very **real** universes of knowledge, experience and possibilities not apprehended through linear processes.

William James saw a progression for a religion evolving from the mystical experience of a seer, through a codification stage which begins to develop logical constructs for the mystic's vision, and on to a final *institutional* stage which is constructed for the consumption of the masses attracted by the mystic's vision. It is the mystic's vision which is enervating, exciting, life-giving. But his vision can not be apprehended by the rest of us. His vision must be captivated, and shaped into something translatable for the rest of us. And finally it is institutionalized into a form which, while fixed, stable, and in a sense *dead*, the rest of us can cling to, something we can ingest without getting indigestion. Jesus was the founding mystic whose vision so captivated the masses; and Paul was the initial *codifier* (though perhaps he was himself a mystic with his Damascus road experience and his ascent into the third heaven) who began the process of shaping Jesus' vision into something the rest of us could grasp and cling to. And the bishops of the third and fourth centuries were the institutionalizers who built it all into a *church* that Constantine and the rest of us could live into. In essence, only the mystic, the visioner has the deeply *religious* experience, the face-to-face encounter with The Other, which the rest of us, in whatever insipid ways, attempt to emulate, in the light of which we *warm* ourselves.

****

Reciting the creed

Every Sunday we stand up in unison and recite together the creed. The Nicene Creed of course, that ecumenical statement of what we, the whole church universal believe. That tersest, densest, briefest definition of *the faith* constructed by the bishops of the early church at the behest of the emperor to unify the church. That *hedge* which protects the church from false beliefs and divisiveness, that says, "To believe inside this hedge is safe, okay; adhere to this; but if you believe outside this, you perish, **eternally**." It tells us that **believing** is what this religious stuff is all about, holding tight onto a linear (more or less) statement of facts (some material, some immaterial) about the construction of this metaphysic. That is what is crucial, clinging onto THIS basket of words, lined up in THIS order. *Knowing* God, having intercourse with God does not enter into it.

This credo was composed in the fourth century, phrased in the metaphors and imagery of the fourth century, with all the metaphysical and physical and biological assumptions of the fourth century built into and standing behind it. The earth is flat and has four corners. There is water underneath, land and water here, and above the dome of the sky more water. Hell is a physical place somewhere down there, and heaven an equally physical place up there somewhere in which God lives. And this earth is the center of the universe, and man the most important creation in it, the apex of all God's creation. And the male carries the seed, is the sole procreator, while woman is only the incubator, has no part in conception, is a mobile uterus to house the seed until it grows able to live outside the uterus. All of that comes along with this basket full of creedal words, some of which I cannot even pretend I understand. So, when we stand up to say the Creed together, professing that **this** is what we, **all** we, believe, can I do that without biting my tongue? Or am I allowed to cross my fingers so that I do not perjure myself?

Marcus Borg covers himself by saying that he understands this creed to be an historic statement made by the church at a certain time and in response to certain circumstances; and he recites it along with us in that context. And in response to the question, "Is Jesus the second person of the Trinity?" he would answer both "No" and "Yes!" And I think I must nod my head in painful agreement as he speaks. You want a simple, straight-forward answer where I think there is none. I cannot even conceive of what you mean by a Trinity, which is what the Nicene Creed is supposedly about. How can one God be three? The math doesn't work for me. (And to call it a "mystery," i.e., not to be solved, makes it no more apprehensible or useful for me; been there, done [or tried to do] that, didn't work, at least for me.) How can Jesus have been fully man *(which necessarily entails mortality, and all the other human limitations)* and fully God *(which we have always understood to mean immortal and unlimited)*. These two things cannot be one and the same. So I covertly step across the aisle and stand alongside Borg, and mutter the words with my fingers crossed. If you intend these words to mean precisely what they say and nothing else, then I have to quietly confess, "No." But if you might allow that they comprise a sort of window that offers *(in ancient language that is almost entirely incomprehensible to the twenty-first-century Western mind and with a whole set of assumptions that I know to be quite inaccurate and inadequate for today's world and metaphor)* a sort of window that will give the merest vague and ephemeral glimpse of the Eternal which is in reality far beyond our scope of vision and power of comprehension, then I can quietly nod the slightest agreement.

So when we stand in unison to recite the creed, I join in because I understand that the Church has always (since 325 or 381 AD or thereabouts) done this as a token of our unanimity that something beyond our imagining happened in the man Jesus whom we call the Christ, something which gave us the clearest image we've ever had, before or since, of what God is about; but at the same time I understand that these words are **only** the vaguest token of what happened, not a precise and literalist encapsulation of the Jesus event, not the be-all and end-all of faith statements. It is a token, a pretty incomprehensible token, and nothing more. The creed is not a sword to conquer the world, or to fall on. It is a token to hold onto when feeling desperate; and little more. As a statement of all that is necessary to eternal salvation, it is a farce. But I agree to join in with your recitation of it because this church is the spiritual home I have always belonged to, I want no other, and this is one thing we do; we say these words together, to affirm both to ourselves and to each other our belongingness.

But as I have begun to explore, and search, and wander the spiritual world in which I find myself these days, this creed is no guide, and is not even a hedge to keep me safe. (Although it could *hedge me in,* keep me back from any useful reaching out to *know* God, to have intimate intercourse with whatever is *the ultimate*. But then that holding-back might be, historically, the real intention of a creed.)

And what if the God I am coming to know does not fit inside this creed? What then?

But on the other hand, all these words I have just written about the creed comprise a linear, logical, rational world view. And I've written them just after I tried to say a few intelligible words about the *imaginal*. So after I've mastered the creed and all that other seemingly linear, rational stuff, my hunch is that the imaginal is my only route beyond, an alternative to the linear, toward the Eternal. But I'm not much good at the imaginal, am I? So maybe at this point I should say along with Lilly Tomlin, "Oh, never mind!"and get on with it.

****

Easter V, 2008

I made no notes to myself during the sermon on Easter morning. They would have been embarrassing. I've spent most of my lifetime in a ministry for which Holy Week and Easter is the very core, the defining moment, the most important moment of the Christian year. But now I am no longer sure what these moments are about (was I ever sure, or just "putting it on"? And have I *lost* my faith, or merely begun to wander somewhere beyond it?) So my notes would have been embarrassing. I would have admitted to myself that Easter morning is always a let-down for me, always has been,

Chapter 3: My Circle of Standing Stones

has never lived up to the hype. Palm Sunday, Maundy Thursday, Good Friday, even Holy Saturday, these I can get into. These are human events; they are about the very down-and-dirty moments and events of our lives. They are real, and I can dig my fingers and intellectual claws, my emotional claws, into them. So when I wake up on Easter morning I expect more of that, only much more intensely, excitingly. (It's gotta be at least a little better than searching out an Easter basket full of chocolates and an opera cream Easter egg.) But it's not! Lots of wonderful colors and sounds and smells and tastes, with pounds and pounds of frappery and gingerbread. So much preparation and promise, and then, the same old liturgy with a few kinks thrown in. The week was about real, human stuff; but this is about something way outside the human. Something ineffable, untouchable, something beyond. It's about what cannot be said, defined, or described. And the hoked-up celebration just doesn't make it for me. I always hope it does for others. But after all these years I've come to not expect much any more.

So Eastertide begins to drag for me. After that Easter morning let-down, and then six Sundays of preaching about John's post-resurrection stories I began to run dry and wish for some of the Pentecost season readings from the Hebrew Scriptures, rich, powerful, human stories you can really sink your teeth into. And then this morning we arrived at the story of Stephen, the new deacon who left off deaconing and took up preaching and got himself stoned to death for it. Had a vision as he was dying, and as he shouted out his vision, well, I thought, that's what happens to mystics; they get stoned, and then someone accommodatingly stones them to death. Happened to the prophets. Happened to Jesus (except execution by suffocation, shock and exposure on a Roman cross instead of rocks). Now it's happening to Stephen. And others will follow. Mystics are just too off-the-wall, too loose-cannon-ish, too outside the limits, beyond the pale. They can't be tamed, and so they can't be tolerated. They can't be controlled, and they dream weird things, wheels within wheels and hundred-eyed indescribable critters, things that point beyond the texts, beyond the codified experiences, beyond the expectable. And those dreams point toward mysteries not captured *(perhaps not even hinted)* in the holy writings, mysteries more indescribable than trinities, mysteries more fundamental than even YHWH.

And I, fool that I am, have a yen for some mystical experiences. I think they might open understandings deeper and richer and more elemental and more extensive and more profound than the tales of Hebrews and their images of the eternal. I would hope for glimpses, mere glimpses mind you, of the chasms and abysses that illuminated and motivated Jesus. Souls are willing to be stoned to death for things like that, and some people are always willing to accommodate them.

****

Part I: The Pilgrimage from There to Here

Feast of Pentecost and Mothers's Day—May 11, 2008

Nancy and I took Ed and Marvine to their church this morning, a small, very country church with an average age of about seventy-five. Found myself reflecting on what a different circle of standing stones this was. A country UCC church, farmers and such, just coming off a short, bad pastorate with a gal they should never have called, now being interimed by a senior pastor who'd served here before, but only as long-term Sunday Supply. She fits them well, seems as country and down home as they are. And I reflected (though I'd been here before and reflected on this community before) how different an experience this was from our normal St. Luke's, Episcopal experience. No formal liturgy here to speak of. But lots and lots of family. What happens in this circle of stones? A reinforcement of this as a chosen extended family. These folks **seem** to like each other, feel at home around each other (I've no hint what ancient animosities and dividing biases separate them; they keep those monsters hidden even from themselves). The first minutes were taken with greetings around the room (time is deliberately or *accidentally* given for this), and the formal service began after this was completed. The pastor began with a folksy litany built around "This is for mothers who . . . ." Folksy, country stuff that said "You're okay, we're okay." Not stiff Anglican liturgical material. A lot of (*hidden*) stuff was going on (*I felt*). Not clear how much of it was Christian. The words of the service were built around the Pentecost readings, but I was not clear that the underlying messages were; they seemed to me more American, mid-Western, farming country messages, and I suspect you need to be a seasoned member of this community to comprehend the underlying, subtle, not explicitly voiced messages. But values were being reinforced. And the pastor knows how to talk with them, country-folk. So a kind of matriarchy was going on. At announcement time one mother touted her son's perfectly pitched baseball game the day before, seventy-five pitches for the whole seven innings. A round of applause felt appropriate, though not given. As a preacher she seemed to me somewhat scatter-shot with Pentecost messages about getting some mission going, and the Interim's messages about some things that need to be happening here, get with it! Not my kind of tight and obviously erudite piece of scholarship. And no Communion; but that was missed only by my Anglican fixation on Eucharist. But these were folks who were enjoying seeing each other for an hour, and then anxious to get on homeward. This circle is about such different things than my St. Luke's that it is kind of amusing *(though to say that would sound deprecating, which I do not intend)*. And I can only hunch what things are given voice and enactment within this circle; I'm deaf as a post to their language, unable to hear what is being said in between and underneath the words. This is not my circle of standing stones.

Perhaps at St. Luke's we are reaching out to touch the **numinous** in our very stiff and formalized, ritualistic, liturgical ways; while here they seem reaching for family, farm community, for *keeping-it-together* kinds of things through a very loose, flexible, transparent kind of liturgy.

****

My Circle of Standing Stones

So each Sunday I make the pilgrim trek to my particular circle of stones *(I pass two other Episcopal ones enroute, one because the pastor is a proudly self-proclaimed redneck who preaches a funny, backwoods version of Americanism with some gospel stuff occasionally thrown in; and the other because the now-moved-on rector chased Nancy and me away with her incompetent temper tantrums)* and wonder, "What am I getting from this community, circle of stones?" and "What is this community, this circle of standing stones needing or wanting of me?" I know I am trying to reach far beyond what this circle can open to me. I can still enjoy and engage in the intellectual musings of this community; they are fun, but in the end insufficient to fund my searching. And I've thus far found no one standing in this circle whom I trust to search alongside. So that is not its drawing for me, not a place to deepen and extend my search for the eternal.

And the liturgy? Well, it's mine, it's what I grew up with (despite the superficial changes of the 1979 Prayer Book revision), it's what I was trained in and practiced professionally for so many years. I am accustomed to and feel most comfortable with it; it is my liturgical home. And it is **a** *limen* for me, in its own way, a doorway that opens in a **very** limited way, to whatever lies beyond, a tiniest, halting baby step toward an *Eternal*. But I have come to understand that liturgy is a communal thing, it is done to foster the community; it cannot, is not designed or intended to feed the individual's soul. No one has told me that; I have gradually uncovered that for myself, and I do not know if that is true for anyone else around me, or whether anyone else has ever discovered it. So my **soul-feeding** must happen elsewhere, through some other *limen* or imaginal. Liturgy has become comforting, but not illuminating, and is instructive only to a minuscule degree. It is a comforting metaphor, but I am unclear for what.

And while I like the people who gather in this circle, and enjoy being with some of them, this is a **very** artificially chosen extended family for me. They are not intimate family or friends for me. But then I am a very alone person who has, or needs very few intimates or compatriots.

So what is this circle for me? I am no longer sure. It draws me back, and I willingly participate. It yields me some little time, some little place, some little focus to muse, to recall, to re-sort, to review and reframe. It causes me to pay enough attention to ask, "What is happening here? What is this about?" and "What is it pointing toward? For what is it the metaphor?" Probably without this time and place I would not take the time to wonder, much less to ask. It does that much. And perhaps it does much more. Perhaps it reminds me that there is something much more than what is happening here, something to which I, Jack Bowers, need to be paying attention. It invites me. But to what?

And what is this circle of standing stones needing of me? I've so little notion of what I have to give, and even less a clue as to what it is in need of. What do I bring that it wants, or needs?

****

A Saturday—September 20, 2008

And now I place one foot outside my standing stone circle, and begin to wonder, perhaps to wander. Odds and ends begin to pile up, bits and pieces, and to join up, and to form a vague alternative to this particular circle, a not-yet-viable alternative, an only vague one.

I've been scouring, even teaching Jack Miles's book, **God: a biography**. He tracks the YHWH of the Hebrew Scriptures, from Genesis through Chronicles, watching simply what He does and says, and asking "Who is He? What is He?" The portrait that emerges is not pretty, from a majestic and then bumbling creator-friend, into a demanding family protector, then on to a violent and sometimes cruel war-god and coercive law-giver, compact-enforcer, next a jealous and loyalty-demanding overlord who moves on to take up international roles, and then, when his covenant with his chosen people fails, a half-insane *(manic-depressive?)* God who, alternately pleading and then abusing, abandons his people, condemns them into exile, and after they return, becomes an increasingly absent God who, while not totally abandoning, fails to make any significant difference. I have not done a similar study of the God of the Gospels and early Christian writings, but at a first glance, the picture is only slightly more attractive.

I've been plowing my way through Karen Armstrong's book, **A History of God**, in which she tracks the development of the several images of God in Judaism, Christianity and Islam, just barely touching Buddhism and Hinduism. It is fascinating to watch the evolution, from familial and tribal gods, through Scriptural presentations, and as those prove insufficient, through further evolving images. I get a portrait of a God who, when frozen into Scriptures, wanes insufficient, and is then further explored with philosophic *(on the rational side)* terms and in mystics's *(on the imaginal side)* terms. Several things become clearer:

1) Armstrong points out (and others echo) that the mystics's ways are for the few, that not many of us can achieve mystical vision, but that on the other hand, religions begin with the mystics's visions full of energy and magnetic excitement, but that as the mystic's vision is codified into a religion it becomes frozen, static and unmoving. The religion is the lay (i.e., non-mystic) person's effort to respond to the mystical vision,

but it is doomed to fail (i.e., to not be as inspiring and motivating as the mystical vison itself).

2) Each *major* religion has evolved its own mystical side, but that side is always on the fringe, too radicalizing to be at the center, and while it may subtly and gradually shift the focus or direction or center, it is at the same time threatening and at odds with the center.

3) Those mystical visions often wander off in directions quite different from the center's vision, and are sometimes even antithetical. The God of most mystics is quite unlike the YHWH of Genesis-Isaiah. And

4) Armstrong, along with others, points out that Christianity in the West has been **taken captive**, and held hostage, by rationalism, spurns the non-rational, the irrational, the imaginal. We in the West have little patience for the mystical visionary, we give him only slight berth, and certainly ignore his wisdom, while most of the rest of the world, particularly Islam, values his contributions and leadership. We are, religiously, out of step.

And I've forced my way (with elbows and shoulders and knees) through William James's lectures, **Varieties of Religious Experiences** a book I should have read thirty-five or more years ago. While those lectures are now a hundred years out of date, in some ways they are still seminal, in other places they've not yet been heard. On reading him I momentarily understand the fundamentalist mind set (not completely, not really, certainly not sympathetically). James divides us into two sorts, those of "healthy-minded" or "mind-cure" religious experiences (not so positive as those words might imply), and those of "sick-soul" experiences (sometimes as unhealthy as those words imply). Or in other words, those of us whose faith grows slowly *vis-a-vis* those whose faith, like Paul's, is marked with a dramatic conversion experiences. And as I read James with twenty-first-century understandings and insights, I can only wonder to what extent our religious experiences are *hard-wired* genetically or hormonally etched into our neurological pathways. Is it possibly written *in my bones* that I will have or require a conversion experience, or that I will not and will instead slowly mature into my faith? Or that I will have no faith at all, no aptitude towards a god of any sort? (I am not referring to the recent discourses about the possibility of a *religion gene* within our DNA; until it is proven otherwise I think that a stupid notion.)

And I wonder about the imaginal. There is a part of me would have liked to be a mystic, to experience the God directly, without any mediation. I understand that at my age, and lacking as I do the essential discipline, and being probably completely without aptitude, that is not a possibility; but those reasons do not appease my yearning. Yet I can imagine. And I think I could learn to accept my imaginings as another reality.

As I reckon up this small pile of odds and ends, clods and droppings, I begin to wonder about the *whether* of Christianity as **the** religion. Is this belief system any better that any other. Or is it simply the one I grew up with, the one scribbled on my tablet by my parents, and the neighbors (most were Catholic) and the culture. Could I have been just as content (or discontent) as a Muslim? Or a Buddhist? Or a Kabbalist? Is this Christianity no more than one way godward among many? Is it mine simply because it was the most marketable religious system in the fourth-century Mediterranean world? I think that might be. A system grown out of the mystic Jesus' experiences, codified by the brash, enthusiastic genius of the mystic Paul. Did it simply **make the most sense** for the most people throughout most of the Mediterranean basin in 200 AD? Was it simply better coinage than the state religion and folk piety of that day? I remember Dr. Solomon at Bexley Hall commenting in an aside about *folk piety*. Though I cannot recall his words, I do not remember that he disparaged folk piety, rather he seemed to be alerting us to it. I had never heard the term folk piety before, but had come to Bexley deeply imbued in it. Christian folk piety was my religion when I arrived, and I was in the process of exchanging it for a much more intellectual, and intellectually acceptable religion, orthodox Western Christianity. But in retrospect, was the orthodoxy any better than the folk piety? And was it any closer to a relationship with God himself? Or was first century Christianity simply the more marketable folk piety of its day? And converted by those early Church Fathers into a supremely acceptable (for its day) intellectual religious system? And I inherited it. And it's no closer to God that the other stuff, loved mainly because it could claim a real, live martyred human Jesus as its founding mystic?

I am wondering. And wandering. But **not feeling lost**!

****

XIX Pentecost—September 21, 2008

Arrived at church a quarter of an hour before the service, greeted warmly Drew, now a cancer survivor, and settled in to muse a few minutes. Ed Burdick sat down beside me, asked if I was working on my sermon. Notes were appearing, scribbled on the front of my bulletin. It was a productive morning, the musings just kept coming, so cryptic notes kept filling up the blank spaces on the bulletin cover.

I get occasional glimpses. Susan says she doesn't give a hang for the unseen God. And while I sympathize with her disinterest, I do *(and just how-hard wired is that need, I wonder?)* I am curious, but more than just curious. There is a vague yearning, one which I suspect will never be satisfied, at least in this life, to experience God for myself. My occasional glimpses are so vague as to be indescribable. The divinity I glimpse is not the very personal, but very incendiary and inconstant, very human and anthropomorphic YHWH of Hebrew Scriptures. Nor the warmly loving Abba of Jesus' gospels. The God I glimpse *("It," I am inclined to say)* seems remote, impassive. I cannot tell from this perspective whether It has concern for me, for us. My yearning is to see Its face, though, as in the Hebrew writings, to see Its face may be to die. So far I've glimpsed only what seems to be Its backside and I'm still alive. Still, maybe in some sense I have died; at least that ancient, childish comprehension of God has died, and the more matured, Christian comprehension has died as well, along with my clinging to those. In the glimpses I get the God does not seem to care that I am peeping at It, yet I *sense* It may care in some vague sense. I read others's words, that everything exists within God, and that somewhat expresses what I sense, and yet It is transcendent, *out there*, separate but still united with the creation.

Then I suddenly realize how much my thinking, my intuitions have been so shaped by the culture, by what I've learned, by all the forces that have gone into the shaping of this being, of this mind which I hold at this moment, that I don't know what to trust. Which images of God arise out of my glimpses of *the infinite* and which lurch out of the muck of my own unconscious shaping?

Still Pentecost XIX—September 21, 2008

As Ed Burdick joked about my making sermon notes, I remembered what I'd learned long ago, that the word "sermon" in the Latin (which stands far-distanced behind our use of it) meant a conversation, a discussion, a talk. And I recalled a story about a rigged dialogue sermon Jack Bishop and Bill Jamison cooked up for one Sunday morning four decades ago, when Jack climbed into the pulpit and purposely wandered off into a slightly tangential, uninteresting direction and on cue Bill, then the Senior Warden, stood up and said loudly enough to be heard throughout the nave something to the effect of "Bullshit," and Jack reacted, and they proceeded to hold an across-the-nave dialogue centered on the topic and direction. I thought, what a creative and daring way to engage the congregation, and why can't we do that every Sunday morning in the sermon time? Hold a real dialogue, wrestle with the issue(s), allowing everyone to grab hold and go home convicted by their own words? And celebrating our diversity! Why should I get up there in the pulpit every Sunday and pretend that I know what they need and ought to hear? Make the sermon a **real** sermon, a dialogue, a discussion, a multi-logue? But, alas, I was never daring enough to try it. Too bad!

And maybe that had been possible in the very early years of the church, that the elder could facilitate the members's sharing about the Scripture readings among the *saints*. But then Constantine legalized us, and the Constantinian need for us became that the elders shape us into *good citizens* of the empire, loyal, obedient, faithful, subservient, conforming citizens. And for the elder, in loyalty to the emperor, to instruct us in our duties and behavior as good citizens. Oh, what a seduction was in that! And, **still today** we preach **at** the people.

And in the midst of my musings and Stephen's sermonic monologue these words sprang into my consciousness, "From your perspective, young man, that may make sense, but from mine, as an old man, it does not make much sense." And I have NO idea what those words were about!

But I still yearn for a richer, deeper, fuller, more complete, less conflictful experience and sense of "It," of God. And I know that will never happen within this comfortable circle of standing stones.

****

Pentecost XXII—October 12, 2008

This morning at the coffee hour discussion Brad Bateman framed his discussion about the relatedness of religion and the economic life by citing a sociologist of religion who posited that what we get out of our religious life, out of church is a 1) sense of the *transcendent* along with 2) rules for daily living. He underlined that by confessing that is what he gets through the liturgy of the Episcopal/Anglican Church. And as I ruminated this morning, sitting in my circle of standing stones, that made sense to me. For me a combination of liturgy and intellectual life of this Episcopal Church offers transcendence, and the force of this circle of people offers a sense of what they and I (and therefore God?) think would be good, useful, beneficial behavior on my part, and what would be outside the pale of acceptability, what would be unhelpful, or even destructive behavior from me toward them (and beyond). Transcendence, that which is greater than me, than us, than all of this; and rules for daily living within and beyond this circle.

****

Pentecost XXVI—November 9, 2008

The first reading today is Joshua 24:13, the covenant renewal ceremony of choosing for YHWH. But the reading asks me why I choose YHWH. And that throws me back to the paradigm of mystic-codifier-institutionalizer. Joshua was the codifier, the people were the institutionalizer. In that day the religion of the leader was automatically the religion of the people. In 1 and 2 Kings and in the eighth-century Prophets the leaders are apostate, so people's devotion to YHWH languishes, which is the ultimate sin, the failure to devote oneself (i.e., the nation as a unit) wholly and solely to YHWH.

The discussion at coffee hour today was about death. Scattershot. Ed Burdick states the key, we have no way to talk about death. The wall is unbreachable We can know nothing about the other side. All the talk about death/heaven/afterlife is metaphor, really talking about here/now/us. Giving structure-meaning-direction to my life, to this community, to my living in this community.

Chapter 3: My Circle of Standing Stones

****

Advent I—November 30, 2008

In the reading this morning the prophet pleads, "Oh that thou wouldest rend the heavens, that thou wouldest come down, that the mountains might flow down at thy presence, as when the melting fire burneth . . . .when thou didst terrible things . . . . Thou meetest him that rejoiceth and worketh righteousness . . . .behold, thou art wroth; for we have sinned . . . we are all as an unclean thing, and all our righteousness are as filthy rags . . . .we are the clay, and thou art our potter; and we all are the work of thy hand. Be not wroth very sore, O YHWH, neither remember iniquity for ever: behold, see, we beseech thee, we are all thy people" (Isa 64:1-9). He pleads with God. For why? What has he seen? What has this prophet heard?

I suspect that this speaker, this prophet is a visionary, that he has just had a vision so earth-shaking and so unspeakable that he cannot tell it to people, it is undescribable, inexplicable. He can only plead back toward God on behalf of the people of his birth. And I can hear his anguish. But I cannot see his vision.

And what shall I make of that? As I step back and ruminate, I can hear, and almost touch, smell his horror. But it is not mine. Nor was it productive for his people. They were still exiled (perhaps already so at the time of this vision). Perhaps this is a tiny bit of evidence that there is an inexplicable God. But I cannot make much more out of these words, except, perhaps, that we **ought** to be paying more attention. And this prophet certainly is describing, pointing toward a different God than J, E, D, or P.

****

Christmas Eve—December 24, 2008

Just finished reading Betty J. Eadie's book, **Embraced by the Light** the story of her **second** near-death experience. She spends some time in the afterlife, and comes back to tell us about it. Nancy warned me that it was an easy read, and she was right. I do not mean to make light of it, but I was not much informed, or impressed. I am certain that she had a truly visionary, mystical experience which was life-changing for her and her family. But her take on it, her apprehension and comprehension and explication of that experience are similar to others's stories, no more informative than them, and a bit *thready*. Bill Byers's[1] take is deeper, more inclusive, and more confidence-inspiring.

My first impression is that hers is a thin metaphysic, it is insufficient to take in, to sustain much of the heavier, darker side of life and reality, at least as I see it. While she does step outside the Christian box, her metaphysic is too simplistic to be inclusive

---

1. A friend from seminary days, also a retired priest, active in healing ministries and a practitioner of reiki, who through regression therapy has experienced several past lives.

(that judgment from a mind that loves, craves complexity). It is too *sweet* and *light-filled*. My sense is that she is searching for a clear, and very simple, single *core-truth* to all reality and life. And that, having had a very deep and thoroughgoing mystical experience, her mind grasps at a few very simplistic themes to make sense of and to explicate that profound experience.

Hers is an educational model of after/other life. The goal of all life is to learn, to grow. But the whole is founded on, boils down to love. The outcome is too neat, too nice, too simple. While not quite Christian Scientism, her metaphysic could take in and incorporate Christian Scientism. Looking at her story from a psychological point of view, given the little bit she tells us of her personal history, there is no surprise in her metaphysical interpretation of her experience; while, in my ignorance, I do not see any traces of her Native American background (my only touch stone is Tony Hillerman's Navaho-describing detective stories), I can sort out traces, bits and pieces of her Roman Catholic and protestant histories which she has bundled together and used as pitons to anchor her interpretation of her mystical experience. A few, carefully selected, Christian niceties seem to be her foundation stones. But for myself they are insufficient. They strike me as a nuclear family oriented comprehension of metaphysics, exactly what I might expect from her background. But they cannot cope with Hitler-and-holocaust, Mugambe sorts of realities, with the ongoing dynamics of unrefined evil that drive much of the world. Her tiny and insignificant finger-hold on evil (a personal satan who attempts to seduce individuals away from good-doing and is easily defeated by good spirits) will not stand up to the real world I witness. So I quail at some of her verities; "Insincere prayers of repetition have little if any light [i.e., power]" is a pitifully superficial and ignorant careen from contemplative prayer and folk-religion, and discourages me from taking seriously many of her broader assertions. Only the similarity of her over-picture to the metaphysics offered by a few others keep me from discarding hers altogether.

****

Still Christmas Eve—December 24, 2008

I find myself in a very strange place this Christmas Eve. This has become a secular holiday celebration for me. We will go to church this night, sing the songs, enjoy the mysteriosity of it all. But the birth of Christ feels oddly empty for me. Have I turned some corner?

****

Chapter 3: My Circle of Standing Stones

Epiphany IV—February 1, 2009

I can't recall what sent me off wandering this morning, some prayer, some tiny bit of liturgy, some word from Stephen's mouth. But it sent me wondering. What was the church to me when I was young? a lad? What did I expect when I turned my attention to it and began to imagine myself a priest within it? And then, what was the church to me during my professional life. And what is it to me now, now that I am retired, and old, and reflective, and more thoughtful, less dutiful? And then I wondered, what are these others expecting out of this? A touch of God? A vision? A hint of transcendence and a rule for living?

****

Lent V—March 29, 2009

When I studied Jack Miles's book, **God: a Biography** I was struck by the similarities between the YHWH of a particular book and the needs of the nation: during the enslavement an ombudsman, organizer, leader; during the early kingdom a family friend and moralist who stood to the side, during the eighth century a critic and pleader and then an anguished but unrelenting judge, and finally after the exile a disappearing absentee. So it is a simple step to reasonably turn all that around and see that changing of YHWH not as any variation in the godhead himself, but rather of the people's perception of God. Maybe, after all the study and ingestion and rumination and regurgitation of Scripture, our perception of the God is hardly more than a projection of our needs. A collection of the best we can imagine and the tiny scraps of wisdom we can glean and gather. God, or rather our perception of a God, may be simply a collection of what we hope for in our best moments and the hazy axioms we intuit about how best we live together on this planet.

This is not to say anything about the existence of God, only that what we perceive about that God may be far more projection than verifiable observation or deduction.

****

Palm Sunday—April 5, 2009

We do this quirky little oxymoronic liturgy of palm branches and triumphal entries, and then move swiftly into the reading of the whole passion story, and a beginning of the last week of Jesus' life. Nineteen hundred and seventy-five years ago this prophet *cum* seer *cum* healer *cum* teacher became too threatening for the Judaic authorities to tolerate, so they put him away, publicly, with lots of show and denunciation and renunciation and some Roman cooperation. And today I stand here *celebrating* that, commemorating. How odd!! What did he, this Jesus guy, do? What did THEY do? What was this whole scene, this doings all about? And what happened then? The resurrection? I mean, if I had been there, with my twentieth-century slightly-scientific understandings and methods of perception, what would I have perceived happened? And what difference would it have made? I suppose much, or an incalculable amount of this last-week story is historic fact, that it did in fact happen. But did it have some objective, supernatural effect? Or was it **only** metaphor, was it only **impressing** upon us a difference rather than effecting some objective, **out-there** difference? Some eternal forgiveness of sins?

****

Pentecost VIII—July 26, 2009

I have begun reading Robert Wright's ***The Evolution of God***. So far a re-sorting of ancient historical theology. Makes great sense, but blasts enormous holes in the Scriptured story. Follows man's earliest notions of gods/spirits through hunter-gatherer cultures, shamanism, chiefdoms, early city-states, empires: a multitude of polytheisms gradually become a polytheistic pantheon, then a monolatry, and finally monotheism. I've got far to go in the book, but it's making profound sense. Wright taught philosophy at Princeton, then religion at Pennsylvania. He started life as a hard-shell Baptist child, got the altar-call, was baptized, and now no longer calls himself a Christian, but refers to a *moral compass*. Neither affirms nor denies a God. But tries to align himself with the moral axis of the universe. Wright puts me in a new place, a place of saying, "Yes, it really is all metaphor, and it gives us no clues as to how the metaphor relates to God."

So I find myself sitting here this morning asking from a different posture, from outside the metaphor if you will, "What is this all about?" If Wright is correct (or at least more correct than wrong), then what is this, my circle of standing stones, all about? What is going on here? This morning we baptized an infant Owen into this congregation and church. Why? And what did we just do? What difference did it make? To Owen? To us? To this community? To this church? To this world? Surely it was a very pacific, and harmless initiation rite. Was it anything more than that? I think so, but am unable to say what more. I'm puzzling, what is this church stuff really about? What difference can it possibly make? What is its influence? And on whom? And to what end? The preacher (the infant's grandfather) proclaimed that we were **not** doing magic, that this was a *beginning* that we were not about making a better citizen of Owen or providing moral direction for him. But he did not say what we are doing.

So I find myself wandering through a strange landscape today. For sixty-five years it had been a familiar landscape, and through the years had been increasingly filled with landmarks and sign posts and direction markers that I could read with ease. It was a landscape I knew well, and better and better as I aged and grew wiser,

Chapter 3: My Circle of Standing Stones

one which I knew well enough that I could give others some direction and guidance. But today it is an unfamiliar and different landscape. The markers and signs are gone, obliterated, or erased. And it is somewhat a wilderness. Not a frightening wilderness, just a not-as-well-featured-as-before wilderness, a place where the only markers and sign posts are the ones I discern for myself, the ones I set up, a somewhat barren wilderness. And I am wandering, searching out my own way. Yet I do not feel lost. Just a little lonely. Squinting toward a tiny light on the distant horizon, looking toward a small, somewhat unconcerned figure far way on my horizon whom I cannot make out clearly, and who glances back at me from time to time, with a little curiosity. A quiet and small part of me may enjoy being out in this wilderness alone.

****

August 29, 2009

Much water over (or perhaps under) the dam since last I wrote to this. Primarily Robert Wright's book *The Evolution of God*, a fetching, though somewhat misleading title. He's not really talking about God evolving, but about our image(s) of God evolving.

Wright is not so much a scholar, though a prolific reader, as a journalist. He collects and disburses information, vast quantities of it. But so far as I can tell he does not do much digesting of it, more like regurgitation. With an interesting beginning, as a Oklahoman Southern Baptist background in his teens, including the traditional altar-call, self-dedication and dunking (as though an adult) baptism, then on to a first year in a fundamentalist college, next moving to Princeton and a thorough going eastern, head-trip education. He writes. And sufficiently well that he has been invited to teach undergraduate courses in religion and philosophy. He seems at this point in his life enamored of *cultural evolution* and *game theory* and in his work he seems to base his study and reporting around those two foci. So he reads pretty traditional but quite up to date historical criticism of both Hebrew and Christian Scriptures through those two lenses, cultural evolution and games theory. It makes for an interesting and unsettling read. I have read him. I am now occupied with ruminating. This cud requires heavy-duty and long-ongoing rumination, re-chewing all I've read, studied, and thought over all these years. I guess I see my theological understandings and formulations as in flux these days, and myself as wandering through, as re-making-sense-of. I have announced to Steve and Stephen that, while willing to celebrate Eucharist, I am no longer able to preach, that there are no more sermons in me, at least for now, **and** will not be until I emerge with a new understanding of it all, and some things worth being said, both to myself and to others. But for now I am in preacher's limbo with nothing in hand or head or heart to be said.

Where do I start? By reciting what I've read. Wright leads through prehistoric understandings, images of god(s), and traces the evolution of spirits to polytheistic god-images through these stages of cultural evolution understanding that it is the *facts on the ground* that drive our understandings/images of god(s), and probably not any mystical, god-driven revelations that shape man's understanding. And who can tell whether the god(s) are evolving? Instead Wright is pretty clear that he is uncovering the culture's evolving needs of god(s) and whether the god itself is evolving is moot and non-discernable. Then he moves on to the evolution within Hebrew Scriptures from polytheism (the worship of many gods simultaneously) through monolatry (the insistence of devotion to one god exclusively in the midst of many co-equal or hierarchical gods), and finally to monotheism (the conviction that there exists only one God), a late, third to second-century BC achievement in Hebrew devotion. His primary tool in doing this is the JEDP schema, unraveling those threads and putting times to their authors. What emerges is that those four authoring sources, writing in different periods, have differing needs of god, imagine the god differently in both word and deed. And Wright sees an evolutionary pattern in those differing images, a gradual movement, albeit in fits and starts, toward greater transnational and transethnic inclusiveness.

He sees this pattern continuing in the early Christian writings, Paul's letters being the earliest (first generation), then Mark (*circa* 70 AD), the Q source, Matthean source, Lucan source, and finally John (probably post 100 AD). Wright sees Jesus as very much in the prophetic-healer mode (preaching the immanent, Isaiah-like kingdom). In Mark Jesus uses the word "love" only once, in the Great commandment (Love God, and neighbor as self.) Jesus' God is not the Christian God of love we have received, but rather a God of judgment. Without Paul Jesus would probably have been forgotten and his sect lost within a few generations. Paul introduces and emphasizes the love theme, building his new congregations around love, i.e., transnational and transethnic inclusiveness, a *taking care of each other* (e.g., "See, how they love each other"). Paul's version of Jesus is probably more important than Jesus himself, what he taught and did. It is those caring communities which Paul created in the urbanizing and industrializing (impersonal, oppressive, dehumanizing) Roman empire that made Christianity so vital and attractive. And Wright also points to the alternative, competing versions of Christianity (Gnosticism, Marcionism, Ebionism, *et cetera*). Paul's Christianity was one of several (many?) versions, all competing with other mystery and pagan religions across the Roman Empire. The *facts on the ground* were that the empire had stopped conquering and was in a consolidating, unifying mode, and Paul's version best met those needs. And then Wright tracks the evolution of the dominant theological doctrines: Jesus as savior, the kingdom as heavenly (vs. earthly and militant), born-againness, original sin, *et cetera*.

With all that regurgitated, where does the experience of reading his book leave me? I think Wright and I handle the Hebrew and Christian Scriptures differently. He seems to treat them mainly as fabricated (albeit unconsciously) fictional history, though he allows they might be *inspired* without exploring how that might be or what that might mean. He does some obligatory light wrestling with whether God really exists, remaining agnostic and coming to no conclusion. He allows that he cannot believe in the Judeo-Christian God, though he is fairly convinced that there is a moral directionality to history, and to cultural evolution guided by non-zero-sumness, and that there is a moral axis built into the universe, and finally that his *good* consists of aligning himself as well as he can with that moral axis. And that is as close as he can come to allowing a God.

Most of what Wright reports I find makes profound sense to me. I probably should explore his authorities on the dating and unraveling of JEDP, just to satisfy myself that Wright's reporting is accurate. He does fairly thoroughly rip the Scriptures to shreds, and leaves those shreds in a disorderly pile. I found that *ripping apart* process somewhat disconcerting for me, although it does not offend my sensibilities, but rather lends some grounds for my own wanderings away from the Scriptures and orthodoxy and toward the mystical.

I would guess that my own growing sense is one of assurance that our Scriptures (Hebrew and Christian) **are** inspired by mystical visions, and to that extent are *validated*. But they are no more (nor less) *inspired* than the holy writings of other major religions (Islam, Buddhism, Hinduism, Confucianism, *et cetera*). And I'd go farther to accept that the reporting and interpreting of those mystical experiences are certainly **very** shaped by the facts on the ground in their respective moments. And while I can empathize with Susan's not giving a hang for the invisible God, still I yearn to touch God for myself, fully aware that whatever that experience might be, it cannot be communicated to others by any means, and that however I apprehend it will be violently shaped and filtered by the facts on the ground as well as my own *ground-into-my-bones* training and sensibilities. It cannot be otherwise.

****

Pentecost XVII—September 27, 2009

A string of Marcan teachings, including "He who is not against us is for us." Margo commented on my taking notes during the sermon. I was arrogantly self-assertive enough to disabuse her, "No, I've already preached that text many times." I had been starting notes on prayer, a knotty topic that I need to address. But in overhearing Stephen's preaching, I was reminded that I've not yet come to any useful (to me) conclusions about the function, the purpose of the sermon, just what is that monologue (or dialogue) about? Throughout my active ministry I considered the purpose of the sermon to be the explication of the gospel text for the day. I began my ministry with the understanding (however mistaken or misguided) that people knew very little about our holy Scriptures, and that one of my primary tasks, if not the paramount task, was to acquaint them with the texts, at least as I understood them. So my goal was to present them with a viable twentieth-century understanding of the scriptural text of the day. My imagined (coached by Herr Spielmann) concept was that in the early church, in the dark of the morning as the congregation straggled in (there being no alarm clocks and Sunday, the Lord's Day, being a working day in the Roman Empire) the elder, presbyter, forerunner of the priest, interpreted the Scriptures to fill the time as the congregation amassed, following the synagogue's precedent. So I saw my task in that light as interpreting the Scriptures to the gathered congregation. I told the story, offered the latest critical understanding and some thoughts, or at least a couple of questions about how it might be applied in our lives. A noble model *(I mused to myself)*.

But with my present sense of my faith, of **the faith** of understanding the story, the Scriptures, the whole ball of wax to be not fact but metaphor, without a clear sense of exactly what stands behind that complex of metaphor, I'm very unclear what I have worthy of being preached. Perhaps, as Wright suggests, the closest I can get to God is as the moral axis of the universe; then the most I have to offer from a pulpit is my sense of how I think that moral axis is tending at this moment, in this circumscribed situation. And, Lord knows, my sense of that right at this moment is no better, no more guiding than anyone else's *(though perhaps a scuidgeon better than Dick Cheney's but with nowhere near his self-confidence)*. So I'm not feeling I have any right to preach, nor any **thing** to preach these days.

So what is the sermon? A moment of moral guiding? But by whose authority?

****

Pentecost XXIII—November 8, 2009

Musings: after William James's, Jack Miles's, Karen Armstrong's, a couple of Jack Spong's, and Robert Wright's books I find myself left with a creator and a moral axis and all the rest is a metaphor which ill-defines the creator and the moral axis. Maybe the deists had it right: the creator made it, set it to running and walked off, leaving us a moral axis by which to run it. Good luck! And it's up to us to sense the direction in which the moral axis is pointing and then make it happen.

So a sermon then, is a conversation in which I prompt the people to discover along with me the directions in which the moral axis prompts/points/compels us. But it's my (the preacher's) responsibility to first discern the moral axis and in which way it's pointing, and then in conversation to direct their attention and thoughts in that direction. And all the while I feel no more apt *(perhaps even less apt that many of the wiser of them)* than the rest of the people to do that discerning and to point their attention and thoughts in the right direction.

****

CHAPTER 3: MY CIRCLE OF STANDING STONES

Advent 1—November 29, 2009

We talked about Luke's Little Apocalypse (Luke 21) at coffee hour. My take, that we need to not bother asking historo-critical questions about it, but instead step back and ask what was the prophet's mystical insight, and what is that saying to us today? In the words of behavioral psychology, that all behavior has consequences; in the prophet's metaphor that there will be a payday, there will be a reckoning; in Robert Wright's words that there is a moral axis to the universe, and that it will prevail! All the other speculation is adulterated manure, not even suitable for composting.

The sermon could not catch my attention (nor Nancy's), so I wandered Are we the final product of all evolution (preposterous!) And then what do we need to be watching for? And what is our moral responsibility toward that? Will our preclusion be even perceivable to us (evolution happens so slowly). And if that is the case, then how is God active in the world? . . . and **how** active is God in the world? And then, my poor, nettlesome, demented cardinal, compulsively flying at my window *(one male cardinal has concluded that its reflection in my office window glass is a territorial competitor and he has spent most hours of every day this whole summer throwing himself frustratedly against my window)* a tiny bit of God's magnificent beauty gone irritatingly awry!!

****

Easter III—April 18, 2010

I have finished my interim ministry at Chillicothe (only Sunday Supply December 1, 2009 through Easter 2010) where I presumed **not** to preach any sermons, but rather to reflect upon their situation and condition. And now I am back to **my** chosen circle of standing stones, St.Luke's in Granville. And I mused this morning during the sermon. I think my own *faith* has traveled a fair distance since last I wrote to this collection. I think Robert Wright (***The Evolution of God***) was the last nail in the coffin of my former *faith/belief* system. He is assuredly not a scholar, but a journalist, with a capacity to engorge a huge bodies of information, and after barely beginning to digest, disgorges, almost as projectile vomiting, so that you have to digest the mess yourself if you want it. But he did bring me to conclude, not so reluctantly, that the sacred writings we have received are indeed a hodge-podge collection of politically motivated scribblings by YHWHists. Perhaps they thought them the mutterings of the deity, but perhaps they were very self-consciously aware that they were creating out of whole cloth sacred writings which they could attribute to the deity for emphasis/authority's sake *(I know not which)*. But Wright pointed in the direction (though he could not himself authenticate the pointing of his finger) of understanding the pieces of Holy Scripture therein gathered as wholly politically motivated and shaped (e.g., J, E, D, and P were written at different times in different situations, and betray quite different viewpoints and messages, even though jammed together by the redactors as though they were one and the same). And on my own I make huge leaps of faithlessness to conclude they have little more, perhaps even slightly less spiritual utility than the sacred writing of some other religious bodies, of Islam, of Buddhism, of Hinduism, or perhaps even Confucianism or Shintoism, all merely point vaguely and unauthoritatively in the vague direction of whatever it is that we may call God.

So this morning, instead of wondering what was happening within my circle of standing stones on this Sunday morning, I concluded that I am present with these others within this circle of stone precisely because it is the circle of standing stones that I have chosen, not because of what is going on there this morning, or any morning, but because this Christian stuff is indeed my circle of standing stones; and I have chosen it, not consciously or deliberately, but culturally, because it is my birthright, because I was fed it from age eight (and earlier) and because it has fed me through all these decades. And because I have suddenly come to recognize that it is merely one among several dominant religious metaphors, that does not make it any less **my** metaphor, the only one I know well, the one that has gotten me this far in life, and the only one so far that is pointing me beyond itself. I am much more comfortable intellectually with the few, feeble understandings I have of Buddhist thinking than I am with traditional, orthodox Christian rationalizations; and much of the Christian metaphor is repugnant to me, less than useless; certainly many of the rabidly reactionary, far-right ravings of self-proclaimed Christian groups/cults/denominations/sects are positively demonic to me, so far off-target and misdirected as to be dangerous, both to themselves and to others. Still Christianity **is** my metaphor; Buddhism, however desirable it may look to me, is **not** my metaphor, nor could I ever make it mine. I might like it, might become enamored of it, but it can never become my metaphor, at least not in this lifetime. So for now, I stand within this circle of standing stones, and **know** it to be mine; and within this circle I am able to wrest my freedom to wander spiritually in the directions many different winds are wafting me. Many breezes are gently pushing in many different directions, but all (my metaphor tells me) are the breath of God.

This morning I listened to what of the guest preacher's sermon I could tolerate, knew it was far, far too literal and embracing of Scripture and orthodoxy for me, and could only wonder "Has she nothing of her own to say? What does she see out there where she lives? Or is she simply too young, too inexperienced to have anything yet to offer?"

****

Easter IV—April 25, 2010

At coffee hour we talked about John's **Revelation** and were fascinated with the details. And that's the trap! The devil is in the details! The message is **not** in the details, but in the overall tone. I realized as I listened to it read during the service that this book almost more than any other, needs to be listened to, not read. Stay away from the details, listen to the tone. Listen broadly, without questioning. The devil (temptation, misdirection) really is in those details, they will lead you astray.

And then, keep in mind that this corpus was penned in the first century, under Roman oppression, by one who thought himself **sorely** oppressed, and was written about **that** time and oppression. But it is merely a curiosity today, has **no** relevance! It is not future-telling. It is hope, it is vengeance, it is a dreaming. But John foresaw nothing that others were not hoping, dreaming, yearning for "Vengeance on these *fucking* Romans!" My theory: either John had some mystical experiences which he seethed in his hatred of the Romans and Roman oppression, and shaped them as predictions about God's coming vengeance; or they were pieces copped from existing Hebrew writings and cobbled together into this format and given a **very** vaguely Christian overlay (in as much as the book shows **no** knowledge of the Jesus of the gospels or his God). But whichever of these two (or any other option you want to offer), this revelation is dead and irrelevant now, and was so when it was adopted into the canon by Athanasius in 374 AD at which time Christians were legal and pagans illegal, irrelevant even then! So, it was a mistake to include it.

And, I reflect farther afield, it must be nice, for some, to hold the certainty and sureness of this gospel (i.e., the good news of Jesus the Christ), but I think the details of that, too, are often misleading, misdirecting.

Susan loves the stories (Hebrew and Christian), and trusts them to tell us about human nature, about who we are and what this world is. And I agree with her that they are good stories. However I think they are Rorschachs, ink-blots, projective images onto which we project our own sensibilities, our moral directions, our own sense of the direction in which morality points. I do not trust the stories, but use them as tools, to elicit out of myself and help others elicit out of themselves their hunches, their sense of the moral axis of the universe, the only thing of God that we can lay hand on.

While not a mystic, and even less a student of the mystics, I think I trust the mystics's mystical experiences, but hold their expressions (verbal or visual) to be shaped by time and culture, the crudest and most inexact statements of what the mystic experienced. Once again, the devil is in the details, misleading and misdirecting.

****

Pentecost VI, 4th of July—July 4, 2010

Reciting the Nicene Creed today, I found myself asking "What mean these words? What this ceremonial, what these formularies? What means all this? These words? These gestures? This fish-wafer dipped in red wine?" And I was driven back to several weeks ago when something out of my fantasizing asked me,

PART I: THE PILGRIMAGE FROM THERE TO HERE

Q. Is this the true faith? Should I believe it? Can I receive it as valid?

A. If it works for you. Does it urge and enable you to be a better person, and to align yourself more closely to the moral axis of the universe? Does it help you see reality more clearly? Does it put in your mind the presence and compassion of the others around you? If it is yours, then it is true, believable, valid.

Q. Is it all relative? no absolutes?

A. Misstated question! For you it is absolute, if it works, if it's yours, if it aligns you. For you it may be Christianity, for someone else Islam, or Judaism or Buddhism.

****

Feast of St. Luke the Evangelist—October 18, 2010

Patron Day, with a full house, thirty in the choir, a brass quintet accompanying the organ for the festivities and the rededication of the building after all the work. But earlier this morning I considered that, given all the craziness, greed, power-mongering, senselessness, amorality and madness rampant throughout the world, I could easily conclude that man is nothing more than an evolved mammilian, no soul, no more immortality than the fish in the ocean from which we probably evolved, even though we might have a touch more self-awareness or self-consciousness, albeit we have no clear evidence; it may be that some other creatures may have some degree of self-awareness as well. The evidence Robert Wright sees which suggests there is a moral axis to the universe is so sketchy and vague to my eyes, so unreliable and inconclusive that I have to stretch my credulity in order to concur. And when that is stacked against the horrors and amorality in this world that seem unchecked in any way—given the amorality of even our own leaders *(their only ethical yardstick is to get re-elected)*. Then I wonder if there is any moral force for good to be reckoned with. Or are we as a species morally adrift completely, unanchored, wafted by any breeze, any whim?

****

Susan suggests that Freud thought the first stage of development is the naive, unknowledgeable innocence before the child begins to differentiate. Could then the mystic be doing naught more than remembering his intra-uterine experience, which most of us cannot recall?

****

Chapter 3: My Circle of Standing Stones

Pentecost XXII—October 24, 2010

At the Grounds for Discussion Coffee Hour Stephen started to share his learnings from the courses he took on sabbatical. He titles his presentation "The Once and Future Church" and intends to lead the conversation into the issues of how we should be reshaping St. Luke's to move into the future. But I am in a different discussion. I'm not concerned with how we should reshape the church. I'm asking the much more basic questions for which I suspect there are no answers. And I have no notion what the responses should, or even could be. What **could** the church be, what **should** the church become, what **ought to be** the mission/task of the church today and tomorrow?

I think that saving the world for Christ, and selling Jesus to every human being have become stupid missions. We need to radically rethink just what Jesus wanted us to be about, and what **we** think we ought to be about, religiously and morally. Convincing everyone that Jesus is the way, the **only** way has become dysfunctional, counterproductive, dangerously divisive and antagonizing. It's not merely repackaging the product that's needed. It's rethinking what we're trying to accomplish. Jesus is no longer the product we're selling. It's whatever Jesus and Buddha and Mohamed and Moses were all about, what they hold in common, what is the root of all religious thought and action.

****

Pentecost XXIV—November 7, 2010

I think it has become time for me to start writing, but how to start? Maybe with the linchpins I have in hand today (I seem to be swinging ape-like, from one set of linchpins to another, towards something, or just indiscriminately?).

(1) I am reading about mystics. They seem to be among the great innovators, redirectors of the church, of the faith, in other religions as well. But I wrestle with "What are they?" Rare persons who really can be in touch with god, the divine, the Absolute? Or merely special persons able to do . . . . What? In deep contemplation to put things together, develop insights, experience? Or re-experience prenatal comfort/memories? What are these mystics? They seem to provide some common ground across religious boundaries.

(2) Robert Wright makes deep sense to me, debunking the Scriptures, talking about cultural evolution, sensing a moral compass built into the universe. But where do you go with that?

(3) I see/hear/experience the Dalai Lama, a person with a truly remarkable comfortableness, humility, an informed naivete, some very profoundness, but in this world extremely improbable/impractical insights. He truly makes (Tibetan) Buddhism sensible, more sensible than the Christian gospels. It all makes the Hebrew

YHWH seem quite childish. Yet the Dalai Lama is silent about God, as though God makes no difference *(which may be correct)*. Buddhism is a system about **living** not a metaphysic about pre-universe. Attractive, but not my circle of standing stones. Our Scriptures are a Rorschach; ergo *tradition* must move to the center, replacing the Scriptures, traditions about the **hows** of interpreting Scriptures, i.e., what and how to project without violating (whatever).

(4) I become more and more convinced that Christianity is just **one** expression of what lies beyond, one expression among many equally valid expressions. But what does lie beyond?

(5) Sin is an outmoded, unuseful, misleading notion. Buddhism's interdependency and intertwinedness is a much more functional model, but does it sufficiently cope with the *evil* in the world? Really need to work on that.

(6) All religion, all religious ideation/language is purely metaphorical. Yes, but how to more adequately conceptualize what lies beyond the metaphor? And so I need to completely rethink what our religious language and ideation means in this twenty-first-century world/universe. And especially re-think whatever the mystics are trying to convey to us.

(7) The main business of the *church* is to stay in business. The truly religious/ spiritual/ spiritually enervating things happen outside the church, at the fringes of the church, and **never** can be at the center. When the main, dominating mission of the church is to stay in business, to survive into the next millennium, then any mission emerging out of spiritual insight **must** take place outside the church or it will simply be overwhelmed, swallowed up by the survival efforts of church.

****

I've spent my life's work theologizing, and I simply can't turn it off. I can stop *priesting* and *sermonizing* but not theologizing.

****

Advent I—November 28, 2010

So, as I wrote John Kauffman, the Christian metaphor has gone dry and dusty for me. I can bemoan and grieve that, or I can move out into the wilderness. It seems useless, non-productive and pretty stupid to waste my energies screaming about inconsistencies, inaccuracies, misdirections and such. Instead, the real and productive challenge is to look *through* the storied metaphor as a lens that may help see beyond the physical, and learn to search out what lies beyond. I know the God is not in the story. But what clues does the story give me to what is beyond? And to see beyond the God, to see what is it about?

CHAPTER 3: MY CIRCLE OF STANDING STONES

****

Epiphany VI—February 13, 2011

Another take on this morning's gospel reading, Matthew 5:21-37 (from the Sermon on the mount). I need to begin with a footnote: the Buddha lived and taught some half-millennium before Jesus. There is only the vaguest, unlikeliest possibility that some of his teaching may have reached Jesus' ears. It is only a slightly less vague possibility that, both being mystics, they taught similar things. And further, it is similarly the distinct possibility, nay, probability that Jesus' followers wildly misunderstood some of his teachings, and in particular this set of teachings. End of footnote.

Matthew the Hebrew, preaching to an orthodox Jewish community, presents these teachings like a reformist Pharisee, as intensifying the take on Torah and the concurrently developing oral midrash. He fills the law up thereby making it so much more stringent, so much more as to make it impossible to keep. That take I think quite misunderstands Jesus' intent. I think it quite perverts his intent and misdirects our attention. I think what Jesus is trying to teach is not a more stringent law which we are doomed to fail, but rather a wholly different understanding of **law**, of the sweetness of Torah (sweeter than the honey-lemon lozenge the rabbi places on the child's tongue to give her/him a taste of the sweetness of Torah). Following the gaze of Matthew's misdirection we come to understand law/justice and mercy as opposites, as mutually contradictory, oxymoronic. Instead I think what Jesus alludes to is a wholly different understanding of *law* and of *grace*. When we live in right relationship with our fellow man, then mercy and law are the same thing; when we live in love among ourselves, then we fulfill Law/Torah without thinking about keeping laws, without intentionality, without any need of being restricted or directed. It is a matter of basic attitude toward our fellow-beings. When we live in whole, healthy relationship, then there is no murder, no adultery, no false witness. Those simply are not options within such relationship.

The Buddha rejects our concept of sin or sins, understanding instead in its place *ignorance* of the most basic reality, that we are all one, that we are totally intertwined and inseparable, that only when we live in deep compassion with our fellow beings, with the whole of creation of which each of us is merely a tiny intertwined fragment (i.e., an emanation of the whole), only then are we healthy, whole, unignorant. I have to stretch very hard to grasp that notion, but I confess it makes far greater sense, invokes a far greater sense of the integrity of human existence than Augustine's damned fancy for *original sin* or our more common Christian notions of sins and sinfulness, which I am convinced are themselves completely debased and worthless coinage. And in its place the Buddha reaches out to grasp *compassion*. If we live with and in compassion, then there is no need, there is no occasion of murder, adultery and false witness. Jesus too calls us, not to greater stringency and purity, but to the deepest compassion.

Part I: The Pilgrimage from There to Here

****

Epiphany VII—February 20, 2011

At coffee hour discussion we heard about Mormonism. John Smith was fourteen when he had his first vision *(still in testosterone drenched puberty)*. At the age of twenty he had published his translations of the eighteen plates. Why should we put any credence in the religious ravings of a pubescent male? I can give no credence to that foundation of Mormonism. And yet in reflection, why should I put any greater credence in Christianity? I come up with three reasons why my Christian stuff feels so much more credible.

1. It's mine. I grew up with it,
2. Smith's stuff is just too radically revisionist, and
3. His stuff, and the rest of the Mormon stuff is just too bloody convenient (e.g., regarding visions about polygamy and race).

Definitely mystical stuff, but weird, deviant formulations, going off in its own direction. Compare to Norwich *et alia*. The choice is **mine**, not the divergent.

****

My journaling ends abruptly here, but the wondering and wandering did not. Several months after this entry I had my one session with John Kaufman and learned that my wandering was not so odd, not so heretical. In fact I seemed merely to be growing spiritually, growing beyond the boundaries of conventional doctrine, though not beyond, nor out of synch with where others have been before. Some months later I discovered a group of people who were also wandering in this wilderness and who seemed ready for conversation about the reaches of our several pilgrimages. We dubbed ourselves the Beyond Orthodoxy group and talked for three years. Then I began to write this book.

Part II

My Review of Christian Doctrines

Chapter 4: Sin, for One Last Time

PREFACE: I FIND MYSELF compelled to scrape together all that I have ever said and thought about sin and write it down; then I must close the book on that subject, never to return. My project is to put it all in order, to make some sense out of it all, and to arrive at a comfortable judgment, i.e., to make some reliable appraisal of sin.

Why begin these analyses with sin? The notion of sin has long gone empty for me, become debased coinage. It strikes a dull thunk instead of a clear ringing, and the face on the coin is so worn and faded as to show me no image. Economists say bad coinage drives out good. That is true in theology as well. The debased coinage, sin, has driven out of my sight and mind that previously useful Christian understanding of what in man is so destructive: of myself, of community, of the world. Sin has been the linchpin of Augustine's fourth century system, the theology the church and our Book of Common Prayer that I have grown up with. So I seek here to jerk that linchpin clean out of the system and see where the other pieces fall, and then to search out a twenty-first century understanding of that complex of issues we formerly labeled sin.

Framework for This Conversation

Sin is somehow related to evil, but the relationship is not entirely clear. Sin may be the willful doing of evil, but that again is not completely clear. Sin would seem to involve some willfulness. There is some hurt, some damage to others, even evil involved. And God is somehow proximate. Sin is unnecessary, unnatural, and may be malevolent. The only parcel I can grab hold of in all of this is "evil." So I must start with that. I observe that there is evil afoot in this world. I would be a fool to deny it. But I would be just as much an idiot to unthinkingly accept evil as simply as it has been presented to me. I must make some distinctions about evil first, and then I must sort out a twenty-first century understanding of sin.

What We Call Evil Changes[1]

Hitler was just coming into his full power when I was being born. By the time the U.S. entered the war I had already been taught to smell the evil that he embodied. As

---

1. The notion of evil has always been in flux. In its earliest use it meant something like "uppity." In Old and Middle English it mean anything bad. Now, for me at least, many **bad** things I cannot consider "evil," such as natural occurrences, as earthquakes, tornadoes and such, and other random events such as pure accidents. "Evil" has become a fairly murky and ill-defined notion.

a child of five I could not understand it. I could not even begin to comprehend it. But I could smell it. I went with my mother to help fold gauze bandages, an appropriate way for me to fight that evil. We knew with a surety, and with passion, that evil was over there, in Germany, among the Nazis, **in** the Nazis. And in those days the Russians were our friends, our allies in fighting the Nazi evil. The war ended with the Nazis and the *Japs (sic)* defeated, and we entered a new world, a revised world. Now the Russians, the U.S.S.R., the Communists became the enemy. They were the new evil, and we were terrified of them, or we were at least supposed to be terrified of them, prodded by McCarthyism. And I should have wondered then about the nature of this very threatening cloud of evil that was morphing, changing form and location, and still supposed to be our enemy. But I was still young and that evil was still an absolute. Then my campus roommate stumbled onto a stash of sixteen-inch vinyl public relations War Department recordings, ordered destroyed but instead secreted after WWII, which talked about us driving down the right side of the road into Berlin, while the Brits drove down the left, and those crazy Russians drove right down the middle. And I was confronted with the changeability of the absolute evil. I began to realize that the evil I'd always known as an absolute, instead came in degrees, and sometimes even morphed. I could not really count on it. And through the intervening years since I've learned that evil is often a fairly relative thing.

Gradations of Evil with Ill-Defined Edges

Evil is not as simple as a huge basket into which we can throw everything bad. I discern that volcanoes erupting are not really evil: destructive, killing, bad, but entirely natural. Unavoidable. How then can they be evil in any objective way? And earthquakes! If you're caught in an earth-quake I'm sure it feels overwhelmingly evil. But it is a natural event, an act of nature. Hard for me to call that evil. Hitler? He was evil, no doubt. And Stalin? Yeah, probably evil. But the Communists? Not so clear a call. Idi Amin? Yeah. Jeffrey Dahmer (the serial killer who ate his victims)? Oh yes, that was palpable evil. But what about accidents? I mean real accidents, not somebody's negligent misstep, but real accidents. They happen! And are they evil? Well, they're — they're accidents. Hard to call them evil. More like "random." And gradually I have come to realize that the world I live in is not made of blacks and whites, but of innumerable shades of gray, with never a true white or an absolute black among them. Always some shade of gray. And randomness. Not everything is intentional. Or caused. Some things just happen. In Newtonian physics everything is predicable, but in quantum physics probability is more like it, and now the physicists are playing with string theory in which even probability becomes improbable.

Chapter 4: Sin, for One Last Time

Evil Is What's Left

So I must define evil and to do that I start by paring off the things we thoughtlessly call evil, but which are really not. First the random things: they feel bad, may actually have quite bad consequences, but are not evil in themselves, only random, natural, mostly unpredictable: earthquakes, volcanic eruptions, tornadoes, hurricanes, landslides, mudslides, floods, rock falls, droughts, blizzards, avalanches, diseases, mental illnesses, epidemics and such, the natural disasters caused by very real, physical, measurable, sometimes even predictable forces of nature, though sometimes unpredictable, unforeseeable. Yes, they are destructive and injurious and leave a path of pain and even death and other forms of human misery behind them. But I cannot call them evil; they are natural, unavoidable, unescapable. Certainly not willful; they just happen.

I find a subcategory here: the things caused mostly by forces of nature, only slightly avoidable and rather unpredictable. When my first wife was diagnosed with cancer, I could almost feel the evil that was her tumor, it felt palpable in the room with us, it had an odor and color and, in my mind's eye, a form and shape, so that while it was hidden deep within her body, I could almost touch and grasp it; it had some presence in the room. Yet in my saner, more reasonable moments I knew it was not a demon, not a touch of satan, certainly not an act of God; a single cell had mutated out of control and reproduced endlessly until it consumed and killed her. These are the factors, events, elements of the natural world in which we live, of which we, at least our bodies, are actually a portion. Their results may feel evil to us, but themselves are natural.

And next I pare off the accidents, true accidents, randomly happening accidents, not of willful intent. Bad consequences, but again acts innocent in themselves. I cannot call these evil either. Newscasters agitatedly misname them tragedies, calamities, but they are not really evil; rather they are naturally occurring events, perhaps influenced by the randomness built into the universe.

Randomness

Several decades ago a friend handed me an issue of the magazine **OMNI**, and in it an article which continues to fascinate me entitled "Connoisseurs of Chaos." It was about the discoveries of physicists who study chaos. They learn that chaos is not chaotic at all, but instead that all motion is organized around three forces: the *fixed point attractor* which defines homeostasis (a fixed or stable state), the *limit cycle attractor* which defines simple and complex harmonic motions (a rhythmic and recurring motion such as a swinging pendulum), and a *random attractor* which introduces an element of randomness into all things. I do not understand the complexities but this understanding suggests to me that randomness is built into the universe, into all things, and into all life. It is the driver of the genetic mutations fundamental to Darwin's thesis of the natural selection of the species. And next, as a theological speculator, I interpolate that some of what we experience or call evil is simply randomness, an unpredictable, unforeseeable twist of events which usually has an undesirable result (when the result is favorable we call it good luck or God's blessing, but I think it is still randomness). In his book ***When Bad Things Happen to Good People***, Rabbi Harold Kushner theorized similarly that many bad things are not God's will, but merely randomness.

Now I am Left with Two Categories of Things I Feel Justified to Call Evil

Jeffrey Dahmer, carefully selecting his victims, killing them with such thoughtfulness and planning that the murder goes undetected, and then eating the body parts of his victims. This is evil, tinged perhaps with an unimaginable psychological aberration, but quite unadulteratedly evil. The willful drunken driver who, having been tagged five times goes out once more to drink and then drunkenly drive, killing a young girl walking along the street. There is willfulness here, an unreasonableness, and, if not a deliberateness, then at least a knowingness and willingness: not as simple as negligence, but maybe deliberate negligence. There is evil here too. It does not smell as pungent as Jeffrey Dahmer's evil, but still is well within the category. But bounds of this category are mushy, it has an unclear, ill-defined edge. While the Dahmer event was purely individualistic, there is a societal complicity with our drunken driver. These exemplify one category of evil, but there is another. There is the Hitler syndrome.

This second category is much more problematic, more greatly impactful, and leads to the heart of my problem with sin. The evil that remains in the basket is communal and cultural: poverty, oppression, racism, violence. I have lived through the war with Nazi Germany, the S.S. Troops, and Hitler's effort to exterminate all Jews from the face of the earth, the Holocaust. And I saw the latter years of Stalin's U.S.S.R., of his and his government's efforts to dominate and to eliminate persons and populations that were in the way, his cruel oppression and murder of his own people. And I am living in the aftermath of George W's preemptive war against Iraq, his eradication of Saddam Hussein and his government, and the resultant unleashing of the conflictful, bloodthirsty clans and tribes and sects within the culture which Hussein had understood how to keep in check through the use of cruel oppression. And I am watching the deliberate enrichment of the wealthy at the expense of the poor and middle class in this country, and in the mid-East the oppression of dispossessed Palestinians by the same Jewish people who had been so cruelly oppressed by the Nazis and others. The litany can go on; I am well aware of this evil in this world. I am a systems person, I believe in and understand social systems. And this evil is systemic, not individual. It is deliberate, social, even though perhaps unconscious (or pre-conscious or subconscious); and it is deeply embedded in the social system. We build together and then live within a social system which rewards and punishes for no obvious or reasonable cause, or for deeply hidden causes. And we do nothing about it. We allow that evil. We may even quietly, silently, unwittingly enable it. We are complicit, sometimes ignorantly, but always voluntarily. We cooperate with that social system. In our prayers we pray abstractly **about** poverty, but we do not pray in ways that actually change or alleviate that poverty; we pray and then let it be. Therefore many go hungry, or homeless. And we allow it. And we do not consider that a sin for which we are individually culpable, in need of God's forgiveness. And that is the heart of the problem. Hitler may be the embodiment of evil, but the reality is that we vote for him, and cheer for him at rallies, and readily or reluctantly and unresistingly, do his will. Again, the boundaries of both these categories are only vaguely visible, and fade into invisibility.

When I study these two categories of evil, one word resounds within me, **malevolence.** There is a will to do harm, injury, oppression, neglect, however conscious and deliberate, or unconscious and complicitous that will might be. **Malice.**

The Trivialization of Sin

Into the world I've just sketched I invite you to talk with me about sin. This is the framework within which I am questioning, "What is sin?" Mine is a world in which there truly is evil, but in degrees and gradations and maybe even in layers. And where often things that appear evil, may not be; but are just bad, or destructive. Or simply random. Unpredictable. Unforeseen and unforeseeable. Even though damaging and hurtful.

In this world the notion of sin has been trivialized beyond significance. The sin we talk about these days in church is individualized, putting the locus entirely within the individual. Since earliest Christianity we have focused on versions such as the seven deadly sins: wrath, greed, sloth, pride, lust, envy, and gluttony. I note that these sins all require me to look within myself, at my interior life. But in reflection I note that Jack Bowers's sins are puny and nearly insignificant when I confess them alongside a Hitler, a Stalin, an Idi Amin, a 2014 Tea-Party-driven U.S. Congress. The Hebrew Scriptures had it right when they placed the locus of sins mainly (though not exclusively) at the national level, when they sent the scapegoat off into the Wilderness of Zsin bearing on its head the collective sin of the nation. Yes, we may be complicit as individuals in the evils of the national sin, but Jack Bowers is not the paramount sinner. It is true that we can *smell* the evil of some individuals e.g., a cannibalistic serial murderer, and that we, the society, need to be protected from that evil. But mostly we need to be rescued from the evil of national sin, for we are both victims and complicit collaborators in that: hunger, poverty, inequity, oppression, abuse, functional slavery, destructive and self-serving governance, greed. To encourage myself to be focused interiorly on my own petty sins as an individual is to be seduced away from any awareness of the sinfulness of the nation or culture (which awareness might lead to reform and change, repentance and newness of living). Using Walter Breuggemann's metaphor of the Empire, to focus on **my** sins serves to imply the sinlessness or incorrectability of the Empire, and thereby serves to isolate me, disempower me, to make me less important to the community and the Empire.

This individualized sin has become less than useless, and instead rather dysfunctional and misdirecting, even counter-productive, because it blinds me (makes me inattentive) to some larger realities of this world, our attention is diverted from the greater evils in our world. Thereby some far greater forces of evil are safely hidden from our scrutiny and we become unwitting collaborators in those greater evils, complicit, enabling them by allowing our eyes to be diverted into watching the puny evils on our own hands while ignoring the greater evil, or by thinking ourselves too small, too powerless, too stupid and inept to be able to do anything about them.

Evil Reprised

At the risk of being repetitive I need to back up and be clear what I am **not** talking about when I say "Forces of evil." I am not talking about the natural forces of this physical world which cause events we thoughtlessly or hyperbolically call evil and tragic: Those events themselves I cannot really label evil. Let me lay those to the side as not part of this conversation.

On the other hand, I do need to restate firmly that there is evil in this world; evil is not a fiction. My burden in this chapter is not to identify all the evils, but to point in their direction and examine how sin is related to those evils.

The boundaries enclosing what we can call evil are mushy, unclear, muddied. I cannot draw them specifically. Only one word from my thesaurus rings true for me: malevolent. Evil is human-caused, not natural or random; it intends to do ill, mainly to other but sometimes to self; and it involves some willfulness, however consciously and deliberately, or unconsciously and seemingly accidental (not really so).

The History of Sin

In the Hebrew Scriptures

For myself I must start from our deep cultural roots in the Hebrew Scriptures. I have found profound insights in those writings, though mixed with stuff peculiar to that age and culture so no longer applicable, and also with stuff uninsightful *ergo* stupid, insipid, sometimes dead wrong (e.g., erroneous reproductive biology, misogyny, women as chattel property). So I read those Scriptures with great caution, taking away what has been insightful across the centuries, considering what might be useful when translated into twenty-first-century realities, and discarding the useless and flat out wrong.

Chapter 4: Sin, for One Last Time

The Vocabulary

In Leviticus we are given a fundamental Jewish understanding of man. First, a little midrash: the student asks, "Rabbi, why is the *bet* doubled in *lab*?"[2] And the rabbi's response is "Because the heart *(lab)* has two *yetzers* (impulses), the *yetzer ha-rah* and the *yetzer tov* (the impulse to evil and the impulse to good)." In the Levitical law it is clear that YHWH understands man has built into him both impulses, and that man must be choosing between them. And it follows inevitably that sometimes man will choose the impulse to evil rather than the impulse to good. Understanding this, YHWH gives man in the Levitical law a means for coping on those occasions when man chooses the evil impulse, namely the sacrificial law through which the evil is undone and the impurity washed away. So the purpose of the Levitical law is to enable man, when he commits sin, to return to YHWH with the impurity expunged so that he can again be in right relationship with YHWH.

The Levitical law[3] recognizes two types of sins: injunctive sins (*aseh*) "Thou shalt love YHWH elohim ..." and prohibitive (*ta-aseh*) "Steal not." The law also recognizes three categories of sin:

1. *Khet* (in the Hebrew '*ṭḥ* meaning "to miss the mark"): inadvertent unintentional sins, mistakes, errors, and

2. *Avon* [also *zdon*] (in the Hebrew *m'l* meaning "to act unfaithfully, treacherously, to trespass"): advertent trespasses (crookedness) e.g., a man is hungry and eats the available pork knowing it's against dietary law e.g., probably the sort of thing intended in the Lord's Prayer "lead us not into temptation, but deliver us from evil," and

3. *Pesha* (in the Hebrew *'šp* meaning "to rebel"): demonstrative sin (rebelliousness, breaking a covenantal relationship) e.g., Absalom raising an army to usurp his father's throne.

So some sins are seen as unintentional, others as intentional but not earth-shaking, and some as very heinous, basically rebellious, and ultimately rebellious against YHWH. The Levitical law, recognizing those gradations, then prescribes specific sacrifices for the first two gradations, *khet* and *avon* but has none for *pesha*. It appears that *pesha* must instead be publicly confessed, which would seem to then reduce the *pesha* to the severity of *avon* for which sacrifice can be made.

---

2. Six of the twenty-two consonants in Hebrew are "doubled" when they appear as the first consonant in the word. By "doubled" is meant the consonant in pronounced in its hard form as opposed to the softer form. But in the case of the word *lab* (which means "heart," both the physical organ but also the mind, character, determination, courage, understanding, the interior person) the bet (one of those six "double-able" consonants), appearing as the second consonant should be pronounced as a "v" sound, but instead is always pronounced as a hard "b" (hence "doubled").

3. The detail of this study I take from Anderson and Culbertson, ATR LXVIII:4 303-328

1. The verb "to sin" (*'ṭh*) is much used, the noun less so (but then Hebrew is a verb-based language). What does the word mean? Brown-Driver-Briggs **Hebrew and English Lexicon** says that the core meaning is "to miss the mark/goal/way/path, to do/go wrong, commit a mistake." The Holladay **Concise Hebrew and Aramaic Lexicon** makes the verb "to be at fault, offend" and "be blame-worthy." It would seem to carry no shading about intent or guiltiness. It refers to an action, not an intention or a motivation. One hurls a stone with a sling but misses the objective, Goliath.

2. The verb "to trespass" (*ml'*) is less used in the Hebrew text. Brown-Driver-Briggs cites the core meaning as "to act unfaithfully, treacherously," while Holladay altogether fails to cite it. In noun form this root means "an unfaithful, treacherous act." And,

3. The verb "to rebel" (*šp*) Brown-Driver-Briggs translates as "to rebel, transgress" and is used much more frequently in the noun form to simply mean "transgression" though in several degrees of severity.

The other word crucial to our understanding is *kaparah* (atonement), (in the Hebrew *rpk*) which means basically to wash away (i.e., ablution) and in some contexts is translated "ransom." In the Pi'el (the intensive mood) *kiper* is translated "to cover over, pacify, propitiate."

In the Levitical law the commission of sin causes uncleanness to accrue to the sinner. That uncleanness is not in itself evil, rather it renders the person **impure**, therefore unable to enter the presence of YHWH to worship. The uncleanness itself is amoral, without moral value or implication (e.g., leprosy is neither immoral, nor the result of an immorality, an infraction of the law. It is simply an uncleanness which would contaminate others and must be quarantined. Likewise a nocturnal emission and menstruation are not bad or immoral, but simply unclean, i.e., rendering the person too impure to withstand the purity of YHWH's presence). The uncleanness must be washed away before approaching YHWH's presence. In the atoning sacrifice the sin is not forgiven, nor does the sacrifice remove responsibility for the sin. The offence must first be restituted/redressed, and after that the accrued uncleanness can be washed away, removing the impurity of the offering-bringer so that he can enter YHWH's presence.

One other word *shuv* (in the Hebrew *šub*) should be reviewed, one which we regularly translate "repent." The Hebrew verb *shuv* means basically "to turn" or "to turn aside" or "return," hence to change direction. One is walking the path and chooses to take the left/right-branching path. It implies a choice, an act of the will. It is sometimes translated "to repent."

Chapter 4: Sin, for One Last Time

Two Sorts of Laws

Scholars have been clear there are two strains within the Hebrew law. One I judge to be concerned about the orderliness of tribal living; it sets standards and limits and sanctions to enforce those limits. The other (Lev 17–26, dubbed the Holiness Code) is concerned about the purity of the nation, the quality of its worthiness to be YHWH's people. If we intend to pay attention to the Mosaic law (e.g., by citing it as reason for our biases, phobias and irrationalities), then we need to be very clear that these two strains of the law, while woven together in the Hebrew text somewhat seamlessly, are quite different, serve different purposes, and are dealt with in different ways. The infractions of the first strain, those that disrupt relations within the tribe are *sins*, but infractions of the holiness code are *abominations* (**not sins**), offenses which render the tribe so impure that YHWH will not (or cannot?) relate to it (e.g., a man lying with a man as with a woman is not a sin but an abomination, because it is a form of worship in the temple of Astarte, the goddess of fertility who is YHWH's primary competitor in Canaan). Conversely in the holiness codes a *wayward son* should be stoned to death, not to sanction such behavior, or deter others from so acting, or to maintain the integrity of tribal affairs, but to remove impurity from the tribe, in order to regain sufficient purity that the tribe will qualify, become again pure enough, to be in relation with YHWH.

Consequences, Not Intent

I find neither the tribal code nor the holiness code much concerned about intent[4]; but I do find both concerned with act and consequence. The underlying attitude seems to me, why you did it is of little consequence, but **that** you did it, and that so-and-so **was injured** by your so doing is of consequence, to me, YHWH, because it harms the well-being of the tribe. In order to redeem the sin some fair, equitable restitution must be made, and then the impurity erased. This seems to me a reasonable stance. Contrariwise I perceive the judging of intent in our culture to be a most precarious undertaking.

Focus is Community, more than Individual

But in the cases of both the tribal law and the holiness code I deem that the focus is on the tribal community much more than the individual. It is the community which is at risk. On Yom Kippur, the Day of Atonement, it is the sins of the nation which are of greater concern and are put on the head of the scapegoat and carried out into the

---

4. Negligence may be considered in levying the restitution, so, if an ox gored a man then the ox is killed, but if an ox gored a man and it be known the ox is a gorer, then both the ox and its owner are killed (Exod 21:28–29). But intent seems not a concern, only the act and the consequence.

Wilderness of Zsin to be taken away. By focusing our Christian attentions regarding sin on the individual, we have lost that national focus entirely.

The Shift from Community to Individual Focus

And then one more final notion while I'm still loitering in the Hebrew yard. I noted above that the two core concerns of the Mosaic law were the maintenance of tribal coherence and harmony, and the tribal purity (acceptability to YHWH). In the earliest historical period as the tribes unified, the tribal issues morphed into concern for the nation. But in the latter portions of the Hebrew Scriptures, and thence throughout the Christian writings the emphasis turns away from the nation and the larger community and onto the individual. And my probing mind will not leave it alone; how comes this shift from the national to the individual? There are two defining events in Hebrew history, the exodus and the exile. We Christians recognize the exodus and play with it within our own Christian traditions, but we do nothing with the exile. We ignore it almost completely. Yet it is as central as the exodus to Judaism. What are we missing? As I watched (setting aside the special case of Gen 1–11) the Hebrew Scriptures pass in front of my eyes in Jack Miles's **God: A Biography** I found myself watching YHWH morph from the private chaplain and benefactor to Abram's lineage into the ruthless, furious, relentless warrior of the exodus vying for the faithfulness of the twelve tribes and then of the earlier kings, then flip-flopping into a bi-polar sanctioner of the post-Solomonic apostate kings, finally retreating into internationality and delivering his chosen people into exile, and then gradually withdrawing, until in the closing books of the *Tanach* he has become remote, increasingly absent and finally gone altogether, and in his place we discover individual heroes who are the saviors of the nation (but don't really **save**, only rescue). And as that exilic and post-exilic period evolves, under the influence of first Babylonian and then Hellenistic cultures, I detect a shift from concern for the nation, which literally no longer exists for the Jews, into concern for and focus upon the individual, so that the post-exilic writings focus primarily on the behavior and piety of the individual rather than on the cohesiveness and purity of the nation. In Jesus we see, I think, a confusion of the two strains, social concerns for justice and mercy toward all people, but with a semi-Pharisaic fixation on individual behavior and piety. So two strains. And the first Christians appear to pick up the individual focus, but, being themselves a dispossessed people under the heel of Rome, do nothing with the national concerns. And because of this focus Christianity successfully appeals to the oppressed, the disenfranchised of the empire.

Summary

I find no consistent, tight definition of sin throughout the Hebrew Scriptures. The Eighth-century prophets assume sin is a moral offense against God, that God requires

Chapter 4: Sin, for One Last Time

of us a moral life, and that repentance alone for offenses is not sufficient; sin contaminates, which contamination must be removed/covered over with sacrifice. Sin in various books of the *Tanach* is described as defiance of God, imputed (moral) offense, rebellion against God, infidelity, apostasy, social injustice, profaneness, and blindness. It may be transgression of a regulation, unwitting or willful non-obedience. The root seems to be "to miss the mark," which for me implies being less than or different than ought to be, and the referent for that oughtness is YHWH. It appears to me that in the earlier portions of those Scriptures sin is mostly concerned with tribal, or later national, cohesiveness and harmony, but in the post-exilic portions focuses more on individual piety and behavior. While shame may well be associated with sin throughout the Hebrew Scriptures, I am fairly convinced that emotional guilt (*vis-a-vis* moral guilt) was no part of sin in the Hebrew Scriptures.

Early Christian History

Now I turn the page to take a very quick look at the first Christians, though my deeper concern is with Augustine at the very end of the fourth century.

The Gospels

The curtain rises on John, baptizing in the Jordan wilderness and preaching a baptism of repentance (i.e., *change of mind*) for the remission (i.e., *sending away*) of sins. When John is jailed Jesus comes striding onto the scene preaching the "... Good news of the kingdom of God: the time is fulfilled and the kingdom of God is at hand. Repent ye, and believe the good news" (Mark 1:15). I note that their separate messages are roughly similar. Both speak of repentance (changing of mind) and where John's referent is remission (sending back) of sin, Jesus' is the kingdom of God (purity). Neither speaks much of the Father's love; both are heavy on judgment for offenses and endtime stuff. And I note in passing that in John's gospel sin is itself abstracted into the failure to recognize God's presence in Jesus.

The Pauline Letters

Saul, renamed Paul after his mystical conversion on the road to Damascus, is a character interesting to me (though I do not much like him or most of his interpretation of the message). A zealous, anti-Christian, fire-breathing Pharisee on his way to arrest some Christians, he is struck blind by a light from heaven which claims to be the Christ. My irrelevant fascination with Paul is simply this, that the man I see after his mystical experience and conversion is exactly the same man I had seen before the life-changing road-to-Damascus event; the same zealous, fire-breathing, driven man, only now pro-Christian instead of anti-Christian. But unchanged.

Part II: My Review of Christian Doctrines

Paul brings two geniuses to the movement: his ability to organize and shape communities, and his reframing of Jesus' message into a language of love and community life. Sin seems to me not so central a part of his message as a tool for managing community life. But in him, the first Christian writer, son-of-God notions and why the necessity of his death are already starting to take shape in his letters. The prophetic teacher and healer Jesus is in the process of being elevated to something super-human.

The Apostolic Fathers

And after Paul begins the Apostolic period of trying to figure out "What in the world has just happened to us?" In the next generation of the Early Church Fathers, Christian belief begins to evolve in a plethora of different, and hotly debated directions and shapes. I am not a student of this period, in fact am barely aware that it all happened. And while sin is certainly part of the debate, the primary focus seems to me determining the nature of this Jesus event. Interpretations fly in a multiplicity of directions and the clamorings begin to say a loud "No" to some of those directions (e.g., Gnosticism).

The Pelagian Dispute[5]

Now I leap ahead two and more centuries, past fanciful squabblings, debates, arguments, fights and outright battles over just what this Jesus event was, and land in the lap of Augustine of Hippo.

Biographies

Augustine was born of a Christian mother (and a coarse, violent, pagan father) and, refusing Christianity himself, was trained as a rhetorician and professed himself a Manichæan, i.e., a dualistic, ascetical fatalist who thought himself no damned good. Hearing Ambrose preach, he had a mystical experience akin to Paul's and converted to Christianity. And I would suggest that, like Paul, he changed jackets, but the man inside remained quite unchanged. He still thought himself unable to do any good, and like the fatalists, unable to change that. He founded a monastery, was presented by others to be ordained, and in 396 AD was consecrated bishop of Hippo. His early training in rhetoric served him well. He successfully countered two issues troubling the emperor, Manichæism and the Donatist Rebellion, and with those feathers in his cap took up his pen against Pelagius. Jerome, crafter of the Vulgate, had already crossed swords with Pelagius and Augustine joined the fray. Throughout the subsequent back-and-forth the two never actually met, but conducted their arguments by

---

5. My discussion of the Pelagian controversy is based on Rees, **Pelagius: Life and Letters**, *passim*

writing books at each other, and in that process Augustine's very systematic theology emerged.

When Pelagius was ultimately declared a heretic, almost all his writings were trashed and what we have been told about him came from the lips of his detractors, Jerome and Augustine (how reliable or unbiased might those sources be?) Jerome declared Pelagius a fat Scot (he is claimed by Scots, the Irish, the Welsh and English), and the bit of his writings which we can confidently ascribe to him indicate to me that he came out of some kind of monastic training; at least he betrays a monastic leaning in his teachings: that you can, with diligence, persistence and discipline, improve yourself. (Bowers's take on his brief encounter of monastic life is that there's no reason to endure such a demanding discipline if you are convinced you can't do life better.)

Their Theologies

I have merely dabbled in Augustine's writings, and know only what I have heard and read from others. So what follows is merely my opinion. Augustine's theology evolved as the controversy proceeded, each restatement getting a little more extreme and audacious. It appears to me that three dynamics colluded at this point: 1) Augustine's internal dynamics (his self-loathing and proclaimed inability to do anything good of himself), 2) the emperor's need for a unifying meta-narrative in melding the divisions within his empire, and 3) Augustine's growing esteem coupled with his drivenness to become the premiere theological[6] voice of the empire. As his thinking developed, original sin became the centerpiece of his system. That notion had been around for a while, but was not widely or eagerly accepted. Augustine made it his centerpiece. It justified his own no-good-ness, and at the same time suggested to his hearers that they too were no damned good and were abjectly needful of the protecting guidance of the God-ordained emperor. And sin thereby became the linchpin in the theological system of the universal church.

I was taught that in the case of heresies, it is usually the heretic who is innovating, reaching beyond the already established for a more complete and integrated understanding. But in this case it would seem that Augustine was the innovator, putting together previously unconnected pieces that had been circulating, but were not widely accepted, into a tight, coherent, and very useful system. Pelagius, from the little we have received from his hand, was teaching some very common, unexceptional, fairly traditional stuff (how to behave morally in an immoral world) which sounded much like what a monk would say. But in denying a few points of Augustine's emerging

---

6. I do not suggest that Augustine consciously set out to become the premiere theologian of the church and empire; it just happened because what he was saying fit the needs of the empire at that moment in history; nor do I think that he consciously selected sin as his centerpiece; that too just happened to fit both his personal needs and the needs of the emperor in governing an unruly world, all very unconscious stuff.

theology (Prof. Bob Page taught us that the heretic usually gets in trouble, not for what he affirms, but for what he denies), Pelagius fell askew Augustine's emerging system and was thereby skewered as heretical, even to this day, I note.

Summary

At this point the issue of sin begins to warp in the Christian writings. I judge that the driving consideration was a trying to make sense of the Jesus experience, particularly his inelegant death and being subsequently re-experienced by his followers as alive. Ideas fly, and in every direction. By the time of the Nicene formulation in 325 AD the man Jesus has been elevated to God, but the notion of Jesus' execution as the sacrifice in expiation/propitiation for men's sins has not yet gained universal acceptance. That notion gets nailed down with Augustine's formulation and his positioning of original sin as the linchpin.

This is what I have received from our tradition and have come to understand as the core of our Christian meta-narrative: because of Adam's sin,[7] sin has been passed on (in accord with the fourth-century misunderstanding of reproductive biology) to all humankind, we are all damned (to hell?) as too impure to survive in the purity of God's presence; but God, in his justice-mercy enables the execution of his only son (though YHWH previously had spared Abram's son) as a temple-worthy sacrifice to expiate/propitiate our inescapable sinfulness, thereby redeeming us back into his presence (for final judgment?) While probably useful in its day, now this is garbage! Albeit garbage with a nostalgia. But all merely garbage.

The Translation in Moving from Judaism to Christian

The first Christians, the apostles and their followers, were predominantly Jews, with a few gentile believers mixed in. But Paul and his bunch were regularly tossed unceremoniously out of the synagogues wherever they went because their messianic message was too radical for most in the synagogues. Their greater success was in forming new communities out of predominantly non-Jews. We think Paul had been trained a Pharisee, but those who came after him were not. So within one generation the Jewishness of the early Christians began to evaporate. Further, while Pharisee-trained, some of Paul's own evolving theology breaks with Jewish tradition, initiating the slide away from traditional Jewish understandings. Hellenistic and Roman thinking begins

---

7. I dabble in some thought-play: Was Adam's sin the eating of the forbidden apple? Or his disobeying the single restriction not to eat of that tree? or simply being a misogynist who passively follows the woman's lead? (*Nota bene* Eve and the serpent [who is not *satan* but rather the consort of YHWH's primary competitor in Canaan, the fertility goddess Astarte] are the dialoging theologians in the story, and ha'adam is a passive drone.)

Chapter 4: Sin, for One Last Time

to seep in and some understandings quite different from Jewish thought begin to emerge.

Sin Became Simplified

In the paragraph on vocabulary above I described the complexity of the Hebrew understanding of sin: two kinds of sin and three different intensities. In our Christian tradition all this complexity has been boiled down to one simple word, "sin," without the nuances the Levitical forerunner saw. It seems to me a lot was lost in the translation. As a result, in our own American jurisprudence system we have multiple levels of complexity and intensity, but in the church we simply sin. One other observation: in the Levitical eyes the law is the gift of YHWH to enable the man to return to purity and relationship with YHWH. So to act against the law, to sin is to act against the dictum of YHWH; the sin may involve damage or injury to another which needed to be restituted or repatriated, but the greater force of the sin is the disobedience of YHWH's dictum. But the notion of restitution has been lost in translation and we are left merely with our disobedience of the perfect and wrathful YHWH's dictum. No restitution to correct the sin. And no sacrifice to make atonement. I think we lost quite a bit in that translation.

Repentance Transformed

Both John and Jesus strode onto the scene preaching "Repentance" (the Hebrew verb *shuv* means "to turn aside," or "return"). But the gospelers wrote in Greek, and so the action *shuv* was translated into the Greek with *metanoía*, a compound word which means literally, a "transformation of the mind," an interior, internal change of mind. While the Hebrew might imply a willful act, a choice, the Greek implies quite differently a change within the non-physical portion of myself, in my soul, my spirit, my mind, whatever. Seems to me the idea of repentance got quite warped in that translation; the part of me that **shapes** intentions, the mind, got dragged into the equation. And in the Christian church lots of guilty feelings are invoked along with repentance, perhaps to motivate or accelerate the repentant. I believe the emotive load to be a Christian overlay.

Guilt Piled On

And while I'm still loitering in this from-Hebrew-to-Christian transition, I will toss one other concern onto the heap. The Christian church has shoved a whole lot of guilt onto this sin notion *(I recall from my tender years Bishop Blanchard telling us newly ordained priests that guilt was quite an appropriate tool to use in the church, and that we should apply it liberally; I blanched at that recommendation)* and in the process of guiltifying we intensified concerns about intent. Our American justice system has become wired with a complex system built around intent (so, multiple degrees of felonies and multiple degrees of misdemeanors). The driving dynamic is guilt. **How** guilty one is becomes a product of his intent. There are bad intentions, worse intentions, less onerous intentions and accidents. Once again I trot back to the rabbinical midrash I cited earlier. "Rabbi, why is the bet in *lab* (Hebrew word for "heart") doubled?" Answer: "Because there are two *yetsers* (impulses) of the heart, the *yetser ha'rah* and the *yetser tov*, the impulse toward good and the impulse toward evil." It appears to me that Freud, while detesting his Jewish religious roots, borrowed from this midrash when he identified the *id* as a mass of undifferentiated impulses. His purpose is the same as the rabbi's, to place the impulse outside the purview of morality, but to put the choice, whether or not to enact the impulse, at the very center of morality. I chuckled when the President of the United States Jimmy Carter admitted that he had lusted in his heart. He implied guilt, while the rabbi did not. Instead the rabbi implied that both good and bad impulses are results of God's creation. Impulses are amoral. Our choices are the arena of morality. Impulse all you want, guilt does not apply, but choose only the good, the beneficial. I suspect God was not the least upset at Jimmie Carter's lusting in his heart. God might have even enjoyed that sexual urge. Along with the rabbis and Freud, I would not consider intent or impulse as having morality, but would see the choosing, whether to act out an intent or impulse, and how to act it out, that **is** morally laden. Culpability derives from the doing, not the thinking. I consider that God does not much care morally about our mental lives, but does care morally about our behavior, where we interact with others, and in particular about how our behavior affects those around us; is our behavior loving and good (beneficial), or unloving, self-centered and harmful (evil, destructive, injurious)—not in intent, but in effect, in result?

I recalled reading ages ago that there are really two guilts, but we fail to distinguish between them. One is moral guilt. By offending or transgressing moral convictions and injuring or harming another one becomes morally guilty. The judgment of moral guilt is reasonable and rational and without emotion. Determining moral guilt is an act of the intellect, and deciding to make reparations is also an act of the will. Not emotionally driven. The other guilt is **emotional**, and is **not** a natural emotion but a manufactured, compound emotion which seems to be composed of two separate emotions crammed together: a sense of loss (perhaps of self-esteem), and anger (perhaps at the loss of self-esteem). It is intended to induce shame, and thereby to deter (bad behavior) or to motivate (change or good behavior). In my own appraisal I judge this emotional guilt to be useless, dysfunctional and usually destructive. I think it almost invariably demotivates and usually fails to inhibit, tending instead to focus the individual's attention on his inner life rather than his behavior. I do believe that we (as a culture) fail to separate these two guilts and instead co-mingle and thereby confuse them, ending up paying much more attention to the emotionally laden guilt and often failing to recognize and then act upon the moral guilt. The result is diffuse and unanchored emotion (largely undirected or misdirected anger, but also shame and lowered self-esteem) with no objective or discharge: very corrosive stuff (I mean that literally, anger does bad, corrosive things to the physical body). It is this emotional guilt which we have piled onto the notion of sin (see the beautiful language of the general confessions in the 1928 Prayer Book).

I now Vault over Sixteen Hundred Years into the Middle of the Twentieth Century to Talk about Sin Today

My Induction:

When I was born and introduced into the church, these words held sway: "We have erred and strayed from thy ways . . . followed too much the devices and desires of our own hearts. . . offended against thy holy laws. . . left undone those things which we ought to have done; and we have done those things which we ought not to have done; and there is no health in us[8] . . . ." It had to be true, because it's in the Prayer Book and we were saying it with great solemnity every Sunday. But I had a hard time contemplating what this young teen had done that was **this** bad! And for added effect we'd pray in Holy Communion, ". . . We acknowledge and bewail our manifold sins and wickedness . . . most grievously have committed . . . provoking most justly thy wrath and indignation against us . . . . are heartily sorry for these our misdoings; the remembrance of them is grievous unto us; the **burden of them is intolerable**[9]. . . " I searched through every nook and cranny of that teen life trying to root out whatever I had done that had so offended. We repeated it every fourth Sunday; it had to be true. But search as I would I could find no faults that were so condemningly grievous. Nor did I feel as burdened down with such huge guilt feelings as the words told. For what? Unless it was the masturbation I was discovering; but my own father did not condemn that act as sin nor did he imply it was a fault. . . he simply coached moderation, in that as in all other things. I continued to struggle through my mid-teen years avidly, hungrily, greedily to ingest and make mine that Prayer Book understanding of sin. Ultimately I failed! Many years later I learned the proper churchy Latin for all this, *"Mea culpa, mea culpa, mea maxima culpa,"* my fault, my fault, my most grievous fault. So I struggled, with declining success, to make sense of all this both for my life and for the lives of my parishioners. Near the end of the twentieth century a new awareness began to dawn upon me as I discovered through my study of Celtic Christian spirituality that there are other ways to interpret all this Jesus stuff. I began to consider, seriously now, whether the Loving Father would do this to his Son, and to us?

---

8. 1928 ***Book of Common Prayer*** Morning Prayer, "General Confession" 6.
9. Ibid., 75

Part II: My Review of Christian Doctrines

The Questions

Doug said to me quietly one evening that he does not think himself so grievously a sinful man, feels not a bad man, does not go to bed each night bewailing the day's evil he's done. I nodded that I feel much the same. Not a saint, but neither a Hitler nor a Stalin nor a Dahmer. I feel my sins far less grievously than Augustine had his. I may be wrong in that, but I am thoughtfully so. So I am forced to raise several questions.

1. Is man fatally flawed? Are we all, without exception, born with original sin weighing down our souls? Are we so flawed, as Augustine claimed, that we are utterly helpless to better ourselves? Is it **only** the "grace" of God that enables us to do anything good at all?

2. Is man so horrid, so defiled, so grossly corrupted that he cannot exist in the presence of the pure and all-good God, that he must be utterly purged, his sins completely washed away "in the blood of the Lamb" (or burned away with a refining fire) before he can survive the presence of the all-loving God?

3. And is man's defilement so totally corrupting that it can be purged away only by the self-sacrificing death on the cross of God's own all-perfect, flawless and sinless, only begotten son, that God's perfection coupled with our complete evilness requires the sacrificial death of God's very own son? E.i., "The precious blood of the lamb?"

That theology does not come to life in me. Nor does it ring true in my world. Throughout my ministry I have had to preach **around** that theology instead of proclaiming it. While I do not consider myself wonderfully good (nor even above-average good) that theology does not inform my life or the way I live. So I am forced to use all my trained critical-thinking tools to examine it.

The word sin has become debased coinage for me. The word has been used in so many different ways, set in so many trivializing contexts, imposed with so many punitive intents, clothed so much with emotional guilt that I am no longer sure what sin means; or rather, I am very sure I do **not** know what it means. Once upon a time I was sure that I could know. I had done those things I ought not to have done, and I had not done those things I ought to have done. There was no health in me. But as I've aged and experienced, as I've also learned, and become more muddled, as I've looked beyond the obvious and into the murk, and as I've listened to so many bad preachers rant about others's sins, I've become less and less sure.

Definitions:

My ***Random House Dictionary of the English Language Unabridged*** suggests:

Chapter 4: Sin, for One Last Time

> **sin**—*n.* 1. transgression of divine law 2. any act regarded as such a transgression, *esp.* a willful or deliberate violation of a religious or moral principle 3. any reprehensible or regrettable action, behavior, etc; great fault or offense 4. *v.i.*- to commit a sinful act 5. to offend against a principle, standard 6. *v.t.* to commit or offend sinfully 7. to bring, drive, etc. by sinning. **Syn** 1. trespass, violation 2. wrong, wickedness 4. trespass, transgress.

A little useful, as far as it goes, but it needs much tighter definition. The ***Oxford Dictionary of the Christian Church*** in the article on sin adds:

> "The purposeful disobedience of a creature to the known will of God. Unlike moral evil it is a fundamentally theological conception.*(I wonder what that sentence can possibly mean?)* In the Old Testament it is represented as a constant factor in the experience both of God's people and the world from the first transgression of Adam and Eve in the Garden of Eden onwards. Its power was aggravated by the moral and ceremonial precepts in the law of Moses, which both increased the occasions of sin and developed a keener sense of moral responsibility. The teaching of the Prophets with its emphasis on the heinousness of injustice, lack of mercy, and idolatry deepened the sense of sin in another way. The Psalms and Jeremiah, by their stress of the heart as the seat of sin, were marked by their penetrating insights into its personal and emotional effects. In the NT teaching on sin is summed up and deepened by the clear recognition that its roots lie in man's character. St.Paul expounds it as a breach of the natural law written in the conscience of man. St.James stresses its origin in the human will. . . ."

And the beat goes on. I'm not too sure this churchy definition is horribly accurate historically, and I might quibble with it in several places, but overall I find it marvelously unhelpful. The word itself is still completely a stumbling block for me.

So I go back to my Greek:

In classical Greek noun *hamartía* was a failure, an error, a sin, and the verb, *hamartaínō* meant to miss the mark, *ergo* to fail of doing or of purpose, to go wrong; and in the New Testament was clearly expressive of the above Oxford Dictionary sense of sin.

One more challenge rises up in me: Random House stipulates a "transgression of divine law." Somehow God is tied up in all this sin stuff. I posited a willful commission of evil without reference to God; but the church has always tied God into all this sin stuff since, in the eyes of the church, it is transgressing divinely given law that effects sin. But what, I will suggest, if the law is not divinely given? What if the law is humanly devised (with the best of intentions, or even with the most surely divinely-inspired revelation) and lately attributed to God? I have elsewhere in these chapters suggested that **all** this religion stuff is metaphor, that even Scripture is metaphor, and that while God stands somewhere behind all this metaphor, still we cannot assume that the law as received in Scripture, in the Ten Commandments and 643 laws embedded in the Scriptures, is in detail God-dictated, but instead should understand the law as man-created and then otherly attributed. Robert Wright suggests that god might be the moral axis of the universe, which feels a reasonable but unarguable inference to me. And while we can hope that the law is an accurate approximation of that moral axis, is well aligned with that axis, we cannot be sure, nor can we use the law in any literalist way; we cannot be sure when this particular transgression is an overstepping of the fuzzy edge of the law and therefore equal to sin, or that overstepping of the fuzzy edge is not a transgression of the law and so is not-sin. It really is getting murky. And moreover it begins to imply that the determination of what is sin and what is not-sin is in our ball-park, not God's. **We** have to discern what's aligned with the moral axis, and not merely accept a so-called God's-law, literalistic definition.

I come away from all that very little enlightened. Missing the mark *(an archery term?)* is about all that helps or gives me a mere toe hold. So much for others's definitions. In my present state of mind, sin is not a useful or functional notion. I could scour each of those above definitions, but that would gain me nothing. I need first to find my own place to stand.

My Understanding

I understand Augustine and Pelagius to have been wrestling with (among other things) the tension between fatalism and free-will. Augustine, with his Manachæan roots stood with one foot, or perhaps both feet, firmly planted in a fatalism: we just can't do any better of ourselves, only God (i.e., God's grace) can enable us to do anything right at all; we are incapable of willing it and carrying it out of ourselves; we are terminally flawed by Adam's sin, i.e., disobedience. But at the same time Augustine had to assure himself and us that man is completely free to choose, that though fatally flawed, he is still free-willed and therefore culpable.

Pelagius on the other hand would seem to have had the monastic's take on things. . . we can, if we try hard, if we are deliberate and persistent, improve our behavior, break the **habit** *(Pelagius's word)* of bad behaviors, be more like what God wants of us *(come closer to the mark?)* And he rejected (probably) Augustine's notion of original sin.

On the one hand, are we hopelessly flawed, fettered with original sin, or on the other hand, are we endowed with free will and able to break out of bad, habitually sinful behavior? I find both Augustine and Pelagius correct in small ways but in most larger ways quite wrong. In my experience it is not as easy or simple as Pelagius would have it; but it is not as hopeless as Augustine makes it out. Yet I am not merely ruling out the extreme ends of this continuum and accepting the midrange.

Chapter 4: Sin, for One Last Time

Straw Definition of Sin

Let me here posit a straw definition of sin which, though quite insufficient, is a place for me to start. I will stipulate that sin is the **willful commission of evil**, whether by action or inaction.

Evil

And then I must dither with evil. I stipulated in the opening framework statement of this chapter that there are forces of evil in this world. I have never yet met a demon, so I do not believe in them. Demonology was the prevalent mythology (or I would say, metaphor[10]) of Jesus' day. We use a scientific, a medical and/or therapeutic metaphor today. Nor have I ever met a satan[11], a personalized force of evil. That again was a metaphor of the inter-testamental period and of Jesus' day, one which the church has tried to keep active. But I believe that in 2016 the satan metaphor functions only as an escape hatch, a way of avoiding responsibility, and of avoiding the effort and change it would take to overcome the real forces of evil.

I also wrestle with right vs. good. As in plane geometry there can be only one right angle to a line at a given point, I reason *(this may be an imperfect analogy)* that there can be only one right, correct way to do, or be, something. All else is **almost** right or correct, but not quite. But good on the other hand translates into "useful, beneficial," and I notice that in a specific situation there might be several possible goods. So choose your stance: does God require us to be/do right, or good? Quite different things in my mind. And is sin then the voluntary or involuntary failure to do as God wills, and doing evil instead? But still, I'm merely quibbling.

Freewill and Choosing

(Prof. Ron Santoni suggests that free-will is no longer argued, but that instead we must talk about choices and choice-making. I yield to that. It is a softening, a graying of the issue, and I still end up wrestling with how open or limited the choices may be.) In my thinking, whether we're talking about right or good, intellectually the issue revolves around the choosing, i.e., do we have absolutely free choice, or are we fated to be hopelessly flawed and unable to freely choose to do good? *(For lack of better, I plead hackneyed lines here.)* If we are not truly free-willed, then can it really be sin? Or if we have somewhat free choice, merely limitedly free choice, then is it sort of sin, or limited sin? Or does God write the law, and then create us such that we cannot keep

---

10. I use the word "metaphor" throughout my writing in my own peculiar way. See paragraph "Worldview" in Chapter 8 (216–17)

11. The Hebrew **satan** translates as "adversary," and first appears in the Hebrew text in the fourth century BC post-exilic book of Job (1:6) to identify one of the sons of God

it, or worse yet, create us flawed (i.e., disobedient), and then require us to keep a law we cannot possibly keep. This would seem a demonic God, sardonic, sneering at us. But the basic problem for me goes even deeper than this simplistic, fourth-century understanding. I start with that which I deem us to be.

How free are we to choose, really? To the extent we are free, able to choose and do, to that extent we are, or may be held, responsible, culpable, accountable. But to the extent that we are not free to choose, or only somewhat free to choose, then can we rightly, fairly be held completely responsible, accountable, culpable. . . or only somewhat responsible, accountable, culpable? Can we be called to account if we had no choice in the matter? So one issue for me is, how free are we, really?

I am inclined here to labor through the layers upon layers of hard-wired and acquired patterns that shape not only our behavior, but even our very perceptions and data-management systems. The fact is, I *feel* pretty free to make choices and decisions. The reality may be that my freedom of choice is very, very narrowed and limited. The whole issue of free will may have been functional in the fourth century, but today it is a red herring, useful only to draw us away from an on-target tracking of reality.

Impediments to Freewill and Choosing

In the following consideration I finally find one place to put my foot firmly and push off to a start. In my younger years we understood that, psychologically, the newborn exited the uterus and began life a *tabula rasa* a blank tablet, a clean slate; and onto that blank slate were then etched our accumulating experiences, which in turn shaped who we were becoming. But the *tabula rasa* has been shattered.

Genes and Hormones

In the last century we began to realize that some mental illnesses seemed to have a genetic component; that some of us were born with a tendency toward that illness. Perhaps I do not after all choose for myself a mental illness, or maybe it is not caused by an unknown virus, or does not happen to me by pure chance. And soon after that we began to realize that many parts of our personality might have a genetic component, that we may enter this world with a tendency toward this or that. In the Myers-Briggs way of measuring my personality-type (my ways in decision-making) I am an INTP; and that is not simply a matter of conscious choice or preference (there are some very useful, beneficial aspects of being an INTP, but some serious drawbacks as well); but it's not clear how *hard-wired*, i.e., genetically caused my INTP-ness is, or how much it was shaped by hormones (*in utero* and/or *post-utero*) or by my early life-shaping experiences (etchings on that *tabula* not-so *rasa*) I am only aware that while my INTP-ness was probably not a matter of my conscious choice *(I am not aware of having ever*

Chapter 4: Sin, for One Last Time

chosen it) although how closely-adhering to that personality type style I live today **is** somewhat *(an indefinite!)* a matter of personal choice. . . how free am I, really?

For example, we are learning that one tendency, a proneness to violent, sometimes uncontrollably violent behavior **may** be related to a genetic anomaly identified as XXY (too many or mutated sex chromosomes), but how much might that control this or that individual's tendency to violent behavior? We are not sure, it's not clear. And we are learning that children who are severely abused (whether physically, sexually, or psychologically) may themselves become violent, sometimes uncontrollably violent. How much choice have they, even in adulthood? How truly insane was Adolph Hitler? Insane enough that he sometimes fell to the floor and chewed *(so we were told)* on the rug? Insane enough to order the invasion of Poland? Insane enough to inflict WWII onto Europe? Insane enough to inhumanely slaughter six million Jews, gays and gypsies? How insane? And if insane, then how controllable by himself might his disastrously destructive impulses have been? Was he in any reasonable sense responsible for the evil he escorted into this world? Or to what degree might he have been responsible, culpable? We know he embodied evil, but how willful was that embodiment, and that enacting? And did it make any difference to those six million Jews, gays and gypsies to what degree Hitler was willful in his evil, his perhaps insanity-driven evil?

We (nationally and internationally) debate furiously and to no avail the goodness or badness, the evilness or okayness of homosexuality these days. But scientific studies now show that gayness is not a matter of choice in any way (a gay friend of mine asked rhetorically, "Jack, who in his right mind would **choose** to be gay?"), but is genetically influenced, caused by hormones *in utero* causing differences in the structure of the brain. No conscious or even unconscious choice involved.

Scientists are now suggesting that the genome does not specifically determine, but rather is the blueprint for each individual, and that (following my imperfect architecture metaphor) the building site and the materials and the craftsmanship are just as important in constructing the person who emerges. Whatever. Know that the genes and hormones are important in shaping the outcome.

Choice, Yes, But from a Limited Menu?

The following is taken from an article in BBC News by Jason Palmer:

> "A growing idea holds that the chances of our choices are written in our brains. The free will that humans enjoy is similar to that exercised by animals as simple as flies . . . . tests show that animal behavior is neither completely constrained nor completely free. . . . Choices actually fit a complex probability. . . in humans . . . perceived as conscious decisions . . . . Experiments . . . with flies *[have]* shown that although animal behavior can be unpredictable, responses do seem to come from a fixed list of options. . . . More and more people are

realizing that it's *[i.e., free will]* a biological property, a trait; the brain possesses the freedom to generate behaviors and options on its own.... *[Scientists]* have used mathematical models to simulate brain activity on a computer, finding that what worked best was a combination of deterministic behavior and what is known as stochastic *[term of statistics: randomly determined observations of samples from a probability distribution]* behavior—which may look random but actually... follows a defined set of probabilities.... the strong, Cartesian version of free will—the belief that if you were placed in exactly the same circumstances again, you could have acted otherwise—is difficult to reconcile with natural laws."

This tickles my curiosity into wondering whether we too are choosing from a limited slate of options? A list we can amend, certainly, if we only stop to think about it and generate additional options, but initially, a short list of unconsidered first options? And how many of those are hard-wired, i.e., pre-determined?

Replicating Parental Models

Has freewill been a delectable fantasy which we told ourselves was a fundamental truth? I remember my first wife telling me how much she did not want to replicate her mother's parenting, and then she was exasperated when she caught her mother's exact words coming out her own mouth, and realized she was doing exactly what her mother had done despite how fervently she wanted **not** to do and say those things. Sounds like St.Paul! And when I looked closely I could see that I too was doing and saying what my father had done, the things that had made me cringe (and when I catch myself doing them I cringe again). The reality is that we learn from our parents as the primary models and teachers of parenting, and we will follow their models almost exactly, simply because they're the only close-up models we have. Sure, we watched, and sometimes envied other kids's parents, but our own parents were the only ones we saw up close, in detail, every day, all day long. So we learned them, incorporated them into our fibers, into our very being.

Is that changeable? Can I learn to parent differently? I think to some degree that may be possible, but I suspect *(really I am damned sure)* it takes very hard, very deliberate, very conscious effort to change even an iota, a jot or tittle. In this case Pelagius had it right: we can do better, but only through careful, conscious, very deliberate and persistent effort to break the learned *bad habits* I've watched my step-daughter parenting; she is an absolutely, marvelously great parent. We should bottle and sell *(no, give away)* her parenting skills. I think even her own mother will admit that her daughter has improved upon her own parenting skills (which are pretty impressive). Throughout my years I've watched parents work hard to improve upon the patterns they've learned from their own parents, but I see little significant success. Parenting is hard, particularly if you've learned from the poor skills of your own inept parents.

Chapter 4: Sin, for One Last Time

We learn from our parents, however well or poorly they modeled for us; and deviating from that model is hard, hard work. . . harder than most of us can manage

The Influence of Social Dynamics

St.Paul talked about "principalities and powers" (Rom 8:38) *(his metaphor, not mine)*; his world was peopled with those kinds of spiritual beings, while mine is not. To be sure, Paul looked out upon a quite different spiritual realm than I do. Nonetheless, I think I understand in the twentieth century terms of my own metaphor some of those principalities and powers, those invisible but very powerful forces he saw at work. I believe that they are very real, and that to a certain (i.e., uncertain) degree they shape and motivate both our world **and** our Selves.

Shortly after my seminary years I spent time in what we then called T(for training)-groups, an educational model for learning about group dynamics, the unseen forces that drive the evolving life of every long-lived group. That was a major revelation to me. It was unsettling to discover that when I place myself in a group setting, there are forces, dynamics at work within that group setting that will drive and shape my participation, my very behavior (not completely, but forcibly, and without my awareness). I become somewhat unlike myself in that setting; I become somewhat another person unlike the person I was as I crawled out of bed that morning. I have not changed, the person who I am; but my behavior, even my emotions and thought processes are to some uncertain and indefinable degree shaped by the life of the group, the dynamics peculiar to that very instant of the evolving life of that group. That surprised, and rather stunned me.

And next I began to learn farther, about the dynamics of *social systems* (i.e., any set of relationships which persist over time, for example, a parish). Goals, purposes, behavior norms, limits, expectations, dress codes, customs, legends and myths, standards, totems and taboos, attitudes, values, rituals, customaries (an almost endless list of impositions pressed by the system or subsystem upon the individual), all of which can vary considerably from one sub-system to another even within the same system. They all affect behavior! A person whom I know well outside a certain system presents himself quite differently when I encounter him inside that system (e.g., a close friend at his work place). I began to be amazed at how narrowed freedom can become inside a system. While we might fancy ourselves to be free choosers and controllers of our own behavior, in truth much of our behavior, and to some degree our emotions as well, in any setting, are shaped and driven by the dynamics at work in whatever group or subsystem in which we find ourselves at that moment. We are not really free agents, we **are** shaped and driven by our environment and the dynamic forces therein. Perfectly reasonable people can be caught up in the frenzy of a lynch mob and behave in ways that will appall them upon reflection. Paul's principalities and powers are still very much alive.

Are they inherently evil? I think not. Those forces seem to me amoral, not capable of thinking or judging or willing; they have no capacity to know right from wrong, good from bad. But they can drive us, nonetheless, toward good or toward evil. And yet we are not helpless. We can, recognizing and paying attention to those principalities and powers, those group and system dynamics, turn and direct them and/or our Selves toward good or toward evil. Am I hereby suggesting that some evil in this world is the result of how man/mankind chooses to direct these dynamics (and I include not-choosing, simply allowing myself to be driven willy-nilly. . . which is itself a choice)? That may be the case; I've not thought that possibility all the way through. And to what degree then is the individual truly accountable for his behavior within that system? When the Nazi officer claimed in his Nuremburg trial that he was only following orders, how free was he in fact to choose action counter to those orders? (he was found guilty as charged); and if he were a non-commissioned officer, low in rank, then **how** free was he to act counter to the orders?

Factoring in Cultures

And then when we look beyond the group, the family, the neighborhood, and the social system, we find other pressures and limits are being imposed: the culture (e.g., American vs Western European vs Far Eastern) and the subculture (e.g., Slavic vs Latin vs Germanic). And in addition, what might be sin or evil within one cultural sphere might not be sin or evil in another (e.g., *honor killings* quite abhorrent to the Western mind, but mandatory in some parts of Eastern cultures). I began to realize the innumerable layers of dynamics are pressing down on the individual, limiting, shaping, directing.

Language as a Limiting Factor

I am a student*(albeit lapsed)* of Latin and Greek, then of Hebrew, (and a little English as well) and I became aware in those studies that the texture and shape of the language shapes the way in which the individual thinks, and even limits what he can think about and how he can think about it. (E.g., there was no word or concept of homosexuality in the Latin, Greek or Hebrew languages, so no way a person of that classical age could even think about that syndrome. Yet today, after the recognition of the syndrome and the coining of the word in the late 1800s it became an explosive topic of debate.) I expect I could go further in this facet of the examination, but I think the case is stated; the language in which we think and speak itself limits and shapes what we can think and say, and so affords us somewhat truncated freedom, and a very uncertain amount of choice within whatever sphere we live.

For example: the Hebrew (along with all Semitic languages) is verb-based with most nouns and the few adjectives made out of verb roots. The verb leads the sentence, so the language focuses attention on actions. Romance Languages on the other hand are noun-based, and the subject leads the sentence linked to the predicate with a verb. The Hebrew uses as building blocks action words, the Greek and Latin use concepts. As I attempt to understand the impact of that fundamental difference in the languages, I envision the Hebrew mind sliding from action to action with diminished attention to defined concepts, while the Romance mind strings together well-defined concepts linked with verbs of secondary importance to the meaning. I believe that thinking in two such different ways creates two quite different senses of the world and even of reality. It's no wonder to me that we Westerners have such trouble relating to the issues of the Middle East.

Complex Scenerios

Yes, I can make choices. I **do** make choices. But there are still several problems for me. I make choices, and I am liable for the results of those choices. Consider: the pedophile molests a young boy. We assume he has voluntarily chosen to do that molestation and therefore we punish him. But on closer examination I wonder how he would make such a choice. Or does he? Would he, by any rationality, voluntarily choose to commit such an abusive act knowing full well that it is wrong, injurious to another, contrary to the *mores* of his culture, perhaps contrary to a morality even more universal than that of his culture? Is he really choosing? Or is he responding to a compulsion, to an urge so powerful and so deep within himself that he is unable to resist? We abhor his act for both the physical and the psychological damage that act does to his victim (and also for its "ick factor"), and so we punish him for it, in the hope that such punishment will cause him to never do that again. But he will. Is he choosing? I do realize he is undoubtably a damaged person, that there is some complex of forces within him that pushes him to commit such acts, forces which, however hard he might try, he cannot resist. In some ill-defined sense he is compelled, not choosing. He is damaged, from all appearances irreparably. That cannot be sin. Most likely not really a choice. He is damaged. He commits a horrendous offense against another person. Repeatedly. I know I should not use him as my example. . . he is not normal. But he is a human being, just as I am. He is a member of the community, just as I am. He is in some sense my equal, and I need him to be responsible for his own behavior just as I am for mine. But he is unable to be completely responsible. I could look at him and mutter, "There, but for the grace of God, go I," and consign him to the waste bin. But that doesn't work. He is one of us. . . unable to make healthy choices, but still one of us. He sexually abuses boys. Another (damaged?) person serially murders people. I cannot comprehend how he could possibly make that choice. But he does. Perhaps out of passion or rage. More likely out of some sociopathology or psychopathology. Perhaps in an acute and violent episode of mental illness. Whatever. It is beyond my comprehension. Another murders, then eats the body of his victim. I am astounded.

It is against all morality, against all that is decent. But he does it. Has he made a choice to do it? I struggle with that.

The lawyer mutters, "Bad cases make bad law." And I nod my agreement; these are most certainly bad cases. So I cannot build sound moral structures out of them. I am fairly certain these aberrant persons are not choosing freely, reasonable, rationally. And if I **must** call it a choice, then they are making **compulsively bad** choices, destructive choices, choices no reasonable person would make. . . I consider farther. . . (*I feel like Tevya!*). On the other hand, they are not far from me. They have a pathology I do not, but otherwise they are as human as I am, as much a member of the community as I am. I judge that their choices are compelled by their pathology; and I am forced to wonder in response, to what degree, and in what ways are my choices also compelled? Or limited?

Four decades ago I learned the error of our assumptions that we are born either male or female, and that homosexuality was an aberration. Instead, I learned, there are eight gender determinants, five of them anatomical, and the other three psychological, and that very few of us are exclusively male or female; almost all of us lie somewhere along a continuum stretching from wholly male to wholly female. . . we are nearly all of us of somewhat mixed gender. So in that light I asked, what is homosexuality? Probably just some confusing segment along that continuum. But no! Next I learned of several studies that indicate that the brains of gays and straights are actually somewhat different physiologically, that the brains of gay males are more similar to straight females than straight males, and the brains of lesbian women more like straight males than straight females. So gayness is not a choice, but a physiological given. And if such human basics as gender and gay-straightness are givens, I can only ask what other choices might also really be givens?

I go farther down this path: an anatomist once taught me that, given a scalpel and my permission, he could lay open and show me in my own neck the vestiges of the gills that had started to grow at an early point in my fetal development. At another point in my fetal development the genetic codes told my developing body that I had evolved beyond the water-breathing fish, that I would be living in the air, was developing lungs and would not need those gills. So the gills stopped growing and withered; but the vestiges are still there. . . in my neck. They did not completely go away! In that instant teaching I realized that as we human beings evolved, we did not exchange this for that, we did not replace one physiological feature with another. We simply overlaid one atop another. We did not subtract. We simply added on!! On another day I learned that neurologists identify the developmental stages of this brain inside my head. . . the more primitive portion of my brain they call the R-complex (for reptilian); it is the part of my brain which I share with reptiles; the seat of my more primitive mental tools. . . the sense of smell, the territorial urges, and such. Growing, quite literally, atop the R-complex is the limbic system, that portion of my brain which evolved in the early mammals; it houses some higher functions, some refinements of the senses, and

Chapter 4: Sin, for One Last Time

emotionality (the fight or flight mechanisms) that distinguish mammals from reptiles. And atop that, the neocortex, the *new brain* which enables me to reason and plan and value. My brain is not a single organ but a complex of layer upon layer, added on, built up. That is how evolution works. This is not exchanged for that; this does not replace that. Rather this is added onto and supercedes or even utilizes that.

Expanding upon that model, I see myself (and you too) as an evolution. I began life at the joining of a sperm and ovum, the last time I was a simple being. Cells multiplied, differentiated, formed the various parts of my physiology and I was birthed. I grew, continuing to develop until around my twenty-fifth year when physiologically I matured. But some of me kept growing, learning, adding experiences and comprehensions and learnings. Layers upon layers. As an infant I had begun to absorb that set of dynamics peculiar to my family.

> *(E.g., my father was, unrealized by the family, an alcoholic whom my mother managed to control with a soft but very firm discipline until their very latter years when his addiction became obvious and destructive. My mother's father had divorced when she was a child and she determined that would never happen to her children, and so rode it out with my father until his death when it became too late to do other. I grew up an outsider at the center of the family, observing but trying to stay out of the center, with two sisters eight years to either side. . . one of three only children, in a cluster that prized males far above females. A peculiar set of dynamics which were the norm for this child, the only set I really knew, the set that still lives inside me.)*

And at the same time I began to absorb the *mores* and morals of the family, the sub-cultures of my Irish-German Catholic neighborhood, and of my very provincial suburb within a very conservative city *(the Queen City, Gateway to the West, Porkopolis)* in the conservative mid-west of a country just emerging from the Great Depression by dint of the Second World War, the most murderous war in human history. Layer upon layer of mini-cultures and subcultures within the macro-culture and shaped by history. And I am aware, in the midst all of that, of a six year old boy, trembling, terrified by **The Inner Sanctum** radio story of the horrifying thing that slimed out of a hole and sucked the life out of the innocent who was unwittingly lured by mournful cries into that dark corner of the basement. . . that small boy and his fear still live inside me *[I quieted that particular fear actually only two decades ago, though it still cowers somewhere inside me]* I know that small boy, he did not go away, we have evolved together over this three-quarters of a century, he and the other boys of each of my other ages.

I am a very complex being, though no more complex than you. We are all complex, layer upon layer of physiology, and psychology, and embedded cultures and *mores* and on and on. It seems to me that if I started peeling away the layers, as of an onion, I would never reach the center, the core . . . I could even wonder if there is a core, but only more layers, or emptiness, or infinity? And taken all together, that complexity gives the shape and direction and impulse and energy to my living. But in the giving of direction, that complexity, those layers upon layers, also limits... it limits who I could be, what I can see, how I experience, what I absorb and learn. It urges me ahead, but with invisible and unknown, usually undetected blinders; and it steers me (how much?) There is much going on around me that I cannot even notice, am unable to pay attention to, can not consider as I examine the options (and all the while I am **un**aware of most of the other possible options), and weigh (on some internal, unseen scale) the few that finally come to hand, and select the right one for this moment in my history. You see, I have to wonder how limited my ability to choose might be. I am not a pedophile, nor a murderer; their pathologies do not limit and drive my choosing. But I am very unclear how really free or how limited, biased, and compelled my choosing might be. I cannot tell because I live **inside** this skin, not as an outside and somewhat objective observer.

This I do know: the wisdom-seekers of the New Enlightenment thought that rationality should be the decision-making tool, for individuals and for the corporate society. We should choose wisely, insightfully, but most of all rationally. And I nod vigorously in agreement. But as I look at the murky stuff inside myself, and as I look at those around me (whose insides I cannot see), and as I look out at the community, and farther out at the larger communities I see that plainly rationality plays a minuscule and insignificant role in our decision-making and choosing. I see that, while I (who prize my rationality) try to make reasonable, thoughtful, careful choices, beneath that thin veneer of rationality lie layers and layers of thick and murky *stuff* shaping and hiding the deeper forces of that choosing. As I look around me I see little rationality in the choice-making of others. I am overwhelmed by the irrationality of our senators and representatives who claim to be making choices out of their conflicting ideologies, but who are really (it seems abundantly clear to me) choosing in light of the whims of the money-givers who are funding their next campaign so they can win and sit again in the legislative halls, so they can get more money to campaign another time and win and sit some more in the legislative halls. I watch the raging battles in Syria, and Egypt, and in the infant nations in Africa, and I see... no rationality. I agree with the wisdom-seekers that rationality **ought** to be the operative tool. But the reality is, it is not. And there appears little possibility that rationality could ever become the operative tool of decision-making and choosing, in the world around me, in the circle of my community, even within myself.

The Cumulative Effect

Some time ago I mused about Bernie Madoff. He betrayed his people (i.e., the Jewish community), his cultural heritage and the individuals who trusted him. Did he sin? Was he a sinful man? Did he sin against God and man? Those are probably stupid and irrelevant questions in today's parlance. It makes better sense, it is more useful to say

Chapter 4: Sin, for One Last Time

that Bernie Madoff was/is probably a sociopath, has no conscience, feels no remorse, nor even any sense of responsibility. A grossly flawed personality. (What could sin mean in this case?) But what does count is that society needs to be protected from him and the likes of him. The Wall Street mess, with everyone in bed with everyone else, living out some subcultural morality apart from and different than the morality of us middle class folks, a subculture somehow believing it's alright to do anything to make these huge bucks, even if it means someone else, some dupe, some pigeon like me ends up paying the bills,. . . it's alright because everyone in that particular bed seems to think it's all right. Deceiving (even oneself), betraying, with the government's compliance, silent assent, even collaboration and tacit permission, complicity. . . .and now, in the after-the-fact, finger-wagging, bail-out time, it's still quite alright to quietly, even if by acts of omission rather than commission, set the stage for it to be done over again with slightly different rules and a slightly different setting and a slightly different *modus operandi* and a few different, as yet undiscovered people. In another instance our glorious leader George W lied and lied and lied us (and evidently himself as well) into an unwinnable war but it was okay because it was in the name of God and democracy. Saddam Hussein bullied, oppressed, stole because it was his privilege, maybe even his responsibility, as the leader of an unleadable aggregation of bitterly divided peoples. Hussein managed to hold in tension and at bay the hatreds and aggressions of the several tribes and sects within his domain, even though he did that (necessarily?) with incredible cruelty and oppression. His rule was evil, but exactly what was the sin? Or is to utter sin equivalent to trivializing and diminuating the actuality and the real dynamics? Has our fixation on sin been in order to deflect our attention, to avoid staring at the real dynamics and factors (perhaps in order to hide from ourselves our own complicity in those dynamics and factors)? My mind now wanders in a host of directions. We need to talk about accountability, how we are to be held accountable for our behavior, especially sinful behavior, and how much accountability if there is only a small but undefinable amount of choice involved. Am I to be held accountable and punished for that which I barely chose, or had hardly any choice at all? Justice and mercy get all confused.

And all that is just the beginning of this conversation. Knowing not how much we are shaped, even unchangeably and irresistibly hard-wired by our genes, by the hormonal mix that saturated us as fetuses and as pubescent children, we are also educated by neighbors, friends, peers, school-teachers, perhaps ministers and such other influential people as struck our fancies, and then pressured, pushed, shaped by the various cultures and subcultures imposed upon us, by the dynamics that constantly flow around and immerse us, floating us through the mainstream, roughing us in the white-water rapids of our lives, by the events around us, the world-altering events. It all shapes who we are becoming, and who we are at that very moment, and so influences how we might choose to act at this instant in this specific and unique situation

I do not want to imply that it's all fated. We are not completely forced, but we are not totally unlimited either. . . we are pushed and shoved and shaped and enticed and lured and even seduced by myriads of forces and factors, and offered a billion options (if we pay attention), then limited by our blindnesses, our inclinations, and the biases of our almost-sorta-random impulse generators. . . almost all of that unconsciously. And finally we choose from what's left.

With all the aforegoing I have, to my satisfaction, pulled the linchpin, the simplistic notion of sin, in Augustine's theological schematic, which has been the core of Western Christian theology. But without the burden of dragging that cartload of sin about, I am left with horses harnessed and running free, a swirl of thoughts which I must force into some logical or reasonable system. I know for sure only what I am not looking at, namely sin. And what I am looking at is a muddle, a murky puddle. So I must start afresh.

Accountability

I must offer one more set of thoughts. When I threw aside the notion of sin, a few turned and asked, "What about accountability? If we don't have sin are people no longer accountable?" And I must offer a few thoughts in response. First, my intention is not to remove or mollify accountability, but rather to increase accountability, and to refocus it.

I perceive that we have already **three systems of accountability** in place, and all are failing miserably:

a. Since I have been loitering in the churchy, theological playing field, that first: I perceive that we have a system to identify malefactions (sins), to confess them, and to do penance for them. The system fails in all three parts for several reasons.

   i. I submit that if we ask the average pew-sitter to name what sins he had committed in the last few days, he would be hard pressed to identify anything significant (Jimmie Carter lusted in his heart). We might revert to the medieval Seven Deadly Sins which are hardly relevant today; and we priests have not been very clear with our congregants which sins they should be on the outlook for in their lives. And I would further submit that the average Episcopalian might not in his recent days have actually committed any significant sins. A friend who was chaplain to a convent for several years told me there was nothing more boring than listening to the sisters's confessions; "They've not done anything to confess." I imagine that most things people might find to confess would be infractions of the legal system, not sins, or wrongs against others so minor as to be hardly worthy of mention.

   ii. We (Roman Catholics) grew up with the pattern of confessing our sins in the privacy of the confessional booth to a priest who was supposed to not know who we were. Hardly a system of accountability. We (Protestants) further mollified that practice by making it non-verbal and communal so that I did not have to be explicit about my malefactions, and instead I said them aloud to no one, only confessing **in general** and anonymously with a public prayer. Accountability?

iii. We (Roman Catholics only, please) did penance as assigned by priest, most likely a recitation of some prayer. No contrition. No Restitution. No correction of the malefaction.

iv. The above system developed out of an early Celtic monastic practice of conferring periodically with one's *soul-friend* another monastic who, similarly to a contemporary spiritual director, coached the fellow-monastic's spiritual life. That early practice evolved into a more regularized system of confessing minor malefactions (e.g., dropping the communion wafer), and being assigned some spiritual exercise as "medicine for the soul" to encourage the monastic not to do that again. Not really penance or an act of contrition. The end product is our confessional system which is of little benefit to anyone, is certainly no means of holding persons accountable, or of encouraging the bettering of behavior.

v. The whole confessional system, while it might have some minor spiritual benefit to the confessing monastic, is of no advantage socially. It is focused on interiorities, and entirely on the individual. It has no communal focus or impact, though community is where the greater evils occur and impact. Instead it may divert our attention from those larger and pervasive systemic evils which are very much in need of correction.

vi. The church has tried to devise a moral code over the centuries, and the Roman Church has made great effort to force that code upon its members, and often on the larger society and culture as well. However the church's stance seems to be that such morality, as it applies to the individual, is universal and unchanging. That code tends to be rather Medieval and unresponsive to contemporary discoveries and understandings. On the other hand, that moral code has been fairly adaptive to the evolving social structure and affairs, so that while proclaiming the sanctity of all life in individual matters, it holds that there can be a just war provided certain conditions are observed, i.e., "It's alright to kill *en masse*." Overall I judge the church's moral codes to be vague (apart from the Ten Commandments), outdated, out moded, and while rigid toward the individual quite adaptive and accommodating toward the social systems. The one exception to this judgment is Pope Frances.

b. Following the example of the Roman Empire, we have built an extensive legal system. We believe in the rule of law, that is, that the law stands over man and regulates his activities. Our legislatures compose the laws, our police enforce the laws, our courts adjudicate infractions of the laws, and our penal system punishes (or purports to rehabilitate) the law-breakers. Each part of this system is quite complicated and exceedingly expensive. And altogether it is only marginally effective. We could harangue about the parts and about the whole at great length and to little avail. We could note several dysfunctional characteristics of the system: it is racist (punishing those of color in preference to whites), it is classist (punishing those of the lower classes in preference to those of the upper classes), it is over-incarcerating (we have the highest incarceration rate in the whole world), it is highly recidivist (it deters few from further law-breaking activity), and the criminals enmeshed in it overwhelmingly believe themselves far more guilty of getting caught than of breaking the law. It does keep a lot of lawyers extremely well-paid. And it quite effectively enables and protects the wealthy. I am not a student of our legal system, so here I will simply identify two flaws of the system most obvious to me, both of which greatly reduce accountability.

i. **Individualism**: e.g., "Red-light cameras" which photograph and automatically ticket drivers who run red-lights have been effectively out-lawed in many of our cities by requiring that each camera be attended full-time by a patrolman, a prohibitive expense, despite the fact that they have been documented to decrease the running of red lights, and they have reduced the accident rates at those intersections. Two complaints about them are voiced: 1.) That they are intended simply as fund-raisers for the city budget (it's quite acceptable to hate supporting the cost of government), and 2.) that they invade privacy. What is going on here? I believe the underlying issue is individualism which prizes the rights and freedoms of the individual over the rights and responsibilities of the community; and therefore people often experience the enforcement of law as an infringement of individual rights. While an act may violate the law, that act is deemed acceptable unless the individual is actually caught red-handed breaking the law. Evasion of law-enforcement of minor infractions seems to be quite acceptable

ii. The **Right to Privacy**: The right to privacy is nowhere stated in our Constitution; the Supreme Court has had to discover that right by reading in between the written lines. The right to privacy would seem to be a sacred, God-given right. I have never understood that. To my thinking such inviolable privacy would serve mainly to grant me the ability to hide from others whatever I do that is illegal or immoral. It protects me from being caught doing what I should not be doing. If I am keeping the law and acting morally, then the only reason for privacy at all is to avoid being seen naked (preserve my prudishness), or expressing affection (or other naked emotion.) I suspect that most demands for privacy are really to eliminate my accountability for immoral or illegal acts I commit outside of public view, i.e., allowing me to break laws with impunity.

c. And the third accountability system we have in place is cultural morality, but that too I perceive is flawed and ineffective. First, it is not universal, but rather is a collection of different and conflicting moral codes. E.g., for a third-generation family on welfare, bilking the welfare system is a way to make a living; it is not only acceptable, it is essential. But to the laborer working hard to house and feed and educate his family, that third-generation welfare family is free-loading, draining the system, and is immoral as well as illegal. And to the plutocrat that welfare family is taking money right out of his pocket; he's not only immoral and illegal, he's an outright thief. We live amidst a patchwork quilt of diverse moral codes, originating from different sources, accountable for different things, and accountable in different ways and to different degrees.

My unsophisticated view is that accountability is very unevenly and ineffectively applied throughout our social system. I think I observe one very general rule about our systems of accountability: that the higher in the social structure the malefactor is, and the greater, the broader the impact of his malefaction, the lower his accountability. In the military we had a saying tantamount to law, "Rank has privilege." That would appear to be in force in the civilian world as well.

The Twenty-First-Century World Viewed in Twenty-First-Century Understandings

I am a child of the twentieth century, and I must search out the real world I live in with twentieth- and twenty-first-century eyes and understandings. It is clear to me that I view the world through the eyes of science. What the church fathers feared when Galileo first published has come to pass; the world has turned from the first century world view and metaphor to another which they could not have imagined then.

New Framework

Now I must pause, and begin another tack, with a few yea's and nay's.

Using Mixed Metaphors

What has become clear to me through this writing is that I have been mixing metaphors in my thinking. Sin is a theological term of the fourth century when church fathers were absolutely sure that they understood clearly the unchangeable human nature and the fixed human condition. And they used theological terms of their day to describe those: sin, free-will, fatalism. But I also notice that after I faltered in the opening paragraphs of this chapter, I finally found a place to plant my foot and begin my own thinking. That place was not amidst those fourth century theological concepts and words, but in a messy porridge of psychology, sociology, cultural anthropology, and group and systems dynamics. I had waded out of the theological stew to find firmer ground in a porridge of contemporary human sciences. And in reflection I realize that, for me at least, the fourth century theological concepts and words have become outmoded and debased coinage, that they no longer work, are no longer useful. The *lingua franca* of this day is **not** theological, but scientific. The metaphor of science (physics, physiology and medicine, psychology and sociology) has displaced the metaphor of theology and religious language as our working meta-narrative. Science has proven more accurate for describing the physical reality in which we find ourselves, and a more useful metaphor for building our way into our future. But science does not know sin, and has limited ability to handle non-material realms So sin, and free-will and fatalism are not wrong, rather they have simply become irrelevant, insipid, unuseful terms for grasping and understanding the physical reality (though they may still serve a function, i.e., to obfuscate a clearer view of reality.)

But this conclusion does not solve the problem the fourth-century theologians were struggling to manage with their notion of sin. That problem is certainly still with us. I see it a little more clearly, still somewhat befuddledly, but more clearly with my scientific metaphor than I could with their fourth-century metaphor. So now I find myself at the very beginning of the productive part of this conversation.

God's Role

Earlier I allowed that we might see the God's law as not so much divinely inspired as humanly devised and then attributed to the God to garner authority. At this point in my thinking I can not attribute that possibility, but rather must adopt the assumption of the law as a human device as my working platform. For the moment I must write the God out of the sin issue (or whatever my alternative to the sin issue turns out to be). I am standing solidly in the twenty-first-century scientific metaphor, and the unknowable God, or YHWH or Abba seems to have no standing inside this metaphor.

The Function of Sinology

And next my mind starts to examine the function of sinology *(my invented term, which has nothing to do with China)*. What has been it's purpose? (Obviously the notion has served some pragmatic function, elsewise we would not have held onto it past it's original functionality.) Why have we, following Augustine's lead, continued to use his understanding of sin? I deem that God (to the degree I think about God) is probably so little bothered as to be not upset by our individual behaviors, (although the self-serving machinations of the leaders of our corporate being and macro-culture may be somewhat more troublesome to the God, or at least to me.) But when we heap up our individualized sins into one pile, the mass is so trivial as to be not worth the sacrifice of God's very son. Why hang onto this fourth-century notion?

I understand our whole preoccupation with sin to be mostly related to social control, that is, with the community's need to inhibit the socially harmful, destructive effects of both its individuals's and the subcultural systems's behaviors upon the larger social fabric. Pointing and saying "Sin," is one social, nonviolent way of attempting to control harmful individual behaviors, i.e., invoking God's wrath to make the individual quake in fear of a larger-than-life punishment. But is it anything more than that?

Yes, perhaps it is. I strongly suspect that the more real, the greater, the very hidden and inside-out function of sinology is to deflect our attention, to misdirect our awareness, to keep us from lifting our eyes and becoming sufficiently aware of the greater sin, the corporate sin, the communal sin, the cultural sin which comprises the greater evil, i.e., rampant social injustices. In restricting our attention and social awareness to our individual internal processes, we are kept from developing an awareness of what Walter Breuggemann's Empire is doing to us, and deflecting us from acting to effect change, to bring justice-mercy to bear. Sinology may be one of the empire's primary tools to keep us gathering straw and digging clay to make bricks for their towers.

Mysticism

One important body of corroborating witness has been the great Christian mystics; but their testimony has always been gibberish to me. Several years ago I discovered why this is so[12]. At this point I simply affirm that I now hold the testimony of the mystics to be of similar origin and type as the transcendental awareness experiences of incipient schizophrenics, and of psychedelic drug users, and of persons in extreme sensory deprivation, and of Eastern monastic mystics. Their experiences are not self-authenticating as Evelyn Underhill claimed, nor see I any reason to assume they are all from or about God. When William James told us religious experiences tended in two directions, toward healthy spirituality (the Mary Baker Eddy, "It's all fine, just gotta think positively" guys), and the sick soul guys I realized the proto-type for the latter was Augustine with his "I'm no good and there's nothing I can do about it" presupposition. My take-away is that what the sick-soul guys have been telling us all about sin is out of their own presumptions and they have not told us anything particularly useful or pragmatic or insightful. I conclude that the mystics have little useful to teach us about sin.

---

12. That explanation is detailed in Chapter 5 (134) and Chapter 2 (29–30 & footnote #5)

Part II: My Review of Christian Doctrines

My Lens Resolves to Confusion

As I look about I also notice that what we had once thought were bold, black lines connecting all these issues and drawing clear boundaries around them have become faded grays, fuzzy, sometimes broken or dotted lines. I am no longer talking about sin, but instead an incredibly complex array of evils and trespasses and diversions and missteps and misdeeds. Augustine's clarity and tightly woven system has become inadequate in the face of an increasingly complex understanding of what this human creature is, how it is put together and how it and its social fabric function. Jesus has become confusing, sometimes more Pharisaic than the Pharisees, sometimes so anti-Pharisaic that he gets himself crucified, occasionally focused on the national sins, but most times narrowly, intensively focused on individualities.

The Dalai Lama points out that we are **all in this together**, that our worlds are so delicately and complexly and completely intertwined and interrelated that events cannot be isolated and reduced to singularities. We are all in this together. I am in some way complicit in virtually everything that is happening. And there is so much complexity and intertwinedness that I become certain of nothing.

Warning: Jack Bowers lives within a world composed of grays. I see infinitely complex shades of gray. I am comfortable amongst grays. Whites and blacks tend to make me nervous, even a little anxious, and very resistant. So all this confusion I am experiencing could possibly be of my own making. Because I am more comfortable with grays than with black and whites, it could well be that, in my searching out of things, my very inner biases make me see more grays than there really are, and I may be blotting out many of the blacks and whites that others see. I acknowledge that possibility, but being the arrogant bastard I am, I also tend to doubt it.

In the Real World (i.e., the World in which I am Actually Living my Life)

Having set a very loose framework, I now try to establish some foundations, throw out some anchors.

Definition of Evil

I need to define evil, not in some general usage sense, but with reference to what I used to understand as sin, in order to discover some other way of understanding that notion instead of trivializing evil into insignificance by calling it sin. As usual I start with my **Randomhouse Dictionary**;

> 1. *adj.* Morally wrong or bad 2. Harmful, injurious 3. Characterized or accompanied by misfortune or suffering; unfortunate; disastrous 4. Due to actual or imputed bad conduct or character 5. Marked by anger, irritability, irascibility, etc. 6. the devil, satan *n.* 7. That which is evil; evil quality, intention or conduct

Chapter 4: Sin, for One Last Time

8. the force in nature that governs and gives rise to wickedness and sin 9. the wicked or immoral part of someone or something 10. harm, mischief, misfortune 11. Anything causing injury or harm 12. A harmful aspect, effect or consequence *adv.* 14. In an evil manner; badly; ill.

Not terribly helpful for my purposes; but then dictionaries reflect common usage, not tight philosophical or theological definitions. So for my purposes here I must reach deep into my own, very idiosyncratic understandings.

Evil (at least evil as it previously related to the notion of sin) seems to me to describe: destructive, injurious, harmful, damaging, destroying, even death-causing outcomes. But that sin-related evil also implied some human agency, thus ruling out natural occurrences such earthquakes, hurricanes, floods, volcanic eruptions, illnesses, psychoses, cardiac infarctions... all things which result from the forces of the natural world without human intervention or causation. They have bad consequences for people, but I would not term these evil. I go two steps farther in outruling things from my understanding of evil. I think true accidents (not the results of human negligence or intent), while destructive, are not evil. (*E.g., driving within the speed limit I hit a patch of black ice and spun slowly into the guardrail. Destructive. Undesirable. Costly. But I did not experience that event as evil. Merely maddening.*) Accidents seem to me more related to the randomness I experience in the physical world. Nor is randomness itself evil for me. And the last I would rule out are impulses and intentions. More about that below.

Somewhere in my head echoes the word "malevolence," the will to inflict injury, harm, suffering. I wrestled that notion to the ground and concluded that it is **evil results** I am concerned about, and I have really laid aside the issue of willfulness. I suppose that echo provides a proof case. Yes, we dislike, avoid, flee from ill-willing people; and yet it is still their behavior, their choosing and acting I am concerned about, their acts which cause harmful consequences. I may dislike being in the company of their ill-willfulness, but do not consider that to be evil in itself; distasteful, repugnant, dislike-able, undesirable, but not inherently evil. Our culture tends to identify ill-willfulness, bad intentionedness as evil, but I consider that a misunderstanding and diminuation of real evil. After I have sorted through all of this I am left with "malefactions," i.e., choices and actions designed to cause injury. So regardless of intent, malevolence involves a deliberate choice and action intended to cause pain, harm, injury, death.

Impulses and Intentions Are Amoral

I did chuckle when President Carter "lusted in his heart." He thought that a sin, while I did not think God was much concerned about it. Freud seemed to think those *id*-generated impulses had no morality; what mattered was not the impulses themselves but whether and how those impulses were acted out. . . that is the arena of moral choice, the acting out (albeit Freud was little concerned about morality.) The *id* (for lack of a better term) is a random impulse generator which simultaneously monitors the input from the external scene, surveys the interior landscape, perhaps analyzes a bit, and then instantly generates (or selects from a list of options) a handful or more of impulses from which I can choose (or I can choose none-of-the-above and deliberately generate some more.) Perhaps some of us have more prodigiously random generators than others, and some may have impulse generators that are not-so-random, but slanted, inclined in certain directions, such as impulses toward hyper-violence. The rabbinic lore did not think the impulses themselves good or bad, but rather thought how one acted upon the impulses was where moral choices were made. Along with them, I would not consider intentions or impulses as having morality, but would see the choosing, whether to act out an intent or impulse, and how to act it out, that is morally laden. The culpability is in the doing, not the thinking. I consider that God is not greatly concerned about our mental lives, but does care fixedly about our behavior, where we interact with others, and in particular about how our behavior affects those around us: is our behavior loving and good (beneficial), or unloving, self-centered and harmful (evil, destructive, injurious), not necessarily in intent, but in effect, in result?

We have been preoccupied in the Western World, perhaps the Christian world, with intent. The jury is required to debate and decide whether the murderer intended the murder, and how deliberately he planned the murder, thereby demonstrating intent. But my observation is that the Mosaic law cared not one whit about intent. I care neither why you do something nor why you think you are doing something, but what you do and that the consequences of what you do have effect upon my life. If you kill someone with a loving heart, that person is just as dead as if you had hated. And in the material realm it matters not one whit how much the murderer intended the murder; the murdered is the same amount dead whether the murder was intended or not, and his survivors must tussle with the same exigencies whether the death was deliberate or accidental. "If an ox gore a man. . ." (Exod 21:28-36) seems little concerned with intent, but completely concerned with effect, with result, with damage, and therefore with restitution. Consequences of behavior seem to be God's concern, but I see no evidence that the intentions are of concern to God.

And in this I stand with the rabbinic understanding that impulses are a part of the naturally occurring mental processes, in their language "God-given," and therefore amoral. Neither impulse nor intention, but choice, act and consequence are the realm of morality, behavior that affects those around us. Contrary to Matt 5:28, I think God was not much disappointed when Jimmy Carter lusted in his heart, but was happy that Jimmy chose not to act adulterously. Morality is concerned with what we do and how it affects others, with results, consequences, but not with impulses nor even intents.

Chapter 4: Sin, for One Last Time
Evil Differentiated from Randomness

Earlier I stipulated that there is evil afoot in this world. I am still hard pressed to define clearly the edges of that evil. . . what is evil and what is happenstance, accident, complex messiness? . . or simply randomness which we choose to label evil? Hitler unquestionably embodied evil. But when Vesuvius erupted, suffocating all the inhabitants of Pompey, was that inherently evil, or rather a random, natural, destructive occurrence with horrific collateral effects for 20,000 people? Sometimes it is hard to say where the fuzzy edge of evil leaves off and chance, i.e., randomness sets in. Or on the other hand, is much evil only in the eye of the beholder, a purely subjective call? And if evil has fuzzy edges, and the commission of evil must be willful or somewhat advertent, how do I go about determining culpability? "Malevolence" rings for me, yet I hold impulses and intentions to be amoral. So I continue to conclude that impulses and intentions are amoral; it is behavior which is moral, and then, the choice of behavior. The evil is in the choosing and in the acting out.

The Vocabulary

If the notion of sin is out, I need to figure out what notion to use in its place

A Playful but Useful Exercise

I focus on the word "sin" in the Lord's Prayer: (This may seem picayune but might be useful.) I find myself stumbling over my tongue these days as we recite the Lord's Prayer together on Sundays. I have become accustomed to muttering the modern translation (for its greater accuracy) while others are proclaiming in unison the traditional translation. But since I started writing these pages I no longer want to mutter the word "sin," even though I understand the congregational muttering of the prayer to be symbolic and nonliteral. So I've been searching for a replacement word. Most often the old "trespassing." But it doesn't work. I recite the modern version just to my own ear so as not to disturb those around me, and instead of "sins" I mouth "trespasses" and I am instantly caught up in the traditional version, unable to find my way back to the modern one before we get to "lead us not into temptation" and I am completely unhorsed from there on. Discombobulating at the least. And vaguely irritating. I mean, really!

So now I attempt a semi-serious study to find a workable alternative to use in my prayer-muttering. As is my custom I start from the Greek original. Matthew and Luke have slightly different versions *(Mark and John do not have this prayer)* Matthew consistently uses the Greek root *opheil–* (translates "owe, be indebted"). Luke mixes it up first using the root *hamart–* (translates "miss the mark") and then *opheil–*. Matthew's version would point us toward the standard Protestant translation "debts/debtors." My

PART II: MY REVIEW OF CHRISTIAN DOCTRINES

Liddel & Scott Lexicon[13] translates the verb *opheílō* "to owe, be indebted to, have to pay, be liable, be under obligation"; and the impersonal noun form *opheilétais* simply "debts." My Bauer New Testament lexicon follows the same course but adds "commit a sin" (I take that to be a rabbinic and Christian overtone.) Luke in the first clause uses *hamartías* ("sins"), but in the succeeding clause uses *opheíloni* ("everything owed"). Clearly in the original the oblique notion of sin (as I have received it from my forebears) was not primary, and was at best an undertone. For precedents one can wander back to Mosaic law in which usury was prohibited to fellow Jews, or to Levitical passages about the Jubilee Year in which all debts and land-holdings were forgiven. In that context these Matthean and Lucan versions could, narrowly taken, refer to little more that the forgiveness of financial obligations within the Christian community, or, taken more broadly, could refer to forgiving all sorts of (restitutive) obligations within the community. The translation "sin" is hardly indicated unless you translate very narrowly with God as the referent, and the obligation as caused by a violation of God's law/will, and therefore requiring restitution (repayment in some kind) or atonement (in place of blood sacrifice).

As I read Jesus' prayer it is primarily about community relations (my bias). Thus (in my thinking) the harm my infraction of God's law/will causes to you is not the sole or even primary concern; more important is the harm my infraction causes to our community. In that context forgiveness of a restitution is possible, especially since the earliest church expected the end of the world momentarily; and, if we can take Acts 3:44-46 as what was really going on, since all goods were held in common and shared, then restitution would be unreasonable and quite forgivable.

Clearly my mind rules out "sin" as an acceptable translation, regardless of how Augustine and Cranmer might feel about that. Why do I say that? Because the notion of sin passed down to me arrives encased in a heavy overlay of emotional guilt. I need only refer you to the 1928 Prayer Book general confessions in both Morning Prayer and The Lord's Supper which I cited above. My own appraisal is that emotional guilt is both useless and demotivating, hence destructive. Such guilt is certainly not the intention of God, at least of any God to whom I am willing to give obeisance. So I find sin not a good word to mutter as I recite with the congregation. "Debtor" is a close translation, one I find useful if taken in a very broad sense.

One other Greek word comes under consideration here. Both Matthew and Luke use the verb *aphíēmi* in both clauses, "forgive us our debts, as we have forgiven our debtors." That needs just a little parsing. The Liddel & Scott Lexicon translates that verb with the root meaning of "to send forth, to discharge," and from there, "to send away, let go, set free, dissolve or disband, acquit, and let pass or give up." The sense of peeling away guilt is not part of this verb, rather a simple releasing, letting go, undoing of obligation. "Debts/debtors" seems simpatico with remission.

---

13. I prefer the classical Greek lexicon because it includes all the undertones and overtones which Christian lexicographers of koiné Greek tend to eliminate or ignore.

Chapter 4: Sin, for One Last Time

I scanned the alternatives to "sin" in Roget's Thesaurus. There are a slew, but none with the brevity, fullload and impact of "sin": to transgress: overstep, disobey, violate, break, infringe, trample on, trample under foot, disregard, deviate, lapse, disobey, offend, trample, ride roughshod. "Trespass" yields: intrude, obtrude, encroach, invade, impose. I like both trespass and transgress. But neither has the heft of sin. The word "sin" has the impact of a ballpeen hammer striking a iron anvil, a sharp, ringing sound, and an impact that reverberates through one's fiber and being. But that heft has accrued through two thousand years of tradition, and there is no other word that can match that. So I may be stuck with "debt/debtors," as little as I love that root. Now I'll see if I can train my tongue to utter that as readily as it used to mutter "sin."

Result

This exercise **informs me little** in my search for an alternative word for sin. It does point me to the original language of a "debt or obligation owed." That in turn suggests to me a required restitution being unconditionally forgiven. Such would be a radical departure from the Levitical atonement theology; but Paul made several such radical changes in his transitioning from Pharisaic Judaism to the emerging Christian theology, so I need not be surprised at this one. And it does lead me toward the current coinage of forgiving trespasses without any kind of restitution or reparation. Just let it go, a notion which I think breeches what is not just a Levitical requirement, but in healthy psychological, interpersonal, and societal relations a necessity for the sound healing of offenses, i.e., reparation is a key step in the healing process for **all** the parties. So it bends my thinking toward what I have come to see as an important **misstep** in early Christian thinking.

A Buddhist Alternative

Now a different sort of thought. I am slightly entranced by the Dalai Lama and his Tibetan Buddhism. I deem him a holy man (I've been in his presence and felt his holiness, though I know not what "holiness" means) who giggles at our notion of sin, thinks it a silly and unuseful metaphor. Instead he talks about ignorance: our ignorance of the way reality really is, our ignorance in acting other than in our neighbor's best interests, which are, in Buddhist reality, **our** best interests because of our intertwinedness. I am fascinated. He suggests for example, that the search to discover "Who I am" is doomed to failure because who I am at any given instant is not who I was just an instant before, nor who I will be an instant from now. The Self is not a constant that can be located and identified and tied down and tracked slowly evolving through time; instead the Self is changing, **constantly** changing, is in the process of becoming. He talks about the intertwinedness of all creation, and how **what** I am at this very instant is the **intersection** of the million vectors of forces and dynamics and influences and persons, as though I am part of, though not trapped in, an infinite web of persons and things and events and dynamics that intersect in this one instant that is me-at-this-very-instant, and which then will be changed because everything around me is in motion and is changing. And so am I. The Self that I search for exists only for a fleeting instant and then evolves into something else, the next fluid intersection of the next million new dynamics and influences and persons, which intersection exists, again, only for another instant. Change is the constant. There is no other constant. How's that for intertwinedness? And in that world sin has no meaning. What does have meaning is compassion, the compassion that grows out of the understanding that we **are** all in this together, and that I have no idea what vectors came together to cause him to do that thing, that horrible thing, and neither does he. But the **useful** response, the beneficial response is compassion which draws him and me away from the horror of that thing he did and back into a life lived in compassion. So three things: 1) ignorance of how things really are and how to live in this mess, 2) the intertwinedness of all this universe and ourselves in it, and 3) living in compassion as the only useful way to live with and for all. I do not yet understand how those three fit together to build a life of peace and harmony. But it appears to me that the Dalai Lama does know how to do that, because when I was in his presence, it **did** all make sense, it **did** fit together and it **did** appear to build the life of peace and harmony which I witnessed in him and which I felt in his presence as I've not felt before. I came away from his presence moderately convinced that sin is a very silly notion around which to build one's theology and one's spiritual temple.

The Dalai Lama's notion of ignorance does not have the heft and strike that sin has accumulated over the centuries. It feels a little light-weight, almost too easy and unpunitive, and I suppose that causes my reluctance to accept his ignorance to replace my sin. But as I ponder the two, ignorance is a much cleaner and somewhat more elegant notion, and it feels more workable. And perhaps it is more realistic, closer to the real world in which I live.

Accountability Revisited

I spoke earlier about accountability. I need to revisit that issue. I need to be exceedingly clear that the disastrous flaw in our several systems (sin, the law, *mores* of accountability) is that they are all focused almost exclusively on the individual. The givenness of that individual focus may go all the way back to the earliest hunter-gather groups searching their way out onto the savannah for food. We live in a macro-system, a nation that is rife with malefactions against select groupings within the culture: the most obvious is racism, and next the enforcement of poverty, of classism; my list could go on at great length, but no need, point made. But we have so designed our macro-system that the system itself is unaccountable. There simply is no way for the system to be held accountable. Individuals, yes; but the system, no. My fantasy traces back to that alpha male of the hunter-gatherer group for whom "Might made right." The accountability of the mini-system was on him and it was simply measured in the survivability of the group. I next visit the authoritative chiefdom where the vested power figure was still the solely accountable entity, and the only accountability was still the survival of the system, not the welfare of its members. And then my fantasy leaps to the kingdom and its royal leader, and still the driving concern was survivability, not the welfare of members. It is with the Enlightenment and the decay of authoritarianism that the welfare of the individual came to the fore. But the issue of accountability for the whole system did not come along with it. We entered the age of individualism in which accountability accrues almost exclusively to the individual, and that, as little as possible. Our founding fathers, obsessed with individualism and liberty, built us a macro-system with the individual solely in charge of his own welfare, and no handles for holding the system itself accountable. Each husbandman is alone responsible for his family and their welfare, and the success of his work ethic is his primary accountability. So, I am a racist (but not the system), and if my family is impoverished it's because I don't work hard enough. For the macro-system which establishes and amends the conditions within which he must exercise his husbandry, there is no accountability. We can elect and un-elect our legislators, but there is nothing built into the macro-system that causes those legislators to act for the good of the members of the system. No hooks. No handles. So the individuals **may** be held accountable (depending on their class, race, wealth, etc.), but the system cannot be. Major flaw.

Now, Looking to the Future I must Attempt to Reformulate the Whole Scene.

Theological Issues

The physicists and other scientists are mastering the material/physical world, but they provide no God, no understanding of sin nor fatalism nor any other crucial, non-material elements of any theological understanding. So I come to wonder, since they cannot touch it, do I need to look for a non-material realm where such things exist? I have a consciousness which physicists nor psychiatrists can describe or explain, and I know not what it is or how it works. But I know it is. And that alone suggests to me that there is some non-material realm, or realms beyond the known material, the physical, the scientifically-understandable. Some wonder quietly whether those non-physical immutables exist in some other realm like Aristotelean archetypes, and somehow have irresistible sway in this physical realm. It appears there are some reasonable questions for which the sciences have no answers and which might point toward some non-material realm(s).

Part II: My Review of Christian Doctrines

If God is Unknowable?

After studying William James and Evelyn Underhill and Jack Miles and Karen Armstrong and Robert Wright, and then scanning all I've studied over my decades about the Hebrew and Christian Scriptures, and all I've studied within those Scriptures, and trying to study tomes such as the **Anglican Theological Review** quarterly, and looking deep into my own life and experiences, I have slowly and rather reluctantly concluded that the YHWH of the Hebrew scriptures and the Abba of the Christian writings are projections, a visualizing and anthropomorphizing of what we want and think we need. And for me the God which may be out there has faded beyond my conjecturing, has become ultimately incomprehensible, outside of my knowing. And so finally I ask myself, what if the God is in the end unknowable? What then? Bonhoeffer's words echo, that we must learn to live as though God were not a given. I grew my post-adolescent theology in the midst of the God-Is-Dead movement, and now I seem to have become at one with it.

My good friend Steve Williamson, though dead now, is still whispering in my ear, "Jack, we must pray as if everything depends upon God, and then we must act as if everything depends upon us." So I am slowly turning my head and starting to study, "If it all depends on us, prizing the best insights of Christianity and the other major religions, what do we need to do to set our world aright?"

And so I must ponder anew the old ponderings. It used to be that God gave meaning to my life. . . or so I thought, though I was never clear why God bothered to create humankind. Perhaps God wanted some one to relate to (but for me it was a one-way relationship). Or God wanted some one to enjoy his creation (yes, but then why the pain?) Someone once suggested that God made us in his image so that God, who has neither mirrors, nor anyone to give feedback, could discover who he was, what he was like, by watching us. But if God has become truly unknowable for me, then those meanings and any others the hidden God had seemed to lend also evaporate and disappear. And I am left to wonder anew, why am I? The scientists, the philosophers have no clue. It could be that there is no answer

Rethink the Jesus event:

If we believe in Jesus as our Lord and Savior *(whatever that might once have meant)* then we must begin by re-interpreting the Jesus event. We cannot reinterpret what happened in 35AD. That history is too far behind us and the data far too sketchy and unreliable for anything useful to come out of such an effort. The searching-for-the-historical-Jesus boys have quite adeptly demonstrated that. Instead we must leave off prating-while-ignoring the twenty-five-hundred year old stories (we have learned too much since then to think they could tell us all we need to know) and place our

Chapter 4: Sin, for One Last Time

thinking firmly within the twenty-first-century framework and then ask ourselves how to understand the Jesus event in reference to today's events?

With the God an unknown, I take the Jesus event to be the central metaphor of Christianity, and ask what that Jesus metaphor stands for, what stands behind that metaphor which needs to be central to our thinking and acting today? Marcus Borg and his company identify the historical Jesus, the pre-resurrection Jesus as a prophet, teacher, healer and miracle-worker. I can certainly recognize those themes in the Christian writings. It seems to me that the scientists and medicos have taken over the healer and miracle-worker roles. And that leaves the teacher and prophet roles untended. The teacher observes reality and tells us about it (or perhaps helps us to observe it for ourselves); the prophet heeds what the teacher teaches and tells us what to do about it.

For me the teacher-prophet role is at the center of what I understand the Jesus event to be **in this** day. Within the Jesus figure reside the core values and the Jesus figure keeps observing the reality surrounding him, digesting all he is seeing, and telling (or showing) us what we need to be doing about that reality. And to do that he reaches down to his very core-most values. The reality he observes is the here-and-now and not pie-in-the-sky.

Because we live this life in community (we cannot survive [as individual entities or as a species], much less thrive without it), and because it is human community (i.e., community composed of individual human beings) which will survive into the future, and not we separate individuals, we live not for ourselves but for each other and for the community. And given that, we must value every single member of our community (and our community is swiftly becoming a global village) and both prize and utilize the unique gifts each member brings to the community. That in turn commands that we care for the least as well as the greatest among us and give attention to the most needy.

The Moral Base

If God is unknowable, then it seems distinctly possible (or even probable) that the Scriptures may not be God's words or Word, but mankind's scribblings subsequently attributed to God. So I must look elsewhere to find a base for the morality that was scribbled into the Scriptures. Darwin's genius was voicing an ultimate goal, the survival of the species (and then discovering its means). Jesus' and Paul's genius was pointing in the direction of how to live together so as to enhance the probability that the community composed of our species will survive, and even thrive. It seems to me that morality is first of all the how-to of community survival. Then what is the moral base? Survival of humanity? The welfare, the benefit, the good of humankind?

The notion of sin grew up in the time of authoritarianism (totalitarians, chieftains, despots, kings, tyrants, warriors) a time when whichever Saddam Hussein happened to be in charge could put you to death for smiling in the wrong way, no questions asked. Augustine devised his Christian theology anchored to the notion of sin in the context of that autocratic world. "Might made right" in those days (a conviction which Vladimir Putin and the hawkish Republicans are striving to take us back to), and there was scant moral limit to the kind of might that could be utilized. Augustine's theology was, in part at least, a reaction to that cruel authoritarianism. The Renaissance and the Enlightenment started to lift us out of that authoritarian world, fomented reaction and revolution, and moved us in the direction of individual rights. In our Western world authoritarianism lost its grip and the various forms of governance which fostered individualism began to take hold. Individualism has flourished and along with it the various -isms that feed on it: capitalism, conservatism, liberalism, libertarianism. And as the pendulum has swung further away from authoritarianism, individualism and its fellow -isms have gone crazy, become completely unfettered and irresponsible. It has become a "Me first" world. And unfortunately we have indoctrinated most of the rest of the world with those same -isms. The notion of sin has become dysfunctional, no longer the deterrent it was intended to be, but instead merely a diversion from the greater-than-individual forms of evil. What has been abandoned and lost is any sense of responsibility and accountability to that which keeps us alive, the community. And I am well convinced that without that sense of responsibility and accountability to each other and to the whole community, we are treading down a path to self-destruction and social failure.

The time has come when we need to construct a morality that pays attention equally to the needs of the whole community as well as of each individual; I am utterly convinced that we are all equal; and the alternate way of stating that value is: the community exists for the survival and thriving of its individuals, and the individuals exist to embody and enact the responsibilities of the community, i.e., we are all inseparable. So a functional morality is one that directs and protects with equal zeal the actions of both the community and its individuals.

No Salvation in Some Hereafter

It is clear to me that early Judaism was about the here-and-now, perhaps Judaism's profoundest insight. Resurrection and afterlife are abstractions built merely upon unevidenced hope. To be sure, I too hope some knowing part of me will continue after my body has been buried in a grave and molders (the Dalai Lama suggests it may be consciousness that survives). But I have no evidence, certainly no proof, and, after observing the life-processes around me, only the vaguest intuitions. And a vague hope. But that salvation-in-the-hereafter piece is most of all a diversion to divert our attention and energies from the here-and-now. If one's here-and-now is shitty, then maybe that diversion is a pleasant and desirable relief. But it is not productive, only ameliorating. An opiate of oppressed masses. And a disastrous distraction. I am pretty

Chapter 4: Sin, for One Last Time

clear that all the Jesus-saves-you-into-eternity stuff is mostly (dare I say "entirely"?) a diversion. Out of the intertestamental period it grew into Christianity's first decades because of the need of an oppressed people who were defined by dashed hopes of ever again being a free and powerful nation, i.e., their need to find relief from the overwhelming distress of their reality. And when the church became the lap-puppy of the emperor in the fourth century, then the salvation-into-eternity morphed into... what? A social control tool? An enticement to obedience and loyalty? A hope of eventual relief from the still-present oppression?

And I am exquisitely clear that the real work of this life is the here-and-now: to enjoy it, to appraise it, to do something constructive and corrective about it, to live in it, though not necessarily overpopulating it with progeny. The useful insights of our religions are those that help us understand ourselves and the world we live in, and urge us to do constructive change where the here-and-now is less than beneficial.

The World We Live in Today

We edged from the jungle out onto the savannah as hunter-gatherer groups, grew into tribes, then chiefdoms and city-states, then nations, and now we are becoming a one-world global-village. Formerly the leaders ruled with military might; today global economic entanglement has pushed plutocrats and oligarchs and mega-CEOs into positions of power and decision-making, hidden from sight and accountability, and mired in slime. They have become the new aristocrats convinced that they know best as proven by the wealth they have accumulated *(shades of Puritan Calvinism; you will know the righteous by the wealth with which God rewards them)*. And they are dedicated solely to the morality of lining their own pockets.

The World Post-Sin

Augustine *et alia* built their theological system around free will, sin and original sin, and Jesus' self-sacrifice; the church has wrapped itself in that system ever since. And the system has proven itself inadequate (if it had ever been adequate) to cope with the realities of the twenty-first century and is completely eclipsed by twenty-first-century understandings of the human critter and its social systems. That sin coinage, if ever of value, is now worthless. Whatever they meant by sin has been trivialized into insipid pap and fails to include most of the evil in this world. The notion of original sin collapsed with the discovery of how reproductive biology actually works, and we are left with the flawed human. The sacrificial theology which, prompted by his followers's experiences of a resuscitated or spiritualized Jesus, euphemized his ignominious death into a expiating sacrifice by God himself through his very-flesh Son, has become hard to swallow in a world long without temple sacrifice. And free-will has shown to be not very free at all, hedged and impeded by layers of biology, psychology, social dynamics and culture so that we are left with an indeterminant amount of choice.

What's Left Is a Basket Full of Malefactions

(Please note, while the **Randomhouse Dictionary** *defines a malefaction as necessarily evil or criminal, I take the word in its root Latin sense, i.e., "a bad doing;" not necessarily evil or criminal, just one with bad consequences.)* Some malefactions are evil, (i.e., designed to cause harm, injury, loss, even death and worse; but I lay aside intent as an amoral impulse which can be chosen or not. The deliberateness of the choice is as important as the bad consequence, "I choose knowing, or even wanting the bad consequence"), others are merely bad (i.e., also causing harm, injury, loss, even death but not by deliberate or malicious choice, though perhaps by poorly thought out or ignorant choice), and others simply matters gone awry (i.e., not much choice involved, but an action/deed with an unexpected, unanticipated twist. . . bad things happening to good people). I leave out of this basket events of nature (earthquakes, tornadoes and such which are not in the least man-caused, though when a skier precipitates a snow avalanche by skiing in an area marked off for risk of avalanche, I would want to hold him liable), and randomness, the randomness built into the universe, i.e., the random factor in the physical realm, e.g., cancer.

This full basket includes a lot of things not formerly known as sins. That is my intention. I am not now mucking about morality or the realm of moral choosing. I am including as completely as I can all bad consequences which have some human choice component, wherever there is some human control, however slight. Remember that I understand impulse and intent to be nearly irrelevant, but behavior which has consequences as the arena in which human interaction matters; when what I do impacts you, the consequences for you and for me and for our community are what count. They make a difference. And that is the arena to which I think we need to pay attention. That is where my choices need to be thoughtful and considerate; that is where I have some control, where my behavior counts. Whether we once called it sin or not, I do not care. Malefactions and their consequences are what I'm chasing down.

An Attendant Issue

What is the function of **punishment**? In addition to the failure of the church's sin *schema* in my layman's estimation I'd suggest that our current judicial and penal system has become almost entirely ineffective. We need to appraise the functionality of our penal system. I hunch that the punishment we mete out to malefactors is really an avenging, and not a useful social tool; instead it is a dysfunctional way to clobber the perpetrator into never doing that again, (which seems not to work since his real mistake, he believes, is not what he did, but that he got caught.)

Chapter 4: Sin, for One Last Time

A recent study indicates that our penal system has in fact effectively reduced criminal activity over the last two decades; the prison population has skyrocketed (in this wealthiest and supposedly most advanced nation in the world, ours is the highest rate of criminal incarceration in the world), and the incidence of crime has actually decreased. But, the study concludes, it is the removal of malefactors from the general population that has reduced crime, not any punishments *(our prison system has become our version of France's Devils Island)*. And our prison system has become insupportably expensive. We need to re-think the whole juridical and penal system.

It seems to me that the underlying issue (rather than sin or punishing or rehabilitating malefactors) is our need to protect the society, both the social fabric and individuals, from actions of malefactors. In many, if not most cases, the rehabilitation of criminals is ineffective (recidivism rates are on the grow) and we need to look toward some other solutions and means of protection. Two thoughts come to my mind. In the ancient Celtic tribal system the punishment for killing (for example) another member of the tribe was seven years of exile; in a tribal system in which the individual's very existence was dependent upon his place within the tribe, that was indeed a severe sanction, but it did protect the tribe for a period from his destructive behavior, and it did give the killer time and space to reflect upon his action and to change his behavior. On the other hand I also recall France's Devil's Island off the coast of French Guiana whither French criminals were transported. With minimal guards the prisoners were largely left to cope for themselves, a very cruel and unusual punishment which mainly served the purpose of removing the criminals from the general populace. A cheaper system than ours, but abandoned in the mid-twentieth century. There are alternatives, and we need to get just as creative as the ancients were.

Systemic Malefactions

And I lay down one more specification. We need to include not only my malefactions as an individual; we need to include even more **our** malefactions, as community, and as any sub-set within that community. Too long we have left out of serious consideration the community's malefactions. For example, we talk incessantly about racism. But we talk about it only as an individual's malefaction: "I did something racist," or "I am a racist." And we get very little traction. Because racism is a systemic problem, not merely an individual's bigotry. And until we deal with it as a systemic problem, we are only blowing hot air. I cite racism only as an example. I could weave as well about poverty and impoverishment, about class and financial inequities, about social control and violence... about a huge host of issues. We make noise about them, but that's all, noise, because they are all systemic problems, only minimally an individual's sins. So, I include in my full basket my malefactions, your malefactions, our malefactions, and the malefactions of the community, of the communities, of the mega-community. That has become a big, full basket. And I propose that the whole of it is what we really must deal with, and not allow ourselves to be limited to whatever trivialities I might dredge up to confess to my priest in the private sanctity of the confessional.

Community Accountability

As I noted above, our founding fathers shaped for us a macro-system within which there are no ways to hold the system itself accountable. But the malefactions we need most to cope with are not as simple as socially controlling individuals; they are mostly systemic, built into the very fabric of the system. And that makes those malefactions difficult to see, difficult to comprehend and understand, difficult to problem-solve, and immensely resistant to change or correction. I have no profound insight as to how a system can be held accountable to itself and to its members. The few exercises we have seen of systems trying to do constructive self-appraisal end up being terribly short-sighted, uninsightful, and blinkered, unable to see even the most obvious. But some such means of appraisal and accountability is the charge. Otherwise we are merely swatting at mosquitoes.

Our Need for a Functional Morality

I seem to have slipped into eschatology. Amazing! My focus is fixed on how to live in the here and now, and I find myself, like Jesus, mucking around in thoughts of the last days. How does this happen? I'm playing with you, of course. But I do find myself mucking around in last days kinds of things. It goes like this. If I take the God out of the system (because the God is unknowable for me and I can't base my system on an unknown), then I'm left with no reliable, trustworthy, sanction-capable foundation for building a god-free morality. I've kicked sin out of the system as a failed and dysfunctional, even destructive factor. Kant suggested "The greatest good for the greatest number." But that doesn't go far enough for me. It doesn't deal effectively with the long-range realities I think we are facing: the population bomb, irreparable destruction to the environment, exhaustion of natural resources, and the desolation of our insular planet. Nor does it deal with even the shorter range realities: the violent rush of the underdeveloped nations to seize some share of first-world goodies, the directionless rush to endlessly develop thoughtless and mindless technologies driven solely by the profit (translate "greed") motive. And who's looking at the long range issues? Anyone? I find myself pondering: how to effect the survival of the species? What kind of a nut sits around worrying about whether humankind is going to go extinct and to be survived by the next step in evolution. . . i.e., cockroaches? But that's where my mind wanders. I think we, as a country, as a species, are running pell-mell towards self-destruction. And how do we live so as to survive? No one's looking out for the whole of the population, everyone's looking at the very, very short range, next month's bottom line; no one's tending to the long-range good.

Chapter 4: Sin, for One Last Time

Our country has become the world's leader in how to live in greater and greatly nonsensical luxury *(actually we've lost the lead in recent decades)*. But we've done it at the cost of despoiling the environment and distressing, (oppressing?) pissing off much of the rest of the world. That can continue only a little while longer. I may not see the reversal, but I think my children and grandchildren surely will. It might be possible for the innovators of technology to stave off that downhill turn for a few decades, but the trajectory is already in place. Unless we repent, (i.e., *shuv*, change course). And the kingdom of god that is nigh is either the wrath of the environment which will despoil us in return, or an entirely new way of living together. Sound radical? I suspect it is more radical than even that. What would it look like to live in harmony with all the world? I'm going to need a little help in that.

I Wonder about Our Moralities

At the Market Street Food Pantry a young man, well tattooed, came in, no identification nor any of the papers he needed to qualify for food. But with authentic fervor he presented his clear need, reinforced with several varying stories, to make immediate assistance all but mandatory. We thought him lying, but had neither the means nor the will to prove it. He should have left without any food, but he persisted, and left with some food. We did not appreciate his obvious lying, though we did not resent his leaving with some food. I pondered that. The whole of my moral fiber resents lying *(I've been accused of puritanic honesty; I hold truth-telling to be fundamental to community.)* Truth-telling is built into our moral structure. Lying is destructive to trust, to loyalty, even to love. Yet I was willing to allow this young man's lying. Why? I opine: he is of the underclass we have created in this country, a loser, one of the hoards of losers we need in this culture to enable (I am no economist so do not understand the mechanisms involved) the thriving of the upper class. Somewhere in his twenties, he will never be successful (an unfair but, given his tattoos, his clothes and the way he presented himself, an irresistible appraisal), always barely surviving: by lying, by scamming, by conning, by stealing, and by doing whatever it takes to scrape together just enough to survive into the next day. **And I wondered**: truth-telling has always been fundamental to me, but pondering what I had just experienced I had to wonder whether honesty is not so fundamental after all, but simply a facet of the culture we have built to support the upper classes, a facet which does **not** work to the benefit of the underclass, but instead keeps them in the underclass? And if one is living on the ragged edge of failing-to-death, is lying permissible?. . . morally justifiable (e.g., Jean Valjean's theft of a loaf of bread)? I have long wondered: is morality a **luxury of the survivors**? Or might honesty be a tool used by the survivors to keep on thriving by keeping the underclasses, the non-survivors, in their place, i.e., losing, barely scraping by? I worry about what passes for morality in this country, this culture.

Part II: My Review of Christian Doctrines

I keenly remember the character the actor Michael Douglas played, Gordon Gecko, an excruciatingly successful financial manager in the movie **Wall Street** strutting in front of a huge class of young, up-and-coming financial managers, teaching them, "Greed is good." And I remember clearly the chill that ran through my bones in that instant; Douglas was presenting his character quite believably. And that chill was my realization that our culture has come to accept and to believe that sound bite as a moral standard, greed is good. I remember contrarily in a theology class as we touched on ethics, Alden Kelly teaching us that the then current understanding that the end justifies the means is incorrect, that the means must stand on the same moral foundation as the end, and must be itself morally justifiable. And that made sense to me... still does as I watch evangelists lying in order to save souls for God.

I have grave concerns about the morality of this culture built on capitalism and consumerism. No, that is too soft a statement; mine are not grave concerns, rather my morals, my deepest values are more than offended by consumerism, a system of selling goods rather than producing, with products deliberately designed to deteriorate quickly so the sucker (oh, I should say *consumer*) will soon have to purchase another (I grew up in the age of durable goods). Capitalism is just as bad (perhaps evil), increasingly shunting money into the coffers of the already-wealthy while trying to convince the rest of us that the trickle-down economy works, and the super-rich are the real job-makers whose growing wealth therefore we dare not inhibit. My uneducated perception is that capitalism, and the individualism which is required for capitalism to work, initially helped topple the autocracies and raise up the lowest classes, fostered industrialization and now undirected technological innovation, all of which have given us goodies we did not need and which ultimately may prove fatal for our species. And capitalism has unfettered itself from serving the needs of the middle and lower classes, and has run amok. We surmise that great wealth (one form of power) being in the pockets of the few has ushered us into an era of undisclosed rule by plutocrats who are completely unaccountable to others and who appear to have concern only for their own enrichment and not the welfare of society. E.g., the financial markets are rigged in favor of the super-wealthy. But I rant.

These concerns made me uneasy about unfettered individualism becoming its own moral code, overriding care for the neediest of our greater community. And I began to sense that the libertarian voices I was hearing with greater frequency these days was individualism taken to its extreme (I am inclined to say *ad absurdum*). I sense it is all very destructive of community, which is fundamental to survival.

All of these -isms sound quite silly when I consider our need of strong, supporting and lasting community. Despite our seemingly clinging to the gospel, I think we are morally unanchored, adrift, and in peril.

Chapter 4: Sin, for One Last Time

Conclusion

Given the above, I conclude that we must discard fourth-century and contemporary notions of sin. In focusing our attentions on the trivialities of personal sin we hide from ourselves the larger and more destructive evils which both oppress us and are leading us toward the ultimate self-obliteration, i.e., the destruction or despoliation or collapse of the social structure we need in order to survive. Meanwhile the evil, some of which we thought was sin, remains. We need to discover new frameworks for identifying, comprehending, and controlling the destructive choices we are making as a society, as a culture, as a community.

Postscript on Grieving

After I have tossed aside most of the old theology, and approached some sort of new but very tentative and vague conclusions, I still have occasional nostalgic moments when I mourn the loss of my old naivete. A certain hymn resurges an ancient, sympathetic chord deep within me, and I wonder to myself, "That was nice, when I once could accept it for what it purported to be"; but even as the chord re-echoes the old, warm, comforting, but lost nostalgias, my mind has already begun to reluctantly parse the words, struggling to discover what reasonably stands behind that particular metaphor today. If I could only let it be again, just for a few moments. It's mostly hymns that choke me up and stop me short, and make me yearn. Though sometimes it comes out of the words, the sights, the resonances of the congregation reciting in unison, and in harmony with my inner self. The feeling passes. And will well up again.

Chapter 5: Talking about the God

Nota Bene: *In this chapter I consistently refer to "the God" instead of our usual "God" (sans definite article) for a specific reason, to remain clear to myself and to you that I am not speaking about YHWH of the Hebrew Scriptures, nor God/Abba of the Christian Writings. I speak to my rejection of those two, and I am clearly searching for some other understanding of the term "God." Hence I use "the God" to hold that focus.*

Methodology

My friend, the philosophy professor Ron Santoni has muttered quietly several times that talking about God is difficult. Difficult? Yes! So in preparation for this chapter I set myself an exercise to discover how Jack Bowers thinks his way through complex issues such as this one. I need to lay out for you some of my discoveries out of that exercise because they have become the underpinnings for this discussion of the God.

I learned that, though others seem to see me as fairly logical using straight-line thinking, underneath that overlay I am really a fairly associative thinker: one thought prompts another, and that another. Not straight line at all, but instead a meandering, discovering ideas as I go. And when I sense I have likely discovered all of value to the issue, I gather related material into aggregations, and then study each of those to discover both the minutia and the emerging patterns, all I can about each of them. That done, I've arrived at the threshold of rationality, of struggling to make sense of each aggregation, and then sorting them all together, in various ways, to see what they might stack up to be.

That said, I will lay out the terminology of my thinking processes.

Sources: Whence do I Obtain my Data? (while this may involve some rational searches, it is largely an associative process)

a. My **perceptions**, i.e., my experiences, that knowledge which I receive directly through my five senses which are my only avenues to the world outside my skull,

b. Others's **witness**, whether directly from other persons, or through the several media (books, magazines, etc., TV and radio, social media), and

c. My **innards**, i.e., my feelings, emotions, introspections, opinions, and memories (the sum total of my knowledge).

Processing: What do I Do with the Gathered Data?

a. **Evaluate**: weigh the verifiability, reliability, or plausibility of the data,

b. **Sort** through data, recognizing patterns (a most basic tool of the brain), and

c. **Filter out**, as best I can, all the presumptions and biases I bring to the data and to this process (this requires that I honestly recognize and acknowledge my own biases).

Appraisal and Concluding: how do I weigh the emerging patterns?

a. **Inclusivity**: Does this pattern incorporate all of the selected data?

b. **Rationality**: is it sensible, reasonable, logical *(I am surprised that as much as we prize rationality, we have no clear definition)*. Ron Santoni and I agree on two questions to appraise rationality: "Does this make sense?" and "Is it coming together?" Another test is intuitiveness, does it fit well and reasonably in the larger scheme?

c. **Standards**: What are my standards in appraising and accepting the data and the conclusion? High? Low? (E.g., in a criminal trial the jury is directed the standard of "Beyond a shadow of a doubt," but in a civil trial the standard is "a preponderance of evidence.").

Problems:

In talking about the God I am wandering in the realm of the non-physical, the non-scientific or extra-scientific. And while I am clear in my conscious mind that scientific rules do not apply (verifiability, measurability, duplicatability, only hard data) in this realm, and are instead limiting and disabling, yet I find my basic critical training and personal propensities are in that direction. Verification is impossible. The soft, anecdotal, unmeasurable data are incomplete, unreliable and fairly implausible for me. This causes serious liability for me in this discussion, maybe even a fatal flaw.

Methodology (continued)

My exercise gave me the courage and energy to do this aloud thinking about the God which I've lost and would like to regain. So now I pick up my broom and begin to sweep together into little piles all the about-God flotsam and jetsam that has floated into my world. These are the scraps of my life, the ravelings and wood chips, the leftovers of living. You will see that the data accumulates in piles sounding like *plops* which are reminiscent of cow pies, or soggy clods of mud. Each plop is not a datum, but describes a collection of what seem to me similar data (the details of which would take many chapters), data that together appear to compose a pile, a heap of similarities. Hidden within will likely be some dross, garbage to be disposed. In the second section I'll voice some considerations, things that condition, affect, color, and probably somewhat disable or limit my thinking (i.e., my data-collecting, and analyzing). That done, we'll commence the sorting, examining, putting things together, starting to see patterns which point to tentative conclusions. Next, to check my process, I'll attempt one experiment. And lastly I'll offer the meager conclusions I think I can legitimately come to.

Sources: Whence Get I my Notions about the God?

Unspoiled Nature

The other night I watched a video on the Faroe Islands's website which reminded me of the most important reasons I want to believe in the God. I visit that website with some infrequent regularity. The Faroe Islands (in the North Atlantic, midway between Scotland and Iceland and warmingly embraced by the Gulf Stream) were the unintended destination of a paltry of Celtic monks who climbed into a coracle (a round wicker boat of tarred cowhides) and pushed off from Ireland without any oars to go wherever the God might take them. I, like them, am drawn to lands-end kinds of places. In my fantasies I'd like to visit the Faroes, so their videos are enticing to me. One video reminded me of the **brute beauty and magic of the unspoiled natural world**, the one the God supposedly created. I am struck by its magnificence and by my yearning for a god who would create such stuff. And I am mindful that Celtic monks were committed to god-forsaken places because they found the God more easily there. They thought nature to be their primary scriptures, and the written Scriptures only secondary. Makes sense to me. The Faroes yield a *feeling* but no intellectual or collatable data. A place to put one foot tentatively.

My Own History

Plop and Plop: I suppose my love affair with **Christianity began for me when** my mother discovered that my father had been an acolyte in the Episcopal Church in Oil City in his tender years, and on that basis she (her family had been atheistic socialists, so she had attended a Lutheran parish on her own) decided the family would start attending the Oakley branch of Episcopalianism along with our closest family friends, the Clarks. So I was baptized at eight years of age, and soon was acolyting. St. Mark's was a small mission, so it offered enthusiastic welcome for the very few young folks my age. And there I first became acquainted with the God, the grand old white-bearded (though invisible) gent dressed in glistering robes, seated upon a cloud, or upon a throne, or upon something, somewhere, but not here. I learned my elementary theology in Sunday School discussing with Mr. Thorpe, our layreader (we had no priest), the St. James Series handouts which were our text, and by the time I was fourteen the congregation knew I was headed for seminary and the priesthood. (That was probably a premature decision on our several parts, but one already made.) And eventually I took that old white-bearded gent off to seminary with me. But my liberal arts undergraduate work had taught me to ask critical questions, and the **seminary** taught me a few tools for sharpening those questions. The white-haired old gent never made it out of seminary. He got lost there, maybe slain. And I came away from seminary with a fuzzy and much disarrayed picture of the God, and only the vaguest notion of the Blue Blur (my moniker for the Holy Spirit), but an intriguing, evolving picture of this Jesus guy, the one they called the Son of God (how his divinity could be has **always** been a confusion. And I must admit, the math of the Holy Trinity never really worked for me.) And then I proceeded to practice my priest-craft over the next thirty-four years. But my relationship with the God was mostly an intellectual one, because that's what I am, an intellectual. And as my comprehension grew, my (unacknowledged) confusion about the God grew as well. I studied the Scriptures. I examined my own (unfulfilling) spiritual life. And I ruminated. Endlessly. And I preached. (As an intellectual I prized preaching and teaching above all else). But I can see in hindsight that during all those thirty-four years the doubting had constantly nibbled at the edges of my theology, so that when I retired and was no longer required to spout orthodoxy, I discovered that what belief I had left in me was quite raggedly frayed. And, no longer tethered to orthodoxy, my critical questions began to range deeper. Which got me to this place. Through it all I largely believed in the God, even though the God was largely absent from me. This plop is lots of soft, mushy, inconclusive data.

Nature

Plop. Along with the Celtic monastics, out in the natural world, out in my ***dysert***[1] was where I most thought I found the God. The church building was where we worshiped the God, but the God was not housed there. The God was out in the world, and was particularly perceivable in the world of nature which the God had himself created. And we reasoned that in as much as he could not possibly have created something contrary to his own nature, the natural world must necessarily reflect the nature of the God which created it. Or so I earnestly believed. Like those Celtic monks I best found

---

1. A *dysert* (i.e., desert) for the Celtic Christian monks was an isolated place away from the monastic community to which the monk could retire and live for some days, weeks, months, following the model of the Egyptian Desert Fathers of the fourth century.

the God when I was alone, in a desert (unpeopled) place with an infinity of time to watch without considering. Even today I can glimpse a brilliant cardinal perched on a branch at the tree line and know I am seeing a tiniest particle of the God's brilliant beauty. My memory wanders back to a pre-teen boy on a blistering summer afternoon, and to the coolness of the embankment of a specific bend in the small creek in those woods I inhabited so many of my hours; the earth smelt sweetly sour there, like fertile soil. And was soooo cool. The God was with me there, in those moments, in that place. Oh, I knew even in those tender years that creek was mainly the runoff from an industrial plant at the far edge of those woods; sometimes, when it ran milky white from their waste, the God was not there. But some days it did run clear and cool, and then infant crawdads would come out to watch me as I built a mud dam across the creek. And they too seemed to enjoy it. And then the God smiled. I could cite a zillion such instances that informed my childish experiences and understandings of the God. The God has always been most present in the natural world which he created. Even today. This plop yields only tiny bits of hard but still uncollatable data, but it does offer a sense of orderliness.

But I am an **urban person**. I've always lived in cities. Not huge cities, but cities. So the world of nature where I might most find the God was always at a distance. A place I visited. For only a few hours. Across the street in those woods. Not the place I lived. And I've never understood how anyone could find the God in the concrete jungle. And that may be the reason I never developed the kind of faith (and faithfulness) those Celtic monks did. My God was usually afar, not up close and warmly enveloping. Not so explicitly comforting and supportive There is a thread of distrust running through the Hebrew Scriptures, an anti-urban thread. Those Bedouins had found the God in desert places: on mountain tops, and in deserted valleys, and wildernesses. They inhabited the villages, but they lived out in the desert places. I harmonize with that discordant thread. The city is a place of chaos upon which the humans must impress some sort of order; and at best, we do that only poorly. Chaos seems to be the primary theme of the city. So being an urban person I can know the desert places in my mind, and know in my mind the God who dwells in those places; but I do not live out there. So I suppose the God which is out there, somewhere, becomes for me mainly an intellectual thing, not something I live in close company with, daily, in my ordinary moments. The God is something I turn my attention to, and wander out to, but only for some moments. I find few traces of the God in the city; and those are screechingly fleeting.

As Science Sees

Plop. I have been talking about the romantic world of nature, where I can be alone, and freed to wonder, to taste of the God. But in reality most of my hours and days and weeks I live in a different natural world, an unromantic one; **the world which science**

investigates and describes and defines. And while it is a fascinating world to me, it has no God. There is no seat at the table for the God when the scientists sit down together to discuss. They observe (but can't see the God), and measure (the God can't be measured either), and hypothesize, and then replicate in order to prove (but the God is not replicatable, so can't be proven by them). I tell over and over again that the physicists can talk us all the way back to within the tiniest fragment of a second after the Big Bang, but at that point their laws break down, and they can not advance the next nanosecond back to the Big Bang itself, much less to whatever was before it. And they can only wonder, what was on the other side, before the Big Bang? Some notions, but no proofs, not even any reliable hints. Some people keep hoping that the physicists will eventually get clear back to the Big Bang, and maybe even get a glimpse beyond it, a glimpse of the God, the Maker, the Creator, the Unmoved Mover, working feverishly in his shop getting things all set up for the Big Bang. But I am convinced that will never happen. There is no place for the God in the scientists's language. The God is not of the physical realm; he is somewhere other, of some non-physical realm. So the God cannot be described or known in the languages of that physical realm. And the scientists, however desperately we want them to, cannot show us the God's house, or introduce us to the old white-haired gent. The God is wholly non-physical, wholly outside their realm. Those scientists, the priests of this modern, technological world have not the slightest clue about the God. We'll have to seek him out without them, and often against their protestations. This pile yields hard, intellectual but mostly negative data. The God is not here!

Man a Special Creation

Plop. The Hebrew Scriptures teach us that **mankind was a special kind of creation**, different than all the rest. The God in the first story creates by sheer utterance, first this, then that, then that. And finally, at the end of the very last day of creating, after all else, as a kind of pinnacle or end-statement of his creating, the God creates humankind in his own image and likeness *the only creation so described*. We are special. We are different. And we alone can relate directly with the God. In the second creation story the God stoops down and takes up a handful of mud and molds it into a lifeless body and then breathes his own breath *(the Hebrew ru'ah can be translated as "wind" or "spirit" or "breath," or maybe all three at once)* into it and the mud figure becomes *ha'adam* the mud-boy. And then because the mud-boy is lonely, the God makes another, this time with a different, again totally unique way of creating; he takes a rib from the mud-boy and fashions it into the woman, *Havah* the mother of living (a.k.a. Eve).

These stories tell us that humankind was, and still is, a special, a different, a unique kind of creation. And we have eagerly bought into that; it made us better than the wild, dumb beasts of the desert. But Darwin and the science boys have eclipsed that notion. They have shown us that we are part of a seamless evolution reaching back to the earliest bit of protein-complex that exhibited what we might call life. We are not unique; rather we are, for a short time, the momentary endpoint of an evolutionary process, with no notion what will next evolve into dominance (cockroaches?) So I am not unique, but an inseparable part of the whole. Creation was not in six days piece by piece by piece, but a slow and seamless evolution, starting from stardust and mutating over seven billion years into this body and person. I do not stand apart. Nor am I better than. I am simply part of. One step in some unwritten, some thoroughly experimental and undesigned discovery process, an on-going evolution.[2]

We hear the science boyos jabbering at us otherwise, but we've still all completely bought into the dream of the old Hebraic stories. We approach our world self-assured that we are different, better than, and charged (or at least unrestrained) to dominate (to whatever end we chose, even to our own mere self-aggrandizement and the destruction of everything else.) But the physical world is telling us back, "You are no better than, but only part of, and a very self-centered, unforesighted, and thereby stupidly destructive part of us at that." *(But I wander afield and prate about morality,[3] instead of the God.)* So the Hebraic stories, and the Christian theology built on them have told us untruths (from the scientific point of view) which we are eager to hear: that we are different, better, superior, unaccountable dominatrices, when all along we are merely an evolved headland, a sandy cape which might get washed away by next tide, maybe even by a tide of our own creation, a tide of waste and destructiveness. *(The morality pops up again. This morality thing begins to feel like whack-a-mole. Mmmm. I'd best pay attention to that.)*

The first creation story makes us in the God's image and likeness. The second creation story makes us out of mud. We are both, suppose. And I get the mud stuff, I know what it means that we are made of mud. But what does it mean that we are made in the image and likeness of the God? Intriguing sparks flash out of that metaphor, but like other sparks they instantly flare out and I'm left very unsure what it means that you and I are in the image and likeness of the God, or whether that tells me **anything** about the God.

---

2. As an aside, I then must wonder: **consciousness**. I have it, though I know not what it is. And if I am merely a step in the seamless process of evolution, does that imply that the rest of the creation must also have some sort of consciousness? Is consciousness too, seamless? Jung suggested a "collective unconsciousness" *(I am not a student of Jung's thought so I can righteously claim to know not what he meant by that phrase. Nonetheless, the phrase itself mutters suggestions into my ear.)* Or am I indeed a special form of creation, the only one with consciousness? I will put, and then beg this question.

3. (Or am I really afield? Perhaps the world-driven morality is a portion of the God!! The world made [i.e., evolved] us. Dare I suggest the "the world equals the God" made us, that the God and the world are in some way synonymous, different facets of, different metaphors for, but the same identity? [No, not pantheism, not even pan-en-theism, something else, I know not what.] Only different ways, different languages, different metaphors to identify the same thing? But I'm getting ahead of myself. I'm still sweeping the droppings together into piles. Hold onto this thought, and we may get back to it later.)

Chapter 5: Talking about the God

The Evolution of YHWH

Plop. I suppose that the earliest **version of the God** probably emerged with primitive, survivalist man trying to control his environment in order to enhance his chances of survival. Weather gods, gods of the hunt, gods who smiled or looked on disparagingly, gods who moved the sun, the moon, the stars. Gods who fought alongside to bring victory, or sometimes defeat. Gods who pledged to control for man the things man could not control himself, but who failed to deliver! Were they pure fabrications? Merely projections of wants or needs? Or was there some non-physical reality in them? Was the physical realm peopled with myriad spirits as the pre-Christian Celts had thought? I have not experienced this material realm as peopled with spirits, though I'm not absolutely sure. Maybe. Sometimes?

YHWH himself, as he leads out of Egypt, appears to have begun as the god of some volcano somewhere; he belches clouds of smoke and fire as he leads out of the Reed Sea; thunder and lightning accompany the God as he meets Moses atop Mount Sinai. YHWH morphs into other forms as the national drama lurches along. But the story had begun (setting aside for the moment the late add-on myths of the first eleven chapters of Genesis) as the God sought out the nomadic Abram. In those early pages the God paints himself as a pretty powerful critter, but his actions (or rather, inactions) betray that the God might be just a solitary, a rather insignificant god, maybe an outcast from the ruling clutch of gods who have already won their sycophants. He seems to be searching for someone to become his adulator, in order to gain him some authority, some respectability, and thereby some power. Maybe he is little more than a genii, looking after the Abram he had sought out and selected. When we leap centuries ahead to the Moses era the God has evidently learned his warrior craft. He knows how to dupe masses into following him, while not quite giving him the allegiance, the fidelity, the faithfulness he's demanding and yearning for. He's now not merely a con-artist, he actually can produce some results. He can offer his people victories, whether by trickery, deception, or outright violence. And though he has mastered the intricacies of inter-tribal warfare, he does not seem to have mastered the leadership skills of keeping his own folks in line. He is clearly not the omnipotent creator of the first creation story. Instead he seems a more polished version of the bumbling super-human of the second creation story. He controls, but in very limited ways; not quite what that tribe of hunter-gatherers struggling to survive in a harsh environment would have first imagined. The story evolves in curious ways. A close parsing of the story seems to suggest that YHWHism remains a minority sect throughout most centuries. The kings are not faithful to YHWH, much to his grief. Through the prophets YHWH rails at the people in charge, the monarchs and oligarches and plutocrats; he rants and raves and pleads, but they seem to pay little attention. He is in many ways sidelined even then. He retreats into the international scene (second term presidents do that too), hauls in the Nebucadnezers and Cyruses to unwittingly carry out his will, punishes, decimates his people for their faithlessness, and finally exiles them. And gradually he retreats even farther, becoming invisible, his actions indiscernible. A petty moralist, muttering about how we should live. But no longer acting, at least in any massive, god-like ways. He becomes a spook, concerned about spirituality (without telling us what "spirituality" is.) Curious. Maybe YHWH had not been a god at all. Maybe he was a figment of the national Hebraic imagination, the God they thought they needed, or would liked to have had. And maybe all the time the real God is lurking elsewhere. Maybe YHWH was, after it is all over, a diversion. Maybe.

Stephen preached one Sunday on the Jacob's Ladder story. He reflected some on Jacob's character. A very unsavory character. Deceitful. Conniving. Not a person I would want my God to select as the progenitor of the Chosen People. Moses, YHWH's hand-picked agent, was a murderer and fugitive. The great King David, again the boy YHWH hand-picked: early on a battle-skilled war-mongering rebel and but later a cuckold, murderer, an incompetent ruler entrapped and paralyzed in a court full of Byzantine intrigues. Clearly the YHWH of the Hebrew Scriptures is not the God I envision. He might have been the one the invading and occupying Hebrew tribes wanted and needed. But **YHWH is not the God I think can do us any good** in today's world.

Outside the Physical Universe

So I need to look elsewhere than the Hebrew Scriptures for evidence of the God. But where? Plop. It appears to me, taking the physicists's conclusions as having some weighty authority with considerable reliability, that there is no place, **no space for the God within this physical** universe. The physicists, and the rest of the scientists describe the physical reality without reference to the God. And in describing physical reality without reference to the God, they have created a metaphor (i.e., worldview) and language that has proven exceedingly useful and functional. Not because they eliminated the God, but because they did not use the God as an escape hatch, a convenient out, a final way of describing without need of further elaboration or elucidation, "The God did it." The physicists theorize that if the God does miracles, i.e., by-passes, subverts, countermands the laws of the physical universe in order to give favors to followers who beg, then the God must be inside of and part of the physical universe, and must be subject to the laws of the physical universe and therefore cannot countermand them: a contradiction. And if the God is outside of, apart from the physical universe, then how could the God reach in and manipulate the physical universe which he created and imbued with working laws (of physics) by breaching those same laws without leaving any physical evidence? But while that whole argument **seems** to make sense to me, I also have a vague and very untrackable feeling that it does not hold up, that there is something unexamined in its premises that renders it, like the ontological proofs of the God, unsound logic. Yet in the end I have come to hesitantly agree with their conclusion, that the God is not a part of, nor anywhere within the physical universe.

And so I must figure out how to look for evidence for/against the God who is outside of the physical universe. Is that possible? Certainly. There are lots of immaterial things outside but still operative within the physical universe. Consciousness. Social dynamics. Mathematics.

Pseudo-Scientific Arguments

I am mildly amused by the **pseudo-scientific arguments for the God**. A few have tried to prove the efficacy of prayer; does the God change the course of events in response to persons's prayers? Anecdotal data are tabulated and the analysis usually shows that there would seem to be some very slight preponderance of evidence to the effect that the God does indeed (sometimes, but unpredictably) respond to our prayers and change the course of events (usually this anecdotal research is done in medical problems). Others cite the so-called near-death experiences, as proofs there is a heaven, an after-life, and therefore that the God must be; I would myself classify those near-death experiences as mystical-like experiences, akin to those of meditators, psychedelic drug users and schizophrenics. All have similarly describable experiences, and none, even though deeply moving and sometimes acutely insightful and life-changing, are self-authenticating, and do not qualify as proofs of the God. Such experiences might move a person to believe in the God, but are not themselves proofs. I find such pseudo-scientific attempts unsound, misguided and (please forgive my crassness, but in this conversation I must let the chips fall where they may) slightly pathetic.

My own understanding is that when we begin to **talk about the God, we have stepped outside the world of science**. I use my own term *scientific metaphor*[4] (not in its usual literary sense), or *world view* to connote this. I understand that we have available to us several sets of eye glasses (metaphors, worldviews) through which we might view the world. The scientific world view is one of them, an exceedingly helpful, useful, practical metaphor. But like all metaphors (e.g., rose-colored glasses, world views), its vision is limited. It sees reality from one perspective, through one framework worldview/metaphor, and that perspective necessarily limits; there are some things which happen outside the framework of that perspective, things to which it is therefore blind. It simply cannot see them. For science, I think, the God is one of those things outside its perspective. Science has no words or language or concepts with which to think or talk about the God. So Jack Bowers must try to lay aside the scientific metaphor when I begin to talk about the God (perhaps impossible for me to do). And I must divine what are the words and grammar and etiquette and logic for the God-talk metaphor.

---

4. See my discussion "worldview" in Chapter 8 (215–16)

Part II: My Review of Christian Doctrines

Mysticism

Several times I had tried to read from the great Christian mystics. Their writings have always come out gibberish for me. Others seem to get something from them, but for me, only dyspepsia. After ingesting Evelyn Underhill's book, **Mysticism** (in which she stipulates one **can not become** a mystic, you either are one, or are not, though William James disagreed, and I add to his conclusion the testimony of Buddhism in which the spiritual life is built on meditation), I remained skeptical of mysticism: I even wondered whether such experiences are simply those of a few persons with such powerful recall that they could remember their *in utero* experience?

Having concluded that the God is unknowable to me through the Scriptures and through others's re-telling, I still wondered if I could have a direct experience of the God for myself. I had barely dabbled in centering prayer with no success, and though skeptical I'd accumulated a few minor experiences which I would have considered the most superficial edge of the mystical. But I thought that before I gave it a serious (i.e., disciplined, persistent and prolonged) try, I would seek out some even-handed (i.e., not founded on a knee-jerk bias against religion) psychiatric appraisal of mystical experiences. No one was able to direct me to any such thing in the literature. After a couple of years's search I finally found that one source that yielded a scientific description and appraisal of such experiences, Julian Silverman's paper.[5] While most of the papers in this volume are concerned with what I deem simple meditation, four papers did give me some insight and understanding, and in particular the last in the collection, the paper by Silverman. The conclusion I draw from his study has become germane to my thinking: I deduce that I need not be necessarily accepting of, nor trusting of mystical experiences, nor accepting that they are of God. I am myself no longer drawn to them.

The Numinous

Let's talk for a few moments about things even more vague.

> **Numen**: divine power or spirit, deity; esp. one presiding locally, or presumed to inhabit a particular object.
>
> **Numinous**: *adj.* 1. of, pertaining to, or like a numen; spiritual or supernatural. 2. surpassing comprehension or understanding, mysterious. 3. arousing one's elevated feelings of duty, honor, loyalty, etc.

Abram slipped out of his tent in the velvet blackness of the night to cover his feet *(a euphemism for urinating or defecating)* and looking up at the blanket of stars experienced

---

5. Silverman, "On the Sensory Bases of Transcendental States of Consciousness" in **Psychiatry & Mysticism**, Dean, ed., 365-92.

Chapter 5: Talking about the God

the numinous, which spoke, whispering into the ear of that aged and heirless wanderer a promise of progeny as numerous as those stars. Abram became a believer.

Plop. I suppose we have all experienced **moments of the numinous**. I certainly have. The pre-Christian Celts thought this world quite peopled with spirits: rivers, trees, large rocks. For them all parts of the natural world were inhabited by myriad hosts of spirits. Even today in Ireland and Scotland all significant features of the landscape still have names, large rocks all have names, as though they might still be inhabited, or in some sense might be spirited. Those Celts knew themselves to be surrounded by the numinous, swaddled in the numinous.

As I consider the matter, I would suppose those moments of experiencing the numinous are **akin to mystical** experiences, moments when we know ourselves to be enveloped in The Great: sometimes transcending us, cold and vast and empty; sometimes immanent, warm and lovingly enfolding; sometimes huge and overwhelming; most times small and vague and barely noticeable; and occasionally offering whisperingly deep, earth-shaking insight. My pre-teen self, enjoying the sourly sweet smell of the embankment at a particular turning of the creek, knew that something was present; my young man, strolling down the unlighted Middle Path alongside his father, looking up at the Milky Way surrounded by uncountable stars you just can't see in the light-filled city, was amazed, and gazed back billions of years beyond. Those are moments of weight. And of value. Fused into our memories. They render us momentarily transfixed, caught up in wonder, beyond ourselves and embodied in that which is so much larger. And they seem very important.

Generally I have considered those numinous-filled moments to be **experiences of the God**. I think many people do, though some do not. I expect I am conditioned to so consider them. I am a person whose life-work has centered on thinking about the God. It's reasonable that I would consider those experiences of *numena* to be about the God. And since, as I learned when I explored my ways of thinking, I am a person who values his own experiences above the testimonies and witnesses of others, I am inclined to take those numinous moments as evidence for the God. But at that precise point I become ambivalent, **bifurcated in my thinking**. I know myself to be preconditioned, that as prefix to my very first premise is hidden an unexamined and assumed pre-supposition which colors every premise that follows; every fibre in my body (and mind) knows before I start that the God is. I am probably quite unable, however much I might doubt and challenge and argue and shred, to begin without that pre-supposition. So I suppose that my search is ultimately not so much a denying, but rather a searching out of what? What is the God? How can I give some shape to my knowing of the God?

And the other side of my bifurcated thinking is **my scientific mind** *(not that I am a scientist, but that scientific ways of thinking are infused into me as my primary tools)* which looks askance at these experiences of the *numena* and responds, "Curious, odd, unusual, out of the ordinary, but not verifiable fact, not reliable evidence, so not proof, though sometimes plausible." In my own experience these events seem always (with perhaps rare exceptions, though I recall not one) to have double explanations. The procession of the fifteenth-century Benedictines into the Caldey Island chapel ruins was also light rainfall on the slates above[6] my head. The God shouting in my ear "Shut up and do your studies" as I knelt in seminary chapel was likely my exhausted-with-wrestling subconscious. The God, I think, may always be an alternative explanation, an additional explanation, but not (dare I say "Never"?) an exclusive explanation. My scientifically inclined mind says, "Not God-or, but maybe, possibly God-and, given that the God is a different sort of explanation, a non-scientific explanation." The question can be put, "Are the *numena* real?" And my mind replies, "Not realities of this **physical** world, but perhaps **realities of some other realm** outside the physical, beyond the physical, the realm for which the physicists have no language." The rain on the slate roof was just rain, nothing more. Which is not to say that the fifteenth-century monks processing into the chapel ruins were not real, but implies that their reality lies in some other, some non-physical realm. Perhaps the same realm as those experiences of the numinous.

I stand with each foot in a different realm, a stance which makes for **precarious footing.**

And there are other kinds of vague but exceedingly compelling experiences that seem to point in the Godward direction. When I was a child the Christmas Eve celebration was so very special. And powerful. In the midst of that midnight celebration it was impossible to not believe in the God. All the specialness of that night sang out the God. That midnight celebration has remained central to my religiosity. What piety I have is build of that and ten-thousand other instances of identically similar stuff. **Moments of intuition, or of insight**: e.g., fifteenth-century monks processing as the rain lightly brushes the slate roof. Individually those moments point only hestitatingly Godward, like a compass needle **very** unsure where the north pole is to be found. But pile up half a myriad of those instances and they come together to point without variability in the Godward direction. But they are all soft, emotion-laden, illogical, extra-sensational; and even taken all together they are not terribly weighty or reliable. Indicators. Pointers. But not proofs. And it could be, at the end of this chapter, that such indicators are all I'm going to get. Pointers.

Culture

And there is another glob of sources for my Godwardness. I mentioned my **family's bias** above. I grew up swaddled within that bias. It was most of the warp and weft of which I am woven. I suppose I could have rebelled against that pattern, that design,

---

6. See the description of my experiences on Caldey Island in Chapter 1 (5–11)

but that would have been to go against my very self. The Godward bias is an essential part of my upbringing. But that is not the all.

I grew up in a **neighborhood** of mostly Catholics, a mix of German and Irish Catholics (there was but a single Catholic parish so they had to manage to get along with each other despite their propensities otherwise). There were only a few of us "publicks" (we went to the public elementary school along with the few Catholics unable to afford the Catholic school). Later in my middle years I learned that the very parochial suburb which my neighborhood was part of was itself quite over-churched, a reflection of who that suburb was. The **God was in the air** of Oakley; you could not inhale without absorbing the God. Again I could have rebelled against that; but why would I have wanted to do that? And I grew up in the post-WWII era, surrounded with foxhole and foxhole-like conversionism; church boomed, the Godward was in vogue. Faith in those days was not in the statements of a creed; it was the faithfulness which came of being inspired with Godwardness in every breath and in every turning.

It is not a surprise that I was bent Godward. It would have been extraordinary if I were not.

Wishful Thinking

Perhaps it is only **my wishful thinking, my hoping, my yearning** that makes me seek out a God. I have been in many, many holy places, seeking. I have occasionally, in a few standing stone circles, felt something emanating from a stone, though I know not what that something was. I have washed my face in a multitude of holy wells. I have wandered and mused and pondered in far off, lonely places in Britain and Scotland and Wales and Ireland where saints have been known to trod before me, and I have sensed the veil between this physical and the spiritual realm was very, very thin indeed, where some *thing* or some *Other* was silently, unidentifiably present with me; but I cannot say what or who. I have managed to barely glimpse behind the seen, to hear beneath the flutter under a cardinal's wing. Every fiber within me seems to be saying there is a something I can call "God." But I cannot put my finger in that scar, I cannot say what that something is. Yet, deep within me, from far beyond the distant, I feel the *mustness*. Maybe it is simply a yearning deep inside me for a God greater than the YHWH who has wandered off. But I am by no means sure.

The Witnesses

I have rarely given much credence to the witness of others, having concluded long ago that while their witness just might be an accurate statement of their own experience, it is not mine and therefore has not as great credibility, not the force of reality that my own experiences have, mine being founded firmly on my own *(ordinarily magnificently infallible)* senses and sensibilities. However, on occasion, I stumble across some witnessing that sounds familiar, that strikes chords within me, that echoes down my hallways. And then I pay heed, I lend some credence *(at least temporarily)* I listen, and faintly enjoy.

A Miscellany

Emily Dickinson suggested, "They say that God is everywhere, and yet we always think of Him as somewhat of a recluse." And Joseph Campbell: "We keep thinking of deity as a kind of fact, somewhere; God as a fact. God is simply our own notion of something that is symbolic of transcendence and mystery. The mystery is what's important." Robert Desnos: "I do not believe in God, but I have a sense of the infinite." Terence McKenna adds, "For monkeys to speak of truth is hubris of the highest degree. Where is it writ large that talking monkeys should be able to model the cosmos? If a sea urchin or a racoon were to propose to you that it had a viable truth about the universe, the absurdity of that assertion would be self-evident, but in our case we make an exception." *(All copped from the October 2013 Issue 454 of* **The Sun***, p.48.)*

John Spong

In **Why Christianity Must Change or Die** Spong seems to have a much better handle than I on what he **can** say about the God. He uses a number of phrases:

being	not bound	external presence
Being from beyond this world	infinite center	universal presence
beyond	reality	inviting presence
divine	center of life	source of vitality
ground of being	internal reality	source of life
emerged out of life's very depths	intense personhood	source of love
depth and center of all	life-giver	transcendent
core and ground of all	which gives life	never apart
infinite	vitalizing force	
expansive	profound presence	

I hear his words, they are vaguely simpatico for me, but not entirely; he whispers an image of the God, but so quietly I cannot quite hear the words. *(I may need stronger hearing aids)*.

As Spong speaks in his book these phrases appear to be sufficient for him, adequately expressing his sense of the non-theistic God. He grew up under Tillich's tutelage; I guess "ground of being" still works for him. I tasted of Tillich's writing while in seminary, but he did not suit my taste then, and the "ground of being" sounds good,

Chapter 5: Talking about the God

but still does not work for me. It feels to me a bit of psychological stuff or a cipher. In my ear it promises something, but on my tongue it has no taste.

Where Else do We Look for Evidence of the God?

The God of the Gaps

In ***Your God is too Small*** J. B. Phillips wrote about the **God of the gaps**. He wrote in a world increasingly defined by scientific understandings, a world about to become technological but not quite yet. Phillips pointed out that if we defined God as the doer of things not understood by science, the God of the gaps in between scientific definitions, then our God was gradually being defined out of existence. That God was too small and getting smaller. Instead we need to discover our God not in the gaps in between scientific understandings, but as larger than science, overarching, transcending, the God who gives us science and everything else. If we pray for the weather, if we pray for medical miracles, then our God is too small. I cannot recall what Phillips offered as a viable alternative, though he surely did. He was certainly right in what he challenged. But I suppose this is for me a non-source rather than a source. This is where I should not look for evidence of the God, in the shrinking gaps.

A Critique of Prayer

If I recall correctly it was Ronald Hepburn[7] who posed this **critique of prayer**. He offered a scenario, that, caught in difficult straits, you are told to go out in the darkest part of the night to an opening within the trees of the wood, and there behind a large but unspecified tree near the center will be someone waiting (no appointment needed) who can give help. Don't go around the tree to see the person, just stay put; he'll be there. You are to tell him what the problem is. He won't say anything, but he'll let you know what the solution is, what you are to do, or he may even do something about it. And then you go home, mission accomplished.

A fairly accurate analogy for much intercessory prayer. In most of my own prayer life, when I envisioned my prayer as some form of communication with the God, whether intercessory or other, I have felt as Hepburn suggested, alone, in the dark, speaking to the unseen, and getting no identifiable response. The up-close-and-personal God our Christianity promised us offered no clear or identifiable indicators of his presence. My prayer life has not been a source of any evidence of the God.

---

7. I read this during my senior year in seminary. It is etched in my brain, but I have long ago forgotten and lost the original source in Hepburn's writings.

Part II: My Review of Christian Doctrines

Meditation

I have dabbled in a few efforts. I cannot say that I have made a really serious attempt at any kind of meditation or contemplation; no disciplined, extended practice. I have merely dabbled. But out of that dabbling I have, however unfairly, concluded that for me these offered no evidence or proofs of the God. There is a huge body of evidence offered by mystics, but, in light of Silverman's analysis of *transcendental awarenesses*, I conclude that these evidences are not self-authenticating as Underhill[8] implied, and in light of similar experiential descriptions by at least three other groupings, I judge the mystics's witnessing to be of low reliability; when I weigh their witnesses against my own meditative non-experiences of the God, I find the result utterly inconclusive. Another non-source for me.

Concepts have Evolved

Looking over what I've written here thus far I realize that I've been way too Protestant in my methodology leaning heavily on the Scriptures and what I am thinking at this moment, and I've failed to take a serious look at what transpired between then and now, I've not looked at the tradition and **how our concepts of the God have evolved over the ages**. In remediation I take a second look at the history of God, to see if that history has traced an observable arc whose trajectory might direct my search somewhere. Karen Armstrong's ***A History of God*** is my text. *(In these paragraphs I have no authority, and instead am merely exploring Armstrong's book, learning from her.)*

- She suggests that the story starts in pre-history with a sky-god creator which has no relationship with man, is just an absent creator, one who's gone away. The next step is the more attractive tribal gods, e.g., the Mother Goddess (fertility), and man is seen to be of the same stuff as the gods, only lesser.

- Hebrew texts begin to take shape in the eighth century BC. While *Marduk*, *Ba'al* and *Anat* were not expected to involve themselves in the ordinary, the Hebrews's YHWH begins his history with Abram, involved very much in the ordinary as a close family friend. In the exodus YHWH becomes a very partial and murderous god of war, a tribal deity who inspires terror and insists on distance, reopening the gulf between man and the divine. But in the Axial Age (800 to 200 BC) as the major religions emerge, YHWH is changed into a god who is on the side of the impotent and oppressed, inspiring an ideal of social justice.

- In India the gods were no longer important, but were superseded by religious teachers focusing on an inward realization of truth; the Upanishads evolved a concept of godhood transcending the gods and found intimately present in all

---

8. In ***Mysticism*** Underhill depicts experiences so profound and life-changing as to become self-authenticating. See throughout, but particularly her chapter on "The Unitive Life" 413-43

Chapter 5: Talking about the God

things. Reason is not denied but is transcended. Some Buddhists object to the concept of God as too limiting (theistic?) to express ultimate reality. Language is inadequate to deal with the reality beyond concepts and reason. Theology, beliefs are interesting but unimportant, the good life counts.

- The Greeks push into logic and reason. Plato posits a divine, an unchanging reality beyond, one static and changeless. The universe is rational. Aristotle contributes (among much else) the unmoved mover, pure being, eternal, immobile, spiritual, attracting all things to itself, but which does not direct the world, is indifferent. Aristotle and Plato were concerned with the individual conscience, the good life, and social justice.

- In 742 BC Isaiah in the temple sees *kaddosh, kaddosh, kaddosh* (otherness, otherness, otherness), a *mysterium terribile et fascinans*. YHWH is no longer mere tribal deity or war god, but fills the earth: transcendent power, lord and master of history. The encounter is one with a person who interacts, who has presence, and who drives his people out into exile. Moses' YHWH was triumphalist, Isaiah's is full of sorrow, on the side of the weak and oppressed. The covenant turns out to have been about responsibility, not privilege, about *ḥesed* (loving-kindness, going the second mile, see Matt 5:39–42). The Exile pushes the Jews into a new religious awareness, from a national religion into one more private and toward a more abstract speculation, one of wisdom, revelation replacing logic, and the synagogue becomes more like a school of philosophy. YHWH is intimately present, so doctrine is quite out of place, each individual experiences YHWH in his own way, and social dealings become sacred encounters.

- Christian disciples, awaiting Jesus/messiah's return, experience Jesus as mysteriously still alive, and his powers embodied in them. They think him the incarnation of the God. Jesus revealed a God placid, mild, good, excellent. God becomes (unlike YHWH) mysterious, unknowable, but known to the soul. Christianity becomes urbane (with a welfare system), then a state religion demanding conformity. The continuing intellectual, doctrinal struggle is over who was Jesus, why did he have to die, what does his resurrection mean? The Trinity evolves, creation becomes *ex nihilo*, Augustine makes sin, original sin, the center of his and the Roman Empire's theology. Christianity becomes misogynistic, kerygmatic, dogmatic.

- Mohammad (610 AD) knows the God as a moral imperative, more impersonal, only glimpsed in signs of nature; imaginative efforts can see **through** the world messages for the rational. Islam stresses intelligence, attentiveness to the world, reason, and curiosity. Islam was intended to be unifying. God-consciousness, immanence, and presence in the believer. Islam is politically active against the establishment. God is absolutely omniscient and omnipotent. Then Islam collides with Greek rationalism.

Part II: My Review of Christian Doctrines

- In ninth and tenth centuries the Arab world is in contact with Greek science and philosophy, and Islam enters a renaissance/enlightenment with a rationalistic, objective outlook. Rationalism and faith, revelation and science are seen as consistent, a prophetic philosophy, but Islam sees deeper than rationality. Deep understanding of self is the kingpin. God is the ineffable, incomprehensible, Uncaused Being, Unmoved Mover. Islam becomes strongly mystical. The discussion of God blended philosophy and mysticism, informed by critical intelligence and philosophy.

- Judaism, Christianity and Islam all develop a personal God. All develop the mystical, in which that God becomes normative. **Sufi** (Muslim): mysticism aims at returning to origins, God is one with the ground of each person's being; imagination is the chief religious faculty and there is no objective truth about God. **Kabbalists** (Jewish): emanations from the inscrutable depths of the unknowable Godhead. **Eckhart** (Christian): refuse to be enslaved by any finite ideas about the divine; God is essentially inaccessible, shrouded in impenetrable darkness. Mysticism and rationality conflict, and reason is inadequate to study God. But Europe moves to see God in even more rationalistic terms.

- There are reformers in all the religions: Shia emphasized unconscious and psychological religious faculties; knowledge is not in information but in the process of transformation. God cannot be known objectively. Kabbalists are clear that their stories are not literal, but only hints of the indescribable. Protestants preach absolute sovereignty of God; God is utterly transcendent and inaccessible. Muslims stress the mystery and inscrutability of God, Greeks the paradox, and in the West a personalistic view evolves. Christianity becomes a rational system, a new literalism.

- In the Enlightenment the new myth is progress. God is absent. **Descartes**: the cosmos is godless, chaotic, there is no intelligent design, no mystery; God is revealed in the eternal laws. **Newton**: God becomes reduced to a mechanical system, you know God by contemplating the world. **Spinoza**: God is the aggregate of all governing, immutable laws, is not personal, is inseparable from reality. **Judaism (Mendelssohn)**: a personal God, of wisdom, goodness, justice, ḥesed, and intellect. Islam goes into decline, stepping back from mysticism to rationality.

- In the Great Awakening: God is literally active in the world (anti-intellectual).

- The Death of God: **Hegel**: God is not separate from mundane reality; the divine is a dimension of humanity. **Formstecher**: understands God as the Soul of the World, immanent in all. **Cohen**: God is not an external reality, but an idea of the mind, symbolic, an ethical ideal. **Rosezweig**: God is the ground of being, a divine dimension underlying each of us; God is not a Being. **Weisel**: the challenge of the holocaust to conventional ideas of God.

- The Future of God: **VanBuren**: do without God and hold onto Jesus of Nazareth. **Tillich**: personal theistic God must go; the ground of being, the ultimate concern. **DeChardin**: evolutionary struggle as a divine force, Christ the omega point of the universe, the world is progressing. **Whitehead**: God is inextricably bound up with the world process. **Rahner**: God is the supreme mystery, Jesus the decisive manifestation of man's potential.

Preliminary Summary

I perceive that there certainly is an arc here, a trajectory. It does not appear to be smooth or regular, but moves by forward leaps and regressions, with swerves. Beginning from an absent creator to the more up-close, friendly, swayable gods of the primitives, and then the tribal gods with particular foci, especially gods of war and of fertility (the essentials of survivability). In Isaiah's vision we see a sudden swerve toward transcendence. The gods merge and the unity becomes more far-reaching. And that trajectory of transcendency seems fairly consistent into the present. The driving forces seem to be rationality (with growing abstraction) and the non-rational (revelation, mysticism, imagination). And the direction of the trajectory seems to be toward further abstraction, toward increasing ineffability and decreasing knowability. The contemporary, momentary swerve of the trajectory would seem to be a wholesale movement away from any kind of theism, toward a notion of the God as unlike anything we have thus far imagined. Karen Armstrong notes that in times of social upheaval there is an urge toward fundamentalism, literalism; that seems a reasonable interpretation to me and would seem to be the key **under**current in the current decades.

Conclusions

In seminary I was gently but firmly urged to cleave to the Scriptures, but with only a nodding acquaintance with the tradition. And all my undergraduate work had impelled me toward a critical rationality. And that sufficed throughout my active ministry because I was bankrolled to cleave to orthodoxy. My break with that mode came with retirement and my gradual awakening that there are other ways to perceive and interpret the data of life. And as I look at the above I judge that I have been somewhat caught up, and am sort of in the present trend of that contemporary trajectory: so not alone, not so lost, and certainly in interesting company. This locus urges me not to look back, but gives me no clues about where from here.

I can only wonder what other sources for evidence have I overlooked?

PART II: MY REVIEW OF CHRISTIAN DOCTRINES

Considerations that are Probably Formative

I assume that I walk into this exploration with certain presuppositions that may be actively shaping my very perceiving, my thinking, my concluding. If I am not clear and conscious of those, they will surely warp the whole effort without my awareness, prohibiting the possibility of objectivity and rationality. My intention is to follow wherever the data leads, but to do that I must be as clear-minded and unblindered as possible. These are the pre-assumptions I can identify:

What Kind of God?

The first consideration I need to be clear about is the **kind of God I have hoped** to find, because if I'm not exceedingly careful, these particular, older yearnings will cloud my present awarenesses, perceptions, processings and concludings. So, what is it I have wanted in the God?

I am first of all a child of the Christian church, and that piety has promised us that the God loves us, cares about and for us, protects us, and will in some sense receive us back (after all, we are of God's breath). What else can I say about the God of Christian piety? That he is just and merciful (there is the sense in the Hebrew writing that justice **is** mercy). That he is most of all supposed to be personal, which is to say, the God deals with me as a person, as a special being of value to the God. If I cull through all that and pick out what I want in the God, I come up with only a few attributes: powerful, compassionate, understanding, warm (caring, loving), conversational (in some sense), and above all personal. I have sought a God with whom I can relate. I have sought a God who knows **me** as a unique individual, with whom I can deal. And one more knowledgeable than I.

I must also be clear that I have already, before starting this process of digesting the raw data, tentatively concluded that the God is ultimately unknowable: that the YHWH of the Hebrew Scriptures was more a projection of the national need than an objective perception of an Adonai, that the God of the Christian writings is a metamorphosed version of the Hebrew YHWH, and may be as much a projection of need as a discernment of the teachings of both Jesus and Paul (two **very** Jewish teachers), and that the gods of mystics are probably little more than their own projected *(and unauthenticatable)* insights.

This is the centermost *platz* of my starting.

I Came of Age Theologically in the Year of the Death of God School

That was a movement easily, readily misunderstood, and consequently passed by without much comment or notice given. Most people took the words literally, and bemusedly wondered how anyone could think the immortal god could die. It was just a nubbin of nonsense to them. Others thought the words bespoke of atheism and therefore simply rejected such talk without consideration. It was also the year of ***God's Frozen People*** and ***The Comfortable Pew***. I understood the whole movement to be saying that the old images of the God had gone dead, no longer had meaning or power, that we needed to be searching out new, more vital, more life-giving images of the God. I reverberated to that notion, even in my seminary years. So I suppose it should come as no surprise to me that today the conventional God of the church has died for me. For me it had been dying half a century ago.

Cultural Underpinnings

I spoke briefly above of the cultural stuff that is so deeply a part of me and my thinking: family, community, regional, national, mega-culture; layers upon layers of cultural stuff washing over me in my formation, impressed upon me by my community, fondled by me again and again and however unwittingly adopted. It is so much a largely unconscious part of me that I suppose I can not possibly factor it all the way out of my thinking and processing. My culture, the agglomerate of the factors and dynamics which shaped me as I grew up includes a deep, foundational, perhaps unshakeable belief in a God, some God, some super-being which gave shape to this world and which in some undefined way still shapes our lives. That conviction is at the bedrock of our culture. And while I can challenge it, I am unable to simply walk away from it.

Meaning-Giving

It is my sense that we (excluding the Buddhists) look Godward to discover the **meaning of life**. But in both the Hebrew Scriptures and the Christian writings I find that YHWH and the Abba are not specific or clear about the meaning of life. The Scriptures make lots of suggestions about the hows of living, some of which suggestions are destructive or even dangerous garbage in the twenty-first century (e.g., women are self-propelled incubators of the male seed and therefore appropriately are chattel property). The only purpose-filled commandment the God gave us was to "be fruitful and multiply and replenish the earth." But other than that I find YHWH not a very fruitful referent when I ponder the meaning of life and the purpose of living. And without the God as referent and command-giver I find humankind bumbling in the wilderness with regard to purpose and meaning.

Unanswered Questions

My overwhelming sense is that there are so many questions left unanswered, and even left unexamined: 1) How can **belief in God**, the one of Hebrew and Christian writing, be **so central** to our culture, to my own life, and yet, as I now look over the matter, **so**

wrong? 2) If the God is a force from outside (alongside, simultaneous, synonymous) our physical universe, **how can we detect** that force? What tools, what ways of perceiving, and perhaps measuring are available to us? How do we go about identifying, or even detecting that force? 3) With no ways at hand to **perceive**, how can we **describe** the God, or where the God is, or in what way the God is? I know of other non-physical realms: emotionality (though emotions do have bio-physical concurrents), social dynamics (which while not human are embodied in and enacted solely by humans); so it is not unreasonable to conceive of some non-physical realm in which the God is. But I have no cognitive or sensory awareness of such a realm.

Speculation

I have always been a **speculative theologian**, panning for theological gold. I have always reached beyond the conventional, ever since seminary education squashed my image of the old, white-bearded gent, reaching to grasp whatever understanding of the God was just beyond my fingertips, rejecting the debased one in hand. Restless fingertips. Now after concluding that so far it's all been fool's gold, this stream of the conventional church and conventional theology and doctrine seems dry of any god-dust. I'm off speculating in other lands.

The Nature of Our Scriptures

I often refer to the **Scriptures**, more often the Hebrew Scriptures than the Christian writings. At this time of my life I **cannot hold** them to be **inspired** by the God any more than any other Scriptures, or kinds of scriptures. I hold our Scriptures to be the repository of some very keen, deep, powerful, useful insights; but I find that those are mixed indiscriminately with loads and loads of dross and trash, and even rotting garbage. So I think that we must sort through those Scriptures exceedingly carefully, and thoughtfully, and with our eyes wide open to the realities of this world. Not everything written therein is good, beneficial, useful; nor can the Scriptures themselves tell us what to heed within them, and what to pass by, and what to condemn to Gehenna. Along with my theologizing buddy Susan I hold the stories to be the most important, the most powerful, the most useful, the most insightful bits of those Scriptures, not because of what they tell us, but because they are exceedingly well crafted jewels into which we can gaze to project and discover our own insights into this world, and into ourselves as well. So I do not expect them to tell me eternal truths, but I do use them as tools with which I can better discover truths. So I cherry-pick, as wisely as I can. And I try to avoid stepping in the *oompah*.

Further, I do perceive that the Holy Scriptures are for the most part used as a Rorschach. What insights are encapsulated within those writings are insights appropriate to the ages in which they were captured and written, and not necessarily for today. I have found that the richness of those holy writings lies in my engaging them as fully as I can, with all my imagination, probing, questioning, challenging, wondering, and even playing, and then carefully examining all that comes out of that engagement with as keen an eye as I can muster, understanding that nearly all that has come out of the engagement has come out of me, is my own projection, and that buried along with all that stuff **may** be some insight that is indeed worth paying attention to, but that such insight, if it be there, will be buried under piles of garbage, most of which is also mine, and does need to be put aside for the garbage-collector. Not everything I glean out of the holy writings is gold.

And whatever inspiration there may be surrounding those writings occurs in the moments I am engaging them, not because they were written long ago when they may indeed have been inspired, **for that age**.

An Aside about Faith

I concluded, in my second year of seminary, primarily on the basis of one word-study I did of one word,[9] that the Hebrew notion of faith had nothing to do with belief (neither incidental beliefs [e.g., the sky is blue, or the hat is red] nor the core, life-driving beliefs [which I call "values"]) but was about behavior, about faithfulness, loyalty, fidelity. So regardless of whatever I think (and on occasion contrary to what I happen to be thinking), I go to church (nearly) every Sunday, I sing the hymns, I rotely reiterate the prayers, creeds, and such, I stand and sit (and used to kneel). I participate. I am faithful. Why? Not because of what I hold as truth inside my mind (that truth is too feeble and insubstantial and temporary to be of much moment), but because that faithfulness seems to hold together, to knead together, to give cohesion and coherence and force to whatever it is that constitutes the spiritual being which is me, and, more importantly, even enables me to look beyond myself toward The Greater (you must define that for yourself).

Tentative Conclusions

Now I begin to amble, to wander amongst these piles, poking at this to see if it moves, prodding at that to urge it into some sort of shape.

The Odds are "No"

When I look at the whole mess of thinking and experiencing that I've dredged up, cull through it all and toss out the useless, and throw the salvageable onto the balance, it appears to me that the **odds are "no"** to the question of the God; but that

---

9. See Chapter 9 (232)

conclusion doesn't get there. I feel incomplete; without substantial or reliable result. I cannot trust that there are no other sources of evidence, sources I've overlooked, or not yet searched out, discovered. In **Why Does the World Exist?** Jim Holt explores the thinking of philosophers and mathematicians and physicists and theologians across the centuries and concludes somewhat reluctantly that he finds no reliable reason or purpose for the world's existence, and in the process he also concludes that there is no reliable evidence for or against the existence of God. I come roughly, albeit by a quite different course, to the same place. But like Robert Wright I find that result **incomplete, unsatisfying**. I reject out of hand the notion that Godwardness is in our genes; that notion, until proven otherwise, is silly pseudo-science (say I). And I also reject the adamant and hostile assertions of atheists that there is no god; they have no more proof that there is no god than I have that the God is. So I find myself in limbo.

The God Keeps Popping Up

Ron notices that "the God" keeps popping up all over in my writings. I have asserted that I think the God is unknowable, and yet I can't let the issue go. I may be merely validating, or refusing to invalidate the thirty-four years of my life expended in the church. Or am I merely echoing a God-talk language that has been several years dead for me? *(I majored in Latin and Greek, two other dead languages; maybe dead languages are my speciality?)* I know I am trying to get once more in touch with that which is beyond, that which I once thought I knew, that for which I have only the one word, God. So the God, the Beyond, *(or whatever)* keeps popping into my conversation, without my knowing what it might be. Is it proof that down deep, underneath all this meandering and ruminating, I still believe in the God? I don't know. On the other hand, while I have pronounced the God unknowable, I did not absolutely deny the God's existence. While I might be reverently agnostic, I reject atheism as stupid and illogical. How could I responsibly deny the existence of that which I think unknowable? That would be a *non sequitor* an absurdity. So I **do** hold atheism to be absurd, an angry rebellion (and one must ask, "Angry at what?"), but not a logical position. Maybe atheism is just silly, and light headed. So, yes, the God keeps popping up as I speak. Perhaps one day I'll recognize it anew.

What the God Might Be

On rare occasions I get a **vague sense of** what the **God might** be. Let me try. **Datum One**: Plato posited a realm of non-physical archetypes, patterns of which the physical are merely shadows. Aristotle thought that this reality is composed of stuff plus structure. And I reflect that while the stuff is physical, the structure has no physical being, it is non-stuff; it is other, but very much the compelling part of this reality. The deeper physicists delve today, the more they discover less and less physical but more and more structure. And I must ask, "Where is the structure written, etched, fixed?" It is compelling. It is transcendent. It is *Other* (than physical.) Can it, or does it, exist apart from the stuff? Or are the stuff and the structure so intertwined, so interdependent, so co-existent that they cannot be separated, cannot exist apart, the material and the non-material? Are there realm(s) outside of this physical universe where that transcendent structure exists apart from the physical? Or are the tangible and intangible one-and-inseparable and just in this here and now? Or might the physical realm be so shot through with the God, just like the structure, that we are unable to detect it?

Datum Two: Bowers has a sense, a notion, a vaguest picture that there exists somewhere (in a non-physical realm) an ideal of how human society might be structured to accommodate survivability, community, individual, and other. Where might that ideal be **written**? Is **that** the God?

Datum Three: There is a set of values (interlocked, interrelated, intertwined) which, if successfully enacted, would comprise an ideal *(for both the community and the individual simultaneously)* social structure. Where might that set of values be written? *(Note: datum 2 and datum 3 might be alternate descriptions of a single notion.)*

Posit a gazillion such data, bundle them all together. That might comprise the God. *(That is as far as I can go right now with this notion. But check in with the notions below.)*

The God as Metaphor

On other days I get this flash (which fades just as quickly) that the notion of "God" is a metaphoric embodiment, an intuition of **the whole ball of wax**: the physical universe, the life I'm living, the ways to live in harmony together *sans* endless conflict, horror, destruction, to live ideally. Meaning in life. The safe way into a future for us, all of us, us of the ages to come. And everything else. Wrap it all up and call it the God. And in the worshiping of the God, I am simply, in many different ways, saying "Yes" to all of that.

God as the Source

Ron Santoni suggests it might be possible to think of the God as the ultimate source. Of healing: we can enumerate and understand the multitude of factors that go into his wife's healing: the surgeons and nurses, the medications, her own attitude and zest. But whence comes the healing force itself? Is that the God? • We can embroider that theme: the source of living: not so much the life itself which somehow and for some reason emerges from the stardust, but rather the sense of living, the verve of living, that which makes living more than mere mobile life-form? Is that the God? • You can embroider this one: Love? • Morality: humankind builds moralities, but what gives the force and direction, the bent to morality? • Values: definitely a human creation. We build our own value systems, individually and corporately in some kind of concert, but whence the drive and ultimate direction? The bent? The arc? The moral direction? The God as source. As root. As ground of being. What pushes?

God Withdrawing

A Reformed Jewish layman well educated in the Hebrew Scriptures and mishnah and talmud, and whom I encountered in a five-evening conversation with our rector on Moses and the Exodus lays out a very clear understanding of Adonai: that he hand-picked this people, brought them out of slavery, gave them the life-giving Torah to live by, forged them into his people, gave them land, and then **gradually withdrew** leaving them the freedom to work it out for themselves, to learn to live Torah, with the understanding that he had given everything they needed; so now, "Do it!" That depiction queues up with my reading of the Hebrew Scriptures through Jack Miles's eyes.[10] It also has a kind of a deist ring to it. Certainly moving in an Enlightenment direction. And it fits neatly, but only semi-believably, with my own thinking. It is certainly quite unlike the eighteenth-century Pietism that we've come through and which has left its crumbs in our whiskers. Dan's thesis is not unattractive to me, but not really satisfying either.

God as Verb

What if we think of the God not as a concept but as a verb, as action: flowing, fluid, moving, doing, evolving? Such non-concept-based thinking is alien to us, difficult, if not impossible. My Indo-European heritage, my very language and thought patterns are born of and immutably fixed to concepts. We western Europeans think in concepts linked by verbs. Our universe is one of clearly-defined and fixed concepts. So the God becomes a concept in our thinking, a noun: the subject, the object, in a prepositional phrase, or a subordinate clause. And likewise the attributes we have affixed to the God are appropriate to a concept: omniscience, omnipotence, perfection, immutability and unchangingness, love, leadership/guidance; you can make your own list, but those attributes are the descriptions of a fixed concept. And unfortunately that's the only way I've learned to think of the God, as a fixed concept. Can I even conceive of (much less think and ponder about) the God as a bundle of actions, motions, doings, and the God itself invisible and undefinable, only glimpsed as fleeting motions: loving, creating, healing. Delineated only by its motions with no conceptual outlines? Can I learn to watch and interpret the actions, the verbs, the motions, rather than fence in the fixed and motionless concept? The effort seems inescapably mercurial to me, it scootches out of my mind's grasp before I can get even a fingernail's hold on it.

---

10. Miles, *God: a biography*, passim

Chapter 5: Talking about the God

Why bother with the God at all?

I went to a two-hour introductory session at a Buddhist meditation center. You can't absorb much in just two hours, but the little I did absorb was instructful to this conversation. The presenter, Lama Kathy Wesley, stated flatly that there is no god figure in Buddhism. That queues with the Dalai Lama responding that Buddhists don't talk much about the God. A Presbyterian minister in the group asked her how Buddhism can call itself a religion if it has no God? The lama's answer was unclear. My response would have been simply that the God is not necessary to a religion; the reference to the God is always prudential, to lend authority, or to sanction. Religions are basically about how to live in the here and now, and the outside-somewhere-God is at best ancillary; and in those sects where the God says the wrong things he can be quite destructive to living in the present. Buddhism is simply about how to live in the present, with complete compassion for all.

Now I do an Experiment

Let's assume for the moment that the God is. Then what?

First, What might be the givens for this Experiment?

1) The God is not to be found within this physical universe, that is, the God has no physical being within this physical realm. I must look elsewhere. I had to conclude this when my seminary professors killed off the old white-haired gent in glistering robes enthroned upon a cloud, and when I listened to the physicists talking about relativity and quantum mechanics, and when I heard J.B.Phillips mutter in my ear, "Your god of the gaps is too small." I had to look elsewhere *(but was inhibited until retirement by my professional responsibilities).*

    2) So it follows that the God is in some non-physical realm, and therefore manifestations, evidence, experiences of the God should reasonably (but necessarily?) also be non-physical. I know there are non-physical realms. Descartes opined, "*Dubito ergo cogito ergo sum.*" Such thoughts were, and still are, non-physical. We do not yet understand sufficient about the brain to know precisely how such thinking happens within the physiology of the brain, but we can be clear, I think, that the thoughts themselves are non-physical, that is, they stand alone, apart and separate from whatever physical processes within the brain bring them into being. Those thoughts exist in some non-physical realm, though encouched within this physical universe. In a similar vein, consciousness is non-physical. We know less about consciousness than about the brain, and while we may be able to locate some manifestations of consciousness (e.g., awareness) within the brain, it seems to me that consciousness itself is a function of the mind, and I know of no clear identification of the mind within the

physical realm. I allow, for myself at least, that, given these two examples, there are non-physical realms operating inside this physical universe.

3) But the God seems not contained within those non-physical realms I find operating within this physical universe. The God does seem utterly other, outside and apart from the physical universe. Transcendent. For some, immanent, somehow present, though non-physical, yet imbuing, saturating, enfolding, warmly embracing *(not my experience)*.

Where then do I Search for Evidence?

I have no vision and few tools to see what lies beyond, utterly outside this physical universe which the God may not enter. Does the God stand straddled, with one foot in some extra-physical universe realm and the other reaching in, standing upon some non-physical realm which is operative here within the physical universe while not being part of it? Might I see evidence of the God within those non-physical realms? What clues might I be looking for?

Let me tick off some of the non-physical realms I see working within the confines of this physical universe but without any physical being: cultural forces (e.g., tribalism, Western European, Arabian and Islamic, Far Eastern), group dynamics (e.g., family, fraternity) and systemic dynamics (e.g., totalitarianism, pure democracy, industrialization, urbanization), ideologies (unfettered capitalism, libertarianism), moralities (e.g., greed, power-mongering, lust), individual psychologies (e.g., a psychiatric social worker I worked alongside thought that the Holy Spirit worked through the sub-conscious mind), and societal structures *[an incomplete list]*. These are some of the places where God might be influencing without our awareness. But by studying the dynamics and factors in all of these citations I can usually account for everything without using God as referent. None of those has mind, all operate through the agency of individuals and agglomerations of individuals, and historical patterns. And just how might God go about exerting that influence through these? And more importantly to this paper, how would I go about detecting that influence?

One possibility: if in studying the dynamics of a given situation exhaustively, I come up with a significantly different force analysis than would cause the actual result, then I must posit some so far undetected or undiscovered force. And if after further study I can still not account for that significant divergence, then I must conclude that the divergence is caused by some unknown or undetectable force, possibly the God. Problems: this is no proof, not even a significant indicator. It is more in line with J. B. Phillips's god of the gaps, using the God as an explanation where I can discover no other explanation. No good.

Chapter 5: Talking about the God

What Kind of Evidence Can I Accept?

I reiterate that Ron suggests that although I deem the God utterly unknowable, that does not necessarily mean that the God is not influencing me. Yes, I allow that assertion, which in turn suggests that one place I might look for evidence of the God is in the instances when I might be influenced by the God unawares.

A Test Case: I cite once more my experience while praying in the blackness of predawn in the abbey ruins on Caldey Island. I had been led to Caldey by a triangulation, the same message from two unrelated sources; Caldey turns out to have a Celtic Christian history. Was I led there by God's influence? I have no evidence, only my presumptions about *triangulation*. I suddenly hear the fifteenth-century monks processing silently into the choir and I sense presences warm, accepting, friendly. A light predawn rain is falling on the slate roof which might account for the sound of rustling robes; such *presences* are corroborated by Bro. Gildas and Sr. Delores. I am given a prayer I've been struggling to write.

In order to write a set of daily offices in the style of the prayers of Alexander Carmichael's **Carmina Gadelica** I had sought out that ideal place immersed in the Cistercians's discipline and setting. In the mystery of that setting and immersed in the presumption of the God twenty-four/seven by all of the monks intensely surrounding me, was it not nearly inevitable that I would have some authenticating experiences of the God? I understood that a light rain was a scientific explanation of the sound in the chapel ruins as likely as the processing of fifteenth-century monks. I was cognizant that the prayer I'd been given could have been as simple as my subconscious delivering the solution my conscious mind had not been able to solve. God was not the only or even a necessary explanation. At the time I concluded the explanation did not have to be either/or, but today, for the sake of this test, I must make that assumption. To be **solidly reliable** evidence for the God, there can be no alternative explanation. So this test case fails the examination; it is not conclusive, nor even solid evidence for the God. It is at best ephemeral and unreliable.

I could cite and examine many other such experiences: God's voice in the seminary chapel; two other times in Ireland receiving nearly composed prayers; giving my life to Christ at youth conference. But to spare me the writing and you the reading, I simply report that as I scan quickly through the whole set I find they all have similarly double explanations, and so are equally inconclusive, vague and unreliable. And when I pull the whole aggregation into one pile, the result is still exceedingly inconclusive, only very waveringly pointing in a sorta Godward direction.

Reliability of Evidence

I find this the most central, but perilously difficult question. My scientifically biased mind searches for verification, for hard data, for high reliability, for exceeding plausibility. But as I scan, and restudy what I've written here, and all that I've dredged up, I find vagueness, soft and mucky (or murky?) data, double explanations, ephemeral mists. Has it all any plausibility? Only if I allow without challenge all the presumptions I bring to the cause. Reliability? I find only the vaguest senses of reliability, and that often seems more hope that critical judgment. I cannot lay down useful rules for the reliability of my evidences in this study.

> *Note: As I write and re-read, I become more clearly aware of how entrapped, ensnared my thinking is, entangled and confined in between two worlds: one is the world of quantum mechanics and such, a world I cannot see or touch, but a world I understand, with considerable confidence, to be more fundamental, more the basic reality than the other, the world in which I really live. I rap my knuckles on the wooden table where I sit, experiencing its solidity. Here I really live, but knowing intellectually, knowing in my very abstract sense, that the solid, wooden table which I rap is really composed of molecules, and they of atoms, and they of sub-atomic particles, and that most of the solid tabletop I rap with my knuckles is brute space, emptiness, nothingness. I wriggle in that snare.*

Summary

The mystical and the numinous I have found inconclusive. I believe these two to be of one sort, and that sort to be ultimately unverifiable, non-self-authenticating. They are soft data, at best, vague, and fairly unexaminable. While vaguely illuminating, they cannot be demonstrated to be from or of the God.

I note that throughout this writing I have discounted or ignored the Holy Spirit. The third person of the Trinity has always been an anomaly to me, I've never known what to do with it. The three modes[11] of God (Father/Creator, Son as redeemer, Spirit as sustainer active in the present world) is as close as I can get to any understanding of the Holy Spirit, and that's not so very mystery-filled.

I have not undertaken the logician's ontological proofs of the God. My recollection is that all have been disproved, shown to be reliant upon hidden presuppositions. Even if valid they tell me nothing about the God itself.

I am left with my own presumptions, with the cultural biases that have been woven into my very fabric since before I was born. Those too are neither provable nor unprovable, of low reliability, and without hard data. Nothing on which I might make a stand.

---

11. The rejected doctrine of modalism (a.k.a. Sabellianism) is the non-Trinitarian or anti-Trinitarian belief that the Heavenly Father, Resurrected Son, and Holy Spirit are three different modes or aspects of one monadic God, as perceived by the believer, rather than three distinct persons within the Godhead—i.e., that there are no real or substantial differences among the three, such that there is no substantial identity for the Spirit or the Son.

There is then the mass of witnessing from those who preceded me, and of those who now surround me; those that I see and hear are couched in conventional Christian language and metaphor, and when I step away from the Hebrew Scriptures and Christian writings as the most authoritative source, I find that horde of self-authenticating witnesses becomes a mish-mash, an untanglable mess of differences and contradictions, a cacophony of words rushing past my ears with nearly no meaning or content. I step back from them in dismay. And then I cherry-pick to reinforce my own closely held values; but I distrust their presentation of the God.

The Hidden God

I learn belated to this discussion that in all this laboring I've been sharing I'm not alone. It seems that theologians and philosophers have been struggling with the problem of Divine Hiddenness for over a century now. *(Come to think of it, I've heard Ron mumble that phrase, the problem of Divine Hiddenness.)* This revelation came by way of an article in the ***Anglican Theological Review***[12] in which Travis Dumsday reviews the problem and C. S. Lewis's response to the problem. Briefly stated:

> *If there is a loving God, surely he would make his existence apparent to us, and in a way we could not rationally doubt. (Because . . . the nature of love . . . will seek an open relationship with the object of love, . . . [and] . . . our ultimate well-being requires a positive relationship with God.)*

If the God exists, why doesn't he make his existence more obvious, in a way not rationally dubitable?

While Lewis, in his writings, is not responding directly to this problem of divine hiddenness, Dumsday cites many passages in which Lewis does seem to speak to the problem. I will not reiterate Dumsday's whole article, but simply lift bits from it. Lewis finds God's seeming unavailability unsurprising, since God, being immaterial, is inherently inaccessible to our sense faculties. But if God manifests himself indirectly via visible signs (e.g., Moses' burning bush), why not to all people? Lewis responds, the burning bush is furniture within this world and cannot reveal transcendence; Moses at the bush faced a choice, to believe or not to believe. The Christian story is that Christ was initially perceived to be God by very few people. Science cannot discover the immaterial reality *[God]*; a certain faculty of recognition is required, i.e., the conscience. God is accessible via the moral law.

Another mode of recognition might be a non-sensory, intense apparent awareness (i.e., the mystical experience). Lewis thinks this mode has an inherent weakness, that it is not right to produce rationally indubitable belief. Lewis insists on God's immateriality, and that two immaterials (my consciousness and the God) cannot meet except in some common medium which forms their external world or environment

---

12. Dumsday, *ATR* Winter 2015, Volume 97, Number 1 (33-51).

(or conversely, if they could meet without that common medium, they would then be indistinguishable) So **all** contact between the divine and the human mind is without common medium, hence not external, but possibly internal, yet dubitable. The mystical experience has the feeling of absolute certainty but remains rationally dubitable.

After exploring that mode Dumsday returns to Lewis's insistence that God does reveal himself by granting awareness both of the moral law and of its motivating force. The moral law transcends both the material realm and ourselves, and is eternally and necessarily true. The moral law transcends the natural order, indicating there is something beyond, something like a mind. And the content of the moral law reveals a good deal about the character of the giver. The Law points to the Mind in which the Law resides, and that is as immediate a contact with the God as we can have. Lewis's chief example then is *thinking* in general, but in particular moral thinking. That thinking yields us, not indubitable knowledge of the God, but as close to it as we can get.

My Response to Lewis

While it is somewhat **comforting** for me to know that the likes of C. S. Lewis also struggled with this problem of divine hiddenness, I am **not greatly moved** by his arguments (as Dumsday depicts them). Lewis cites two modes of knowing the God, knowledge of a universal moral law appropriated by the conscience, and the mystical experience. Lewis almost dismisses the mystical experience in as much it does not yield a **rationally indubitable knowing** of the God. I agree with him so far as he goes, but I go a few paces farther on that matter, accepting Silverman's psychiatric appraisal that the mystical experience is of the same ilk as episodes of incipient schizophrenia and psychedelic experiences (as well as sensory deprivation episodes); all four can produce profound insight, but none has verifiable or plausible grounds to claim divine origin. I view mysticism as occasionally useful but not particularly Godly.

Lewis understands that our conscience is the faculty through which we appropriate the moral law, that the moral law is universal, and being such is not only clear evidence of the God in whose Mind the moral law resides, but also shows us in its content much about the Mind of the God. It appears to me that his thinking is buttressed by a whole set of quite challengeable presumptions. Being a student of social systems, it is clear to me that the moral law which Lewis embraces is neither universal *(in our world particularism is the standard of moralities, i.e., moral codes are relative to particular societies, so that so-called honor killings are abhorrent to Americans, but are quite acceptable, even mandated in some eastern societies)* nor necessarily of God. Further, I am a child of the era of psychology, and tend to see through those eyes; I understand the conscience not necessarily to be a gift from the God but rather an essential part of each person's psychology (somewhat akin to Freud's superego), which we garner during our formative years from our parents and community and which grows into an integral but malleable part of our adult psychological structures. I believe the moral law which the conscience appropriates is much more of the community's and the culture's *mores* than of the God.

And lastly, being three quarters of a century later than Lewis, I quibble: Lewis seems to believe that thinking, reasoning, rational thought is unique to the human species. Given what we are learning these days about other species and about the seamlessness of the evolutionary process, I judge it presumptuous to assert that only humans can think. We know not how thinking evolved *(at least one neurologist has suggested that the brain is more a chemical factory generating the chemistry that activates and manages the body than a thinking machine, and that thinking is sort of a chance side benefit of the brain)* but both the elephant and the greater whales have larger brains than we, and demonstrate some capabilities quite similar to ours. On what grounds can we reliably assert that only we, not they, can think? I hold that the jury is still out on that issue.

Results

I find the whole of this exploration quite unsatisfying. That should not come as a surprise to me. I expect that down deep inside me I anticipated that I could come to no conclusion. Thousands through the ages have pondered this issue and collaborated to bring the aggregate thinking to this point. I could not realistically have expected myself to overturn some stone they had never before bothered to even kick. I wander amongst these piles of data and find them ranging from moderately to fairly unreliable, mostly a vague pathway cobbled with faint and ephemeral impressions. Overlooking the mass altogether I see that the set of presumptions we bring to the search is the weightiest factor, and when I try to factor those presumptions out, I am left with the most inconclusive of stuff: impressions, hopes, and such. But no place one can firmly place his foot to step off. I suppose the hardest and most reliable data I can lay hand on amongst all this stuff, the most plausible, reasonable and informative, is the brilliant flash of crimson I see as a cardinal flits from branch to branch in my back yard. And perhaps that is enough. At least for today. But how about tomorrow?

Willard Quine's Non-Foundationalism

With the little I know about the human brain, Quine's non-foundationalism[13] makes great sense to me, that all that I can know is as a web, a net, a fabric: not separate

13. In his 1951 essay, "Two dogmas of Empiricism," Willard Quine proposed a non-foundationalist model of human knowledge. He argued that each of our claims about reality – each of our attempted descriptions of it – reflects "the totality of our so-called knowledge or beliefs." This totality is a manmade fabric. At the center of the fabric – the center of that web, that net – lie beliefs or assumptions, that both color our entire outlook and stand at a distance from, and thus relatively impervious to, direct experience. At the edges, or "sensory periphery," of the fabric lie beliefs of another sort, those reflecting our direct experience of the external world. These latter beliefs take shape, however, under

and distinct bits, nor a structure built upon foundational knowledge, but a woven fabric incorporating and relating all I know to all I know. And I suppose that my knowledge of the God used to be near the center of the web, central to my thinking, and thus fairly protected from my day to day experiences and learnings, the peripheral knowings, but fairly influential of **how** I perceived and **what** I perceived. And I sense that my knowledge of God has gradually, with all my critical questioning and pilgrim wandering, migrated, or been dragged away from the center, though not so far as to the periphery; and it still is very important to me as is witnessed by all this writing I've been doing over the last several years. But no longer the very center.

On the other hand, it occurs to me that perhaps my knowledge of the God has not so much been nudged (or tugged) away from the center of the web, as been allowed to subside to some lower level, that the web of my knowings is multi-layered, or three dimensional, and knowledge of the God has slowly and quietly *flumped* downward, still close to the center, but underlying, sagging, and unwittingly supporting the very center of my knowing *(this study has become almost as much about my thinking and way of knowing as about the God)*. That image fits my sense of where the God is today in my living: unseen, unperceived, non-intervening, silent, but watching, curious, mildly amused, and hovering underneath it all. And worried. If the God is speaking to me at all today, he speaks out of his worry!

And Then it Occurs to Me

If the God ultimately proves unknowable; and if the God cannot be defined in any credible or comprehensible or useful way; and if the God, who despite his unknowability might still be influencing me and you and the issues and matters of this world, cannot be in any reliable or measurable way detectible; and if these and other such conditions apply, then of what use is the God? In what way does it matter whether the God is, or is not? If, as Bonhoeffer suggested, we must learn to live as if God were not a given, then why should I care? And then, the God no longer being the law-giver, I must look elsewhere to found any moral or ethical structure, and I must further devise

---

the influence of the former: I might see God in a mother's kiss, you might see nature and nothing more. The whole fabric, or body, of the knowledge we claim to have comes into play when we interpret what our senses present to us directly. In turn, our sensory experiences – especially when they are somehow at odds with our total outlook – affect the whole fabric: due to "logical interconnections" among our beliefs, reevaluation of one occasions reevaluation of others, including those beliefs closer to the fabric's center. Still, the totality of what we claim to know is so "underdetermined" by direct experience that there is "much latitude of choice" as to what beliefs need to be adjusted "in light of any single contrary experience." . . . knowledge is a web or fabric, vulnerable at the edges due to the force of experience, yet obstinate at the center due to the persistence, and relative invulnerability, of our core convictions. Knowledge on this account undergoes constant reconstruction, but the process is immensely complicated, not least due to what Quine calls "our natural tendency to disturb the total system as little as possible."

adequate sanctions to make that structure enforceable. And if that turns out to be possible, then what need have I of the God?

Post Scriptum:

We went to Al Huggins's funeral one afternoon. It started with someone singing "Amazing Grace," and I could only think of how intensely my deceased buddy Steve Williamson detested that song. I find the sentiment of the words . . . *(thoughtful pause)* . . . "stupid" is the only descriptor I can come up with. But behind the tune itself I hear singing inside my mind bagpipes, which I much enjoy. I was drawn in, and for that hour I was a part of **our** community, sharing the grief of Al's family. Frankly most of my conscious attention was focused on Scott Hayes's beautiful four month old daughter as he sat directly ahead of me, new life in the midst of the celebration of a death, her mind struggling to discern, to learn what her eyes were seeing. For the closing we heard a rendition of "On Eagle's Wings," and I teared up some. It sang a beautiful image, a hope. A hope in which I place so little credence; but the community's hope, so who am I to denigrate it? As little as I know about the God these days, it was right to be there, in that celebration. I have said before that what we believe intellectually is of very little importance. (I need to amend that statement to be clear I am talking about theological beliefs, doctrines and such.) That stuff has become not very central to my faith. My faith has to do with what we were doing there in that hour; not so much what was said, but very much what we were doing. And my experience that afternoon affirmed that conviction in me once more, that faith has very little to do with what we think about the God; it has everything to do, with our faithfulness, our loyalty, our steadfastness within the community.

And that is as far as I can go until we begin to dialogue on this matter.

Chapter 6: What Think Ye of Jesus?

THIS CHAPTER MAY BE complicated and iconoclastic. Some of the ancient arguments are complicated, not easy for us of the twenty-first-century mind to understand, but it has been necessary to reiterate some of that in order to be clear how we got from there to here, which in turn helps understand where *here* is. Follow as best you can, and where the details are just too complicated, pass over with caution so you do not lose some point important to your understanding. Be mindful, the ancients argued from a literalist stance, trying to pull together bits of Scripture which are really quite disparate; today many of us reason from a post-literalist stance, and from a contextual and overview stance, so that the ancients's thinking appears to us arcane, obscure, culturally bound, and unduly and complicatedly nit-picky, i.e., flat out unreasonable. Our reasoning might appear the same to them, but it's their reasoning that got us to this place.

This chapter is not comprehensive. I will tackle only three issues which are central to my thinking these days, namely 1) was Jesus divine? 2) Was Jesus' death to atone for our sins? and, 3) What does Jesus mean to me?

My Preface

I have never been able to plumb how Jesus could be fully human and fully divine. Those are mutually exclusive in my mind, so it just has never worked for me. I arrived at seminary with my childish understanding that Jesus was the Son of God, namely something *other*. In New Testament studies I began to get in touch with the human side of Jesus. So in the early years of my ministry I emphasized his humanity, both because that's what I was still exploring, and because my intuition was that most laity were so over-focused on the divine side of Jesus that they didn't really consider his human side. So that was my early emphasis, helping them (and me) get in touch with the human Jesus who could relate to their daily, human lives. One of my earliest sermons was summarized by a not-enthralled parishioner, "Jesus was a loud-mouthed Jew with B.O." My words were blasphemous in his ears. And actually he was not far off target, maybe even right on, though he meant it as an insult. That same year I was invited to preach at the community Good Friday "Seven Last Words" service, a three-hour squishy liturgy that proffered soft, warm, (odiferous?) homilies; I was lucky, I drew "My God, my God, why hast thou forsaken me?" And I preached it to the hilt. No one listened through that sermon without some notion of what it might have been like to die on a Roman cross. I was never again invited to preach at that service. I fairly quickly concluded that most worshipers were much more comfortable with a sweet-Jesus-off-on-a-cloud-somewhere than a Middle Eastern Judæan who preached in your face and seldom had opportunity to bathe. I've preached that sermon at least once to every congregation I've served. The human side of Jesus I understand, a lot like you and me, though living not nearly so comfortably. But the divineness? Never got through to me. Still doesn't. Many Christians claim to have an intimate relationship with the risen Jesus, up-close, warm and cosy. But the risen Jesus has never deigned to even say hello to me. Not part of my life experience in any way whatsoever. Which leaves me free to ponder the divinity of Jesus. How can a person be human **and** divine both at once? An oxymoron impossible to resolve. For me at least.

In Chapter 10 (250–58) I discuss Jesus' resurrection. In short, I conclude that something happened back then, but we cannot know what; the reports are so diverse and incompatible that we can come to no conclusion. We can only be clear that there's no chance it was the resuscitation of a dead body as some bits of Christian Scriptures seem to claim, and from there you can imagine almost anything you want. Now, most Western theologians have been fairly firm that without the bodily resurrection of Jesus there is no Christianity. It's an absolute must. I'm not one of those. I don't do Kirkegaardian *leaps of faith* to believe in the unbelievable. I've no notion what might have happened on that first Easter Sunday morning, but my faithfulness doesn't hang on it anyhow. So, not a problem for me. But it does leave the question hanging, Was Jesus in some sense divine? And that's where I'll start in this chapter.

How Did We Get from 34 AD to the Nicene Creed?

What it Meant back then to Be Divine

Our vision today is obscured by our contemporary notions of divinity. Omniscience, omnipotence, creation, both transcendence **and** immanence at once, compassion, caring: you can expand the list for yourself. But that's all modern stuff, the result of two millennia of Christian and Jewish pondering. The ancient folks's concepts of the gods were not at all like that. The Greek gods (and also those of the Romans who copped almost everything from the Greeks) lived on Mt. Olympus, had a rollicking good time, lots of parties and intrigues, endless bed-hopping, vicious competition and fighting, but very little concern for this world or human affairs. Sometimes they could be cajoled to intervene in human affairs, but not on a regular or predictable basis. The relations between the gods and humans were very arbitrary, and one-sided, god-sided. Those gods seemed much more anthropomorphic than our modern YHWH (or LORD, or *Adonai*, or God, whichever you prefer), sorta like humans but much bigger, stronger, more divisive and self-centered, the way humans would like to be if they thought they could get away with it.

And the separation between human and divine was considerably more permeable than our modern minds can grasp. The separation was even crossable. Sometimes gods came down, took on human form, and walked among us, sometimes even copulated with us. And sometimes the result of that copulation was semi-divine, half human, half divine, i.e., a *hero*, like Hercules, a super-human being. And sometimes a person went in the other direction: the pharaohs of Egypt were divine, Alexander the Great declared himself god, the Roman emperors after Julius Caesar were all divine. I'm unsure how that all worked, but what we need to understand is that "divinity" in the days Jesus walked the earth was different than we imagine today, different than the YHWH, the Abba we think we have inherited. Our understandings are the result of 800 years of Jewish henotheism *(faithfulness to one god exclusive of the plethora of others available)* which gradually faded into monotheism *(there* is *only one God)*. God today is much more austere, regal, heavenly, and nonhuman from our twenty-first century vantage point. But even within YHWHism there had been some gradations between YHWH and humans: angels appeared with some regularity, heavenly critters temporarily became human (e.g., Abraham's and Lot's visitors), Paul's "principalities and powers and authorities," the three humans *assumed* into heaven (Enoch, Moses and Elijah). King David was "my (i.e., YHWH's) son." Late in the inter-testamental period there were evocations of the Son of Man and of a messiah, both heavenly critters. The satan (which means simply *adversary*) of ***Job*** (ca. fourth century BC) evolved into the Satan (fallen angel) of Jesus' day. And there were Sophia and the Logos *(Wisdom principles/personae)*.

So be clear, when the first Christians started talking about Jesus as God, they were talking out of a quite different context than that of our twenty-first century. Becoming god was not so impossible back then as it is today. On the contrary, becoming a god was far from unknown. Didn't happen all that frequently, but it did happen. While it was quite unimaginable for the Jews in Palestine in Jesus' day, it was not unknown in the Greco-Roman culture and mythology of the Mediterranean basin.

Jesus of Nazareth

He was born of Mary in about 4 AD, reputedly without benefit of coitus,[1] adopted (we assume) by Joseph the carpenter. The boy grew up and became an itinerant preacher/

---

1. I have long ago lost my source (perhaps my Hebrew professor, the late Dr. Richard Henshaw), but have been assured by several scholars that this recollection is correct.

Throughout the ancient world the understanding of reproductive biology was that the male (and only the male) provided the ***seed***, which was a miniature and intact version of the infant which would be born in nine months. The woman provided to the reproductive process only her uterus, the requisite incubation chamber in which the seed could mature to birth and become a full human being. Thus the male was thought to be the sole source of human life through his seed, i.e., the semen, while the woman was merely a self-propelled incubator to brood the seed until it achieved viability. The ancients understood that the infant was the child of the father alone, and the mother had no part in the reproductive process.

teacher, and for his trouble was put out of the way by the Judæan authorities with an assist by the Roman procurator, one Pontius Pilatus in 34 AD or so. But Jesus' tomb was found to be emptied,[2] and some time subsequent to that he became God. And just how did that happen?

I need to back up and ask one prior question. Did a Jesus of Nazareth actually exist? Was there once such a person? Reliable historical data is non-existent. We have nothing in hand that proves an actual Jesus of Nazareth walked the roads of Galilee and streets of Jerusalem. In all the annuals and writings that have survived from that period, outside of the body of Christian writings he is mentioned only by the first-century Jewish apologist Josephus (ca. 37-100 AD) who mentions Jesus once, calling him "a wise man" *(but at least one scholar has suggested that is an addition by a later scribe)*. So no hard evidence. But on the other hand the vitality and power of that Jewish off-shoot sect which, when excommunicated from the synagogues, became The Way, the early Christian community, that testimony coupled with the large body of ancient Christian-produced witnessing (**very** biased stuff) suggests that Jesus was very probably a living human being who walked this earth. I have found no cause to challenge that. On the balance, it is a lot more reasonable to conclude that Jesus of Nazareth was a living human being who walked Palestine than it is to deny it.

Are the Christian Stories about him Factual?

I have no reason to believe they are. Historically, three efforts in the last two centuries to find the "historical Jesus" have been largely fruitless. The scholars get close, but they can never get *there*. The search for the historic Jesus has been interesting, curious, sometimes **very** instructive (e.g., the "Jesus Seminar" in this decade), but more for enlightening our contemporary thinking than for any discovery of the *real Jesus*. We have only the stories we have received, and they are unverifiable. The Jesus Seminar may have taken us a few steps closer to what Jesus of Nazareth thought and taught, but that still is not terribly conclusive. So, we may reasonably conclude there was a real Jesus, with some idea what he taught, but we must also realize that all other potential knowledge is buried beneath layers of what some thought they could remember, and of what others thought he might have taught, and of what others wished he had taught though he hadn't.

If Jesus Was a Real Human Being, How did he Get to be God?

And at this point I defer to the book **How Jesus Became God** by the biblical scholar and historian Bart D. Erhman. He's the scholar, I'm the student.

Given this context, in the ancients's understanding, Jesus, born of the virgin Mary, had to be literally the biological son of God.

2. On Jesus' resurrection see my Chapter 10 (248-56)

PART II: MY REVIEW OF CHRISTIAN DOCTRINES

Did Jesus Think Himself God?

Unequivocally, No! The Jesus Seminar attributes nothing to Jesus' lips which might even vaguely imply he thought himself anything other than human. While the gospels put apocalyptic and eschatological messages into Jesus' mouth, the Jesus Seminar attributes no eschatological sayings to him whatsoever; the teachings on the "Imperial reign of God" (a.k.a. the Kingdom of God/Heaven) which occur regularly on Jesus' lips seem to imply God's present reign, not some future or proximate endtime. Matthew puts *Son of Man* references on Jesus' lips seemingly about himself, but the Jesus Seminar scholars think those did not originate from Jesus. Eschatological and apocryphal stuff was rife in that day, had been for a couple of centuries, so it's not a far stretch for others to put those words into Jesus' mouth. On the cross the gospelers title him "King of the Judæans," but Jesus did not think of himself as such.

The Scholars's Thoughts

I have long thought Jesus to have been an itinerant rabbi with a fundamentally eschatological bent, teaching some pretty wise, but fairly traditional, very Jewish stuff (both about social interaction and *mores*, and about the social structure), doing some healings (not clear how) and miracles (really?), and upsetting the authorities sufficiently enough to get himself executed as an insurrectionist in a time and place chucky-jam full of insurrectionists against the Roman oppression. I have adored his values about the poor and the oppressed for many decades. But taking a look at contemporary scholarship, it appears I have been wrong. More likely Jesus was a very traditional Jewish rabbi, a reformer wanting to return to the essence of what Adonai wanted for his people, but probably not very radical at all, concerned about here-and-now living, sufficiently charismatic to get some healings and miracles attributed to him, and somehow getting himself sufficiently crosswise with the very edgy Judæan authorities to put himself in harm's way. I still adore his values about the poor and oppressed. Some scholars have opined that without Paul, the early Christian sect and their zeal for Jesus would have not survived more than a generation or two; it was Paul who breathed some critical revision into Jesus' teachings and gave some solid organizational structure to the young sect and then spread it world wide. I tend to agree with those scholars.

Historically How does Jesus Become God?

I've thus far painted Jesus as a very human figure. He got himself executed, and on the third day they found his tomb emptied. I've referred you to my chapter on his resurrection; I have no idea (rather, I have several very soft, warm, squishy notions) what happened that morning and in the ensuing weeks , but I'm clear in my own mind it

Chapter 6: What Think Ye of Jesus?

was not the resuscitation of his dead body. In these pages I'll carry this issue no farther than that. So how did the man Jesus become God?

For this I defer to Erhman's scholarship. He traces the allusions of Jesus' divinity back as early in the Christian writings as we can go, to the writings of Paul. Erhman is clear that some believed Jesus had been raised from the dead (no uniformity[3] as to what that meant) because they'd had experiences of him alive again, such powerful experiences that they had to reevaluate who (or what) Jesus was. Erhman traces earliest tradition to a pre-Pauline creed which Paul cites, "Christ died for our sins according to the scriptures; and that he was buried, and that he rose again the third day according to the scriptures: and that he was seen of Cephas . . . " (1 Cor 15:3-5) Such belief in Jesus' resurrection (whether physical, spiritual or hallucinatory) was the beginning point of Christology. Erhman next cites Rom 1:3-4 as Paul's recitation of another pre-Pauline creed, " . . . his *(i.e., God's)* Son Jesus Christ our Lord, . . . which was made the seed of David according to the flesh, and appointed the Son of God with power, according to the spirit of holiness *(i.e., the Holy Spirit)*, by the resurrection from the dead: . . . " So Jesus became God in two phases: first, he was the Davidic messiah, and next, he was appointed the Son of God. Erhman holds that sometime before Paul's writing the tradition had already *exalted* Jesus to God through his resurrection. This may be the oldest faith tradition we have in hand.

In Acts (if Lucan, then post-Pauline), Erhman identifies another encapsulated faith statement, " . . . what God promised to the fathers, this has been fulfilled for us their children by raising Jesus; as it is also written in the second psalm, 'You are my Son, today I have begotten you'" (13:32-33). It was Luke's conviction, that Jesus' divinity preceded his resurrection, dating back to his conception (if the author of Luke and Acts are the same.) In Acts 2:36 is another early belief, that God exalted Jesus to be his Son by raising him from the dead: "God raised this Jesus . . . as he was exalted to the right hand of God." Similarly in Acts 5:31, "the God of our fathers raised Jesus . . . This one God exalted to his right hand as Leader and Savior." These earliest Christologies were called "low Christology," (Erhman prefers "exaltation Christology") i.e., that Jesus started out as a mere human being who was raised up, exalted, perhaps adopted ("adoptionism" has long been ruled heretical stuff) to become the Son of God. And low Christology was later overwhelmed by a contemporaneous "high Christology." In post-Pauline writings the Christology evolved farther. In Mark it appears that Jesus

---

3. Paul seems to me at best ambiguous at to what he means by resurrection. Erhman thinks Paul envisioned a physical resurrection: in 1 Cor 15 Paul seems quite clear that Jesus' resurrection was of his human body, just as ours will be of our bodies. Bp. Spong argues in the other direction from the same passage, that Paul in the same passage speaks of a "spiritual body," and being raised up "in the twinkling of an eye," "imperishable," "flesh and blood can not inherit the kingdom of God," must "put on immortality." I conclude that Paul was himself unclear, and I note that Paul knew not the human, physical Jesus, that likely his formative experience was after the crucifixion, according to Luke, on the road to Damascus, an experience that sounds to me like a mystical experience, so not of a resurrected body but of a non-physical presence. Certainly a powerful, formative and life-redirecting experience.

became the Son of God at his baptism. Matthew and Luke were clear some 10 and 20 years later that Jesus became the Son of God at his birth (or conception). John[4] makes him the Son before the creation, an incarnational Christology, i.e., Christ/God become man.

Erhman suggests that rather than a contemporaneous "high Christology" superceding the "low Christology," it may be that the synoptics came out of an "exaltation Christology" (i.e., Jesus was entirely human, but was "exalted" to divinity by his baptism) tradition while John and Paul came out of an "incarnational" Christology tradition, so, not a matter of *higher* superceding *lower*, but of two parallel and possibly contemporaneous, co-existing traditions. Some of his language could imply that Paul saw Christ as an angel of the Lord, a pre-existent divine being, God's chief angel (therefore divine, but not God) which came to earth in humble obedience to God, took on human form, was crucified and thereby bore the "curse " *(i.e., of "hanging on a tree")* of the sins which other people deserved, and was therefore granted the status and honor and glory of God himself.

It would seem that Jesus became thought of as God fairly shortly after his death (certainly pre-Pauline), mainly because the first followers were so convicted by their experiences of the resurrected Jesus, that they had to re-evaluate their understanding of who Jesus was, which in turn led to his exaltation/incarnation. And eventually exaltational Christologies gave way to the incarnational, that Jesus was God before the world was created, was even the agent through whom the God created.

What Did the Early Church Think?

It was not long after Paul and the gospelers that the turmoil began, and roiled on until the Council of Nicea attempted to slam shut the door to alternatives. The issue was simple: in what way is Jesus, the messiah *(Christos)* divine (maybe God)? But the issue is endlessly complicated. Answers to the question were proposed. Accepted. Found faulty (How can a man become the God? How can the God become human?) Then another answer was proposed, debated, refined, and replaced the former which must then become wrong (since there could be only one correct answer), *ergo* heretical. And so the church battled its way through a series of answers, each in turn becoming a wrong answer, hence a heresy. We need to understand clearly that the church was not monolithic in this period, but rather that belief was evolving in a number of different directions, some in sequence, some simultaneously and separately. The early church did not begin with a single position, and the initial differences only multiplied with time. The earliest position would seem to be Marcan, that Jesus was purely human

---

4. In his book ***The Fourth Gospel: Tales of a Jewish Mystic*** Bp. John Spong makes a strong (and for me very attractive) case that John's gospel is absolutely non-historical, but is instead the explication of John's own mystical experiences of the risen Christ. John alone among the five gospelers (including the Gospel of Thomas) makes the earthly Jesus a divine figure throughout (and even before) the story.

Chapter 6: What Think Ye of Jesus?

and was somehow exalted to divinity. Or, alternatively Johanine, that the Christ was entirely divine and only appeared to become human. There was one other possibility, that Jesus was human, and the Christ (a separate being) was a divine who **entered into** the human Jesus for a time. That too was explored.

We must keep in mind, these argumentative folks were all **literalists**, trying to make irrefutably clear sense out of conflictful bits from the Hebrew scriptures and in the emerging Christian writings (we do not get a canon of the Christian writings, the New Testament until 370). I would submit (out of my very liberal, non-literalist posture) that it was an impossible task; but they were determined that they had to accomplish that task. I will not drag you through the series of answers and counter-answers and heresies,[5] and only point out that the Council of Nicea in 325 was con-

---

5. From Erhman in *How Jesus Became God* I summarize the "heresies" and stages in the evolution of Christology (chapter 9):

A. Adoptionists:

  i. Ebonites thought that Jesus was a normal human being, and was adopted by God at his baptism; Ebonites were sometimes portrayed as "Jewish Christians."

  ii. Theodotians held that Jesus born of a virgin, but was a mere, but unusually righteous man, who was empowered by Holy Spirit at his baptism to do healings and miracles; some held that he became divine at his baptism)

B. Docetists (from the Greek *dokeō*, to seem or appear) held that the Christ was divine, and only appears to be man:

  i. I John was written as an anti-docetist letter, asserting that "Christ came in the flesh"

  ii. The Ignatian letters are in part also anti-docetic

  iii. Marcionites held that the Law and the gospel are at odds, that salvation comes not through adherence to the Law, but only by faith in the death and resurrection of Jesus; that there was a God of the Jews and a God of Jesus, two gods. Jesus was not born, but descended as a full adult, and being divine did not really suffer or die.

C. Gnosticism was a Coptic development from the gospels holding that the Christ was divine, and Jesus human, and the divine temporarily inhabited the human, that salvation comes through secret knowledge revealed by Christ to his followers; the creation was by a demi-urge, is flawed, and so salvation is to escape from the physical world.

D. Hetero-orthodox (Erhman's term): Christ is both fully human, and fully God.

  i. Modalism held that there is one God, that Christ is God and was pre-existent; And affirmed the Trinity, three, were all the same, one God in **different manifestations**.

E. Hippolytus and Tertullian held that God is one, that the Trinity is three distinct beings unified in will and purpose. But the Father is greater than Son.

F. Origen (a prolific mainline theologian and writer, was late in his life declared heretical) held that the Christ was the Wisdom *(Sophia)* and the Word *(Logos)* of the scriptures, was pre-existent. But Origen held a unique belief in the pre-existence of souls, some of which fell away and became demons, some remained faithful as angels, and some in between those extremes became humans. The Christ did not fall, but was exceedingly faithful in Wisdom, in Word, in God and became human, in his obedience, to work out God's salvation

G. Arianism: the arguments in Arianism seem obscure and insignificant to me, but were serious and threatening in its day. Christ is divine, but lesser, having been begotten by God; is divine, but younger than God, and being God's Son is inferior to the God.

vened to deal with the Arian controversy and roughed out a "creed," a statement of what the whole church believed *(we do all believe exactly this and nothing else, don't we? . . . .* **RIGHT?** !!) ineffectively slamming the door on all other trends of thought. The church now had one, clearly stated (in fourth-century metaphor) belief about the nature of Jesus the Christ.

But the efforts at Nicea did not end the disputes. Arianism survived (Erhman thinks it was even the dominant belief in some places, at least periodically) until the Council of Constantinople in 381 when the door to alternative understandings was finally slammed shut with excommunications. Other disputes were aired after that, but by this time the whole world (i.e., the Roman Empire under Constantine and his successors) agreed that Jesus was the Christ, the Son of God, second person of the Trinity. How that could happen might be minorly argued, but Jesus' divinity was solidly agreed.

Jesus Becoming God Summarized

And that is how Jesus became God. As a child of the twentieth-century scientific metaphor I find nothing in all of that which is compelling for me. I find it easy to accept that Jesus was a man who walked the dusty roads of Palestine preaching within the mood of Roman oppression and the complicity and distractedness of the Judæan leaders, and against his people's failure to live out the ideal image offered by his Adonai. It seems reasonable to me that his followers, seeking hope amidst oppression, and perceiving that this Jesus had been a truly extraordinary teacher and prophet, and then after his death experiencing something about him they could not understand or explain except in terms of some kind of resurrection (i.e., that their rabbi in some way living again), all that would induce some to shortly begin to deify him. And then a certain Pharisee named Saul, the known persecutor of the followers of Jesus, reversed course to become an also extraordinary leader among them, spreading Jesus' (somewhat altered) message far and wide, among some Jews, but much more broadly and effectively among non-Jews. And following Paul's leadership, along with the gathering tradition, this burgeoning sect came to understand their dead and resurrected leader was divine, maybe was of God himself. For them all this was reasonable. For me it has taken the aura of legend and myth. And I am unable, knowing all religious language to be metaphor, to follow their literalness into their debates about things I also conclude are unplumbable, but which led them to avidly proclaim Jesus to be very God. I have, for myself, concluded that the God, if one there be, is unknowable (at least to me), so to say Jesus became God adds nothing coherent to my understanding that Jesus was a very human and extraordinary rabbi and prophet. Is Jesus God? Before I can answer you must first tell me what you mean by "God."

H. Nicea, convened to counter Arianism, declared that Christ of the same **substance** as the Father.

Chapter 6: What Think Ye of Jesus?

I have Loads of Problems Surrounding the Question, "Did Jesus Die to Atone for Our Sins?"

The Scriptural Bases

Paul quotes a pre-Pauline creed, "that Christ died for our sins . . . " (1 Cor:15:3). This is likely the earliest and cleanest statement that Jesus' death was about our sins. I can find nowhere in the four gospels any interpretation of Jesus' crucifixion that he died to some how make atonement for the sins of humankind. The only other Pauline reference I find is, " . . . when I shall take away their sins . . . " (Rom 11:27), but this is not a reference to Jesus' redeeming death, rather it concerns the eventual saving of non-believing Israel. The Letter to the Hebrews (much later, *circa* 64 AD) states, "So Christ was once offered to bear the sins of many . . ." (9:28) This is a confusing reference for me as I will explain below in talking about sacrifice. In the first Letter of Peter (still later, *circa*. 81 AD) the author says, "Christ also suffered for us, ...Who his own self bare our sins in his own body on the tree, that we, being dead to sins, should live unto righteousness: by whose stripes ye were healed" (2:21, 24). In the First Letter of John (*circa* 95-110 AD) that anti-docetist author says, "*(in re. Jesus Christ the righteous:)* And he is the propitiation for our sins: and not for ours only, but also for *the sins of* the whole world," (2:2) and in 2:12 " . . . because your sins are forgiven you for his *(Jesus?)* name's sake." And yet again (3:5) "And ye know that he was manifested to take away our sins; . . . " I may be in error, but these are the only scriptural references I have found that are specific that Jesus' death was in some way to remove our sins. The pre-Pauline creedal statement links Jesus' death and our sins, but does not say how those are related; by the time we get to the Johanine letter the theology has evolved so that his death was *propitiation* (a technical term regarding sacrifice which I will discuss below) for our sins, . . . sins are "forgiven" . . . and "to take away our sins." The *how* of this taking away of sin will be debated until the era of Augustine who will build it into the linchpin of his systematic theology.

"What Kind of God?"

I am not the first to ask, "**What kind of God** demands, or on the other hand, requires the death of his own Son[6] to remove the sins of humankind?" Paul proclaims a God of love, but it is hard to swallow that the perfect, all loving, omniscient and omnipotent God is either so bound by his own purity requirements that someone or something must die sacrificially to wash away (or cover over) our corruption before we can survive in his presence, or that he is so relentless and merciless as to require that sacrifice.

---

6. In the Abraham story (Gen 22:1-14) YHWH aborted at the very last instant his requirement that Abraham sacrifice Isaac. I had always thought that was an "Ah-ha" moment for YHWH, when he suddenly realized that he did not need human sacrifices like the other gods, that animals were sufficient. Guess not.

I know we human beings are willing to sacrifice our own sons and daughters in order to preserve the security and freedom of our country (or more plausibly to protect our economic interests and energy demands *[pardon my cynicism, but I am striving to speak truth]*). But I would expect something more omniscient and omnipotent from an all-loving heavenly Father. I think, as I have listened to people and to myself, this is the most troubling aspect of the "Jesus died for my sins" theology. While the ancients were able, given their premises, to make some acceptable logic out of this, I find the whole scene less than Godly, instead, quite unseemly. This does not present to me a God I want to worship and adore.

From an Intellectual Standpoint

I am very disturbed by the inconsistencies, irregularities and outright errors of the logic and theology of this "Jesus died for my sins" theology. Jesus was a Jewish boy, and he died, albeit at the hands of Roman soldiers, swaddled in a Jewish culture, and his followers, at least initially, were good Jewish boys and girls. Given that, they got it all wrong! They being so Jewish, I would assume they should do it all in the Jewish way, in accord with the way YHWH had directed that such things be done. In Chapter 10 (259–64) on Atonement Theology is described in detail the Levitical system of sacrifice, in this case for sin. You can read that for yourself. I will summarize and emphasize in the next three paragraphs rather than elaborate in detail here.

First Restitution, then Sacrifice for Atonement:[7]

Levitical Law is very clear that there are two components to sin, the injury (damage, harm), and the corruption (contamination) accrued to the sinner (which renders the sinner too impure to enter the presence of YHWH). And therefore there are two mandatory steps to correcting the sin: fair restitution (reparation) to the injured, and the washing away (cleansing *[expiation]* or covering over *[propitiation]*) of the contamination. Levitical Law is clear that both steps must be taken, and **in that order**. The sacrifice achieves the atonement; that is, the sacrifice washes away the sinner's accrued impurity, so that he, cleansed and pure, is able to approach YWHW's presence, i.e., be at-one with YHWH. The sacrifice does not remove, correct, or forgive the sin; that is accomplished only by restitution (reparation). And the sacrifice cannot cleanse the corruption until **after** restitution is made. In accord, then, with Levitical Law, Jesus' sacrifice was completely ineffective because we were not first required to, and therefore did not make restitution or reparation.

Now I realize this is an exceedingly legalistic rendering of the sacrificial system, and it makes little sense to us not raised in such a legalistic sacrificial system. I simply

---

7. My authority here is Anderson and Culbertson, *ATR* LXVIII, 303-28.

cannot get into it. But on the other hand, if you're a first-century Jew, as Jesus and his followers were (and were absolutely literalist), then this is your system and this is how you must do it. And if you're a first generation, absolutely literalist Christian, a follower of the very Jewish and resurrected rabbi Jesus, then this is still your system, and this is the way you must do it or you are flying in the face of YHWH's Law, the Torah. Sacrifice for atonement does not work without restitution first.

Scapegoat Theology

I must step back from the theology of atonement and look for a moment in a slightly different direction. The language in four of the seven references I list above (Rom 11:27 "**take away** their sins;" Heb 9:28, "to **bear** the sins"; 1 Pet 2:24) "**bare** our sins"; and lastly 1 John 3:5 "to **take away** our sins") is quite bothersome because it bears no relationship to the language in Leviticus concerning atonement sacrifice. As I say above, restitution or reparation corrected the sin and then the sacrifice cleansed the corruption accrued to the sinner; there is no language of "taking away," or "bearing sin." However that language does fit another sacrificial action in Leviticus. Once a year, on Yom Kippur, the Day of Atonement the temple liturgy (Lev 16:5-10) included a separate action for making atonement on behalf of the nation as a whole. In that liturgy two identical unblemished goats were brought to the priest, but only one was to be sacrificed. On the head of the other goat the priest placed his hands, and pronounced all the sins of the nation, symbolically placing those sins on the head of the goat which was then taken out and released alive into the Wilderness of Zsin where it would meet any unknown fate it might. Since the sins of the nation could not be restituted, instead they were symbolically placed on the goat's head and the goat, **bearing** those sins, would **take** them **away**. That goat, called the *scapegoat*, was not sacrificed or killed, but released alive. The other goat was sacrificed, cleansing the nation's accrued corruption and enabling atonement for the nation.

Much confusion here. In some early Christian citations the language of atonement is used (ignoring the need for reparation first) and the sacrifice is intended for cleansing, purifying the offering-bringer. But in the other citations the language is of the scapegoat, but the scapegoat was not to be sacrificed. Either these authors, or the emerging traditions out of which they spoke, were grossly ignorant of the Jewish sacrificial theology (which they appear to be invoking), or they may be deliberately obfuscating that Levitical prescription. In either case, the theology they are devising is quite inconsistent with the Jewish theology in which they are swaddled. Bluntly put, Jesus cannot take away sins like the scapegoat (in which case he must live), and then be killed as the atoning sacrifice. It would require two Jesuses!

PART II: MY REVIEW OF CHRISTIAN DOCTRINES

And Along Comes Augustine with His Spin

I dealt briefly in Chapter 4 with Augustine of Hippo's influence. I will not discuss his contribution here in depth, but must at least point out that he is responsible (in my view) for making sin the linchpin of the theological system Western Christianity has toed up to ever since, and thereby making salvation (from our sin, of course) the most important work of Jesus' death on the cross, blinding us to any other meaning and significance his death might have. In Augustine's system, Christ's resurrection is relegated to a ratification of the effectiveness of his sacrificial death to atone for our sins.

I must fill out that notion by repeating a few words: Augustine was first a Manichæan, which is to say (grossly oversimplified) a self-hating fatalist. He thought himself doomed, unable of himself to better or change himself, and inescapably inclined toward evil (he confessed to scrumping apples from a neighbor's orchard!) He had a conversion experience, studied, was ordained a priest, then consecrated a bishop, and finally became the premiere theologian of Imperial Rome. Through it all, just as Paul had remained an indomitable zealot both before and after his conversion, Augustine seems to have remained a self-hating fatalist both before and after his conversion. I sound unfairly critical of Augustine. I think I am not. He built for us a theological system hung upon the linchpin that mankind is incurably sinful and can do absolutely nothing good of himself. Christ's death on the cross is our only hope. And we are stuck with that dreadful theology. While that theology was much more overt in our penitential 1928 Prayer Book (which I grew up on), and has been softened in our 1979 Book of Common Prayer, it still underlies and dominates our preaching and liturgy. It ignores all the rest of Jesus' ministry, and defines humankind as unable to do any better; and therefore we ought just to live with all this world's mess (and the God will clean it all up, eventually). My sense is that there is little to nothing to commend Augustine's theological system, and much to condemn in it. But that is my rant.

Forgive and Forget

While this phrase is not used in the early Christian writings, it does seem to be the message of our day. Jesus died on the cross, and somehow our sins are thereby forgiven. And we should therefore forgive others and forget the harm or evil they have done us. That certainly is a perversion of anything we might find in the Scriptures, but it appears to me a cornerstone of contemporary pop-psychology/theology. In our Christian thinking we have completely lost the requirement of restitution or reparation which I deem fundamental to the maintenance of healthy relations in the community and social fabric. It seems to argue that we have been forgiven by Jesus' death (without cost to us) and therefore we should forgive others (without cost to them *[how wonderful!]*, albeit perhaps at cost to the person sinned against and to the community *[Oh . . . too bad]*). While *forgiving and forgetting* may be psychologically healthier for the one sinned against than hoarding and brooding resentment and anger (which is very corrosive stuff, both psychologically and physically), it is also at cost to the sinner (who is by that forgiving released from the necessity of making reparations, itself a cathartic act), and at even higher cost to the community which has witnessed the damage (physical and relational) but seen no fair reparation, so no accountability, or justice, which is in turn corrosive to trust within the community. So in *forgiving and forgetting* we focus all the attention on one of the two parties, ignoring the health of the second and being oblivious to the abiding injury to the community.

Need to Rethink

I firmly believe that we need to rethink from the very beginning both the theological system, and the premises and the reasonings, we have received from our history, and the pop-psychology/theology we are trying to operate today. And the place to begin that rethinking is by asking simply, "What think ye of Jesus? In **what way** is he the Christ?"

What, then, is Jesus for Me?

From the above it is obvious that I approach Jesus as fully human. To say he was divine, the Son of God, the Christ adds nothing to my comprehension of him (especially since I reject the "he-died-for-my-sins" theology); since I deem the God unknowable, and not in the least like YHWH or Abba, to claim Godhead for Jesus is to claim something unknowable, and merely obscures the picture. Instead I want to deal with Jesus as a very charismatic, wise and insightful, but quite traditional albeit prophetic (but not eschatological) and itinerant rabbi of first-century Israel. My Chapter 8 tells out my understanding of metaphor, and I am prepared to deal with Jesus as metaphor and try to plumb what truth that metaphor is attempting to reveal or enlighten; to do that I must read far beneath the written lines, aware that I run a high risk of projecting onto that Jesus figure the stuff congenial to myself. These lines are my first stab at this; the result might be quite lumpy, of an inconsistent consistency.

Jesus as Exemplar

Jesus died, executed on a cross, the form of death Rome reserved for non-Roman insurrectionists and which the Jews thought "accursed," i.e., dying "on a tree" as the attempted usurper Absalom. Why did Jesus have to so die? While early Christians used the language of the sacrificial theology of the Second Temple period for his death, it does not fit the Levitical template. Furthermore, since we ourselves left off sacrificing animals and put such sacrificial theology behind us after the temple was destroyed in 70 AD, that theology no longer makes any sense at all to us nineteen hundred years later. We do not live in an era when killing a sacrificial being, whether animal or human, will make atonement for us with the God. As a result, the sacrificial language we use, in the Eucharist, and in the clump of theology surrounding sin, has become worse than empty; for me it has become repugnant. I am repelled by a God who himself demands or whose attributes require the sacrificial death of his own Son for something I did or failed to do. I am accountable for myself. Furthermore I see such first-century thinking as dysfunctional today; it discourages human accountability. "The devil made me do it, and Jesus paid up for everything I did."

But sacrificial language is not the only language available to us. The gnostics saw Jesus as the deliverer of secret knowledge which was the means to salvation. The Western church rejected that image, and for me that rejection was wise and functional. The Celtic church did not completely reject the sacrificial language, but did not emphasize it or use it exclusively. Instead the Celtic church placed its greater emphasis on exemplar language. They saw Jesus as the one who far more than any other exemplified God's will for humankind, how God intended us to live. The tribal and rural Celtic culture being more "spirit" oriented than the industrialized and urbanized Roman culture, paid more attention to the natural world, to the inner life, and to health-inducing human relations. And Jesus exemplified that life style for them. They paid more attention to his teaching and living than to his death. *(Nota bene: the Roman Church trashed the Celtic Church as completely as it could, thereby displacing most of this kind of thinking.)*

I would like to think that Jesus is an exemplar of how to live this life as it was designed to be lived. I am careful to allow that I do not understand his exemplarship literally, to mean that I ought to be trampling the dusty roads of Palestine, preaching to the underclasses. Rather I see Jesus pointing the way to living one's life for others (and not for self), living in such ways as to assist and support a healthy social and relational fabric: turn the other cheek, go the extra mile, care for the homeless and the poor, eschew the self-servingness of authorities. I see a similar exemplarship in the Dalai Lama: live in compassion for all persons and all creation.

As for his death on a cross, John has Jesus say, "Greater love hath no man than this, that a man should lay down his life for his friends." (John.15:13). I hold up Jesus' death as exemplifying his commitment to his values, his willingness to die for his values, and to show the importance of those values to those around him. *(This last notion may be pure projection on my part.)*

Jesus as Embodiment of Values

I would like to think that Jesus holds up and embodies, enacts for me certain values. *(Here I run the high risk of using Jesus as a Rorschach, projecting my values onto him;*

Chapter 6: What Think Ye of Jesus?

so I will try to toe up to the Jesus Seminar's conclusions[8] about what Jesus really said.) I realize that this paragraph is really not worth the paper it is written on. What is required in looking at the values Jesus lived by and taught is an exceedingly careful and thorough study of the gospels, leaning heavily on the best scholarship not only about what he taught (e.g.,the Jesus Seminar), but of the narratives as well, what he actually did and what stories were laid upon him by later followers. That task is long and tedious and far beyond my abilities and time constraints, and may be immaterial (not all first-century values are functional in the twenty-first-century.) I am content in these pages to merely glance in that direction, take a quick and superficial swipe, and point before moving on.

The Kingdom of God/Heaven

At the top of the list of what Jesus was most frequently talking about was this "Kingdom of God." I note well that the Jesus Seminar attributes no eschatological sayings to Jesus, even though that topic had been around and was quite popular amongst Scripture writers for a couple of centuries. Jesus (as the Jesus Seminar defines him by its decisions about what he really said) seemed not much interested in endtime stuff. And when we take that eschatological twist out of the Kingdom of God talk, I have to conclude that Jesus was talking about the here-and-now, about the ideal, the best way we could be living together, the way the God intended us to be living together. So I take these sayings seriously, as pointing most clearly to the values embedded in Jesus' teachings. It would take more pages and time than I'm willing to commit here to plumb these Kingdom of God sayings to be sure what Jesus was telling us; the most

---

8. The Jesus Seminar was a six year effort by seventy-six New Testament scholars from North America and Europe to discover what Jesus actually taught, another piece added to the century and a half of attempts to discover the historical Jesus. They understand that, in addition to what Jesus himself taught, the five gospels (including the apocryphal Gospel of Thomas, an early collection of Jesus' sayings) also include material which the gospelers, the early apostles, and subsequent redactors thought originated from Jesus. Using the thirty-six criteria which the Seminar adopted, the scholars sorted through the over 1,500 sayings recorded in the five gospels discussing each saying, and then voting to place the saying in one of four categories:

Would include unequivocally as spoken by Jesus,

Would include with reservations,

Would not include but might use some content to determine who Jesus was,

Would not include.

The Seminar's conclusions carry no authoritative weight apart from the educated discussions of those scholars and their considered balloting. Readers will differ on how accurately they think the Fellows of the Seminar have concluded; and the Fellows's conclusions will obviously gore many favorite oxen (including one of my own). For myself, after examining their working criteria for the decisioning, I consider this latest effort to discover the historical Jesus to be highly reliable. We can never scrape away the overlays of the intervening two millennia, but I think they have given us a pretty valuable tool, one which has quite impacted my own thinking. The result of their work is published in ***The Five Gospels: What did Jesus really say?***

obvious is that he thought this ideal way of living together would be so attractive that it would take over human affairs. And it would be a new, entirely different way of living together. *(Oops, I may be slipping into Rorschaching!)*

The Poor and the Oppressed

I see embodied in Jesus a cluster of values around **paying attention to the poor, the oppressed, the outcast**, both in what he taught and in what was portrayed in the stories. He championed those ignored or trampled on by the authorities, religious and secular (in his world those were inseparably intertwined). For myself, I sense him reaching back to the eighth-century prophets who supported the poor by railing at those in power. In accord with these values Jesus also taught about the spiritual and communal dangers of wealth, and of power.

Social Relations

A number of Jesus' teachings cluster around **social relations, the hows of living together** with a life-giving level of self-sacrifice and concern for the other. I find this social concern throughout the Hebrew scriptures, so in these values I think Jesus quite traditional, but teaching with exquisite power and pointedness. I may be projecting, but I see Jesus teaching us to live much more for others, far less for self.

Abba

In accord with his social and relational values Jesus teaches **trust in Abba, the Father**. He would have us live more for others, with less concern about self, and in compensation, to trust much more that the loving Father will provide.

Self-Awareness

While Jesus' greater concern is about matters social and relational, he does not ignore pointing to **self-awareness**, particularly where that affects relations. But he was not into navel-gazing.

Reformer

I need to pause here and reiterate so that you are very clear what I am saying. I am convinced that Jesus was very much within the Jewish tradition, was teaching nothing outside of that tradition, nothing radical, nothing revolutionary. He was a reformer. Like the Cistercians, a few Benedictines who thought the Order was getting too

Chapter 6: What Think Ye of Jesus?

worldly and soft, and therefore started that eleventh-century reform movement to return to the central principles of monasticism, Jesus wanted to return to the core of YHWH's Law. And that Law was about **how to live *together***, how to live copacetically as community. Jesus is not about individual spirituality and behavior; he is about community, about living together healthily. And while, being a first-century Jew, he couched it in terms of the relationship with YHWH, or Abba, he and his teaching and prophesying were and are still intensely about social stuff.

Summary

So what is Jesus for me? It is clear to me that Jesus is not *God* in any literal sense. I understand him to have been a human being who actually walked this earth in the first of the first century, who taught some exceedingly important stuff, and who was willing to die for what he believed, held central to living, and was teaching. I am clear that his teaching and life were focused on the social relations and behaviors that were conducive to the health of the social fabric. And I am clear that he is for me one very important (perhaps the most important though not the sole) window through which I can glimpse those social values. To call Jesus "God" is to add nothing to that understanding, other than, perhaps, to emphasize his importance, and the importance of what I see looking through him; it may be tantamount to saying, "This is the best example of the way we humans (individually and socially) are designed to live." (But on the other hand, to call Jesus "God" may confuse or obscure the whole matter.) So I understand Jesus as a teacher of core values, and as in some ways an exemplar of how to live/die. In John's gospel Jesus is made to say, "Who has seen me has seen the Father." In some sense I can hold that to be true; Jesus may be the clearest window through which we can view those values which are most critical to the individual and the social fabric. Did he in any way atone on our behalf? In as much as his values, his example bring us closer to the ideal *(God?)*, yes. Did he take away our sins? I can't see how that would be possible; and the notion is itself dysfunctional because it relieves us of accountability for the mess we're living out.

Chapter 7: Thoughts about the Institutional Church

FOR WHAT I SAY in this chapter many will call me a cynic. Once upon a time I referred to myself as a realistic-idealist. And while I've not completely lost my idealistic side, it probably has been tarnished some with old age and hard knocks. These days I see myself more as a realist. So I approach this topic with an eyes-wide-open attitude. Today I'm not so much interested in the church as it could be, or even as it should. I need to start with the church as it really is. And that will feel cynical to some.

I remember my homiletics instructor saying to me after I'd delivered a harsh assessment of the church as I then saw it, "Jack it's the easiest thing in the world to criticize the church and find fault. It's much harder to make some positive suggestions." And George Ross was right. So here today I'm going to tell it as I see it, not criticizing, nor fault-finding, just describing reality with eyes as clear and as much honesty as I can muster.

In the briefest, the church is in a sad mess, and that's probably irretrievable. First, I'm going to summarize (irresponsibly briefly) how the church got to where and what it now is. Second, I'll weave at some length about the social system we call the church as I see and understand it today. Third, I'll talk about the deception that has kept and will continue to keep the church locked where it is. Fourth, I'll share some thoughts about what the church could be. And finally, I'll share what I think keeps me faithful to this parish church.

I strongly suspect that the discomfort felt by a few of us in our disapproval of the church is because it does not match up to our ideal, to our dream of what the church ought to be and ought to be doing, and what its members, including me, ought to be doing, how we ought to be impacting the world. But if we take that dream as our starting place, we fail to recognize the reality of what the church actually is now, and without that insight as a starting point it's impossible to figure out how to get the church to live up to, or even move in the general direction of our ideals. We listen to what the church says, and what it says about itself but we do not realize that the church's words, though spoken with utmost sincerity, are a mask, and that the reality behind the mask is quite different from the message the church is openly proclaiming. With those framing thoughts I begin with a little dis-adorning of history.

Chapter 7: Thoughts about the Institutional Church

The History

Jesus did not found a new religion. He was a zealous rabbi who sought to reform, or rather to purge the Jewish practices *(I am inclined to picture a roughly administered enema)*, to return to the origins. He was a prophet who, like the prophets before him, also taught and did healings and wonders.

Neither did Paul set out to found a separate religion as he rescued Jesus' memory from fading into a failed prophecy. He too set out to reform Judaism, working *(rather loosely, I'd say)* from Jesus' teachings. But what Paul taught was too radical to be acceptable in the synagogues so Paul and his followers were summarily tossed out. They formed their own communities, apart from the synagogues; and they reached out to the *goyim,* the gentiles, the non-Jews. Just like the other "mystery religions" of their day they flourished, and even outstripped other mystery religions. So large, so ubiquitous that they were perceived to be a perilous threat to the emperor and his government. Persecuted, oppressed, they still burgeoned.

And finally Constantine, in a fit of sheer genius, or perhaps of rank shrewdness, co-opted the church: brought their leaders into the imperial court and into his fold, coddled them with tidbits of influence, and used them as additional help in unifying his divided empire. And so the leaders of the emerging and radically unsecular, counter-cultural church were converted into puppies in the emperor's court. And I believe that we have been so ever since, whether designated as the official "Church of State"(as in England), or simply functioning as the informal and undesignated (but still very significant, as here in the States) church of state.

The then-evolving doctrine, the not yet official dogma of the pre-Constantinian church, had continued to evolve, but after the church was co-opted into puppydom, that dogma, where it served the needs of the empire, was frozen in place and has continued to be the language of the church to this day. I.e., part of the ideology needed to help unify the empire and strengthen the emperor's grip on the people became couched in church language; then a certain **Augustine**, a lapsed Manachæan[1], clawed his way to become recognized as the premiere theologian of the church, i.e., of the empire, using sin as the linchpin of his Christian theological system and adopting "original sin" (to convince us we are so bad and helpless that we needed the emperor's God-ordained leading) as the causation of our sinfulness, and by insisting upon our utter dependence on God's grace *(it goes without saying that such "grace" was effected through the ministrations of the emperor and his housebroken clergy).*

And so the church became, however much we might wish otherwise, **a creature of the state,** doing the state's bidding, whether that bidding had been openly ordered or unstated. In the Middle Ages the church and the state were so intertwined that they were sometimes the same; bishops were often lords of the realm, among the wealthiest, and even raised and led armies. Clergy were by and large the most educated of the

---

1. Manachaeans were fatalists who thought man was no damned good.

populace and were hugely powerful. The Queen of England is still today the head of the Anglican Church, being "The Defender of the Faith".

I could drag this history lesson on, but there is nothing startlingly new to be told, so I will not. Obviously I have told the history through my own biases, and I trust it's sufficiently overstated. The road trip described has clearly shaped what the church has become today; and that severely constrains what the church could ever become even under the most skillfully designed and concerted of efforts.

A Comment

This re-telling may appear negative, caustic, even cynical. I do not experience it that way. **None of this history was deliberate or conscious or Machiavellian.** No conspiracies, no plotting. It just happened. Constantine was no demon, no agent of the satan; he was an ambitious warrior attempting to pull a divided empire back together, and the young oppressed church was quite willing to become his ally. Augustine and his ilk were no demons; he was merely an ambitious bishop striving to serve his God by serving his emperor, and, in the process, to become recognized as the premiere theologian of the empire.

Such stuff has continued to happen, shaping the church we have inherited and shaping as well the good citizens we live among, e.g., the unorganized-militias, the technocrats, the fill-my-pockets politicians, the survivalists, the at-all-costs industrialists and profiteers, and the hordes of me-firsters.

What is the Church Today, in This Place?

Now I attempt to view the church, not with any starry eyes of hope, nor with any cynical biases of negativity, but simply with eyes as wide open as I can. I'll start out with . . .

A (True) Story:

Nancy and I went to church one Sunday morning at a small United Methodist Church in the village of Center, Ohio. Our eight year old unchurched great-grandson lives near there and early that winter had announced to his grandmother, "I want to go to church." And she has been taking him every Sunday since, she who as a stereotypical preacher's kid hated church going. Well, this Sunday was his first stab at acolyting (not so complicated as in the Episcopal Church; his only duty was to light and extinguish the two candles). And we went to witness the event, to give support.

We arrived a few minutes earlier than planned, as it happened, only seconds after the first couple. He was the self-proclaimed "candy man," an elderly gent more than half my age, who every Sunday morning fills his pocket with hard candies, which he casually distributes amongst all the children there (some members accuse him of

Chapter 7: Thoughts about the Institutional Church

"bribing" the kids into church; he just considers it his personal effort to "sweeten" the church experience for the little ones [*actually the candy-giving is a piece of a millennia-old rabbinical practice.*] But the kids appreciate him.) He also seemed the undesignated welcoming committee and made Nancy and me quite well welcomed. He took us inside, pointed out the facilities and swept us graciously upstairs into the worship space. By then several others had arrived and greeting conversations were popping out wherever two or more intersected. It was a curious, very un-Episcopalian scene, more like a highly enjoyable and much anticipated community gathering occasion.

Our daughter had warned us that this would feel very like the Taggarts's (Nancy's parents) church, another small, rural church in Baltimore (Ohio, that is). We had attended with them on special occasions over our years. Those experiences had taught me that the church, maybe particularly in rural settings, can be quite different than my urbanized, Episcopal experiences. It approximates, much closer than St. Lukes, my standing stone circle[2] understanding of the church, a special place where the community **really** gathers to do several kinds of important stuff. Announcement time at the Taggarts's church was a hoot: "Joe's sick, in the hospital. Ya might visit him" and "My boy's pitchin' at the baseball game this afternoon. Y'all come an' cheer him on!" Sitting with the Taggarts in worship always provoked me to ponder very deeply and seriously what this church stuff is, underneath the several layers of veneer, really about. I learned things there not obvious in Episcopal worship.

We arrived at the church in Center that morning a little over half an hour before worship time. And so did much of the congregation. The time was not wasted. Meetings and greetings were popping up all over the worship space, conversations that seemed amazingly inclusive, begging others to join in. If you'd wanted to do some private Anglican type meditation in preparation for worshiping God this was not the place to do it. This was the gathering of the community. Dianne was right, this felt much like her grandparents's church. And she and Bayne were, after just a few weeks, already well known here, and warmly included. Most knew this was Bayne's first stab at acolyting and offered supportive words. One gracious elderly choir member made her way over to greet us, turned to Bayne and said she knew this was his first time to acolyte, that she expected he might be a little nervous (he allowed that he was, "A little.") She told him she understood, that she could remember her first, but that he need not be overly anxious. "Just remember, the worst thing that could possibly happen is you could burn the whole church down." We all laughed, even Bayne. He did fine. And many told him so.

As Anglophiles go this was not a wonderful liturgical experience. Country-style Methodism tends to be pretty relaxed and informal, so there's not great emphasis on precision (of act or word). The Scripture readings were a curious collection. The sermon was . . . well, not something I'd have preached. Rather syrupy and insipid and not very commanding. Encouraging, but not demandingly so. Lots of love with a just

2. See *Gors Fawr* in Chapter 3 (34–35) and also Standing Stone Circles in Chapter 1 (13–15)

a smidgeon of holiness thrown in. But I was aware that what was happening at the surface, in my ears and in front of my eyes, was not the important stuff. There were layers upon layers of more important stuff going on. Interaction stuff. Inclusion stuff. Communitarian[3] stuff.

As we sat down that morning in that small, quaint country church I was keenly aware that we might be sitting in someone's pew. It is a joke amongst pastors of small congregations that the quick, easy way to take attendance is by noting the empty places. Actually, that's true, you can. I always did it that way. In small churches everybody has their own seat. It's not assigned; you just pick out an empty space the first time you visit, and if nobody grouses about it, that's your place. Forever! You see, that's one thing churches are about, allowing everyone to find their *place*. That's not unimportant or accidental. In a growing congregation like St. Luke's the place where you sit during the service becomes a little less possessive and important; but Nancy and I tend to sit in **approximately** the same pew every Sunday, as close as we can without overriding somebody else's choice. And I've noticed you tend to do the same. *Place* is not merely incidental. It is important. Not just your place in the pews, but your *place* in the congregation. Everyone carves out his own niche in the congregation's life, with help from others, his *place*.

Social Systems

For this I must do a chunk of teaching. Longer ago that I want to remember, when Ed Burdick[4] and I were busily learning about group dynamics and how groups develop (read "mature"), we were also learning about *social systems*. And we were learning to see a parish as a social system. A sustained set of relationships that has a dynamism all its own. A parish is a social system. What do I mean by that? Definition:

> *A social system is a specific set of human relationships that are sustained over an extended period of time.*

Two metaphors are better than one. *(When you overlay one atop the other and look through both simultaneously, you can see the ineffable pattern.)*

Metaphor One—A Mobile

My first is a visual metaphor, so you'll have to imagine it in your mind's eye. You walk into a large room and hanging from ceiling center is a large and very complicated

---

3. A recent school of philosophy which holds that individualism must be balanced with care for the social fabric. See a full discussion in Chapter 13 (303–23).

4. The Rev. Ed Burdick has been an associate of mine in this diocese since shortly after my ordination, an unofficial mentor, and a former rector of St. Luke's Church, now retired but still resident, and a member of a parish group I have been meeting with for several years.

Chapter 7: Thoughts about the Institutional Church

mobile. The room is quiet and the mobile is at rest, totally motionless. But mobiles are only fun when they're in motion, so you go over to it and give one of the smaller elements a hard swat. It spins wildly, and immediately, but very slowly, the energy of its spinning begins to be transmitted to the whole mobile, which slowly starts to circle, and the other elements begin to spin sympathetically, the larger elements quite slowly, smaller ones faster. Following the physicist's law of the conservation of energy, the energy you put into this mobile system by swatting that one element is gradually being transmitted equally throughout the whole system. The whole mobile is now in motion, various parts moving at different speeds and in different directions. Each specific part is related to all the others and they are gradually sharing throughout the whole system that energy you had in-put. It is a phenomenon pleasing to watch. You make note that each part is related to all the others through the complicated set of connection strings and balance beams; when one is affected, all are effected to some seemingly non-specific degree. But if you stay to watch the mobile long enough you will witness another phenomenon. As the energy from your swat is slowly diffused throughout the whole system the mobile will gradually slow down, and eventually, if you wait long enough, reverse itself, and eventually return to exactly the same static, unmoving, resting position you saw when you first entered the room. Every element will be precisely as it was before you sent it spinning with your swat. *Homeostasis*, from the Greek for *"the same stance."* The tendency of every system, social or mechanical, is to maintain its interior stability, which is to say, all systems resist change, and when forced to change will seek to return to their original positions.

A social system is an interrelated set of subsystems which interact with each other as a whole. If you change how the Vestry operates, that will gradually have an effect, however great or slight, on every other part of the parish. One major difference between my mobile and the parish as a social system is that the social system is not inanimate like the mobile, but instead will seem, like a living organism, to have a life of its own, independent of its individual members and even somewhat independent of its subsystems. So one of my views of the church is as a huge, complex mobile with a multitude of parts, carefully balanced, all in motion, the parts all dancing in close relation to each other.

Metaphor Two—A Lecture:

That's one metaphor for a social system; now I'll offer a second, this one verbal rather than visual. I define a social system as a set of relationships which persist over a period of time **apart from the specific persons within the system**. There are some quite identifiable elements of a social system:

- It embodies and acts out of certain values (some clearly articulated, others not so clearly stated, and a few quite hidden);

- it has specific (though sometimes unstated and unclear) goals, both ideal goals and operational goals;
- it has its own norms, accepted ways of relating (*mores*, customs, rules, laws);
- it has an established set of status-roles (behaviors expected of individuals in certain roles);
- it has power (authority, modes of influence, hierarchies of influence, lines of communication *(nota: bene information is one form of power),* ways of acting out ideas, etc.); and
- it has established sanctions (patterns of rewards and punishments).

There are also recognizable patterns governing interactions:

- communications (formal and informal),
- decision-making and problem-solving,
- boundary maintenance (identity of the social system, identification-inclusion-exclusion of members, resistence to systemic threats and disruption),
- systemic linkage (enablement of cooperative interaction between and among subsystems)
- socialization (mode of transferring norms, goals, beliefs, sentiments to new members)
- social control (eliminating deviancy or rendering it compatible), and
- institutionalization (gives structure to the social system and makes social interaction and action predicable)

And there are two basic modes of interaction

- cooperation/collaboration, and
- competition.

Now, every item in this list needs a lot of explanation, none of which am I going to dump on you here. I've already said lot more about social systems than you would ever want to know. But I must add a couple of additional comments. As complicated as this model of a social system seems to be, you need to be aware that each subsystem **also** has its own set of these elements and patterns. For example, each subsystem has its own take on the system's goals. The altar guild is concerned about keeping everything in the sanctuary clean, neat, orderly, in its proper place and ready for the action. The acolytes, on the other hand, are concerned about doing properly (so as to avoid negative sanctions) a few select actions, e.g., lighting the candles, with little regard for collateral effects (drops of black candle wax on the sheer white altar linens, to the enormous dismay of the altar guild.) And the choir, on the other hand, is only

Chapter 7: Thoughts about the Institutional Church

concerned about making music, with low regard about how well the vestments are adorning them (cottas are often askew) or where they leave music lying around (to the great frustration of the altar guild). And meanwhile the Vestry, concerned with other practical matters, doesn't give a hang for all these things. The subsystems are moving in different directions with different aims, and with lots of opportunities for abrasions, upsets and outright warfare, as well as collaboration and cooperation.

> ***Now watch the interactions:*** *I remember quite well from my first months as a vested acolyte, that the service was long and boring. But I had just acquired a nifty pair of tiny plastic dogs attached to small magnets, so that if I put one on one side of a page in the prayerbook, and the other on the other side, they stuck together, and when I moved one, the other moved too. A great boredom reliever, and (outside of my awareness) a source of quiet, reserved amusement to the more observant (and also bored) members of the congregation. That is,* **until** *my parents realized what was going on. I quickly learned that one thing an acolyte does* **not** *do is distract the congregation from the stock (and boring) layreader's sermon. There are dire consequences. My goal had been to keep the boredom at arm's length; the listeners' goal was to avoid being distracted from the hard-not-to-get-bored-at sermon.*

Metaphor Three—Place

I recall two stories about **place.** The first is out of my own experience vacationing on the tiny island of Monhegan, ten miles off the Maine coast. Sunday morning we went to the minute Episcopal chapel, took an empty seat and waited for the liturgy to begin. Just seconds before the appointed time a slightly overweight and modestly ugly matron suddenly stood at the end of the short pew, unmoving and glowering vigorously at us. Clearly we were the tourists, she was the native, and we were uninvitedly occupying **her** place. We moved and she claimed her unmarked, but unofficially very designated seat. We did not feel welcomed and never went back.

The other story comes out of the lore of teachings about small congregations. The story goes that a newly widowed woman returned from a grief-filled family visit and found in the pew she and her husband had occupied for years a new couple whom she'd never seen before. Her *place* had been taken while she was away grieving her husband's death. She had a choice. She could glower them out of her seat and reclaim her place; she could graciously give up her place to the newbies, leaving her without place. But she chose a third option: she asked to join them in the pew, shared the story of her husband's death and that they had worshiped in this pew for many years, and invited them to share the pew with her. They were somewhat honored by her revelations and her invitation. They not only stayed, but became friends. She had given them *place* and invited them into her place. That's a touching story. I tell it not because it's touching, but as an illustration of how important *place* is with the life of the congregation, and within the lives of the members. And you must understand place as much more than where we sit on a Sunday morning. It is our place, or places, in the life of the congregation, it is one of our several places in our world. Our church place gives each of us a kind of "place" in our life. So that's another piece of my view of the church. *Place*. A parish may look simple. But in reality layer upon layer.

Metaphor 4—Levels of the Conversation

Let me add one more layer of how I view the church, a parish, this parish. This time an anecdote. More years ago that I want to recall, when we were still learning about group dynamics and group development, Ed Burdick and I went to an Advanced Training of Trainers workshop. *(When you lead a group learning about group dynamics, you call yourself a trainer.)* The method of this workshop was to live out a long weekend of work together in a group without any assigned goal or task except to learn more about group dynamics and development, a very frustrating but informative methodology. I found myself in a group of twelve or so that seemed much more experienced than I (not really the case!) Midway in our second day we became terribly bogged down and unproductive, rudderless and adrift. We called for the workshop leader to consult to us. A fuzzy-headed, bearded old geezer came, lay down on the floor (we were variously postured in a circle on the floor) where he could observe, and watched us try to work without saying a word for about ten minutes. Suddenly he said to us, "You need to look at your sexual dynamics," got up and left. It felt a lot like a two-by-four upside the head. We started talking about what were the sexual dynamics in the group and quickly became aware that there were three moderately attractive women in the group, and all the men in the group were, pretty unconsciously, mostly unintentionally, in competition for the attentions of those women, leaving three other women shunned out in the cold. Wow! The rest of the weekend I paid attention to the sexual dynamics of the group. When brought into consciousness those dynamics were no longer dominating our work, but they did not go away, they were still present and active.

I came away from that experience with a new understanding, not just about the dynamics of a group or a social system, but about language and how the human mind works. I first discovered that if I want to learn about the sexual dynamics of an interaction, I need only listen to the music beneath the dialogue, to the innuendos, the double *entendre*s, watch who talks to whom, and how, paying attention to the non-verbal as well as the verbal, what's going on through **and** underneath the words (approximately 5 percent of communications is conveyed by the words, the remaining 95 percent is non-verbal.) And when I listened with that focus, the sexual dynamics became very clear. So then I experimented. I tried listening for the power issues (same process.) And the same clarity! What I concluded is that it's all there, all the time! We don't stop talking about power and start talking about sex. We're all talking about all of

CHAPTER 7: THOUGHTS ABOUT THE INSTITUTIONAL CHURCH

it all the time. I just need to pay attention, listen and watch for it. So I learned that this mind our ours is much more complex than I had thought. The obvious verbal content is just the surface; and it's **all** going on **all** the time just under the surface. And we're probably **all** listening **all** the time to **all** levels of the conversation, quite unconsciously, and paying attention consciously to the one level most engaging at that moment. Need I say more?

Layers upon layers upon layers. And it's all happening, at once !

Summary

Enough said about the parish as a social system. I do not intend for you to understand the intricacies of the social system; I merely want you to be **aware** that the parish is a social system, and a fairly complex one at that. There are layers upon layers of things going on simultaneously. We need not be much aware of all them, but we **do** need to be aware that it is not simple, or easy. Most of this stuff happens way below the conscious level, and it's only useful to examine it consciously when there is very disturbing and unresolvable stuff going on. Competent rectors do not need to consciously know all this systems stuff, but they do know intuitively how to operate most of it. Outstanding rectors know this stuff well and pretty consciously, and learn how to manipulate these elements and processes to the betterment of parish life.

I view the parish, the congregation as amazingly complicated. Layer upon layer. This particular layer, this way of viewing the parish is as a social system.

An Overview of What the Church is Today

We can describe the church as "the Body of Christ" until we are blue in the face, but that will yield us no helpful understandings. "The Body of Christ" is a figurative statement, a metaphor, and while it may be uplifting and even a little motivational, it is not in the end very instructive. It yields hope, and promise, but no fact. And I am attempting here to deal with fact. So I need to start from the other end of things. The church is a **very** human institution, a human creation (despite whatever the God might have had to do with it). So I need to examine it from human directions, psychologically and sociologically *(I am neither psychologist nor sociologist, so this is going to be crude and cumbersome)*. To understand what the church is, I need to understand what roles it plays, both in the individual's life and in the social fabric.

The Imaginary Separation of Church and State

We need to be clear that from the beginning of the human era the church (that part of the social fabric we call religion) and the state (that part of the fabric that enacts governance) have been one and inseparable. The chief *(Moses)* and the priest *(Aaron)* (by

Part II: My Review of Christian Doctrines

whatever titles they are called) have always been brothers, if not actually embodied in the same human being(s). So the patriarchal Abraham set up a stone as an altar and called it *bethel* (translate *the house of the god*); the dancing King David led the parade bringing the Arc of the Covenant into Jerusalem. The high priest Caiaphas held hands with Pilate. St. Augustine wrote theology the Roman emperor endorsed. Bishops of the medieval church were often lords of the realm. The monarch of England is still "Defender of the Faith."

The Attempt to Separate Church from State

The founding fathers of this country made an ill-conceived attempt to separate the two, writing disestablishment into the constitution. Secular and sacred powers had been intertwined, fully collaborative, incestuous throughout the Medieval Era; the enlightenment brought on the decline of autocratic power and the rise of individualism, two cornerstones of our country. The founding fathers dictated that the state should **not** establish a church of the state, and Jefferson wrote about the separation of church and state. It was a valiant effort doomed before undertaken. We have no official, i.e., *established* church in this country, but Christianity, the several denominations, the innumerable churches have continued to be the unofficial church of state in this country. To verify that you need only go to that small church in Center, Ohio to hear the gospel preached there (or in any pulpit in this country); what you will hear, dressed in gospel words, are the values of Americanism. We think we have separated church and state, built a wall between the two; actually we have merely blinded ourselves to the operative reality.

The Church was Initially Counter-culture

I note in passing that in its early ages **Christianity was distinctly counter-culture** (though Paul did commend believers to be obedient to the authorities; yet we were ambivalent, living out counter-culture values while trying to keep peace with the state). The Roman emperors perceived Christianity to be a threat to their reign and lived, for the main, uneasily tolerant and wary, but at times aggressively hostile and expending efforts to eradicate Christianity. Constantine ended that uneasy co-existence when he co-opted the growing power of the church into his effort to unify the divided and divisive empire (the arguments among the Christians had been part of that divisiveness.).

The Making of Good Citizen

A few scholars have suggested that the very subconscious role assigned that church at that Constantinian point in history was to make of the people good citizens (i.e., obedient, docile, compliant and supportive). In my appraisal that has been the church's

Chapter 7: Thoughts about the Institutional Church

primary, though very, very *sub-rosa* assignment for the seventeen hundred years since. I make my judgment in part on that history, but much more by taking note of the values I hear preached *(yes, out of my own mouth as well)* in the various parts of the church in this country. I have studied our Holy Scriptures enough to flatter myself that I have a fairly good grasp of the values proclaimed and held up in them, particularly among the eighth-century prophets and in the four gospels (feeding the hungry, unoppressing the oppressed, fostering wholeness [i.e., healing blindness, lameness, epilepsy, leprosy, mental illness, and other diseases], raising the dead, caring for widows, orphans and sojourners, freeing prisoners, clothing the naked, loving all neighbors).

I do hear the church, in general terms and with a very modulated voice, ever so tentatively proclaiming a few of those prophetic/gospel values, but gently and with no great push behind them (except in a few corners, to wit, Ed Burdick here, Maurice McCrackin in Cincinnati, and the few of their ilk). But on the other hand I do not see mainline clergy opposing even the more obnoxious or most dangerous and destructive of the values of Americanism, not even the values clearly contrary to the prophets and gospels. Further, as I listen closely through the dissonance between the words and the undergirding music I hear much of the Americanism values (in particular the focus on the individual and the eschewing of any serious criticism of the secular community and culture) quietly echoed even though they are contrary to the gospel values. And I do not consider that the work of some unseen satan: I think that's just a given of the very human institution we are; there are layers of the system's life to which we attend blindly and unwittingly.

We, the creatures of this societal subsystem, the church, are also citizens of the larger system, our nation and culture, and we are very much caught, entrapped, disabled within this network of conflicting values between the two systems (really more than two systems; Americanism is no more monolithic than is the church); and in that crunch the values of the system we have to live in, the secular culture, prevail, overwhelming the gospel values.[5] I dare to voice all that because for thirty-three years I listened to the barely discernable but grating dissonance between the gospel's counter-culture values and the Americanism values in my own preaching. And I suggest that if one dared to preach pure gospel values in this church bluntly and openly, and without heavily blanketing them under a thick quilt of American values, he would speedily be accused of blasphemy. Or worse, un-Americanism. Tantamount to communism.

---

5. Two or more decades ago I made the acquaintance of a very conservative premiere New Testament scholar teaching in the most important of the Southern Baptist seminaries. He reported that he was in fear of losing his teaching position because the right wing of the Republican party (read "Karl Rove and company") was attempting to take over the leadership of the Southern Baptist Church and then use that denomination to advance its political goals, and he was himself marked as not conservative enough to serve their interests. I thought his report rather bizarre, but he did later lose his teaching position, and the political radical right certainly has taken over the Southern Baptist Church and is now using it to serve it own ends. An extreme and obvious example of how the church serves the values of the secular culture.

Part II: My Review of Christian Doctrines

The Sociology of Religion

One direction in which we need to look is the sociology of religion. What are the several functions religions (Christianity being only one of them) have served in cultures? Which of those can we (i.e., St. Luke's, the Episcopal Church) now choose to carry on? Which can we give ourselves to heartily? Preaching the "gospel of Jesus the Christ" may be the ostensibly chosen metaphor, but what behind that is the sociological function, the ultimate purpose, the functional end? One sociologist suggests that religion provides a sense of transcendence *(the sense that there is something, some one out there greater, weightier, more fundamental than myself)*, along with some rules for living. That sense of a transcendent being can come through many voices, liturgy and the beauty of nature being the first two that come to my mind. And it appears obvious to me that we are in desperate need of some reasonable rules for living that make sense for the whole of our populace, not just for an elite few.

I think this suggestion starts in one right direction, but I have no training in sociology, so cannot lead this investigation. The sociology of what the church is about for the culture is one course of exploration we need to pursue seriously if we want to remain relevant, influential, and vital to our culture. There are a few other imperatives I'll point to below.

Transcendence

As I sat on a Sunday morning listening to the marvelously well played and well sung offertory anthem I was reminded of one more thing that both binds me to St. Luke's and points my attention toward the Transcendent: the music, the liturgy, the building, the "decently and in good" orderliness, the tradition: all conspire to remind me that there are finer, more beautiful things in life than the mundaneness of my days. A weekly *pointer* to the fineness that seems to be alive just beyond my reach, and possibly to the reality that looms just beyond my vision.

The Primary Business of the Church

I've concluded that the primary business of the church is as simply stated as "to stay in business." Most of our attention, most of our energies and efforts, most of our dedication and loyalty, most of our finances are aimed at keeping the church in business. Most of the organization and its direction labors at that. We are working hard to keep ourselves (i.e., the churches) in business. And secondarily, the church does most of its business under the commission Constantine issued, to make of us good citizens. If we want to move beyond that then we would do well to assess our real function within the social fabric, and then decide whether that is something we want to do, and that

Chapter 7: Thoughts about the Institutional Church

we think is worth doing. Until then the church is quite completely hobbled between the Gospel and the church's social function.

The Church Trapped and Paralyzed Between Its Commission and Its Primary Business

Matt.28:19 gives the church our **Great Commission**, "Go ye therefore and teach all nations, baptizing them in the name of the Father, and of the Son, and of the Holy Ghost." We are certain those words came not out of Jesus' mouth, but for much of the church they have been the marching orders through the centuries. Evangelize and preach the good news. Or on the other hand, preach Americanism. But I don't think we can effectively do both. Individualism, libertarianism, capitalism, racism run fairly counter to gospel and eighth-century prophetic values. And, let's be real. We are remaining in business to support Americanism. If we don't we're likely to be drummed out of business.

The Church Is Not an Actioning System

One other thing allows me to rest easy (i.e., not become enraged and exercised that the church is not acting out gospel values) with parish life as I understand it. I am pretty clear in my mind that parishes, and the greater church in general, are not designed to be *actioning* systems. The church which has devolved into our hands was not intended to be prophetic, to confront the cultural values, nor make changes. If it had been it would have been designed quite differently. (E.g., I think the whole of the focus on individual sins acts as a distraction to keep us from paying attention to the anti-gospel acts and behavior of the larger community, about which we ought to be quite prophetic.) In fact the *leaders, i.e.,* the primary trained and paid staff, are very vulnerable to the sensibilities of the people, the good citizens they serve. The label we hang around the clergyman's neck is a clue. We call him *rector,* a Latin word which best translates as *school administrator.* We do not expect him, from that position, to prophesy, and if he does he is very vulnerable to our *d'ruthers.* We can simply withhold our pocketbooks, or our presences. He dare not get too far out of line or he will find himself leading no one. If the church were intended and designed to be *actioning* it would be designed to protect and enhance the prophetic and leading roles[6]. Look around at a few action taking groups and you'll see that those are organized quite differently than the normal parish and diocese. My resting-easy understanding is that the parish is designed primarily to be a community (sending care packages to our college-bound children is a community-sustaining activity, it fits into the functioning

---

6. The one exception I am aware of is the Society of Friends a.k.a. the Quakers. I have no close knowledge but understand that the Friends have led a number of efforts to enact some of the gospel values.

design), and to be a place I can come to muse over my values, the core of my spiritual life. Not designed to be prophetic, or to take prophetic action.

The Growth Trap:

Ed Burdick unintentionally demonstrated the dilemma for us in St. Luke's at one meeting of our discussion group. While offering a proposal for action he quietly admitted that the "growth mandate **is** imperative." That translates into plain English: if St. Luke's (or any mainline parish) wants to survive fiscally today, it must grow to such a size that its budget can support its staff, or conversely, if we do not grow sufficiently large, our financial needs will swamp us and the boat will sink. That's the mandate, and the corollary is, if the preacher waxes very prophetic he will chase the larger portion of the congregation away. We, St. Luke's, live with a foot in each camp: we, or at least some few of us, would like to be prophetic enough to impact the world around us in a favorable (to us) way. But to do that would imperil St. Luke's future. It's a Hobson's choice. So I look around me, try to see St. Luke's as it really is, and ask whether that is enough for me. I'm eighty, well past my prime. It is enough.

What Does "Prophetic" Mean?

I have bandied this word, I ought to define it. I obviously do not mean one who foretells the future. Ostensibly the prophet is one who speaks for the God, but in as much as I have declared the God unknowable, I doubt that I can mean that. As I look at the eighth-century prophets and at some of Jesus' utterances I could mean someone who stands up for the values those seem to embody: care for the oppressed, the poor, the broken, etc. But as I read my own words I think I am actually reaching farther than that. I realize that I do not mean simply words or persons or acts that take care of, that tend to the underclasses; rather I mean one who by word and deed dares to have deep insight into the ills of the social fabric, a *clear-seer* who can unbiasedly and probingly see reality as it is, piercing the euphemious veils hiding its ills *(I am tempted to say "evils")* and courageously telling that vision to others, pointing ways toward healing those social ills and moving us toward a more humane, more caring and loving, more compassionate social fabric; one who has the vision to see the whole of the larger social fabric, and to critique it in such powerful and positive ways that others want to change it, to amend that fabric to be more humane; a leading critic of the larger social system.

Faith Development

When I first read Fowler's ***Stages of Faith,*** he made me realize that my spiritual pilgrimage was not causing me to lose any faith, rather it was about growing my faith

Chapter 7: Thoughts about the Institutional Church

beyond the boundaries of orthodox doctrine. Gradually I have also come to realize that the mainline church is necessarily committed to serving those who have, in Fowler's terms, a *synthetic* (i.e., unanalyzed), or **conventional** faith (the fundamentalist churches are, in turn, committed to serving those whose faith has not grown beyond *mythic-literal* toward a conventional faith, but is still hanging onto literal interpretations of the scriptures and doctrine). In my younger years I wrote off the differences between mainline and fundamentalist churches as "different strokes for different folks." Through Fowler's eyes I see that it is more complex. We each serve a different stage of faith development within the quest of Christianity. But it becomes clear to me that the mainline churches, committed to serving a conventional faith, can accommodate and tolerate, but cannot effectively serve those whose faith has grown beyond the conventional without seeming to abandon or be false to those still holding to the conventional. And I do not see that as a limit to be bemoaned, only acknowledged and accepted.

What about Spirituality?

The church's preoccupation is necessarily keeping itself in business, and secondarily, making of us good citizens. Beyond those two purposes, if it impacts the individual worshiper's spiritual life, that is perhaps more accidental than intentional. Very little of what we do has much to do with *spirituality*, which I had always mistakenly thought ought to be the primary business of the church. Frankly, after thirty four years of living and working within the arms of the church, I don't think the church knows all that much about the spiritual life. And in saying that I do not intend a condemnatory or negative judgement on or against the church. That's just the way it is. The church which I have served for thirty four years is dedicated to human needs and ends, working through human means. And what of God? Of God's intentions? Of God's Spirit? Of God's working out his purposes through his church, the living body of Christ? All *god-talk*, all metaphor. We talk of mission, of evangelizing the world for Christ, of baptizing in the name of the Father, Son and Holy Ghost. I am convinced that while that was a functional metaphor in the beginning centuries of the church, it is now defunct. It no longer works for most people (outside of the evangelical denominations); and those in the mainline churches for whom it does still work are becoming fewer. Further, it is increasingly unclear what to **read out of** the Christian metaphor. Science is answering more and more questions for us; the "God of the gaps" J. B. Phillips pointed out is becoming less and less useful, or helpful. We must re-think what we understand out of the Christian metaphor and how to apply that. And right now the church, in its multiple forms, is simply getting in the way of that effort by refusing to go beyond the ineffectual evangelical task. And if it chooses not to be part of the re-interpreting, then the church becomes (or remains) part of the problem. My non-confessing friends think the church has much ill to answer for, and they are right. They say it should have known better; there they are mistaken. But enough of my rant. Some more positive suggestions are needed.

Low Probability of Change

We have in hand in the church only what we have been given, and I believe our power to redesign it and change its direction and being is extremely limited. My smattering of training in organizational development (a sociological understanding of human social systems) has informed me that organizations are changed only, *if ever at all*, under the severest of duress and then with only the most dedicated, strenuous and tireless efforts. And my appraisal of the church today is that it has nowhere near sufficient vision to move it toward serious change or revitalization, and further that it is fraught with sanctions and inertias which would powerfully resist any such visionary change.

The church we have received is much more a proclaimant of the values of the state, of Americanism in all its varieties, than of gospel values. Working as a professional within the church over three decades it became clear to me even as early as seminary that the church, and the parishioners I served, really did not want to hear prophesy from me.[7] They wanted (1) some theological interpretations which would help them be comfortable with, or at least tolerant of, the world they found themselves in, they wanted (2) some comforting of what they were encouraged to perceive to be their spiritual ills, they wanted (3) some assurances that there is, after all, a loving God for them, and most of them also wanted (4) some soft assurance of an afterlife. In exchange they would tolerate an occasional, but only muted outbreak of my prophesying **if** I couched it in very moderate terms. This all stands to reason. We, the church, entered the protection of the empire given a portfolio of making peasants and warriors into good citizens of the empire. I believe that portfolio is still ours. We happen also to carry a portfolio of proclaiming the good news of Jesus the Messiah and the state allows us to do that, even enables us to do that, so long as we do not proclaim that gospel's values too stridently or in preference to the values of the state. My rants against capitalism, militarism, competitiveness, environmental rape, overpopulation, individualism, and senseless, inane technology would never be tolerated from the pulpit. Mind you, no policeman or officer of the state would come into the church service to stop me. That's not needed. The good citizens in the pews would stop me, not overtly but with their pocketbooks and their feet.

---

7. I recall with a chill in my bones the second cure I served, just as the Viet-Nam civil war was heating up and we were sending advanced military personnel in as "advisors" to South Viet-Nam. I thought our participation there ill-advised, immoral and untoward. Heatedly. I was inclined to preach ferociously against our military involvement, and as I preached, there sat, in front of me a young pregnant mother with her child alongside her, the wife of a lieutenant at that moment deployed to Viet-Nam as a "military advisor," and so dangerously at risk. I learned with absolute clarity in that very instant that the preacher cannot possibly be both pastor and prophet.

Chapter 7: Thoughts about the Institutional Church
How Did I Get into This Place?

I came out of seminary wanting to make a difference in the world. Didn't have to be a huge difference; I just wanted my life to count for something *(chalk that up to the DNA of the socialist John Slayton in my genes)*, for a tiny corner of the world to be a little better, a little healthier, a little more in touch with the God. I began small, as curate under an exhausted, burning-out rector, wanting to help people get in touch with the very human side of Jesus. That effort did touch a few people helpfully, but to most others it was confusing, to a few blasphemous! The rector crashed and self-immolated, and I stayed on as their interim rector; they had loved him, so they worked out their wrath at his betrayal by kicking the shit out of me. After a year of that I moved on to a small, struggling, ill-conceived and doomed mission where it took only three years for me to burn out. That eleven-year-old mission needed to grow (though their internal dynamics militated against that), and I was unprepared (there was in that day no understanding of how to deliberately grow parishes) and unequipped (read *"had not the required personality makeup"*) to lead them there. I built them a bridge and, having felt a failure twice, bailed out of parish ministry (this was before we understood *burnout*). Three years later doing a four-month stint as interim co-rector of a parish I discovered that parish ministry can be fun and that I could handle it, so I began to search my way back into parish ministry. That took another four years, and landed me in a small and dwindling county-seat parish in which I could myself thrive even though the parish was irretrievably failing. By then I was no longer hoping to save the world, or even a small corner of it; I was just surviving. My need to make some change, to have some impact had evaporated. It took twenty years to build that parish a bridge and then I retired.

I had left seminary avidly devoted to some of the values of the eighth-century prophets and of Jesus' teachings (most notably egalitarianism, the urge to alleviate the inequities of the poor and oppressed, and to confront the self-servingness of the operators of the establishment). It took only a few years to learn the parish and the church did not want prophets and could not accommodate prophecy, and, more importantly, that I had not the grit it would take. *(I never was a revolutionary: I wanted very much to join the Selma march, but with a wife and two children to support, and a parish not similarly committed, I opted not. At that early point I functionally acquiesced to the church's status quo and unwittingly commended my devotion to revolutionary values into a long and deep sleep from which they are only now starting to awaken.)*

I was at the same time learning that managing a parish demanded all of my energy and left no energy pool out of which to prophesy. I was effectively neutered, and spent the rest of my ministry doing plain old parish life. Do I regret that? Not deeply; and while I'm today slightly saddened at that loss of youthful hope and energy, in hindsight I can still see no acceptable way out of that quandary. That is my personal history in relation to the church's unrealized quandary. Today I am in my eightieth year, in decent health but with gradually declining energy and without sufficient will to engage such a new and demanding prophetic tack.

The Church's Quandary

The church proclaims a set of values out of the Judeo-Christian heritage. Some of those fit my three core values, some do not. So I cherry-pick, as do we all. Add to those Judeo-Christian values some quite American, often antithetical, values. It becomes a quite mixed bag. A prophet could sort them out and hold up a coherent set, but parishes (with rare exceptions) do not cotton to prophets, so we hobble along, trying to speak softly in both camps, voicing some selected Judeo-Christian values, and smothering those with a crazy quilt of American values. The church **could** choose either one, but would have to abandon the other set, an act which does not hold with our assigned and accepted role in the culture. The easier, safer, least risky course is to opt for neither and attempt both just as we have been (the Transactional Analysis therapists of the seventies used to state as an axiom that "try" always translates into *"try and fail."*)

On the other hand we, both as a culture and as a nation, are in severe need of some very forceful goading. The values we profess as Americans are failing us and our social system has begun a descent toward chaos. We desperately need a prophet (or a cadre of prophets) to point out the way for us if we are to avoid the systemic failure that lies ahead *(I realize I sound like the benighted prophet of doom)*. And the church does have the equipment (i.e., value system and personnel) to take on that task, if it could develop the will and the insight. But taking on that task would require massive, deliberate, careful, and painful change. The question at hand: can the church change? John Spong in his ***Why the Church Must Change or Die*** argues that it must; and I agree with him, so far as he goes. But he argues only theology, and while that change would be difficult enough, it is only a minute fraction of what must change for the church to become *(prophetically)* relevant. What is further required is systemic change, so I will now take up that part of the argument.

A Model for Change

I need to start my argument with a model for change; I am here concerned not with whether, nor with the content *(which Chapter 13 on communitarianism will supply)*. In this moment I am concerned solely with the process of change, and for that I need a workable model. One designed specifically for social change would be better than the one I have, but I've no training in that area, so must make with a model I borrowed long ago from the engineers in Procter and Gamble. They, being engineers, worked with a change model that was necessarily mathematical. It read "**A times B times C must be greater than D**," where A is the level of dissatisfaction (or pain) with the way

Chapter 7: Thoughts about the Institutional Church

things are, B is an ideal image of how it should be, C is a do-able first step in that direction, and D is the cost (pain) or risk of making the change. This being a mathematical formula, the product of the first three elements must be greater than the cost, and so if any element A, B, or C is zero, then the product of the three is zero and cannot be greater than the cost. What the engineers showed me was that my dissatisfaction was not enough; I needed also to know how I wanted it to be at the end, and have formulated at least a first, manageable step toward the ideal. And even when A, B and C are workable (i.e., not-zero) elements, if the cost (pain) or risk is too high, the change cannot happen.

It's a very simple model. And there are assuredly other more complicated change models more appropriate to this case, but this one is sufficient for pleading my case this morning. It points out that while Jack Bowers's dissatisfaction with the way things are in the institutional church might be enough of a factor to motivate **me**, I do not perceive that the greater community's dissatisfaction is sufficiently high to motivate a broader change. And while an ideal somewhere in the direction of what the communitarians are suggesting rings for me, I suspect the greater community would find that ideal appalling, completely unacceptable, and absolutely wrong-headed, a gob-strangler. And as I have not yet formulated a first step that might lead in that direction, I couldn't initiate any change anyhow. Finally, I am fairly certain that the greater community would find the cost impossibly high and excruciatingly disruptive.

Discussion of Change Elements:

Element A—the Motivating Pain or Dissatisfaction

Using James Fowler's Stages of Faith, that the mainline church as we know it today is the church of *conventional* (i.e., *synthetic*, **unanalyzed**) faith. It is the faith of the general public (apart from the fundamentalists, caught up in their Stage 2, mythic-literal faith). Those are the people this church serves, and upon whose support and pocketbooks it depends. And its focus is to feed those people, to pastor them, to help their faith be comfortable and even helpful for them. There are a few for whom the conventional, unanalyzed faith no longer works; our faith has expanded, enlarged, become more inclusive and out-reaching beyond the hedge of orthodoxy; we are on the cusp between Stages 3 and 4, or have moved even farther. Our spokesmen are the Jim Pikes and the Jack Spongs who see the need for spiritual growth and are trying to coax us out of the comfortable conventional. They are somewhat prophetic, cautiously prophetic, but not yet challengingly prophetic (like the Gandhis and Mother Theresas). So, I point out, the pain, the dissatisfaction of the church is not general and widespread; it is felt by only a few (albeit sometimes acutely). And the pain, the dissatisfaction of the church general is certainly not sufficient to motivate large and significant change in the motive and life of the church.

Part II: My Review of Christian Doctrines

Element B—A Vision of How We Want it to Be

I.e., an end-goal, a state in which . . . . One problem with the church is that it has no end goal, no ideal image of the way we want it to be. It's all in God's hands. We're mired in original sin, can't do any good whatsoever unless the God infuses it into us. And even then we're not responsible for the outcome 'cause we're so sin-impaired. Jesus talked about the Kingdom of God, but we've transformed that notion into something off in the by and by, or into some internal state that has no external consequence. Jesus and the eighth-century prophets hint at some vision, but it's so vague as to be uninspiring (in terms of change-motivation). I would argue for some kind of real communitarianism, but that's not hitched up to Jesus or the church, so it's not a motivator for change in the church. A long dead friend once remarked to me, "Jack, you can't get anything done in the church because it's time line is the millennium." He was right as far as he went, but he didn't comment on the lack of an ideal image, an end-goal. A vision with sufficient power to motivate must be clear, attractive, and shared. Ain't got one.

Element C—A First Step toward That Vision

There are several first steps already taken; President Roosevelt's safety net of Social Security, then Medicaid and Medicare, now the Affordable Health Care Act. They are feeble, but just starts. And they generate furious push-back. But worst of all, they're not integrated into a plan, a process. Piecemeal and all fairly fragile. And they're all secular. The church had nothing to do with them, and did not noticeably support them. I confess, I have no first steps in hand. I have a vision, fuzzy, incomplete and imprecise. But no first steps in that direction.

Element D—The Risk, the Cost of Making the Change

Finally, I suspect that currently the cost, the risk, however small, might be far too high. My now-dead friend and I once analyzed the resurrection as a change model. It worked, but the cost was radical disjuncture. The old must die, absolutely and completely, before the new can be born. Jesus was dead, his side speared to prove it, and interred in a sealed tomb. Absolutely, positively, finally dead. And **then** he was raised up. Radical disjuncture. And that may be the case for the church as well. It may be that for the church to change, to become prophetic, to be the goad this nation and culture needs, it may first have to die as we know it, and be resurrected as something entirely new and even hard to recognize. And that death would not come easy, if at all; the church is so intertwined with the secular system, that the secular system may need to keep the church alive, in some form, even if nearly terminally enfeebled.

Chapter 7: Thoughts about the Institutional Church

An appraisal: Can the Church Change? Can We Change the Church?

I must confess that I am positively pessimistic about the probability (or even possibility) of significant change in the church. That is in part a reflection of myself, of where I am in my life. I should allow that I am an old man now, and very comfortably retired; I have become a coward, unwilling to seriously risk losing the comforts I have gained. I am no longer competent to lead any charge to radically change the church, or the culture. But my appraisal is also, in part, a reflection of my understanding of the process (e.g., the above "change model") the church would have to engage to effect any real change. The people of the church are comfortably ensconced in their "conventional faith" and are not impelled to want change; the leaders of the church (in our case the House of Bishops) are charged, not with moving the church into a prophetic mode, but with maintaining the orthodoxy and stability of the system; the mission of the church has been effectively compromised since 331 AD.

Is it possible to become more prophetic within the church? There are glimmers of possibility. Martin Luther King, Jr. was certainly a brilliant flash of possibility; but, as I pointed out, he worked within the Black church which expected him to be socially active and was willing and able to follow his leadership. I recall from my childhood a Presbyterian clergyman in Cincinnati, Maurice McCrackin, who was a principled pacifist, civilly disobedient protestor against the Viet-Nam war and who refused to pay taxes to support that war; he led a very small congregation of similarly inclined supporters which was barely tolerated by the Presbytery. *(The prophet must have supporters who listen and are willing to follow and risk; otherwise the prophet is simply killed out of the way, as in the Hebrew Scriptures.)* If we search we can find a small number of examples of prophetic life, usually at the fringes of the church: food pantries, The Open Door Ministry in Atlanta. But those bring no significant change to the social fabric. Is it possible? Perhaps even under the broad umbrella of the church, but most likely near the fringes. But would it be worth the cost? The prophets among us are usually consigned to the outposts and disabled by being labeled kooks, odd-balls, misfits.

The over-arching question: Is the church capable of calling the social fabric to accountability and of moving the social fabric toward embracing and living out the core values voiced by the Jesus and the eighth-century prophets. The jury is still out.

This particular horse I have now beaten completely to death.

What is the Church for Jack Bowers?

I have continually referred to St. Luke's as my circle of standing stones. For me that is an exceedingly apt metaphor, one that illuminates and informs my relationship to St.

Luke's. I've told you that my Welsh guide thought standing stone circles were multi-purpose.[8] For me St. Luke's is multi-purpose.

I've Out Grown it, but This Church is Still Home

I have lately been saying that **what** we believe intellectually (i.e., doctrinally) is not terribly important. I have obviously wandered into a place where the Holy Scriptures and the orthodox dogma are no longer in any way literal for me. I am forced to take them as metaphors, as a set of lenses through which I might discover and study the various levels of reality. (Not the **words** of God, but **perhaps** the Word of God.) So these days I rest easy with creeds and readings and preachings. But contrary to appearances, I have not abandoned or walked away from or rejected them. My sense is, not that my belief has changed or moved to a different spot, but rather that it has grown larger, it includes more, that the margins are much farther out than the encircling hedge of orthodoxy. But the church as I grew up with it, the creeds, the Scriptures, the doctrines, are still my home, my center. I understand them differently than I did before, but they are still the furniture of my spiritual life. And curiously I am not interested in switching or trying out some other Faith. This Christian stuff, as I have learned it and studied it and preached it, is **my** stuff. It is my language. Its metaphors are my metaphors. It is the only set of spiritual tools that I know well enough to use comfortably, and to rest with, comfortably. They are still binding me tightly to St. Luke's and the church, and while I feel far less bound to the greater church than before, I feel very close to St. Luke's. **This** is my circle of stones, and those other circles belong to other clans.

Treasure Chest of Values

My Welsh guide admitted that his stone circle probably had had an astronomical function; likely it told the ancients when to plant and when to harvest. St. Luke's also has such a function for me. Though not unerringly aligned with the "Christian moral axis," it does point at least roughly in that general direction. While I do not hear nearly as much prophetic stuff from the pulpit as I would like (*that seems true for a small handful of other listeners as well*), I find that just the act of being in church, listening to the readings, participating in the liturgy, saying the old words over again, hearing the preacher starts me to musing about matters moral and ethical. I think that for me, St. Luke's in particular is a residing place for values and morals and ethics, a place I can come and take them out of their boxes, turn them over in my hand, study them, and while musing about them watch them sparkle in the light, and wonder how we might move the world (or just this little corner of the world) one millimeter closer to that way of living. And in those moments I can only hope that I am musing a tiny bit

---

8. Again see *Gors Fawr* in Chapter 3 (34–35).

more than just to myself. For me the values I find imbedded in our Scriptures, and hidden (*buried, even*) within our Christian tradition, symbolized for me by St. Luke's, those values which I can touch only with my fingertips, are the very core of my being, the heart of my spirituality. And because I grew up in this Episcopal church, spent my life in this church, I call those values "Christian." They probably are not so Christian; it just happens that there in St. Luke's is where I find them. And because Christian is all I've ever known, that too is probably what so binds me to the church, and more specifically, to St. Luke's. The values seem whispered here. Now I must pointedly remark that not all the values voiced in the Scriptures or in the fabric of St. Luke's are ones I want to hold in my heart. I have no genocidal urges against the Amalakites (see 1Sam.15:1-8). Nor am I moved to stone wayward sons to death. So I am very selective about the values I lift out of our Scriptures and St. Luke's. The Scriptures and the church are not the ultimate source of my values, rather a bin out of which I select my values. And while I have some vague sense of why I choose some values and not others, that "why" is still not entirely clear to me. Someday I would like to explore that.

It's about Community

I'm becoming much clearer that one facet of St. Luke's which is important in my life, is this community of people of similar mind and soul *(I know not what is a soul)*. People ask, "Can you be a Christian and not go to church?" I have never thought you could, I always knew the community was important. But now I am clearer that the community is much more important than what I think about matters doctrinal. This community of fairly similarly minded folks, of sort of similarly intentioned folks, of folks headed kind of in the same direction, and who support me (*as I support them*) in my directions and intentions; that's important. And I mean the whole congregation, not just our small, fairly similarly-minded discussion group. This St. Luke's community is not single-minded or unanimous, but we care about, and for each other, not for any self-benefit, but because we are in community. This community is one great importance of the church, and of this parish.

But this community is about more than just being an aggregation of supportive people. Robert Wright in *The Evolution of God* suggests that there is a moral axis to the universe. That is as close as he can come to calling anything "God," and while I cannot follow him quite that far, I do catch hold of his phrase and play with it, "a moral axis in the universe." As a social Darwinist he thinks the world is ever so slowly evolving, aligning itself to that moral axis. I suspect that is a very vulnerable hope, though it does seem to me as well to ring vaguely true, that this human, social world is **ever-so-slowly, quite imperceptibly, incalculably** evolving to align itself more closely with the moral axis that may be built into the core of this universe (*I **think** we might be today just a smidgeon less cruel and violent than William the Bastard or Genghis Khan or Darius, although I'm not the least bit sure; there are still Idi Amins and Hitlers* *running about these days)*. I might call that moral axis the spirit of God, or **a** spirit of God. And I think that, behind all we say and do and think in church, there is a feeble urging of us toward that spirit, that moral axis. I think the most important function of the church is to be for us and for the rest of the world a moral compass, pointing and urging us Godward. The difficulty for me in all this is that I think the church, ever since Constantine co-opted us into his service, has almost entirely lost sight of that moral direction, and has spent itself mostly serving the Empire. Bowers thinks that the real task of the church (and I suppose that means you and me) today, beyond serving as a community for each other, is to rediscover the moral axis of the universe (*vis-a-vis* the needs of the Empire), and as a community to get on with the business of pointing us truly Godward.

Complexity

My view of the church is that there is so much going on, and it's so complicated, that it's amazing there's room left for anything to happen at all, for any forward movement. But there is. Astounding! I have become clear that within that complexity of those entanglements and interweavings of layers upon layers of stuff, I'd best not look for simple or easy answers and solutions; those would probably be wrong, or, at the best, inadequate. Nor should I allow myself to get caught up and immobilized in all that complexity. Physicists have the luxury of controlled experiments searching for the simplest and most elegant solutions. I do not. I live in a world of moving complexities, and am searching only for adequate solutions that suffice to enable me to move on.

Is the Church Unlike Other Good Organizations?

Given that I reject literal understandings of any of orthodox doctrine, do I view the church as in any way different than any other **good** organization, *i.e.,* one committed to values which I see as similar to the gospel values or mandates? I pause here to consider. I cannot really compare the church, particularly St. Luke's with other **good** organizations, mainly because I've never had a close-up experience with any such organizations. They exist, I know. Some are much more responsive than our church to those needs. But then, they are designed to be actioning, and the church is not *(in my eyes)*. On the other hand, none of those can offer the history (reaching back to Abram), the Holy Scriptures, the two millennia of tradition that the church offers. There is a richness within the church that no one but another religion can offer, and I am not tempted to other religions. Within the church, and especially St. Luke's, I am deeply and sumptuously fed. So I have come to believe that I am better fed here than in any other "good" organization. In that sense the church is quite different than the others. That's a very subjective judgment, but that is where this particular choice is made, in the subjective. That richness of tradition, history, and Scriptures feed my mind, my values (which is to say my spiritual life), and I am tempted to say it feeds my soul, though, as I've said, I've not the faintest notion what a soul is.

I suspect my loss of the literal understandings of the doctrine is not so great a loss for me as others might think. I've lost only the literalism of the doctrines (which means I'm now freed to utterly reject some pieces of that doctrine, such as Augustine's dysfunctionally naive concept of sin), and instead I'm free to plumb for much wider, deeper, more inclusive and meaningful understandings and interpretations of those doctrines. Rather than feeling I've lost anything, I sense that doorways to a wider and richer spiritual world have been opened to me without losing anything of value *(to me)*. My horizon is wider, and yet I still have my center in the Christian stuff which I was born into and grew up with, and which I find in St. Luke's these days.

The Deception

Perhaps I should say "blindness" instead of "deception." I want be clear for you: I don't think anyone set out to deceive the church or to make the church into a deception. It just happened. An accident of history, if you will. The church began as a counter-culture movement, was co-opted into the emperor's service and willingly complied. The church became intimately intertwined with the secular state such that the two eventually became inseparable. And so the church has become an unintentional, un-witting, unofficial creature of the state, invisibly so. And if you listen carefully you will hear, beneath the preacher's gospellish words, a quiet music that supports, or at the very least does not confront or counter the values and directions of the state: e.g., unfettered capitalism *(at the cost of the poor)*, institutional and systemic racism *(at the cost of blacks and Hispanics)*, refusal of gun control *(to the benefit of street gangs, organized crime, drug-dealers, and especially the arms manufacturers)*, rampant individualism *(at the cost of the underprivileged, the handicapped, the underclass)*; this list could go on, you fill it out with your own pet causes. My point is simply that the church **is** a creature of the state, however unwittingly and involuntarily, and the state **will** step in to keep us in line if we step too far out of line (e.g., Jesus, Martin Luther King Jr., the wingnut in Florida who burned korans, and the other wingnut in Topeka who picketed military funerals).

The church's proclaimed mission is to evangelize, to baptize, to spread the good news, to save souls for Jesus Christ *(or whatever, pick your own words)*; I conclude that mission is at best an overlay, a veneer, maybe a cover-task, possibly an outright ruse, not intentionally, not deliberately, not mischievously or satanically, but simply out of blindness, self-deception, a voluntary distraction from the underlying but more germane task, to bring the gospel's justice (**a.k.a. *mercy***) into our worlds. And the church is fairly trapped in that deception; we would like *(some more than others)* to preach and hear the good news proclaimed by Jesus (the blind see, the lame walk, the lepers are cleansed, the deaf hear, the dead are raised, to the poor the gospel is preached), but if we did that with purity and zeal we would become as much an enemy of the state as the early church was to Rome. The church is trapped, and her words must remain muted; or alternately, she must go underground, and I don't think anyone is of a mind to do that. And so the church remains a castrated half-breed, an impotent child of both the Empire[9] and the gospel, so unable to well serve either.

Please forgive my purple prose. I once learned that is difficult to see the forest whilst standing amongst the trees; I labored amongst the trees for over three decades; I have just recently found my way out to a place where I think I am looking at the forest. But I may still have a mote or two in my eye.

If the Church Could Escape its Entrapment, What Might it Do?

I've said many words above about the church's entrapment; here I'll add just a few summary words, and a few givens (spoken from where a Jack Bowers type finds himself on his spiritual pilgrimage) and then I'll talk about some possibilities of what might be useful or helpful in the church.

The Givens

For a Jack Bowers type the givens are fairly few and brief. I can no longer take anything religious as literal: Holy Scriptures, doctrines, even traditions, liturgy, hymnology. It is all metaphoric, figurative, symbolic, pointing not to itself but toward the beyond *(whatever that might be)*. I search, which means I question, I challenge, I probe, I attempt *(however vainly)* to understand, and which also means I more often than not come up empty-handed, or with dirtied hands. But I am reaching for more, for richer, for more foundational.

What Could the Church Be and Do?

Several years ago I had a fantasy conversation with Ed Burdick during coffee hour. I asked him, "What is this all about? What's this church about?"

"Well, it's about spreading the Good News of Jesus Christ, of course!"

"Then why this building, why this vast institutional arrangement? They're not essential toward the spreading of the Good News. In fact, they retard that action. They

---

9. Walter Breuggemann, today's premiere Old Testament scholar, currently uses the exodus imagery of the (Egyptian) Empire, in which, like a pyramid, all power in all forms flows to the top while the oppressed slaves at the bottom do all the labor, reaping no rewards; he depicts the gospel as the "freedom community," the way to freedom from the Empire, but sees the world, and the church, as very much in the service of the Empire and the Empire's values.

sop up vital resources, almost all of our time and money. But we don't need them for that task."

My imagined conversation ended there, I couldn't quite figure out what Ed's response might be at that point. He might agree with me and just shrug his shoulders as Ed often does. And I couldn't fantasize any plausible argument Ed Burdick might come up with for all this building and staff and hierarchy. But my next tack would have been, "What if, Ed? What if it's not really about spreading the Good News? At this moment I don't want to debate for several days about Jesus Christ or the Good News. Let me lay those issues aside just for this moment. I want to ponder, what if those are not the core reason, the underlying reason for the church? What then? The church keeps on going, in many different forms. It has survival power. There must be something or some things, very vital at the core of this church that it keeps struggling on, muddling through, despite the multitude of perversions that strike it. What's that staying power about? And I'm not really interested in the "God keeps it going" arguments. Deep inside my mind I suspect that God doesn't care one whit about the church, one way or another. I suspect it's **our** need, not God's, that keeps this church perking along. So what need of ours is the church meeting?"

But at that point I start coming up with my same old standbys.

1. The church is a values-reinforcer. But clearly these are mostly our culture's values being reinforced here, not much related to Christ or to so-called Judeo-Christian values. Oh, we use catch-phrases and proof texts out of the Hebrew and Christian writings to validate the values we're trying to reinforce. But we're not drawing these values out of the Scriptures, we're just **using** the Scriptures, projecting our values into the Scriptures. In fact, most of the values I find voiced in the Scriptures are repugnant to me. And Jesus stood for some values I would absolutely reject: leaving family and following him, rejecting all riches. The Hebrew writings prescribe stoning to death young girls labeled "adulteress," and wayward boys. Eradicating whole cities. If I threw all those Scriptural values on a scale, I suspect I'd reject well over half of them, maybe closer to 80 percent to 90 percent of them. They're not values amenable to me, not values I think work in this modern world, particularly the western world.

And then I go blank. 2) and 3) and such won't come into my mind.

Psychology of Religion

I spoke above about our need to get a lot more serious about sociology, what role(s) the church fulfills in our culture. Another direction we need to pay more intense attention to is the psychology of religion. I am not trained in this and cannot lead, only suggest. But we should look at what role(s) does the church (i.e., membership, community, faith, belief, values, etc.) play for the individual? Beyond the external effort of integrating the individual into the larger community, what is the internal function of religion within the psyche of the person? While a little less than half the population of the U.S. claim membership in the church, nearly all the people claim they are spiritual. That would suggest that the religious realm seems to serve some utilitarian purpose for most individuals. What is that, and how can we do that more directly, if we want to?

Some years ago when I was a chaplain within a community mental health agency I was immersed briefly in the intersection of science and religion. One problem for therapists and counselors was religious language. Since they were mostly untrained in religious language, it was a barrier for them, and in some cases they interpreted it as causing mental illness. Schizophrenic clients used a lot of religious language. The trick, I learned, was to pay little attention to the religious language itself, but to look **through** it, to understand what the client was trying to tell others was going on inside him by his use of religious language. Understand that the religious language the client is using is a veneer he uses to express what is going on inside himself but which he has no other language to express. Look **through** his religious language, not at it, and listen to the music playing underneath the words. I think we could do a lot more of that in the church, looking **through** the language instead of at it, and see what is going on, what the church and religion can do for and with the members.

Learn the Spiritual Realm

And a third direction we ought to explore more devotedly is the spiritual realm. Who knows about spiritual life? The monastics who dedicate themselves to the spiritual life certainly have some notions, though my stay of five weeks with the Cistercians suggested to me that their notions are too tightly framed within the orthodox Christian metaphor to be of use to this Jack Bowers wandering outside those doctrinal boundaries. The mystics make claim to have some expertise in that (spiritual) realm, though Eastern and Islamic religions put much more emphasis on mysticism than Christianity in our western, linear, logical realm. I have been nudged in the direction of deepening my spiritual life over the past two decades, with great frustration. My frustration was lightly explained when it was pointed out that the whole topic of spiritual life only entered the conversation in the last half century. I have thrashed about for some definition of what we meant by the spiritual life only to discover that we have as yet no working definition of that realm! And by the way, the mystics might be a fascinating physiological and psychological excursion, but I'm pretty certain they can't tell us anything useful about the God and non-physical realms.

Preaching the Gospel Seriously

For whatever reason, I know not what *(perhaps simply because I am a Myers-Briggs INTP, an "intuitive-thinker")* I always considered preaching my most serious task.

Chapter 7: Thoughts about the Institutional Church

Poured a lot of time and study and writing into the effort. I had known of one large Presbyterian Church in Dayton that hired one of their several clergy to do nothing but preach; he was expected to put at least forty hours a week into sermon preparation. I could only assume they got good sermons from him. But I was a small parish priest; I could not devote fulltime to the sermon, nor could my small county-seat congregation have digested it if I did. But I was never really satisfied with my sermons, though a few of my clergy friends were, and occasionally plagiarized me *(with my knowledge and permission)*. I always felt the Episcopal Church did not prize preaching as highly as I did. And as I looked around I did not see that others had much of a handle on what the sermon was really about, what it was for, what its function was for the pew-sitter. Some my sermons were little more that amateurish pop-psychology. I saw my role as acquainting parishioners with the Holy Scriptures, showing them some of the beauty and richness and wisdom (as I knew it).

I think there are some serious gaps in our training for sermonizing. We need significantly deeper insight into what our members need, want, and into how to deliver that to them, not exclusively in the sermon, but more deliberately using the sermon as one tool. And we could learn to be a lot more discerning and self-aware about when we are preaching gospel, and when we're peaching Americanism or the Empire *(or what I sometimes call "cultural crap.")*.

Community

For me, being a non-literal believer, whether in Scripture or liturgy or whatever, community is of very high importance. I spoke above about place. That is an important part of community, allowing, or even assuring that everyone has place, and is allowed or enabled to move from place to place as growth or personal situation requires. But there's a lot more to building and maintaining a sound community.

The Iona Community, Healing the Wounded Warriors

The Iona community off the coast of Mull in the Inner Hebrides of Scotland comes to mind. The tiny isle of Iona had been home to the monastic community of St. Columba in the late 500s, one of the very most important monasteries of Scotland. George McLeod, in the first half of the twentieth century founded a new community there, not monastic but a healthy parody of monasticism. A Presbyterian clergymen out of Glasgow he had watched too many clergy working in the ghettoes of Glasgow and other cities simply burn out and crash, and to meet that need established the Iona Community, focused on the physical task of rebuilding the ruined fifteenth-century Benedictine monastic building(s), but primarily as a spiritual refuge where ghetto workers, the wounded warriors could come away, rest and heal up from their stripes. That community is still alive and vital and is now flung world-wide in ministry, but

Iona is still their place to come and be healed. I think the parish church could be that kind of place, where members doing serious ministry might come and be healed, not with the depth and intensity of Iona, but of that ilk.

Serious Church Growing

I am aware that **serious church growers**, the leaders (mostly clergy) who know how to build mega-churches, of necessity have learned how to build and maintain community. It comes with the territory, and it's the heart of the task. For the most part I absolutely abhor their theologies and leadership styles, but I'm well aware that their success is really founded on their ability to enable community-building and raise up lay leaders who can foster and maintain that community-building. I am inclined to think that is the only thing they do that is worth emulating, but we can learn some from them about community.

A Base for Action

I've said as clearly as I can that the parish is designed to be a non-actioning system. It is designed to be pastoral, and probably becomes quite unstable when it tries to be a prophetic system. But I would think that while the parish itself cannot be very prophetic and actioning, it could provide a base for prophetic voice and for clusters of members who organize to take prophetic action. I am not myself aware of any such operations, but I suspect that a careful search would discover some places where that clearly is happening. St. Luke's initiated and largely staffs the Market Street Food Pantry in Newark to feed the poor. The Church of the Advent in Cincinnati has long had an intense ministry to its inner city ghetto. I've heard echoes of such ministries in a few places in this country and in England. Rather than try to convert the base ministry of a parish, it might be more feasible to enable the parish to be home base for the prophetic ministries of members.

A Base for the Exploration of Values, Morality, Meaning

For myself (essentially as a baptized member, not as an ordained priest) participation in the life of the parish has become (*among other things*) a regularized occasion of spending time pondering values, my own values, the values I hear proclaimed in the Hebrew and Christian writings, and the values of our American culture. Those times are also occasions of considering moralities and moral structures. And for plumbing meanings in living. Those three searches I hold to be the core of the spiritual life, for the individual, and potentially for the community. From my point of view the parish could be much enriched, and could much enrich the spiritual lives of some members by a disciplined or organized program of this kind of spiritual work.

Chapter 7: Thoughts about the Institutional Church

Research: What do Members Want/Need? What Could the Church Offer?

The church has lived with an assumed mission of evangelism, proclaiming the good news. We knew what the people needed, to be saved from their sins. I've suggested above that such a mission is make-work, a cover for what function(s) the church really fulfills within the culture and for the individual. If my suggestions should prove to be the case, then perhaps we are approaching the time when it will behoove us to ask, to seek out what our function(s) within the larger society is, and what might be the needs and the wants of the church's members. It could be that some serious research is in order, that we stop assuming we know better than they what they need and want, and instead do some study to learn, and maybe even dare to ask what they think they need and want in order to fulfill whatever function the church could fulfill in their lives.

Final Words

With all I've said above, one might wonder why I stick around this church, why don't I just wander off in some direction that's more to my liking? I think that is not only a fair question, but it's a question that needs to be explored in closing this chapter. Why, if Bowers cannot believe the tiniest bit of the church's doctrine in some slightly or vaguely literal sense, does he want to hang in?

Faithfulness

I've been clear that I think "faith" is a bad and misleading translation of the Hebrew word *'mn* (aman). It has nothing to do with what we believe in our minds, but is an action word meaning something like being faithful, loyal, constant. Faith became an act of intellectual assent, **belief**, when the bishops at Constantine's behest created the *credo* at the Council of Nicene, a lowest common denominator to help unify the church (and thereby the empire). But for me having faith does not mean believing a particular piece of doctrine, but rather acting in faithful ways, being **faithful**. And so I, accepting in a literal sense absolutely none of the doctrine, can still be faithful by what I do, how I behave. And there is much in the Christian church that calls me to be faithful besides a specific set of doctrines. So, what calls me to faithfulness?

Community

Along with many other preachers I've touted all my life about how the church isn't the building, it's the people. Well, in reality it's both. And I've mused about that before. The community is important to me. It's an artificial community. We don't live together. Don't really have that much intercourse. And yet a community is important. When I was a kid our primary community was the neighborhood. We took care of each other. We cared about each other. We chatted, gossiped across fences. We knew each other. Not so today. I know the neighbor to one side and the one across the street, but no others. Community these days is not in the place where I live, it's elsewhere: at work, at church. So the church community is artificial, but important, probably more important today than when I was a kid. We talk, we laugh, we share. And the matters we talk about are matters I care about.

It is a community of fairly similar minded people many of whom like to use their brains. We are somewhat alike and we somewhat like each other. We are an artificial community (except for the real Granvillians), but I am much closer, emotionally and intellectually, to this community than to my own neighborhood or the small city where I live. I do feel at home among the people of St. Luke's. And it is here within St. Luke's that I found the small group with whom I can freely share my theological musings and meanderings. So in several ways St. Luke's is my community, the one I selected, and which in turn seems to have selected me.

Repository for Values

Robert Wright suggests there may be a moral axis to the universe. I'll buy that notion for now, until we can come up with a better way to frame our morality. And then I add that for me the primary role of the church is the business of pointing us truly Godward, i.e., toward that moral axis. To discover that I look first to the eighth-century prophets in the Hebrew Scriptures for some clues, and then toward some of Jesus' teachings, and next I look around at the world in which we find ourselves and start asking "What needs to be happening on this planet, what must be the social climate of this planet, for the good of mankind?" And with that in mind we, the church, need to become more aggressively prophetic, much more aggressively moral, and quit mucking around caught up in picayune diversions, such as what does the Empire need of us? And, what is Jesus saying to me about me?

I think the most important aspect of church (both the community and the building) for me is that it houses the values. Since Constantine the church has mostly embodied the values of the culture, of the state. Most clergy understand the Christian values to be pretty counter-culture. But the folks in the pews, the folks who will still be there after the rector leaves, the people who really own the local church, they know that the values embodied there are not really counter-culture. The church really is the church-of-state, however unofficially. It embodies the more fundamental values, the American values.

Now I realize that if we scraped together into one pile all the values the churches across this nation embody, **all** the American values, there'd be one hell of a vicious, nasty, bloody cat-fight. So I'm clear that the values St. Luke's embodies are somewhat different than the values the First Christian Church here in Lancaster embodies. And that's probably why I chose St. Luke's and not the First Christian Church; the values

Chapter 7: Thoughts about the Institutional Church

it embodies are closer to those I hold dear than those at First Christian. And I'm also aware that the values St. Luke's embodies are not exactly congruent with those I hold most dear. That's obvious to me when I find myself scribbling notes during the sermon, usually outlining the counter-sermon dribbling out my ear. So the values St. Luke's embodies are in some ways different from mine. And it is possible that the values I think St. Luke's embodies are merely my projection, that I project them onto St. Luke's so that I can have my values validated by some body outside of myself, namely the community of St. Luke's. I know, that is **very** convoluted and self-serving. But it's probably closer to reality than my dream about St. Luke's embodying **my** values.

Now the church, St. Luke's, **is** a repository for some pretty revolutionizing values: feeding the hungry, releasing the prisoners, freeing the oppressed, etc. And the preacher does occasionally give voice to a few of those. But, in accord with the compact worked out between the empire and the early church leaders, the preacher voices those only occasionally, and then not too stridently. We do want to know that, while we, as a parish, as part of a larger church, do not pay too much attention to them, those revolutionizing values are still there, a vague nudging towards a maybe unfulfillable dream. But we should also know that if we really want to do something about enacting those values, then we probably need to build another, free-standing system specifically to do that and not beat up on the church for not doing what we'd like it to do, but which it is designed explicitly ***not*** to do.

A Musing Place

I find myself often when I am in church, musing. For me the church has become a place I go to muse, to think about, to consider, to try to understand, deeply, and profoundly. The church, both the physical place and the body of people as well, seems to encourage my thoughtfulness, my considerations. I realize that is a very individual act, not one the other people there are likely to engage, not part of the liturgy, not something we are supposed to be doing. But it works for me.

My Circle of Standing Stones

Among other things it is a place of transcendence. Like those magnificent cathedrals of medieval Europe, the church reminds me that I am transcended, that there is some Other. And however ineffable it is, I must pay attention.

Whatever I might believe at the top of my head, for a multitude of reasons the **church is still home** for me.

Chapter 8: All Religion Is Metaphor

Most will find the first section of this chapter tough sledding: a little too technical, and just flat out boring. No apologies; I need to lay the foundation. If you must, skip through this first part, though you might have to come back to it. Next I deal with metaphor in Christian religious thinking, and finally I attempt, as an experiment, to pierce the metaphor(s) of the Nicene Creed.

All Religious Language is Metaphor

Some years ago I read the novelist *cum* Roman Catholic priest Andrew Greeley's story of a non-practicing Irish Roman Catholic police detective from Chicago who, vacationing in Dublin, Ireland, was sucked into solving a murder. In the course of the narrative he was exploring his unbeliefs at a cocktail party with the archbishop who responded to him, "Of course, you understand that all religion is metaphor." Now, I do not hold Andrew Greeley to have been an eminent theologian, but that simple thought struck me like a runaway bus and has been haunting me ever since. When we talk and think theology, or any matters spiritual, or about God at all, about whatever lies behind the material world, we are contemplating and uttering things somewhat beyond our comprehension, things certainly beyond the range of our language. Our working vocabulary of words and concepts arise out of the material world in which we live, and flounders when we start making god-talk. We have not the words to describe spiritual things with any precision; the spiritual experiences themselves are usually quite ephemeral, soft and fuzzy, squishy and vaporous around the edges, difficult even to recollect later. And so, being unable to describe our spiritual realms with precise words, we have to speak in metaphors. We describe those spiritual experiences with material images because we have no precise spiritual language with which to describe them. We talk in metaphor. All religious language is metaphor; even our religious ideation is metaphorical.

Definitions

I need to sidetrack to draw some definitions. Just what is a metaphor? Simply put, it is a literary tool for describing; it attempts to clarify what one thing is by comparing it to another, hopefully one better known or understood. Metaphors and similes are

Chapter 8: All Religion Is Metaphor

analogies. A simile clarifies by stating that one thing is **like** another, but not the same as. A metaphor, on the other hand, says they are the same, this **is** that.

> From the ***Random House Dictionary of the English Language***: "Figure of speech: a term or phrase applied to something to which it is not literally applicable in order to suggest a resemblance; something used, or regarded as being used to represent something else; emblem, symbol."

That helps a little, but doesn't really get there for me. I'll try again. This time from Wikipedia a definition of a *metaphor*:

> "a figure of speech that identifies one thing as being the same as some unrelated other thing, for rhetorical effect, thus highlighting the similarities between the two. It is therefore considered more rhetorically powerful than a simile. While a simile compares two items, a metaphor directly equates them, and so does not apply any distancing words of comparison, such as "like" or "as." Metaphor is a type of analogy and is closely related to other rhetorical figures of speech that achieve their effects via association, comparison or resemblance including allegory, hyperbole, and simile.[1]

Metaphor is about Tension

That gets me a little further. A metaphor tells me about one thing *(the tenor, ground or target)* by saying it is the same as another thing *(the vehicle, figure or source)*. But I know they obviously are not the same, so I have to figure out in what way they are the same. "War is hell." Well, I know war is not the same as the hell my fire-and-brimstone preacher keeps pushing at me, but there are some similarities. "War is a chess game." War is patently not a chess game; there are both similarities and differences between the two.

From here we could get very technical, and I don't really want to do that, but I do have to go at least one small step farther to understand how the metaphor works. Sallie McFague[2] is more rigorous and thoroughgoing in her definition of the metaphor, first citing another's definition[3], ". . . when we use a metaphor we have two thoughts of different things actively together and supported by a single word, or phrase, whose meaning is a resultant of their interaction. . . ." and she then herself emphasizes the **insistence** on "two active thoughts which remain in permanent tension or interaction with each other." So, she points out, "when we say 'war is a chess game,' we keep both thoughts in tension. . . war is, but is **not**, a chess game."

---

1. Wikipedia https://en.wikipedia.org/wiki/Metaphor
2. McFague, ***Metaphorical Theology*** *passim*
3. Lakoff and Johnson, ***Metaphors We Live By*** cited by McFague

My understanding from these definitions is that we learn from the tension between the target and source which have been pronounced to be the same. They are not the same; they are analogous, corresponding in **some** particular. "Jesus is the good shepherd." We can be fairly sure Jesus never herded any sheep, may never have even known any. No identity here, so the similarity must be explored. Jesus is an itinerant rabbi, fairly unlike a shepherd. But we might discover some elucidation of his rabbinic role by looking at the shepherd's role, which is what the gospeler John does (10:11-14). It's not that the rabbi Jesus does anything the shepherd does, but in the tension between the target and source we discover some insights about Jesus' role. And, I might note, as I try to unravel in what way the two are analogous. I will probably discover that you, in your unraveling, are discovering some slightly different correspondence(s). That is the richness of the metaphor.

Other Metaphors

There are two other kinds of metaphor I need to identify in passing, simply to be clear about the most used forms. One is the **parable**, an extended metaphor narrated as an anecdote illustrating and teaching, e.g., Aesop's fables, and many of Jesus' teachings. The parable usually intends to make a single message or have only one point of correspondence. The other is the **allegory**, another extended metaphor, this one having multiple points of correspondence and so may have several messages; Jesus' story of the Sower and the Soils is an example (called a parable but really an allegory in as much as there are multiple points of correspondence). In the first centuries of Christianity the interpretation of the Scriptures as allegory was a favored mode of interpretation.

Literality

Before I take another turn, I must take note of one point which I think often confounds us. The simile clearly states that the two being compared are different; this is **like** that. But the language of the metaphor implies they are the same, identical. We know they aren't, but sameness is spoken. Jesus **is** the good shepherd; he's not **like** a good shepherd, he **is** one. To understand the metaphor I must recognize the target and source are different and then step into the tension between them. But we have a problem. In the early years, and for too many centuries since, our Scriptures have been usually understood quite literally. That would be fine if Jesus was **like** a good shepherd; but if Jesus **is** the good shepherd, we wobble. Take it literally or figuratively? I'm sure fundamentalists get caught there, but I suspect that even those of us who have been taught about metaphor wobble a bit at this point. Literal or figurative? Problematic.

Chapter 8: All Religion Is Metaphor

Worldview

Now I take a turn from the metaphor as a simple figure of speech to larger uses of the term. A **root metaphor** is an "underlying worldview that shapes an individual's understanding" of a situation. The Wikipedia article explains the **Conceptual metaphor**:

> "Some theorists have suggested that metaphors are not merely stylistic, but that they are cognitively important as well. . . .metaphors are pervasive in everyday life, not just in language, but also in thought and action. A common definition of a metaphor can be described as a comparison that shows how two things that are not alike in most ways are similar in another important way. They explain how a metaphor is simply understanding and experiencing one kind of thing in terms of another. The[y]. . . call this concept a 'conduit metaphor.' By this they meant that a speaker can put ideas or objects into words or containers, and then send them along a channel, or conduit, to a listener who takes that idea or object out of the container and makes meaning of it. In other words, communication is something that ideas go into. The container is separate from the ideas themselves. Lakoff and Johnson give several examples of daily metaphors we use, such as 'argument is war' and 'time is money.' Metaphors are widely used in context to describe personal meaning. The[y]. . . also suggest that communication can be viewed as a machine: "Communication is not what one does with the machine, but is the machine itself [4]."

This second understanding, root metaphor, is more fundamental for me than the rhetorical one. My friends have noted that I use the term metaphor in two quite different ways; one implying the simple metaphor wherein the target is identified with the source, and the other to indicate a **worldview**, a way of seeing and understanding, a cognitive framework. I'll illustrate.

My initial learning about this goes this way. In my mid-teens my grandfather had a darkroom in our basement and he acquainted me with the rudiments of black-and-white photography. One evening when I was preparing to print some photos I set up my developer and fixative baths but discovered we had no *short stop*; that was simply a solution of 28 percent acetic acid diluted with a specific ratio of water. I grabbed a bottle of acetic acid off the shelf behind me and went out of the darkroom to mix some up and fill the jug we kept the dilution in. I mixed it up and stepped back into the darkroom, set down the jug and turned to put the bottle of 28% back on the shelf. I glanced at the bottle as it slid onto the shelf and the label was blank! I held it under the light. Quite blank! Unsure of myself I puzzled "Did I mix the right stuff? I stepped out of the darkroom, bottle in hand, and read clearly, "Acetic Acid 28%." Slightly confused but somewhat reassured I stepped back into the darkroom and as I again slid the bottle onto the shelf saw it was blank. It said nothing about acetic acid! Again I took the bottle out of the darkroom and the label clearly said "Acetic Acid 28%." But

---

4. Wikipedia https://en.wikipedia.org/wiki/Metaphor

PART II: MY REVIEW OF CHRISTIAN DOCTRINES

I also noticed the label was red lettering on a white label. Aha! I stepped back in the darkroom and put the bottle under the light. No red lettering! Just a red label. And in that instant I learned that you can't read a red label under a red light.[5] My red light was on, and under that light the whole label was red and the lettering didn't show up. You simply can't see anything red under a red light.

    I tell that long story not to amuse but to illustrate a simple and very basic, fundamental point. The light you are bathed in affects what you can see. We talk about "rose colored glasses" to indicate a Pollyannaish person who simply can't see the bad stuff going on, he only sees the rosy stuff. The colored glasses he wears will color everything he sees. And then I generalize: that metaphor, the glasses, lens, worldview one uses to view the world around him will necessarily color and shape his perception of that world, and because of that there will be some things he simply will not see, he will not even be aware they are there; and conversely, everything he does see will be somewhat colored, shaped, affected, distorted by the lens through which he is looking. Jihadists today see the world through a lens that distorts everything so that whatever non-Muslim they see is automatically hateful, conspiratorial, aggressively hostile and threatening to them, all to be destroyed. Call it a worldview if you like. It's a framework, a structure, a window. I would identify this framework as part of what the psychiatrists call our psychological structures, the structures we have each built up out of our experiences over the years and through which we perceive the world, and by means of which we respond to our world. Those structures shape what we see and what we do; they are an essential and inescapable part of us. We cannot survive without them. Worldviews. Mine are slightly different than yours. Ours are somewhat different than a Parisian's, but radically different than a Jihadist's. Our individual worldviews shape and color our worlds.

Another Layer, Language Itself

My thinking here is shaped by my training in languages (Greek, Latin, Hebrew, English). They have taught me that while on the one hand **what** we are thinking to a small degree may shape and push the limits of our language (the words, the grammar, the constructs *e.g., you may have noticed that I tend to create new words when the old ones just don't hack it*); on the other hand our **language both shapes and (immeasurably) limits, sometimes even warps our thinking**. We, at least the most of us who are not geniuses, cannot think very far outside of our language; the words, the grammar, and the structure limit and shape both what we can think and how we can think about it. We need the tools of the language both to give shape to, and then to express our mental ruminations (e.g., the study of "logic" serves not so much to build air-tight "proofs"

---

    5. When developing negatives absolute blackness was required; the faintest ray of light would overwhelm the images on the negative, it was that light-sensitive. But photo paper was not as sensitive and a red light could be used which had almost no effect on the developing photograph.

as to ensure clear and accurate communications). An Einstein may be able to think far beyond the tools of his language (in his case mathematical symbols), but most of us can not; the tools of the language roughly form the boundaries of our thinking.

I'll offer one example out of my own experience of how language shapes our comprehension and understanding. The Indo-European languages which I've studied are noun based; i.e. the roots of the preponderance of words are nouns from which verbs are formed (though conversely some roots are verbs from which nouns are formed). Our language is **concept** based, and as I think about the working of our language (and therefore our thinking, since language is the tool we use to formulate our thoughts) I envision a set of concepts linked (almost chain-like) by verbs. In English the subject is normally first, linked by the second word, the main verb of the clause, to the third, the predicate; that is the regular structure. We have learned to think in defined concepts linked primarily by verbs (actions). But in Hebrew (and all Semitic languages), the roots are almost all **verbs**. Nouns are built on verb roots, and there are few adjectives. The main verb is regularly the first word in the sentence, followed by the subject and then the predicate. So the first notion the reader or thinker encounters is the action, followed by the doer, and then the acted-upon. The Hebrew mind learns to think in terms of actions (rather than concepts). I envision that as watching the flow of fluid actions in which a few concepts (nouns) are floating. Our western mind thinks in terms of a chain or network of concepts linked with verbs. How different a Hebrew worldview must be, thinking primarily in terms of actions rather than concepts.

Several Metaphors

It is my contention that we each carry around within us several worldviews, or what I call metaphors, schemas, frameworks through which we perceive and respond:

The Scientific Metaphor

We live in a scientific era, born of the Enlightenment. We see and understand most things in terms of the tenets of that metaphor. It defines the world as rational, reasonable, predictable. Its fundamental premise is cause and effect; everything has an identifiable cause; and every cause has an effect, a predictable result. There is no room for randomness. And science does its work through reductionism, the process of reducing everything to the simplest, most basic mechanisms and elements. I understand the first human need to be making sense of the world, an orderliness, so that the world becomes predictable and thereby to some extent controllable. The scientific metaphor has done an outstanding job of meeting that need.

PART II: MY REVIEW OF CHRISTIAN DOCTRINES

THE PHYSICISTS'S METAPHOR

This metaphor has been in vogue (though evolving) since Galileo, Newton and Einstein. It reaches in two directions, utmost reductionism and cosmology, sub-atomic particles and universes. This metaphor envisions the world in terms of matter and energy and structure. Its primary tool is measurement. When I rap my knuckles on the table, the physicist knows that the hard and resounding tabletop is not what it seems, but is an orderly structure of motion, of vibrating molecules and whirling atoms and sub-atomic particles and empty space, but mostly space. And the physicist looks in the opposite direction as well, to the solar system, the galaxies, the universe(s), and tells us how the universe came into being and is evolving; much of scientific discovery and engineering development grows out of the physicist's knowledge and findings.

MY REAL-WORLD METAPHOR

I rap my knuckles on the table top. The physicist smiles, knowing that tabletop is not what it seems to me, and instead is a bunch of whirling electrons and nuclei, vibrating molecules, but mostly empty space. I smile back because while I might barely comprehend what he knows and understands, I am clear that I do not live in his world. I live where the tabletop is hard and can hurt my knuckles if I rap too hard. The world I live in is a creation inside my brain out of bits and pieces of momentary perceptions and bushel baskets full of experiences and all the fact I've ever gathered. I create my real-world metaphor here, inside my head, a characturish, cartoonish kind of thing. And it works. It is not an accurate depiction of the unseeable realty that surrounds me, but it does make a usable sense out of whatever really is out there, a sense that is workable, and makes it possible to maneuver and live in this world. I live inside a work-a-day metaphor, quite unlike the scientist's and the physicist's. Everything I perceive and do happens through that everyday, real-world metaphor. Even if it actually is only inside my head.

Only Inside My Head

(*This may not be pertinent to the defining of metaphor, but it feels important to me, and fascinating.*) The physicist's worldview is one thing, but when I get out of bed in the morning, I arise into a different world, a fairly orderly world of substantial things and beings which **actually exist only in my head**, inside my brain, in my mind!! I **create** them there inside my skull, brain, mind! I select certain of the stimuli whizzing around me as I arise from the bed, and I constitute them into a *reality* within which I can live and cope. This is the **one** metaphor I have learned to construct and maintain inside my head through my living of these eighty years of life in order to cope with living in the midst of a reality which I cannot even detect. This is **one** metaphor, **my** metaphor,

Chapter 8: All Religion Is Metaphor

which I alone have learned to construct; you have your own, which is probably fairly similar, but different. Because I built mine out of a set of little bits of perception unique to me that I learned to detect and select (or fabricate out of my fantasies), and organize, and build into the "psychological structures" through which I manage my life in my idiosyncratic universe, therefore my world is slightly unique to me. And in my old age I have come to realize that there are many things out there in the world beyond my eyes and ears which my metaphor screens out, chooses to not even detect because they don't seem relevant at this moment, chooses even not to know they exist (probably because they weren't important to me in the first few days after I exited the uterus and so concluded to omit them from my "select-in" screen). Some of those you may know about while I don't, but there are some I know that you screen out and can't even be aware of. And then together, you and I, as we talk and share and learn from each other begin to build some other metaphors to talk about other things that science can't even conceive of, like consciousness, and the sense of an emotion, or the blueness of blue (a light wave just so many angstroms long but with no color), or the taste of an orange.

A religious Metaphor

And then I sit down to prepare my sermon, and suddenly I am in a different metaphor. It is furnished with the God and Jesus and sin and a Kingdom of Heaven, strange things which can never be part of the furniture of the physicist's or the scientist's or even of my real-world metaphors. I am very clear that "God" is not a word in the physicist's or scientist's realms, not a working or useful concept, is not included in the vocabulary they use inside their metaphors. And while within the context of my everyday, work-a-day metaphor I might invoke the God, in a prayer or meditation or even a curse, those are not the furnishings of my *real world* metaphor either. To invoke the God in that instant I had to step out of my *real world* metaphor and into the religious metaphor. The religious metaphor uses a wholly different language and construct, one unique to itself. But it is a primary metaphor in my profession, one I use to make sense and order out of most of the non-material events of my living.

Several Metaphors (continued)

The religious metaphor is the one in which I spent most of my working life, so it is familiar to me. But I am clear that it is different than the others. The furniture in it does not fit in the others. By straining I could probably identify several more metaphors, world-views I carry around inside my head, but I've already made my point. These metaphors are separate metaphors, worldviews, somewhat exclusive constructs. And they are not mutual. I can be in this one, or in that one, but never both at once; I have to leave one and move to the other. And if I try to mix them together, I get in trouble; things will not work well, there will be confusion, even misunderstanding, perhaps bad mistakes, misjudgments. I must do physicist's work within the physicist's metaphor where the God is not; and if I want to make god-talk then I must step out of the physicist's metaphor and into the religious one. They don't intermingle and they are not simply overlays. They perceive and structure different realities. And like my colored glasses, they enable me to see different things. But be warned, there are things outside their vision as well, things they cannot see. I think I've said enough; I hope you understand.

I Need to Lay One More Caution before You

As I plumb the mysteries of religious metaphor I realize that I am wandering perilously close to epistemology (i.e., what we can know and how we can know it). This discussion requires me to edge up to that precipice. I pick up an orange, cut it in half and share it with you. We savor the segments. But I wonder: are you tasting what I am tasting? Are our taste sensations the same? We have no way of knowing. There is no external touchstone against which we can both check. So we eat the segments and trust that we are both enjoying roughly the same taste sensations. *(We could try to describe to each other what we are tasting, and we might get close to understanding what flavor(s) the other is savoring, but in the end, I fear, we'll never get quite there. The question will still remain, for me.)* And likewise when we step into our religious metaphors together, you into yours, I into mine, we cannot be quite sure that what you are seeing inside your religious metaphor, and what I am seeing inside mine, are the same thing, or even roughly similar; our two religious metaphors may be undetectedly somewhat different (unless you are a Muslim and I am a Buddhist, in which case we know they are quite different and if we want to converse meaningfully then we must check out everything very carefully and very exhaustively). And, as I've already suggested, even if we are fairly clear with each other about the dimensions of our two religious metaphors, we still must be careful and tolerant when we step together into the tension of a literary metaphor, e.g., "Jesus is the good shepherd," because as we begin to unravel the metaphor, you may discover something different than I in that tension; it is the nature of the metaphor that it is deliberately ambiguous. It opens doors rather than slamming them shut.

I Stipulate This: All Religious Ideation and Language is Itself Metaphor

It is a way of trying to conceptualize and/or verbalize a peculiar non-material realm which feels like it may be, and is, actually, beyond our ability to comprehend (or, perhaps just beyond our fingertips). *God* is part of that metaphor, as is *Jesus*. But a metaphor with what? A metaphor claims two things are the same, and in as much as I know they are not, the message lies somewhere in the tension between the two. If Jesus is the one, then what is the other with which he is compared? And if I've no idea what the other is, then how can I find between them the tension where the learning lies, the unseen reality and/or truth the metaphor is trying to illuminate? *(I realize as I am writing this paragraph that for several years I've been misusing the term "metaphor" in my thinking. To say "Jesus is a metaphor" is nonsense. What I have meant is "Jesus is a **stand-in**, a substitute, a code or shorthand for something else, something for which I cannot easily find other words, or which is too complicated to easily explain. What is that something else? What is Jesus standing in for?" Likewise the God, YHWH, Adonai is a stand-in, but for what?)*

When I delve into religious stuff, i.e., theologize, I am trying to understand, to make sense of myself and of you and of us and of the world, of this creation in which we find ourselves and of the God which we hope has something to do with the running of all this world and our lives. But these are not material facts which we can palpate and stack up. We can ruminate about them, but being children of this material realm, of this physical world, we have only the vocabulary and language and structure of material things to guide us through the ruminations of things immaterial, spiritual, religious. Where's the metaphor in this religious stuff? I'm going to play with three topics, the Holy Scriptures, the God and Jesus, to see what I can learn. Come with me.

The Holy Scriptures

I begin with our scriptures, the Hebrew Scriptures and the Christian Writings. Are they metaphor? In what ways are they metaphor? Can any of our Scriptures (Hebrew and Christian writings) be understood as non-metaphor, as factual, or literal?

Fact or Fiction?

It is instructive that Karen Armstrong (***A History of God***) asserts that Muslims understand the whole of the Koran to be metaphorical, not to be understood literally. I leap from there to suggest that perhaps the fallacy of much of Christian thinking, influenced by protestant, fundamentalist, Enlightenment and scientific understandings, is that our Scriptures are to be taken literally. "Fact or Fiction" is the cry, with a failure to comprehend that much, if not most truth lies beyond the realm of fact and fiction, is abstraction from outside, rather than inside, physical "posits." And that has to be particularly true the second we start doing "god-talk." Much of Christendom, along with most religions, throughout most of history have understood that truth, especially religious truth, is not a "fact or fiction" deal. To try to understand the two creation stories as scientific fact is not just misguided, but stupid and wrong-headed, and results in many misunderstandings and horrid fallacies (the foremost one today being "Creationism.") Those stories were never intended to be scientific descriptions of physical realities. Physicists do that kind of stuff. They were intended to propound religious, spiritual understandings of ourselves as human beings, and of the world in which we find ourselves, and perhaps even of the God (though that may be a specious effort). Were there two critters named Adam and Eve? Hardly. They are metaphors for you and me. The story-teller was not propounding his version of the "Big Bang Theory." He was not even foremostly asking about the beginning of the physical universe. He was telling us about you and me and our world using as his metaphor the two most ancient forebears of our line that he could imagine, a first man, the "mud-boy" *(ha'adam)*, and a first woman, the "mother of all living" *(havah)*. And I then extend that understanding of the intentions of the first two stories to cover most of our Scriptures. History, as we try to write and read it today, is a fairly modern creation. The ancients did not write history as we have come to understand it, as the assemblage of the brute facts of a period of time; but rather they wrote recitations of the great deeds of their great leaders. *(And in another vein we can easily argue that there is no such thing, even among contemporary scholarly historians, as an unbiased assemblage of the facts. All modern history is written by the victorious, and about the great deeds of the victorious and the evil deeds of the defeated.)* And our Scriptures, our holy writings, were never purported to be "history" in the modern sense, however much the literalists and fundamentalists might strive to make them into "history."

So what within our holy writings can be taken or understood to be "fact"? Probably very little, nearly nothing. They should all be understood as "great stories" about our origins, about our past, stories that celebrate that past and those origins, stories that attempt to share with us who our forbearing story-tellers thought us to be, where we came from, how we got to this point in time and space; but not as *fact*, not as scientific understanding, not as "history," but as legend, myth, as important great stories which they firmly believed tell us "truth" (i.e., abstract truth, not facts) about ourselves and our world, and maybe about the God. And wherever in our holy writings we happen to discover some bits and pieces that might be historically or scientifically accurate, those are probably best understood as coincidence, happenstance, chance, but not as corroborating evidence.

Then Metaphor:

We could get quite confused at this point. I've been using the term metaphor the three different ways: 1) as a stand-in, substitute for some non-material, and perhaps inexplicable 'other' *(a misuse of the term "metaphor," though I do use it this way)*, 2) as a specific literary tool (Jesus is the good shepherd), and 3) as a worldview. So I need to be clear how I understand the Scriptures to be metaphorical in each of these three ways.

Worldview:

To use the Scriptures as a worldview, I need to step way back from them, until I can no longer see the details, and then view the sixty-six books (of several quite different *genre*) as a whole, as a coherent unity. And from that vantage I can understand our

Chapter 8: All Religion Is Metaphor

Scriptures as indicating, pointing toward a way of living, toward an understanding of what comprises good living, and how this world is put together, and what is my place in this world, what is **our** place. A window, or set of eye-glasses through which I can view and understand the world. A framework for making sense of myself, and of our relations and of the world. I will not attempt to tell you what I see as I look through that particular worldview, that would take several volumes; but I will comment this: that specific worldview, our Scriptures, is two millennia old and needs to be understood as, in light of what we have since learned, somewhat out-dated, so used with care and caution. Some of it may be still accurate and quite applicable, and some needs to be taken as only the roughest of guides; I understand that some people, our fundamentalists and the ultra-orthodox Jews, take it all as accurate and applicable in every detail, but I cannot go in that direction at all.

Metaphor, A Figure of Speech

As I have already mentioned, the ancients favored interpreting the Scriptures allegorically (a particular kind of metaphor with many points of correspondence). But they also understood the text literally. In the light of textual criticisms from many different vantages I can not take our Scriptures literally in any sense. I tend to understand nearly all the text as metaphor. The stories I understand mostly as parable, (a category of metaphor with one central point) through which I must look, gaze, ponder. Some are exceedingly rich. I find the "Rape of Tamar" (2 Sam 13:1-22) one of the most exquisite stories in the whole of the Scriptures, though unquestionably a horrifying story for this and all feminists; each time I ponder that story I discover new dimensions to bring back to my current world and see what they tell me in this light. Other stories are more baffling; Luke's parable of the rich man and his squanderous property manager (16:1-8) drives honest, loyal people a little crazy; or Matthew's Vineyard Laborers (20:1-16) which drives capitalists and profiteers straight up the wall. I think all of these metaphors need to be read first in their own context to discover what Jesus or the author was teaching, and then secondly, in the light of today's world to discover what it might be teaching us today (which, with an intervening twenty-hundred years of discovery, is sometimes garbage.).

In moments when I am honest, I will mutter under my breath so as not to be overheard, much of the teachings in our Scriptures were *apropos* to its day, but have little if any instructive value for us today.

Metaphor, a Stand-in, a Substitute

I'm unclear how this might apply in the reading or use of our Scriptures. I think this usage is fraught with traps and pitfalls; with a stated target but an unstated source the tension is fairly indefinable, and the teaching quite vaporous. It can be an attempt to look through the words and get glimpses of the non-material truths which may lie behind them. But I think it can easily devolve into fantasy, cherry-picking, proof-texting one's own thinking and mindset. While I might ask with all seriousness, "If Jesus is himself a metaphor, then what is the truth to which he is pointing? ..or for which he is standing in?" I would be most leery of asking that same kind of question of any specific piece of the Scriptures.

Rorschach

As I have said before, I see our Scriptures most often used as a Rorschach, a projective tool, an ink blot into which the reader (or preacher) projects his own stuff. When I hear someone proof-texting I can be very sure that's exactly what he's doing, lifting a few words out of the Scriptures and out of context to justify and give authority to his own thinking. I think that a very dangerous and self-serving process. I believe that whenever we draw something out of the Scriptures we must then aggressively and rigorously test it in the real light of day in the real-world in which we live, against the current reality, and see if it then still makes sense. Scripture, by itself, unreflected upon, is a hazard. And the literary metaphors in Scripture, when the secondary reference is not specified, are particularly open to hazardous misuse.

The God

When asked, "If the 'God' is metaphor," how do I respond?

First I Must Lay a Foundation

In starting I confess that I was fairly appalled when I studied (in preparation to teach) the literary editor and ex-Jesuit Jack Miles's book, **God: A Biography**. The YHWH Miles revealed through the course of the Masoretic text of the Hebrew Scriptures is nothing I want to worship. The cultural evolutionist-journalist Robert Wright's book, **The Evolution of God** showed me that the God revealed in our Scriptures is primarily (if not exclusively) the god needed, yearned for at those particular times in history, at those points of the cultural evolution, but probably it bears no relationship to the God of the universe. Karen Armstrong's **A History of God** shows that the images of God which have evolved in the major religions of the Book (Judaism, Christianity and Islam) bear remarkable resemblance to each other. If we bypass the various Holy Scriptures of those religions, then maybe we are worshiping the one and same God. But that God does not resemble the revelations of Scriptures. Evelyn Underhill, in describing the stages of development in the spiritual experiences of mystics in her book, **Mysticism**, indirectly describes a quite different God than any of our scriptures envision, a God which seems to have two faces: on the one hand the mystics experience the God as an overwhelming and all enveloping

Chapter 8: All Religion Is Metaphor

love, and on the other hand as a vast, cold, and impersonal emptiness. And I then find it instructive that the Buddhists have almost nothing to say about God. I have to conclude tentatively (and for myself only) that the God is in the end quite unknowable, and perhaps is not terribly necessary. We may utter the word "God," even realizing that the word is metaphor, but we know very little about God, and even that small knowledge seems to be slowly erased away by the discoveries of physics and the other sciences. "God" seems to point only to that which is *utterly other*. And while some individuals may be able to describe that utterly other in slightly more specific terms, those descriptions seem to me quite idiosyncratic, unverifiable, and often incompatible. "God" is metaphor, but it is beyond me to imagine what reality that metaphor stands in for.

From there I wander farther down this path, wondering **how far** I dare **to push** the metaphor bit. First I notice that when I say "The 'God' is a metaphor," I realize this not a standard metaphor; there is no target-source relationship, no tension. This is what I've called *a stand-in*, a substitute. But I'm given no clues what the metaphor "God" stands in for. The word "God" remains opaque, I can see nothing of whatever is standing behind the word; or rather I should say the notions about the God that I've been offered are unacceptable to me: YHWH, Abba, Allah; I judge them all to be projections out of the culture's need; they are not verifiable or demonstrable evidence, or tracings, footprints of the God *(at least they do not appear so to me.)* But then, my standards of reliability seem to be fairly high.

What then Can I Say about "the God" as a Metaphor?

I did make feeble stabs at defining what "the God" might be standing in for in Chapter 5. But none drew blood. I was, then and now, clear that "the God" does not stand in for YHWH or Abba or Allah. And I became clear in that chapter that I can find no sources I can judge reliable to learn about the God, either out of my own experiences or out of the witnessing of others ("reliable" is the operative modifier). I have no cause to doubt that the God exists, I simply can find nothing reliable to say about the God. I did suggest several possible sources for which "the God" might be the target: 1) the ideal of human living (for me an ideal out of communitarianism), 2) the (unclear, undefined) whole ball of wax, 3) a verbal, non-conceptual understanding of the Other, and, 4) that which is Wholly Other. None of those is very informative or helpful, though the notion of the God as verb-like is curious and opens up to interesting questions.

"The God" as a metaphor remains almost completely a blank for me.

Jesus

Sallie McFague suggests that Jesus himself is a **parable**. I understand her to mean that Jesus is himself a type of metaphor. A real live human being and a walking, talking metaphor. Well, maybe.

PART II: MY REVIEW OF CHRISTIAN DOCTRINES

Jesus as the Target

In metaphors used in the early church to describe Jesus we find these:

> In the four gospels: Son of God, Lord
>
> In John[6]: Word, light, true light, light of the world, bread of life, bread of God, way, good shepherd, true vine, resurrection, life, door
>
> After the gospels: high priest, sacrifice
>
> Post Scripture: lamb, Sophia, servant

(this is not an exhaustive list, but from the scope it's obvious these descriptors can not be taken literally.) These are metaphors in the sense of the primary definition, figures of speech in which one thing (the target) is said to be the same as another (the source). In this paragraph I'm going to play a little with only one of these, the rest you'll have to play out yourself.

What are we saying when we utter the words "the Son of God"? I can understand those words to mean something like "We hold Jesus to have embodied and enacted more than any other human who has walked this earth what we think God wants of us." No divine DNA in his body cells, but divine morality, divine will, divine intention, divine-like behavior (but emphatically not divine DNA). And then what reality does that Jesus metaphor point toward? In what myriad of ways does that metaphor speak to us? And therein lies the main problem, the myriad of ways. In that tension between the target (Jesus) and the source (any of the above) there should be only one point of correspondence. But the one you find is likely somewhat different than the one I find; and the way you interpret that point of correspondence may be moderately different than the way I interpret the correspondence I found. There is room for different interpretations of the metaphor. The beauty of the metaphor is that it can locate and express the inexpressible, but its mischief lies in its inscrutability.

This Jesus was evidently so inspirational, so revered, so recognized as leading or pointing in a God-ward direction (the moral axis of the universe?) that he became dubbed (after his death) "the son of God." An honorific title, but something immensely more than just an honorific. We cannot simply mean "follow his example like lemmings," get executed for insurrection. What then? And finally we need to answer **not** "What did **they** mean when they dubbed him 'son of God?'" but rather "What do **we** mean when

---

6. The preponderance of these metaphors come out of the Gospel of John. That may be more than happenstance. John Spong in his ***The Fourth Gospel: tales of a Jewish mystic*** puts forth the thesis (overwhelmingly attractive to me) that the fourth gospel was written by a Jewish mystic who had no experience of the earthly Jesus, but wrote this gospel to explicate his own mystical experiences of the post-resurrection Christ. This thesis makes sense of John's idiosyncratic style, his radical departure from the synoptic story line, his use of so little of the synoptic material, and his consistent depiction of Jesus as divine and triumphant, particularly on the cross. If Spong's thesis bears out, it would help explain John's greater use of these metaphors unique to him, especially in as much as they are attempts to describe the mystical experiences of the Christ, not earthly remembrances.

we proclaim him 'Son of God'?" One more notion occurs to me: that we use the *Jesus metaphor* to encourage ourselves to aspire to the best that is within us, to live toward, and in compassion with those living around us (literally and/or figuratively).

Jesus as a Worldview:

I hesitatingly offer one other notion. When Sallie McFague suggests that Jesus may be a parable, perhaps instead of a figure of speech metaphor, we should think of a worldview metaphor. This might yield some useful stuff. Jesus as worldview, i.e., look through Jesus' eyes, see the world as he saw it. I'm hearing some values, some frameworks some moral leanings when I do this. But I must admit it does feel a trifle too close to WWJD (What Would Jesus Do?) I'll leave this for you to play with.

The Creed:

We stand and recite together the Nicene Creed each Sunday. I do so cheerily, and with no misgivings. I understand not a single word of it literally. I take it to be metaphor, from beginning to end. Some wonder how I can do that without misgivings. "Isn't that hypocritical?" After all, the congregants are all (so far as we know) reciting the Creed intending it literally, while I, saying it together with them, intend it as pure metaphor. I tell those who ask, "No misgivings," I simply understand that they are living in a conventional (i.e., unanalysed) understanding, as in Fowler's[7] third stage of faith development, while my faith has grown beyond those boundaries, and I am forced to understand those words metaphorically, non-literally.

Marcus Borg suggested that the Creed was a statement from a particular moment in history, a statement which bound the church together through those words which for them had literal meaning. I take him to mean that was the metaphor (worldview) of that age, but that metaphor is now dead. The Creed still has a binding force, a somewhat different binding force from that of the fourth century, but it is still effective. So I repeat the creed with you when you recite it, not as a meaning-laden, literal statement, but as a recitation of the one metaphor which still expresses and reinforces our bound-togetherness.

And all the while we are reciting the Creed together, I am busily translating, saying the words together with you but attaching my attention to what I am hearing behind the words, beyond the words. I understand that the Creed was written and recited as a very literal document; no metaphor there. They thought in those terms. Their Scriptures were literally true. And their theological language was literally true. For them. In those years. But the world has moved on, and we have learned a few things. Most of us no longer believe the universe was created in six twenty-four hour

---

7. Fowler, Stages of Faith *passim*

days. We (i.e., most of us) now think of those two creation stories as the ancients's attempts to tell themselves (and us) who we are, what this world is about and who they thought the God was. With the Enlightenment and the age of reason those literal words have been transformed into metaphor, and we are still learning how to read the transformation. And so it is with the Creed as well.

Behind and Below

And now as we stand to recite the Creed, let me explain to you some of the things I think I hear behind and below those words. I am not going to tell you anything about the Creed itself, that is a different exercise. Only what Jack Bowers hears. Three paragraphs, one about the God, one about Jesus, and one purporting to be about the Holy Spirit, but which ends up being a basketful of doctrinal pieces. *(Note: I've not tried this before, don't know how well or poorly it might come out.)*

> **We believe in one God, the Father, the Almighty, maker of heaven and earth, of all that is, seen and unseen.**

There is one "wholly other." It preceded all of this and will still be after all else is gone. We attribute everything to this author of the material and non-material, and of everything else.

> *We believe in one Lord, Jesus Christ, the only Son of God, eternally begotten of the Father, God from God, Light from Light, true God from true God, begotten, not made, of one Being with the Father. Through him all things were made. For us and for our salvation he came down from heaven: by the power of the Holy Spirit he became incarnate from the Virgin Mary, and was made man. For our sake he was crucified under Pontius Pilate; he suffered death and was buried. On the third day he rose again in accordance with the Scriptures; he ascended into heaven and is seated at the right hand of the Father. He will come again in glory to judge the living and the dead, and his kingdom will have no end.*

A certain human Jesus did walk this earth, did inspire so powerfully, so singularly, that in him, through his living, we got glimpses of what life can be, of an ideal for us. We want to follow in his way. And ultimately his way, because it is the best, the ideal, will triumph in this world.

> *We believe in the Holy Spirit, the Lord, the giver of life, who proceeds from the Father and the Son. With the Father and the Son he is worshiped and glorified. He has spoken through the prophets. We believe in one holy catholic and apostolic Church. We acknowledge one baptism for the remission of sins. We look for the resurrection of the dead, and the life of the world to come.*

The Holy Spirit is an empty doctrine, but somehow the Wholly Other is influencing us, its spirit is moving us. (The rest is simply loyalty oath.)

Chapter 8: All Religion Is Metaphor

As I look back at what I've just tried to draw out of the creed, what I've written seems exceedingly thin, weak, and insipid, but the best I could do. I am disappointed.

I have had to **struggle against a not quite overwhelming urge** as I wrote about the Creed to critique and comment, to dispute and correct, to go through it spewing footnotes line by line, word by word. That might have been an interesting exercise, but it is probably not very informative or useful to teach the Nicene Creed from a post-Christian, non-literalist, fanatically metaphorist point of view. Such critiquing does often happen in the back of my mind as we are reciting the Creed together; a phrase or word snags my attention as we wander past it, and my attention stops to seize on it, to take it in my teeth like a puppy and roughly shake it before dropping it to catch up with the rest of you. I successfully resisted the urge, but found that in avoiding that side-track I had much less to say than I thought I might.

An afterthought: Levels of Consciousness

As I wrestled with all of this, three words tumbled around in my head, behind the scene, as it were: pre-conscious, unconscious and subconscious. Eventually I had to go to my *Random House Dictionary* to discover the difference between them. **Pre-conscious** implies thoughts, mental processes absent from conscious awareness but capable of being brought into consciousness. **Subconscious** means operating beneath or beyond the conscious. And **unconscious** means not perceived at the level of awareness; occurring below the level of conscious thoughts. Why were these tumbling through my thinking as I studied what I could say about religious metaphor? And then I realized that these metaphors I'm playing with happen at different levels of consciousness. "All the world's a stage, and all the men and women merely players..." Shakespeare wrote. That metaphor I can plumb at a very conscious level. Actually, I hardly need to pull the tension into words, the meaning is fairly obvious. It's sorta pre-conscious and easily becoming conscious. But other metaphors are not so obvious (e.g., "Jesus is the Son of God"); in fact, I find some religious metaphor exceedingly difficult, impossible to interpret with words. I get the sense of it, a feeling for it, but the essence doesn't translate into words. It seems to be understood and then interpreted at a subconscious or unconscious level, and is not willing to be dragged into conscious awareness. Which makes it all the more difficult to agree upon. What does it mean? I don't know, but I know it means something important, even if I can't say what it means.

Chapter 9: Faith and Spirituality

First, I must lay out a disclaimer about my ignorance. I am a priest who put thirty-four years into active, parish ministry, and I know next to nothing about faith and spirituality. I recall neither subject being a topic during seminary. I received no particular education or training on either topic. And while I considered aiding my parishioners in their spiritual lives to be an important part of my portfolio, knowing so little about these topics, and being unaware of resources available about either, I sought very little help about them. I remember making a few, very ignorant swipes at trying to help parishions in these areas, but came away feeling they knew as little as I did. I suspect the church has been sufficiently preoccupied with staying in business to have very little time left to squander in these areas. But then, I'm not clear that the church *per se* knows much about faith development and spirituality; monastics might, but the church, no.

Faith

As I set out to write this piece about faith, and I pulled my notes together I realized that for me the topic of ***faith* is so knotted together with *spirituality*** and the *spiritual life* and *doing spiritual work*, that I was unable to disentangle them. It appears to me that what ties them together so inseparably are what I call *values*. I'll start with defining faith, which turns out to have some oddly shaped edges.

Faith Equals Belief

I grew up understanding that my **faith is defined by the Nicene Creed** (and maybe as well by that similar but briefer creed we used in Morning Prayer, the one written by the apostles themselves). Sometime early in the reign of Constantine the Great, it came to pass that faith became an intellectual thing, a matter of what I believed (with the top of my head.) Two major forces were at work here. 1.) The church *(or should I say church**es**, because Christian thinking was evolving in lots of different directions during those first three centuries?)* was struggling to define what had happened. Somehow a Judæan peasant, the son of the carpenter Joseph of Nazareth (with roots in King David's Bethlehem) became God. He'd been hung out to die, but was raised up and lived again, then was extracted up into Heaven. And the church was frantic to figure out precisely how that came to be, and even more precisely what this Jesus

Chapter 9: Faith and Spirituality

now was. And they were viciously avid and determined about figuring all that out. The other major force was more secular: 2.) the Roman empire was in trouble. It had been divided for some decades for administrative reasons; it had become just too big and unwieldy. But the division wasn't functional and Constantine's goal was to re-unify the empire, and Christianity, which was growing like Topsy in divisive ways, wasn't helping matters. A solution: co-opt the church. Constantine, who'd had a battlefield conversion, decriminalized Christianity and took in its leadership. He needed to unify the church(es), thereby eliminating that as a source of divisiveness, and possibly even co-opting the church to help unify the empire. And it worked (to some degree). As the first step Constantine forced a lowest common denominator, a clear statement of exactly what the whole church believed, i.e., the Nicene Creed.[1] And at that very point the mark of faith became adherence to that Creed, or in other words, what one believed intellectually about this Jesus and his God-ness.

Had it not always been this way? I think it had not. As I look at the first three centuries of the church I get a picture of members so committed that they were willing to die for the cause, and some were actually doing so during the few efforts by Rome to stamp out Christianity. But the spiritual life of the church appears to have been scattershot, i.e., diverse and intense. The trick for all Christians was to stay alive, and that meant keeping a low profile in the face of Roman suppression, and during periods of aggressive persecution keeping your head way down. A few professional churchmen were arguing about what Jesus was and how he got that way, but most Christians (it is my impression) were just keeping their heads down while trying to live faithfully, i.e., in the way Jesus had taught. So in those days, while a few were debating those issues, most were just living out the faith. So faith before the Creed was a matter of how you lived, and how you might have to die for the cause.

It's my conviction that at that specific point in history faith was transformed from a way of dedicated living, according Jesus' dictates and in relation to Jesus' God, into intellectual adherence to specified doctrines about Jesus' nature and how it got that way. And we have lived in that doctrinal definition of faith for these succeeding seventeen centuries. Being a Christian has meant believing, affirming, or maybe just accepting (i.e., an act of the intellect) a short list of doctrines: Jesus died for our sins, he was raised up from the death, and he was extracted up into heaven, as God. And thus far, most of those doctrines have been meant, and had to be affirmed, pretty literally.

---

1. The Apostles's Creed was not written by the apostles, but first appeared in France in the fifth century, written in Latin (all the early Christian writings first occurred in Greek) and appears to have been a baptismal creed, intended to affirm an individual's belief at baptism, whereas the Nicene Creed was intended to be the whole church's statement of what the whole church assuredly believes.

Part II: My Review of Christian Doctrines
Bowers's Understanding of Faith

Sometime in my middler year of seminary Dr. Henshaw, the Old Testament and Hebrew professor, assigned the task of a word study. It was to be of a single word (root), within a short selection of the Hebrew Scriptures. I chose the word commonly translated "faith" (in the Hebrew 'mn [aman], the root of the "Amen" with which we end each prayer) in 2 Isaiah (40-62), a manageable chunk of scripture for this second year student. After scouring 2 Isaiah I found that root used only four times. In none of those times could it be reasonably translated "faith" (as we have understood that notion since Constantine), and instead within its contexts seemed to mean something like faithfulness, fidelity, constancy, loyalty. I concluded from that far too short and elementary study that faith had nothing to do with what I believed in my head, but had everything to do with how I behaved, how I acted: faithfully, loyally, trustworthily.

From seminary I graduated into a thirty-four year career in which I was expected to teach and preach the faith, i.e., what Christians ought to believe. Only in the last few years since retirement have I begun to appreciate what I drew out of that short word study, but had set aside: that faith is a matter of behavior. It is what I **do**, not what I think. Faith is a matter of being faithful, of being loyal, of being constant, of being trustworthy, no matter what I think (my thoughts are fluid, and change from moment to moment, and cannot be counted on). Christian faith is a way of living among those around me, and within my community. Faith is behaving such that I can be counted on, trusted, being faithful to myself as well as my community.

Recently I have been saying to people that **what we believe (doctrinally) is not really very important**. I've become convinced that what we **do** is what really counts. How we behave. How we conduct ourselves within the community. As I read the Levitical law and the Hebrew Scriptures I have gradually concluded that YHWH had little concern for what we thought, what we intended, but high concern about what we actually did. YHWH's people survived and throve, or perished, because of what they did, not because of what they intended or thought. As I look around our world, and observe reality happening, what we think, what we intend is of no impact. What we **do**, and the consequences of what we do, that matters. Our thoughts, our intentions have zero impact on the world around us **until** they are translated into actions, acts, deeds, things done (or not done). What I think inside my skull has no impact on the reality outside my skull. But what I do has consequences, makes a difference, for good or for ill.

Belief versus Values

Now I need to **condition what I just wrote**. When I say that what we believe doesn't make much difference, I need to be clear with you that I'm talking about pure **intellectual** beliefs, things like Christian dogma, and whether the hat is red or blue. It's

Chapter 9: Faith and Spirituality

obvious by now that those (neither the Christian doctrines nor the color of the hat) aren't going to change the world. Will make hardly any difference at all. What does really count are our **values**. By that word I mean the convictions that are at the center of our being. The convictions that shape and drive our behavior. Those count. Those make a difference. Those result in actions which bear consequences. So for me, faith is not what I think about how Jesus became God, it's about the values that live at the core of my being, that shape who I am and how I behave, what I do and what I will not do; and simultaneously the values that live buried in the center of our culture, the values that both shape and drive our culture.

I pause for a moment to point out that we do have a minor **semantics problem** here. Some, when they talk about beliefs, are talking about the beliefs that really make a difference in their lives. And I think that what they are talking about is very close to what I mean by "values." So let's agree for a few minutes that we're talking about those beliefs that are the most important ones **in my living** of life, and **not** the beliefs that I think, sorta incidently, at the top of my head, the ones that don't really matter, don't make any significant difference out in the world beyond the surface of my skin.

> E.g., do I believe that the world is a sphere? Yes, but that belief really makes no difference in how I live, unless I happen to be a airplane pilot or a ship's navigator making course from this point to that point and doing so along a great circle because on the surface of a sphere there is no straight line between two points. Then that the world is a sphere is important to me, but otherwise it is of no significance whatsoever. Once again I knock my knuckle on the table top, knowing in my mind that the table top is composed of unimaginably tiny particles and empty space. That I believe because the physicists reliably tell me so, and I choose to believe them. But it makes absolutely no difference in my daily living or in my behavior. I do not live in that realm but in a world which I fabricate inside my brain, a world in which the table top feels hard and when I rap it, my knuckle hurts. That is my reality. And that is the realm where values count, make the difference.

And it is the beliefs so central so powerful, so convictful that they determine how I will live in that fabricated world. Those are the beliefs (which I tend to call values) that I am talking about here. That clarified, I move on.

Spirituality

I seem now to move to a somewhat different topic, **spirituality, the spiritual life, doing spiritual work**. But in my thinking this clump is intimately partnered with faith. I cannot separate faith and spirituality because both are centered on values. I offer . . .

> **A trial definition**: *Spiritual life/doing spiritual work* is the work of tending to that bundle of values, of purposes, of practices and habits and customs which

form the very core of my being, and give me enervation and direction; and the job of *tending* is one of clarifying, altering, applying that which is at my very center and gives me coherence and cohesiveness.

Definitions

I've read others's definitions of spirituality, but most are God-centered, and since I have deemed the God unknowable, to found my definition on the God would be to found it on an unknown. Not terribly functional. So I've gone in my own direction.

Archbishop Rowan Williams and Others

I get the most exceedingly vaguest bit of guidance from a very, very few others. Rowan Williams, the (now retired) Archbishop of Canterbury suggests that "the spiritual enterprise means occupying a certain sort of place, grasping in a certain way where and who you are" and adds later, *(for Christians)* " . . . living in the 'place' defined by Jesus." and " . . . to stand more fully in the place where Christ stands." I can kinda get into that, but not with precise words. Another, Ronald Rolheiser in **The Holy Longing** says, "we are forever restless, dissatisfied, frustrated and aching, overcharged with desire, fundamental dis-ease, unquenchable fire . . . . Spirituality is what we do about that desire, our longings, our unrest . . . " That definition is more purple than my very intellectual definition, but I think it is headed very roughly in the same direction.

Tillich et alii: "The Core of my Being"

That is a pretty vague notion. It may be akin to Tillich's "ground of my being," I'm not sure. John O'Donohue talks about the "inner landscape behind my eyes." And that's the place where my values lurk. Mind you, they do *lurk*. They do not want to be seen, but they do want to be at the ready, close at hand and ready to spring into action. I have learned that while my values are the very center of who I am and what I do, they remain very, very murky, unclear; sometimes feel like they don't want to be rooted out and looked at in the harsh light of day. They are not secretive, but they do lurk.

Non-Foundationalism

I'll try from a different direction, from somewhere in the neighborhood of Williard Quine's[2] **"non-foundationalism."** My very elementary understanding of the

---

2. I am not a student of Quine's epistemology, and have barely a nodding acquaintance with him from two sources, the article on him in the **Stanford Encyclopedia of Philosophy** (plato.stanford.edu/entries/quine/), and a citation of him in Schriven, "Conflict and Persuasion after Foundationalism: Toward a Philosophy of Witness," *ATR* Vol.96 Nr.3 pp.528-30

epistemologist Quine is that he suggests that our total knowledge is like a fabric; "at the center of the fabric –the center of that web, that net –lie beliefs or assumptions, that both color our entire outlook and stand at a distance from, and thus relatively impervious to direct experience." What Quine is describing feels on target for me. And what he identifies as at the very center of the web/net/fabric sounds very much like my values. Not a neat compilation of reasonable and linear statements, but an aggregation (probably fairly primitive and unrefined) of experiences, notions, presumptions and assumptions, urgings, nudgings, impulses, brute habits, along with a few carefully reasoned out, maybe even teased out linear conclusions. And those values color and shape my perceptions, my processing, my concluding, and my translating into action. As those values are at the center I, sense them, similar to Quine, to be fairly impervious to new experiences (which are at the periphery, the open edge of my knowledge net). But they can be consciously, deliberately over-ridden. And they may be alterable, though not easily so; as Pelagius knew, it takes persistent, deliberate and disciplined effort over time to change them, but in some (unspecified) part they can be changed.

Murky Work

And that's what spirituality, or doing spiritual work, is about, clarifying, altering, applying those values. If we don't do that work, then we are simply, and pretty mindlessly driven by whatever winds, with no hand on the rudder. The spiritual work is, like tending the fields, sometimes digging around in **murky** stuff, sometimes even **mucky** stuff (mucky because it is merely an agglomeration *[one which is absolutely essential to us, we* **need** *a center, the center is* **not** *an optional thing]* ingathered early in life, later in life, from a diversity of sources, many of which are **not** reasonable). I struggle with some of my own values. For example, these days I find myself thinking in the direction of, even in some brief and cautious moments talking, very carefully, about the *equality of all persons*. That had not been much a part of my consciousness until I started writing all this stuff several years ago. It may be that the notion has long been a part of me, near my center but very quiet, and now it's bubbling up to the surface of my consciousness more often (as you see in Chapter 5). But I've no idea where the notion came from, what sparked it within me. It would seem to have been lurking in the murk *(pardon my unintended alliteration)*. Or perhaps it comes out of a gene I inherited from my socialist great-grandfather. I know not. This is only one example; but from many such examples I conclude that if we don't tend to this stuff, if we don't do the spiritual work, then we are driven willy-nilly with no idea where that came from and even less choice where we want to go. It's important, but murky, mucky stuff. The center of our living.

PART II: MY REVIEW OF CHRISTIAN DOCTRINES

Stages of Faith

I want to go one more place in this conversation and then I'll sum up. As I have already told you, I had been wandering in spiritual desert lands for several years. John Kaufman, a trained and sensitive spiritual director, and I sat together for several hours. At the end of our session he loaned me John Fowler's ***Stages of Faith***. It was the most helpful book I'd read in many years, it explained what was happening in my pilgrimage. Fowler had done his research across denominational lines, and across religious lines, so his results are not specific to Christianity or any religion (or non-religion). What he learned was that faith is not a place you stand forever, rather one's faith evolves, changes over time and circumstance. I'd heard in my younger years of priests who'd "lost their faith," and while I knew I was no longer clinging tightly to some of the dogma that had been important to me before, I did not feel like I was losing anything. And Fowler's book helped me see that my beliefs had simply grown beyond the borders of conventional Christianity, and my pilgrimage was an exploration out into a wider field of faith. Fowler identified six different stages of faith development, Christianity as we practice it in the mainline denominations being the third of those, the one he dubbed "conventional, unexamined faith." And I had wandered afield out into a more "reflective faith," sometimes foraying briefly even farther out into a "conjunctive faith." I had not lost anything, I was simply growing beyond the conventional belief structure.

Fowler lists the questions he thinks faith addresses:

What are you spending and being spent for?

What causes, dreams, goals or institutions are you pouring out your life for?

What power(s) do you fear? What power(s) do you rely on and trust?

To what or to whom are you committed in life? In death?

With whom do you share your most sacred and private hopes for your life and for the lives of your loved ones?

What are those most sacred hopes, those most compelling goals and purposes in your life?

I find that list compelling and informative. And useful.

Summing Up

Faith as a Verb

Willard Quine thinks that our knowledge is linked to language and so do I: the notion of faith (doctrine, or belief) as we have received it is a noun, a concept, a defined thing. "Faith" as I researched in the Hebrew of Second Isaiah was a verb, an action word, so something you do: not a fixed belief or a concept, but a fluid act of doing. *Faith* is being faithful, loyal, trustworthy, and trusting. So first of all, nowadays I come from a quite different direction than I used to in the conventional church. Faith is not a matter of intellectual belief; faith is a matter of acting out my values.

The God is Not a Backstop

My understanding of YHWH and Abba has been evolving considerably from my younger years. I have come to a place where the God is quite unknowable; and I can no longer expect the God to be the primary actor. I am the actor in this world, you and we are the actors. If anything (good or bad) is to happen in this reality, you and I will have to make it happen. To lean on the God is to beg out and let reality drift wherever the others want to take it. The God will not intervene.

Moral Axis

I am sympathetic when Robert Wright thinks there is a moral axis to the universe. I hope he is correct, but I'm not really convinced: enticed, but not convinced. And likewise when Martin Luther King, Jr. suggested that the arc of history is bending toward justice, I really, really hope he was right; but the evidence of this country, and of this world suggests otherwise. As I look about me, the real world suggests to me that it's a very long, very slow arc. I conclude that if it's going to happen, we will have to make justice and morality happen.

Modes of Spiritual Work

I understand that what I have written about faith and about doing spiritual work is a very intellectual undertaking. That is no surprise to me as I reflect. In the Myers-Briggs Personality Indicator stuff (how one goes about making decisions) I am an INTP (Introverted-Intuitive-Thinking-Perceiver), and when we look at the spiritual life of INTPs we see that they are NTs (intuiters and thinkers), highly intellectual (Thomas Aquinas is the model for doing my kind of spiritual work). In Chapter 3 I wrote about my **Circle of Standing Stones**. Almost every Sunday as I arrive at my pew I begin to ask myself, "Bowers, this is your circle of standing stones. What's going on here today? What is happening? What is the God (or the Whatever) trying to tell you today?" That's one of several ways I do my spiritual work. I also read. I write. I think. A lot. Those are my ways. But they are not the ways everyone should be doing their spiritual work. I have mine. We each need to find the ways that are right for us, the ways we each tend to this spiritual life, our core, the center of our being.

My wife rocks infants at the daycare center.

Chapter 10: Four Other Doctrinal Matters

THIS CHAPTER IS A collection of four discussions on other doctrinal matters: the authority of the Scriptures, what we can know about Jesus' resurrection, whether Jesus' death was an atonement for our sins, and the whole matter of prayer.

The Authority of Scripture

This piece has been a long time happening, and has been stitched together in stages over the course of six years, and you will detect the seams as you read. The bulk was written in 2008, but by 2013 my conclusions had changed remarkably; those appear in the latter part of the paper. And I am amending onto the beginning some opening words about the origins of all these thoughts.

My first Bible was a Christmas gift, as I recall, from my godfather sometime after baptism in my eighth year. As a child, my mother, the granddaughter of a socialist leader in the national party and an avowed atheist, had gone of herself to a Lutheran church but when she discovered that my father had been an acolyte in the Episcopal Church in his youth, she betook the family to the nearest Episcopal parish. I quickly showed interest, hence the gift of the Bible. It was a Revised Standard Version, a fairly new translation in those days. And my mother made it absolutely clear to me that nothing was ever to be put on top of my Bible: not another book, not my glass of Pepsi. Nothing! The roots of my sense of the authority of the Scriptures go back that far. Yes, that was certainly a bit of *folk piety*, but it was an absolute in my young years.

The Bible (the Hebrew Scriptures and the Christian Writings) comprise our "Holy Book." And Holy Books do carry authority. I suppose I got my very first taste of critical thinking about the Scriptures in a college Old Testament course given by A. Denis Baily. Mr. Baily was first of all a geographer, so that course was taught from the vantage of how the geography of Palestine shaped Jewish history and the Hebrew Scriptures. He was respectful of the Scriptures, but clear that geography was as important as God in shaping the Jewish story.

Seminary introduced me to historical criticism and some of the arts of looking critically at our holy writings. Taking Hebrew had been a good way to learn that the Hebrew Scriptures were always ambiguous at best, and were often cloaked in unclarity. My Hebrew professor taught with a rabbinical approach to the Scriptures, playful, teasing out new ideas, always looking for new understandings, never content with any simplistic understanding, ever looking deeper or from a different angle. I came away

CHAPTER 10: FOUR OTHER DOCTRINAL MATTERS

from seminary absolutely clear that our Scriptures are **very** earthen vessels; they may contain the holy, but they are themselves very earthen, very imperfect. And they bear the imprints of their stenographers (the authors, the students, the redactors) all over them. Literalism and inerrancy could **never** be part of reasonable thinking about the Scriptures. And their authority could not be in the text itself; it had to come from somewhere behind the text. The Scriptures might be the inspired Word of God, but could not possibly be the precisely dictated words of the God.

My next lesson came shortly after seminary as the feminist movement began to take shape and gain momentum, and I realized that our Holy Writings, both the Hebrew and the Christian, bore the shape and shaping of patriarchy (and I was a middling feminist). Everything in those Scriptures was written and interpreted through patriarchal eyes, misogynist eyes.[1] And that bias did not set well in my feminist world. My Holy Scriptures had a built in bias that I knew was dysfunctional, flat out wrong. And so my questioning the authority of Scripture began.

---

1. In footnote #1 of Chapter 6 (162) I pointed out the ancients's misconception of human reproductive biology which, if the maiden Mary was a virgin, made it *de facto* that Jesus was undeniably the biological Son of God. But the story does not end with that. It is my long held and very considered opinion that this misconception of human reproduction has had a profound impact on the most fundamental shape of our social structure.

Since the male was understood to be the sole producer of new life *via* the seed, then he was infinitely more important to the survival of the species, or the survival of the clan/tribe, than the female, who only incubated the *seed*, and did not participate in the creation of the *seed*, which is to say, *the offspring, the progeny, the future*. While any woman could incubate (except *barren* women who must, therefore, be faulty, and therefore even more inferior), without the male there was no new life. So a male might come to love his wife, but he was quite clear that she was infinitely inferior to him, less a being than him. I am persuaded that this simple misconception of reproductive biology fueled, or at least gave rationale to, the ancient understanding that women were inferior beings and therefore second or third class persons, in no way equal to the male. We, and our social structure, have evolved beyond that history, but that past has not gone away; like our biological history, it is still part of us. Such a fundamental belief has underlain the whole social, legal and psychological male attitude toward women (and to the degree that women had no alternative understanding, they were involuntary *[albeit unconscious]* participants in those *mores*.) And so it has come to pass that those *mores* have been built into the very bedrock of our social understandings today: in our Holy Scriptures, in our community and social structures, and to some degree still in our individual psychologies and attitudes. I am convinced those ancient roots lie behind and very, very unconsciously feed the misogynous attitudes and social structures still very operative within our culture, and those same misogynous attitudes are even more fervently rampant within many lesser-developed cultures. Look toward patriarchy and you will see misogyny as well (perhaps as a cultural tool to buttress the patriarchal structures.) I frankly believe those misogynous attitudes and beliefs are very powerfully a (if not **the**) subconscious driver behind the jihadists phenomenon in the lesser-developed cultures who have found a religious rationale within their misconceptions of Islam.

Our Holy Scriptures then, written out of a misconceived reproductive biology, were shaped through the lens of the resulting misogynous patriarchy, and, unless the reader is keenly aware of that scriptural bias and very consciously and deliberately and disciplinedly factors it out of his reading, he will be unconsciously urged onto misogynous attitudes. And that fundamental attitude, along with racism, is shot through our entire social structure.

Part II: My Review of Christian Doctrines

June 2008

I've certainly wrestled with the question of the authority of Scripture throughout my ministry. I am by nature, though not sufficiently dedicatedly, a scholarly person, a questioning person, an inquiring person. And *how* to understand our Scriptures (both the Hebrew and Christian writings) has been of central importance to me, in my sermonizing, in my theologizing, in my wrestling with my own religious experiences and intuitions; God gave me both these Scriptures and a strong inquiring mind trained with a powerful education, but did **not** require me to choose between the Scriptures and my mind. I was theologically trained in the early 1960s, so textual criticism was a part of my training, one of my foundation stones. I have never been tempted toward the literalist edge of our American debate over the Scriptures. But I have been inclined to nudge the Scriptures toward the center of the stage in my ministry. I have rarely failed to preach from one of the Scripture readings assigned for the day. I have preferred to teach from and about the Scriptures. I have grown to see the place of the Scriptures as at the center of spiritual life and development. I began my ministry with the understanding that my task as preacher was to interpret the Scriptures to the congregation. I ended my active ministry understanding that my preacher's task is to discern and report what God is saying this day to those people in this congregation through these particular Scripture readings; much more a discerning than a scholarly exposition. I grew to be a *fundamentalist* in my own way, studying the readings with all the scholarly tools and commentaries at my disposal to discern through, in between, and underneath the **exact** words of the text, sometimes even in the silences in between the words and verses, what God is saying this particular day to these particular people, struggling to discern what is new today in this text that was not found within these same words 2,000 years ago or even yesterday.

So in my own way the Scriptures have always been very central to my ministry. I discovered late in my professional life that my primary mode of spirituality (in the Myers-Briggs stuff I am an NT, i.e., an iNtuitive Thinker) is Thomistic, very scholarly, so much so that I was never good at *praying* the Scriptures. I did it the way God designed *me* to do it, i.e., studying; and I did it fairly well (so I was told by people whose opinions I value.) So I did ministry always with an eye on the Scriptures. I was not always obedient. I was not always faithful. But I always was in relation to the Scriptures.

So as I contemplate the authority of the Scriptures, the issue is not couched in terms of literalism or criticism, but centrality. In seminary I was taught Richard Hooker's *three-legged stool* understanding that our *faith* (i.e., what we intellectually believe) is supported by the three legs of the Scriptures, tradition and revelation, the tool of reason being the primary mode of revelation for Anglicans. That made profound sense to me, so I have always tried to carefully hold the three in tension, with the Scriptures always before me on my desk, the tools of reason and rationality to help me understand the world around me as well as the Scriptures before me, and to

Chapter 10: Four Other Doctrinal Matters

understand as well that the Scriptures are informing me both of the world around me and of what God is quietly whispering to me about that world. And while the tradition informs me about the content of my faith, my belief, it also warns me when I am about to step outside the circle of Christian understandings.

But of late I have come to a modified understanding of the Scriptures and of the tensions among the three legs of Hooker's stool that support my faith. I suppose this understanding came to me in a blinding revelation in the blackness of one night as I lay awake, wondering how people can read so many and such radically different things out of the Scriptures. A homophobic soul finds justification for his hate and fear and blind rage at gays. A white racist uses it to justify his fear and hatred of blacks. An American conservative justifies his blind support of capitalism, and a progressive his support of social justice. We use the Scriptures to support a plethora of contradictory and frequently mutually exclusive issues and stances. How can that be?

I have always been clear that our Scriptures are not a single book, but a collection of books spanning over a thousand or fifteen hundred years, books composed, collected, written down, and redacted in a range of different situations and historical contexts, and to a number of unspecified, different purposes. I assume that the only constant within them is the person of a male God, but even that is surrounded by hosts and layers of different, unique theophanies and religious experiences through which God is interpreted to us. There is no single or consistent theology or comprehension of God therein to guide us. We grope blindly through the words of the Scriptures to discover what truths they tell us. No wonder we come away with our idiosyncratic dreams and fears buttressed by them.

And in a blinding flash that night I realized that for us in these days the Scriptures function mainly as a Rorschach onto which we can project almost anything our conscious and subconscious *psychés* desire, even the support of capital punishment and unjust, oil-driven wars. The Hebrew and Christian Scriptures, gathered together, are so diverse and diffuse that somewhere in them can be found support for just about anything, especially if you are willing to **read into** the text *(eisogesis)* shades and colors that another would not see, and are willing to jerk (i.e., cherry-pick, proof-text) words, phrases, clauses, verses completely out of context and interpret them in isolation from the whole corpus of the Scriptures, are willing to distort and twist and contort and abuse the text, and even selectively ignore portions. So where is the *right* understanding of the Scriptures? Can they be read accurately, correctly, or as they were intended? That feels like a resounding, "No!" And how can we know, any of us, when we are using well, or misusing the Scriptures, the words on the page? How can they be *authoritative* when they function mainly as a Rorschach?

I remember a fraternity brother in college who was headed for seminary but had to undergo a psychological examination first. The psychiatrist doing that testing for his diocese used a Rorschach test among other tools. But when this fellow saw all kinds of lusting, sexual things in those inkblots, and feared his answers would

Part II: My Review of Christian Doctrines

disqualify him as too unrighteous to be acceptable as an ordinand, he made up stories of what he saw, nice, clean, non-sexual stories. He failed that examination of course. He confessed what he had done, was subsequently re-examined and told the truth, and passed this time. There are rules about Rorschachs, it seems, about what to report seeing in the inkblots, and about how to interpret those reports. The inkblots themselves are lawless, without rules or authority. It is the psychiatric community that establishes the rules about Rorschachs.

And, I have concluded, there are rules about how to read and how to interpret the Scriptures as well. It was and is the community which surrounds and upholds our Scriptures which has created those rules down through the centuries. And those rules are imbedded in our traditions. I started to learn those rules as a child in Sunday School. I had to unlearn those first, childish rules during my seminary studies, tearing them down to clear a place for building more mature rules with the scholarly building blocks of historical understandings, archeological findings, historical criticism, form criticism, narrative criticism and such. I was taught to use my rationality and all of my intelligence when I approached the Scriptures and to look beyond the words on the page. I have said that I was taught a *rabbinical* way of dealing with the Scriptures; that description may not be accurate. I should rather say that I learned from a Christian teacher who was himself taught in a rabbinical school, so I understand that the study of the Scriptures has a long tradition, older even than Christian studies, a tradition which remembers what other great teachers have thought and understood. I learned to work within the tradition, guided by, but not limited to that tradition. That tradition is my foundation for understanding, for reading the Scriptures, and without it I am clueless, lost, as though asea without compass. Dr. Henshaw gave me tools, rules, guides, and taught me to use both the tradition and the new discoveries still being uncovered, along with all my wits. So I was taught how to continue to learn, to use the commentaries, and weigh the commentaries one against another, to follow the new and evolving understandings of what our Scriptures are, where they came from, the contexts within which they were gathered, written down, and redacted. So when Richard Hooker suggests that *tradition* is one of the three legs that sustain my faith, that *tradition* is very rich for me, and very essential to my understandings. That tradition shapes and forms, though it does not limit, what I believe from the Scriptures about God, about myself and about our world.

I suppose that for me *The Tradition*, as vague as that term might be, is at least as authoritative as the Scriptures themselves, for without the tradition to guide me, the Scriptures are little more than random words strewn upon the page, merely a Rorschach onto which I could project anything I wished and find that wish solidly confirmed: racism, misogyny, classism, tribalism, nationalism, capitalism, communism, whatever "-ism" dwells within me . . . my profoundest hates, my profoundest fears and my profoundest lusts and my profoundest idolatries.

Chapter 10: Four Other Doctrinal Matters

This works for me. My difficulty with others of a more fundamentalist, literalist persuasion is that I have been taught that the protestant radical reformers threw out the whole of tradition as irretrievably corrupt. But now I've concluded that they threw out some crucial parts, the teachings about how to approach and use the sacred writings. Those traditions are as old as the Scriptures themselves, and are probably equally, if not even more, important. Without them you will surely project onto the holy writings anything within you, even the most evil things. Only the tradition along with a very critical approach can protect us from that misstep when they tell us, "No, that interpretation is not consistent with the received tradition." So whatever tradition we (each of us) receive and accept is as important as the pages and the words of the Scriptures.

I suppose that to be faithful to a discussion of the authority of the Scriptures I must clarify (or muddy) three issues within the larger question. When asked, "What do I hold to be the authority of the Scriptures," I must break that down into three sub-questions: 1) how much authority do I ascribe to the Scriptures? To what extent, to what limit, within what bounds are the Scriptures authoritative? and 2) what *kind* of authority does it have, what is the nature of its authority? and 3) on what grounds is it authoritative? The first two of these may over lap somewhat, but I take them in this order.

In response to the first, "how much authority, what limits, bounds," I must admit that I do not hold the earth to be flat, despite psalmic references to the "four corners of the earth." I cannot be a flat-earther. I find the arguments of mathematics and earth sciences and astrophysics to be highly compelling. I've been to sea, I've seen the round horizon, I've watched ships arise from below the curvature of the earth. I am fairly convinced that the earth is a sphere hurling through space around the sun roughly as Copernicus and Galileo described. In confessing that much I betray that I do hold the physical sciences, in as much as they are verifiable, to be more authoritative than the Scriptures, at least in matters that the physical sciences capably describe. I heard recently of a financial advisor who claims he follows the Scriptures in giving financial advice to his clients, claiming that the Bible tells us everything we need to know about successfully managing our finances. I am not inclined to seek that advisor out for financial advice, and if he sought me I would run with all speed in the opposite direction. Further, knowing my personality as well as I do, and my wife's as imperfectly as I do, I would be a fool to try to dominate her in our relationship, or to seek to make her subservient to me in all things as the Hebrew Scriptures and Christian Writings would have our relationship. She and I are very much equal partners, each with strengths and weaknesses. From these few words it appears that I might be hard pressed to state places in my life and world where I hold the Scriptures to be the absolute, or even dominate authority. If forced, I might say that while I take the Scriptures seriously and to heart, only in matters of the spirit and the spiritual life do I hold the Scriptures to be a powerful authority, and even there not the sole or necessarily dominating authority.

And I must add a condition. When we begin to speak of God, and of most spiritual matters, I find language quite inadequate. As complex and expressive as English is, I find it not up to the task. However it may be not the language that fails, but our ability to conceptualize and then express in words. My experience is that God and matters spiritual are really beyond my firm grasp; my mind can not quite comprehend or encompass them in totality. The priest-author Andrew Greeley has one of his characters, an archbishop of Dublin say, "All religion is metaphor." I think that is correct. All religious expression is metaphor, and all metaphor is open to interpretation, in fact open to each individual hearer's interpretation. How then can a metaphor be, in any absolute sense, authoritative? The metaphor points beyond itself, and cannot itself be authoritative.

What kind of authority do the Scriptures then have? What is the nature of its authority? Having said the above, I'm not sure how to respond to this part of the question. It may be that the word "authority" is getting in the way at this point. I understand authority to be one form of power. We **invest** authority in certain persons, certain offices, certain things. We **invest** civil and criminal law with authority, with power over us. That is, we cede power to the law; we individually and as a community give agreed upon laws the power to rule our lives. We invest the law with authority. Perhaps then we can **invest** the Scriptures with authority, that is, cede power, cede authority to them. Ceding that power would be a matter of choice.

I need to take a different direction for a few moments. Living five weeks among the Cistercians I began to learn the power of the Scriptures in a way I had not used it before. The monks set aside an hour each day as part of their daily routine to do the *lectio divina*. That is a particular method of using the Scriptures, not to read for meaning or understanding, but to allow God to speak through the Scriptures. It is a kind of prayer, if you will, reading the Scriptures to listen for God. It is a very individual activity, and it uses the Scriptures in a very powerful (though non-scholarly) way. There are other ways of using the Scriptures for the same purpose, to generate opportunities of listening to God, to allow God to speak to us: the *African Bible Study* method is one of those appropriate to use in a group setting. I am not terribly good at using these methods, but I have used them enough to learn about the power in them. They are ways of finding God, not within the very words of the Scriptures, but through and beyond the words. I can believe that God has inspired the Scriptures, that is, breathed his spirit into the Scriptures (but I do not know exactly what I mean by that), that God has given us the Scriptures as a means of speaking to us, of helping us listen. But I do not believe that God dictated the very words of the Scriptures to stenographers who unerringly copied them down.

Finally, on what grounds is the authority of the Scriptures based? I have heard 2 Timothy cited as the reason for ceding authority to the Scriptures: "All scripture is given by inspiration of God, and is profitable for doctrine, for reproof, for correction, for instruction in righteousness: . . ." (3:16). First I would have to parse this verse very carefully to learn what these words might originally have meant, and then what they probably do ***not*** mean now. Then I have to ask whether that verse alone is sufficient to invest authority in the Scriptures. And my very logical mind says that a self-authenticating, self-authorizing system is not to be trusted. The foundation for the Scriptures must come from outside the corpus of the writings themselves.

As I read what I have written thus far, I am not terribly happy with it. I seem to have divested the Scriptures of all authority. That was not my intent; and that is not my actual practice. I do cede to the Scriptures some authority. What authority and how much authority is much harder to say, but I will try.

First, I find that in my evaluation the Scriptures do often speak "truth," (carefully distinguishing that I do not mean "the truth," that is, facts). The first chapters of Genesis do speak truth clearly to me. I am hard pressed to put into words exactly what that truth is. I think it may be beyond expression in words. They do tell me about human nature, and our relationship with God, about the created world and God's and our relationships to it. But I find that the exact nature of that truth shifts, changes from time to time, depending on the context, depending upon the questions I bring to the text. Obviously those chapters are in metaphor. The astrophysicists's and Darwin's theories make perfect sense to me, so I am free to use these chapters as I think they were meant to be used, to tell me truth, not to relate scientific facts. The gospel renditions tell me much truth. To what extent those renditions are factual or metaphorical I am not clear. To what extent they tell me exactly what Jesus did, exactly what he said, precisely how his community reacted to him, I am **very** unclear. But the story does tell truth, to me at least. And so I have found it very helpful in determining the course of my life and my relationship with God. The "Rape of Tamar" (2 Sam13:1-20) I might take to be a factual story, that is, that it really occurred, and in the way told; but that is not my burden. I do not read it as history. Apart from its artistic beauty as a piece of poetic prose, I struggle to find within the story God's truth, for me and for our time. The factuality of the story is immaterial to me.

Where in the Scriptures do I find truth? I cannot specify. One day in these verses, another day in another set of verses. In the first centuries after Christ the scholars and leaders of the church wrestled with the various versions and sets of the texts in their hands, fought, sometimes viciously, with each other over which texts to include in *holy writ*, and which to exclude, and finally in council (and Susan urgently points out to me that that council was a gathering of male, celibate bishops, not the *ecclesia*, not the Christian community) came to a decision in 382 AD on the canon of the Christian Scriptures, accepting the Hebrew canon chosen by the rabbinical scholars. We live with that decision now as our Bible. The church, in its wisdom, or in its folly, determined in 382 AD that these were the holy writs inspired by God, and no others. I cannot argue with that decision. The Christian community in its mode of decision-making of that day made that decision. I honor it, even though all the particulars of it may not make sense to me on every day. Most days I question the wisdom of including

John's ***Revelation***, as did many of them; but on (exceedingly) rare occasion I might find God's truth even through those words.

So I conclude, for me at least and for now at least, one basis on which I accept authority in the Scriptures is that they tell truth, God's truth about God, and about me and about you, and about our world. The church has historically said that, and I too say that, though I am very hard pressed to say what I mean by "God's truth."

And secondly, I find myself drawn to truth as revealed in mystical insights. I am not clear how much of the Scriptures themselves come to us through mystical experiences. Some works of the prophets appear to come from that source. Perhaps much more was so inspired. And that too lends some authority to those parts of the Scriptures, at least for me. Today anyhow.

As a final comment, I suppose that in our church, and perhaps in all denominations, there needs to be an every-other-generation iconoclast, a respected personage who rattles the foundations to see what falls out. In my younger years that was Bishop Pike. He became an embarrassment for the Episcopal Church. In his younger years he had co-authored the book which described the faith of the Episcopal Church, the content of our beliefs, in our first "Church's Teaching Series." A very orthodox book by two **very** orthodox priests. Later he became a bishop. And still later he began to utter some very odd, unorthodox stuff. His post-teenage son had committed suicide, and Pike was very troubled about that. Somehow he was led into the realm of "channeling" and speaking through mediums with the spirit world. He was attempting to commune with his dead son, and, as I understand it, died in a desert in an attempt to speak with the son. And as I recall, in those latter years of his life he was at such odds with his fellow bishops that he was encouraging a heresy trial in the House of Bishops to vindicate his beliefs.

And now we have John Spong, nipping like a terrier at the heels of the Episcopal Church, harrying us to re-examine the limits of our faith statements and perhaps broaden the reaches and limits of our faith. What can one believe and still be within the Christian faith? When does one step beyond the faith? Can our beliefs, our understanding of truth, be limited to what can be discovered or verified with our Scriptures, the holy writings which were frozen in 382 AD? Is that what we mean by the "Authority of Scripture?"

****

undated

I **do** argue with the choosing of the canon of our Scriptures by a council of our bishops in the fourth century in the midst of deep and sometimes violent debate over what is **the** truth in Christianity and attempts to define the *One True Faith*. That alone admits a bias. But then agreeing with Susan's appraisal that this council was composed solely of patriarchal males struggling to maintain their patriarchal upper hand, I have to question how much did that bias affect their choosing. We now understand that Christianity was **never** monolithic, that it was always evolving in different ways in many different places, many of these with their own writings in addition to what those bishops selected. We are just now rediscovering a few of those writings, re-examining what some of those divergent varieties of Christianity thought and felt and acted out. And there probably were many more that have been completely lost to us. As much as I would like to, I cannot go back and query those bishops, "Why these books? Why not those? What makes you so sure? And for godsake, why John's ***Revelation***?

And because of that I become much less trustful of the Scriptures, wondering what truths those bishops might have ruled out of our Scriptures.

****

January 18, 2013

Today I read again what I had written above and marvel at how far afield I have wandered in the intervening five years. I can no longer subscribe to what I wrote above. If I had to reformulate my stance on *The Authority of Scripture* today I would perhaps say something like, "I think the Scriptures hold whatever authority **you** ascribe (i.e., cede) to them, and no more. I am done arguing Scripture with flat-earthers and homophobes and such. If they want to hide their fears and aspirations behind some "holy writings," so be it, for them, but not for me. I am a child of the twentieth and twenty-first centuries, and my trusted metaphor is the language of science. I find some, occasionally great wisdom within the Hebrew and Christian Scriptures, but the sort of wisdom that is **not** in contested argument with the findings of science, rather, wisdom that informs of realms beyond, outside of, alongside scientific knowledge. Science is about things physical. The wisdom of the Scriptures is about things non-physical, about morality, and spirituality, about attitudes and things of the "mind" (or the "soul" if you will.) So for me today the Scriptures are useful to be plumbed (but not to determine) the things that are beyond scientific reach (at least so far) about you and me and us and our living in this world.

So this closing note: As I reported in Chapter 1 for several years I puzzled over the place of mysticism and mystical experiences. I suspected, along with William James (and with Evelyn Underhill's conviction) that mystical experiences are at the core of the founding experiences of many (perhaps most) great religious leaders and movers: Moses' conversation with a burning bush, Jesus' forty days in the wilderness, Paul's vision on the road to Damascus. Our legends are rife with such stories that changed and motivated and energized and directed religious heroes. But I have come to question the source, the origin, the genesis of those experiences. Mystics claim that their experiences are of being in the very presence of the God itself. But, other than the fact that those experiences are almost universally reported in *god-talk* language, I find no convincing evidence that they are in fact from, or about, some deity. So I was left wondering the source, the meaning and therefore the value of those mystical experiences. And I was left questioning how the experiences might validate the usefulness of the subjects' wisdom, teaching, leading.

Julian Silverman's study, for me, demystified the whole *corpus* of mysticism. I no longer wrestle with their *authority*. The insights that arise out of some are profound, life-changing, even history-changing. The insights of others seem little but bits of gibberish. The real test for me is that some *work*. Their insights are successful in coping with this *ordinary* reality. For me the authority of those insights comes not from their source, but from the fact that they work in this reality. Whether the experiences themselves are of the God or about the God or caused by the God is indeterminate. I accept from catalogers like Underhill and Williams, and from the reports of the mystics themselves that the mystical experiences are exquisitely gizzard-tickling; but for my money they are *throw-aways* unless the insights they yield are useful and beneficial.

I turn back to the authority of the Scriptures. It is obvious to me that much of the Scriptures was written as *holy history* by the persons charged with tending to that holy history. Beyond that some of those Scriptures were written (orally or graphically) by persons who have had mystical experiences (e.g., the eighth-century prophets, Jesus, and Paul). Does that lend them any kind of *authority*? I think not. Silverman's work calls into question for me the source of those mystical experiences . . . are they from the God? Or do they originate within the individual's psychological structures and processes? Their insights have proven valuable across the ages, but whether they are from God is unverifiable. And if that is the case, then I must handle that portion of the Scriptures not as godly utterances, but as powerful insights for **their** age, and which **may** have applicability in my age as well; but their applicability is **not** a given simply because the mystic uttered "YHWH said . . . ." Given that, for me the text of the Scriptures, the insights they offer, must stand on their own. Is it insightful? Is that insight beneficial, helpful, useful, informative, motivating? Does it make our lives a little better?

Resurrection: a Study and Opinion

A few words about the resurrection. Jesus' resurrection is posited as the fundamental truth (i.e., *fact*) of Christianity. Without the physical resurrection of Jesus it all falls apart, agree all theologians *(or so I was taught)*. So I need to ask, in as far as we can determine, what did happen on Easter morning circa 34 AD?

First, the record: In the gospels Jesus is portrayed, after the discovery of the empty tomb, as alive again, but with a body that has both supernatural and normal human properties. And the record is mixed across the gospels; when we view the authoring of the three synoptics as on a time line, there would seem to be some progression, i.e., with the passage of years the depictions of Jesus' body change in nature.

The Sources

Paul

We tend to look first toward the gospels when we start asking questions about the resurrection; that's where the story, as story, is told. We can place the earliest gospel, that of Mark, somewhere between 65 and 75 AD, some thirty-one to forty-one years after the event. But the words of Mark are not the earliest evidence available to us. We can place Saul's traumatic experience on the road to Damascus somewhere between one and six years after Jesus' crucifixion. And some three years later Paul is back on the road evangelizing. So out of Paul's mouth, or from his pen, comes evidence that pre-dates the gospel renditions. Before looking at the gospel testimony we should first look at what Paul tells about Jesus' resurrection, evidence which is considerably closer to the event, and is presumably less distorted or faded with time.

In 1 Corinthians Paul argues that just as Jesus was raised[2] from the dead we too will be raised up "changed, in a moment, in the twinkling of an eye, at the last trump…" (15:51-52). Paul then would seem to offer us a Jesus housed, not in a three-day dead and now resuscitated physical body, but in a body transformed, changed. The process Paul describes: the dead shall be raised imperishable, since flesh and blood cannot inherit the kingdom of God (1 Cor 15:50). "That which is mortal must put on immortality" (1 Cor. 15:54). He talks of a "spiritual body" (1 Cor 15:44). Paul is clear the God has raised Jesus to new life, but is equally clear that new life is not in a resuscitated body. While the letter to the Colossians may not be directly from Paul's hand, most scholars agree it probably comes from a disciple or associate of Paul and likely reflects Paul's teachings; Colossians says, "If, then, you have been raised with Christ, seek those things that are above, where Christ is seated at the right hand of God" (3:1). And in Romans Paul writes, "Christ, being raised from the dead, will never die again…" (6:9-10). But we know resuscitated bodies must eventually die. Paul does not know the raised up Jesus as a resuscitated physical body, but as a body transformed, that will never die, that is at God's right hand: I conclude Paul speaks of a spiritual body.

---

2. 1. The Greek verb here *egeírō* means "to stand up, arouse from sleep or death" (alternately *anístēmi* is sometimes used in the same sense, "caused to arise, aroused from sleep or death") but is used always in the passive mood when referring to the risen Christ, that is, Jesus was made to stand up, something God did for or to him, that he could not do for himself. So when we say "resurrected" we need to understand "was caused to stand up." (Rom 4:24, 6:4, 6:9, 7:4, 8:11, 10:9, and 15:28) But the question central to this search is begged by the Greek verb: was Jesus' dead body caused to stand again, i.e., resuscitated, or was the **very** Jesus (i.e., spiritual, non-physical) raised up in a new body?

Part II: My Review of Christian Doctrines

Paul's Conversion

I need to side track in order to make note of Paul's dramatic encounter of the risen Christ on the road to Damascus (Acts 9:1-21). Luke (if the book of the Acts of the Apostles indeed be from his hand) is lengthy and deliberate in his telling of this encounter; and so important is the story for Luke that he tells it again in equal (though somewhat different) detail a second time (Acts 22:4-16). And Luke mentions it yet a third time in reporting Paul's defense to Agrippa (Acts 26:13-18). It is for Luke an obviously very important authenticator for Paul's ministry. But the (weightier) curiosity is that Paul himself, in all his letters, never once mentions the event.[3] I can only speculate what happened to Paul on the road to Damascus, but I would think that, if he had met a resuscitated Jesus in a physical body on that Damascus road, he would have mentioned it somewhere, to someone. Paul does tell us that he knew a man who above fourteen years ago "was caught up into the third heaven," and another who was caught up into "paradise" (2 Cor 12:2,4). (Was that man Paul himself, choosing not to glorify himself by claiming the experience?) I cannot definitively interpret "third heaven" and "paradise," but they do sound to me like something one might say in trying to describe a mystical experience. Paul may have been a mystic; that would not surprise me. And it could be that in Acts Luke is trying to describe a powerful and transformative, life-changing mystical experience Paul had on the Damascus road, an experience which Paul knew would sound like gibberish coming from his own mouth. If my hunch is anywhere close to what did happen, then the Jesus Paul met on the Damascus road was not a physical body, but certainly a mystical experience interpreted by Paul as of the resurrected, transformed Jesus.

Conclusion

I think it fair to conclude that for Paul, the earliest though not eye-witness account we have for evidence, Jesus' resurrection was not the resuscitation of an executed body, but rather of a transformed, changed, perhaps *spiritual* body.

Mark (16:1-8)

Next I turn to the gospel witnesses. Mark, the earliest gospeler (*ergo* the *[perhaps]* least revised of the four) tells us absolutely no stories of Jesus' resurrection or of post-resurrection appearances! He reports only one empty-tomb story, that of three of women followers finding Jesus' body gone, the tomb occupied by a young man in white robes (who might look like the messenger predicted to announce the end of the world)

---

3. In his letters Paul never mentions his reported blindness, his conversation with Jesus, or Ananias' role in his recovering of sight and his baptism. Luke relates all those some thirty years after Paul's death.

telling them Jesus is raised up and they are to tell the other disciples that he is preceding them back to Galilee. But the women tell no one because they are too frightened.

There is a later add-on, 16:9-20, (penned by whom we know not; we know only that the vocabulary and syntax would indicate a different author) which reports Jesus' appearance to Mary of Magdala, and then another time to two walking a country road (reads like an echo of Luke's "Road to Emmæus" story), and finally an appearance to the eleven gathered for a meal (reads a bit like Matthew's "great Commission" story). This add-on, seemingly added to correct Mark's error in not telling us of the raised up Christ, concludes with a very terse report of Jesus' ascension. This presumably added piece is later than the Marcan text and reflects not Mark's understanding, but an understanding from some later time. End of gospel. For Mark there simply is no experience of the raised up Jesus.

Matthew (27-28:20)

Matthew's telling comes about a decade after Mark's. Matthew in all probability had a copy of Mark's gospel before him as he wrote (he follows Mark's content and time line closely), along with his own copy of "Q" (*Quelle*, the content common to Matthew and Luke but not contained in Mark), and still another collection of sayings and stories known only to him among the gospellers. Even with Mark in front of him, Matthew tells a somewhat different end-story. He tells us that Pilate set a watch at the tomb at the suggestion of the Judæan leaders responsible for Jesus' execution; they had warned of a plot to steal the body. Despite the posted watch two Marys find the stone rolled out of the entryway, the tomb empty, and a single *(end of the world)* angel in brilliant white telling them Jesus is raised, and is preceding the followers into Galilee. As the Marys leave they are accosted by Jesus himself, whose feet they clasp, and Jesus reiterates that he is preceding them to Galilee. Later the raised up Jesus meets the eleven on a mountaintop *(mountaintops are liminals, places where all sorts of epiphanies happen)* in Galilee laying on them his "Great Commission" (28:19). The only pertinent fact I can lay hand on is that the two Marys clasped Jesus' feet. He must have been corporeal. But that by itself is scant evidence.

Luke (24:1-53)

Luke, probably another decade later than Matthew, gives us a longer and more complicated story. He also has Mark and "Q" in front of him, along with another collection of sayings and stories different than Matthew's. The women (not identified or enumerated) find an empty tomb, but this time **two** *(end of the world)* angels materialized to remind them of Jesus' resurrection predictions (no mention of preceding them to Galilee). Then follows Luke's unique *(though perhaps echoed in the Marcan add-on)* story: two followers are fleeing Jerusalem toward the town of Emmæus when an unrecognized person catches up with them, consoles their grief and interprets all the events to them. They stop for the night in Emmæus and as they sit down to eat, that person says the blessing over the bread, breaks the loaf, and in that act they suddenly recognize him to be Jesus. And Jesus just as suddenly disappears! The two return to Jerusalem to tell the others, and as they are reporting Jesus suddenly appears. They think him a ghost so he eats some fish to prove it is he, not a ghost (ghosts don't eat fish). He leads them out to Bethany and is extracted up into heaven.

Analysis of Luke

The witness here is very mixed. In this gospel Jesus' raised up body is first presented as very physical: he catches up with them walking along the road and walks with the two, interpreting to them as they go the week's events in light of the Scriptures. No indication his body is in the slightest non-physical. They arrive at Emmæus and prepare to sup, Jesus (assuming the papa role) says the blessing and then breaks the loaf into chunks; his body is physical enough to perform that physical act in such a way that will not indicate to the two that his body is anything other than a normally physical one. And it is in his doing this that they recognize him. Evidently his physical appearance is sufficiently different now than it had been before his execution that they could not recognize who he was, but something in the mannerisms of his blessing and breaking of bread connects with past experience and they recognize him (though I am forced to conclude that Jesus' body was unrecognizably different than before the crucifixion). And just as suddenly he disappears, something normal physical bodies cannot do. The two speed their way back to the others in Jerusalem to report this event, and in the middle of their reporting Jesus appears among them; again, something a normally physical body cannot do. They think him in a spiritual (ghostly) body, but he says it's a physical body; look at it, touch it. And to prove his body is physical, he eats some broiled fish and honeycomb, which non-physical bodies cannot do. After some teaching he leads the group out to Bethany, one of their former haunts, and after blessing them is extracted up into the heavens before their very eyes, something that has happened only thrice before to physical bodies, to Enoch, to Moses and to Elijah.

It seems that Luke goes to some length to tell us that Jesus' body after he has been raised up, is alternately very physical and also capable of doing things physical bodies cannot do (disappearing, reappearing, levitating). Luke gives us a carefully mixed picture, one that is baffling. For myself, I would hunch that he is trying to explain to the reader something he either doesn't understand himself, or simply can't explain.

John

And lastly I turn to John's gospel. Probably first penned in the late 90s AD. John tells four quite different resurrection stories *(but then, John's whole gospel is quite unlike the other three)*: 1) he has Mary Magdala find the empty tomb and report it to Peter and the "beloved disciple" who 2) run to the tomb and find the body gone (considerable detail is reported.) The two go back home puzzled, leaving Mary at the tomb where 1a) she is greeted by an unrecognizable Jesus who will not let her touch him because he has not yet ascended to the father (I'm unclear what that means, but it implies to me that his body is not palpable, not corporeal; but how ascension would affect that is not stipulated). And 3) that same evening, despite locked doors, he suddenly (without benefit of Scotty's transporter beam) materializes among the ten (all except Thomas who, because he was not there, does not believe it). And 4) the following Sunday evening Thomas is with them and again Jesus materializes, again despite the locked doors, and responds to Thomas as though he had heard Thomas' thoughts, inviting him to touch the wounds.

The Jewish Mystic

I need to pause at this point and offer an explanation to help interpret the Johanine stories. In John Spong's most recent book, *The Fourth Gospel: tales of a Jewish Mystic*,[4] he offers a very well-founded and fairly compelling understanding of this fourth and most troublesome of the gospels. The three synoptics read reasonably well together. But John's bears virtually no similarity to the other three. In the whole of his gospel John tells only three stories similar to the synoptics, the cleansing of the temple, the feeding of the crowds, and the crucifixion, but he puts a radically different spin on these stories. The rest of John's gospel tells stories told nowhere else, and paints a Jesus unrecognizably different than the prophetic, itinerant rabbi we found in the synoptics. Spong's studies of this troublesome gospel have led him to a conclusion I find immanently explanatory and utterly convincing. Spong maintains that this gospel is the product of a Jewish mystic trying to communicate to his community *(in Epheseus? . . . where the [mystic] Paul was known?)* his mystical experiences of the risen Christ. Spong points out in great detail the very, very Jewish roots beneath each of the pericopes in John's gospel, clarifying as he proceeds that none of the stories come out of historical fact nor out of the synoptic tradition, but all grow out of this Jewish mystic's attempts to tell his people of his mystical experiences of the risen Jesus. Since the stories come, not out of history but out of his visions, so all are peopled, not with historical persons such as the synoptic Peter and James, but with fictional characters created to symbolize and enact the themes of his mystical experiences. John's gospel cannot be read like the semi-historical stories of the three synoptics, but must be detached from all history and read as John's telling of the risen **very** Jesus, his telling of the themes of and about the *persona* he comes away with out of his mystical experiences of the risen Jesus. So Spong shows us that John writes not out of historicity, but

---

4. I owe much of my revised understanding both of Paul's reports and of John's gospel to this latest book by Spong.

out of his own mystical experiences; ergo, not *fact*, but the *real* Jesus (of John's mystical experience) who stands behind and separate from what others take to be the facts.

So, John's four post-resurrection stories enumerated above need to be understood as peopled entirely with symbols which do not relate to the facts, but point beyond the facts toward a far deeper reality of Jesus. And as such, John's stories tell us virtually nothing about the physicality or non-physicality of Jesus' resurrected body: the relatings are all symbols out of John's mystical experience.

The Add-on to John

There is at least one add-on to John's gospel. Spong points out that there were three major crises in the life of John's community, and that the text of the gospel was edited or amended after each to incorporate the communal experience of those crises. So there are at least three layers of material in the gospel which are fairly inseparable.

In the add-on (21:1-25) then, some Johanine writer records a last post-resurrection appearance, this time beside the Sea of Galilee where the followers are fishing unsuccessfully. The unrecognized Jesus fills their nets and they come ashore where he is grilling some fish for their breakfast (remember that ghosts don't eat fish). Now recognized, Jesus thrice quizzes Peter and predicts Peter's death. John closes saying "There is much else that Jesus did . . . . " This *appearance* comes of even later origin and bears the stamp of hyperbole. I lay it aside.

Acts and Paul

There are several more reports of Jesus' post-resurrection appearances. Acts (1:1-5) says that he appeared throughout the forty days (i.e., from Easter to the Ascension) to the disciples and taught them, and appeared to Saul (Acts 9:1-5) on the road to Damascus (though I myself count this event, not so much as a post-resurrection appearance by Jesus, but as Paul's own unique mystical experience). And Paul reports that Jesus appeared first to Cephas (Peter), then to the twelve (*sic*: no tradition of Judas' betrayal!), and after that to five hundred at once (1 Cor 15:5-6), though Paul was not witness to any of those, just reporting what he was told. While these appearances do not tell us anything about the nature of the raised Jesus' body, because the *Acts of the Apostles* is (probably/possibly/maybe) Lucan we might infer that it assumes, as does his gospel, a corporeality, and that inference is validated by Jesus' being extracted up into the clouds in the "ascension" (Acts 1:9).

Analysis

And there you have it. I expect that there is little new to you in this gathering-in, though you may never have seen all the reports collected into one spot before; Spong's

Chapter 10: Four Other Doctrinal Matters

spin on John's gospel is likely new to you. Altogether I find the lot very troublesome. In some cases the story-teller goes to lengths to show that Jesus' body is real and tangible: so he eats fish, and invites them to palpate his body. In other cases the body is clearly super-human (or extra-human): he can suddenly appear and just as suddenly disappear, across distances, and in nearly all cases he is reportedly unrecognizable at first. Apart from the vacated tomb there is little consistency among the stories (and to complicate things, some scholars think it highly unlikely that there ever was a tomb for Jesus in the first place[5]). The stories are widely divergent and there are no repetitions (except for a couple of vague echoes.)

It is telling for me that Mark, probably the earliest, reports **no** resurrection stories, has no post-resurrection appearances. And it's curious to me, and more than a little unsettling that the further from the crucifixion we get historically, the more stories are reported, the more detailed they become, and the more the writers depict a resuscitated physical body (while maintaining **some** non-physical attributes). Yet Paul, offering the earliest evidence, seems to speak only of a transformed, changed, *spiritual* body. On examination it appears that understandings close to the event were that Jesus' resurrected body was **not** physical, but as the years and decades pass after the event the understanding moves toward a physical, but super-human body.

Conclusion

What shall we make of it? Clearly the eleven (or twelve) and others around them have had **some** kind of an experience of Jesus after his death; they report experiencing him as alive again. In Jewish tradition and lore fact is established only by the agreement of two witnesses in significant detail. No two of these witnesses agree to *any* significant degree. But clearly, with so many reports, with the intensity of the reports, and with the continued **high** valuation of the reports, **something** significant happened. But exactly what is completely unclear. We may repeat it in the creeds Sunday after Sunday, but that repetition alone cannot establish the nature of the facts. Some have suggested mass hysteria, or mass visions, or a kind of auto-hypnosis or auto-suggestiveness. Perhaps. Further, I suspect, if a clutch of twenty-first century scientists had been on the scene during those stories, they still could not tell us with reliability exactly what happened.

My Contemporaries as Witnesses of the "Risen Christ"

Some will affirm that the accumulated experiences of so many witnesses alive and present today (as well as throughout the course of the intervening history) of the risen Christ in their very own lives is proving testimony of the validity of the resurrection

---

5. Entombment would have been quite contrary to established Roman custom for the execution of an insurrectionist; the body was **always** left for the scavenging birds and dogs in order that there should be no proper burial.

of Jesus in 34 AD. And I can only respond that I have myself fervently prayed, many times in my own life for that experience of the living Christ, I have often put myself in places and circumstances most favorable for experiencing the living Christ, and yet I have never, not even once, had the most fleeting experience of a living, resurrected Christ. So I can only wonder about their experiences of the living Christ. I consider my own experiences (or lack thereof) as valid as theirs; after all, my experiences are part of **my** reality, while theirs are not part of **my** reality. How come, then, the divergence of our experiences? Perhaps such experiences of the risen Christ are given to some but not to others. On what basis is that discrimination made? Why am I deluded and bereft? Or on the other hand, might they be the deluded ones? Is there a living Christ? They have experiences of him (they claim). Why can I not, despite my sincerest of yearning and attempt? I find this contemporary body of witness as mixed and unsatisfying and unconvincing as the New Testament stories themselves. And that in turn urges me to question those of history.

My Conclusion

So, I know not what to make of it all. Perhaps the whole of *resurrection* is simply metaphor. And if so, then what stands behind the metaphor? To what is this metaphor trying to give voice?

Our resurrection

What does all this say about the possibility of our resurrection from death into eternal life? Paul says that if it happened to Christ, it will also happen to us. But the accumulated evidence does not tell us what happened to Jesus, and so cannot imply what will happen to us. Further, I am not as confident about Paul's proclamation as he seemed to be. So, after reviewing all this, I'm left not knowing what might happen to us after death; and further I'm not clear that anything will happen to us. Despite Paul's affirmation of life after death, I note that neither Edgar Casey nor Harry Houdini have come back to tell us about the other side, though they both promised they would. So, I can hope. But I know it is only hope. The Dalai Lama thinks that our *consciousness* will survive our death. That sounds pretty good to me.

But this is as far as I can go.

Atonement Theology

My source for this understanding of the Levitical Sin Offering is Anderson and Culbertson, "*The Inadequacy of the Christian Doctrine of Atonement in Light of Levitical Sin Offering*" ATR LXVIII:4, which reports from a portion of a seminar on various aspects

Chapter 10: Four Other Doctrinal Matters

of Christology among a group of Christians and Orthodox Jews in Jerusalem, October 1984, gathered by Dr. Paul van Buren, the National conference of Christians and Jews, and the Shalom Hartman Institute for Advanced Judaic Studies in Jerusalem.

In Leviticus 4, 5 & 16 YHWH lays out the template for temple sacrificial offerings for sin. In the fall of 1986 the ***Anglican Theological Review*** included an article reporting a seminar between some Anglican and Jewish scholars around the topic of "atonement for sin." That article was enlightening, enervating and utterly convincing.

The seminar made clear that in Levitical sacrificial theology making sacrifice at the temple in Jerusalem was **not** intended to take away or forgive sins. The logic of sacrificial theology ran thus: *sin* has two components. The first and most obvious is the damage or injury done to the one sinned against (offended, injured, damaged); and the second but less obvious was the *corruption* or impurity that accrued to the sinner in the act of his sinning. The first part, the damage, was corrected with some specified restitution or reparation to the sinned-against which was deemed *fair*. And for the second part, a blood-sacrifice was made in the temple in Jerusalem (a sheep, a pigeon, whatever; the **blood** of the sacrificed animal splashed onto the side of the altar was the efficacious part because the "life" *[which belongs to YHWH]* is in the blood [Lev 17:11]). But Leviticus is clear that the temple sacrifice was in no way related to the appeasing ("erasing" *[expiation]* or "covering over" *[propitiation]*) of the sin. It had nothing to do with the sin itself. The blood-sacrifice was intended to atone, i.e., to cleanse the holy place, i.e., the temple, of the impurity, the contamination, the corruption brought by the sin-offerer. The sacrifice in no way obliterated or removed or forgave the sin itself, it cleansed the holy place. Further, Leviticus is very clear that the restitution, or reparation and then the sacrifice must be done in that order; atonement, purifying the temple so God can be present, cannot be accomplished before restitution was made. So for a sin, first restitution, reparation, amends, and then at-one-ment with YHWH. Both steps accomplished, the sinner was absolved (cleansed).

Our forebears got it quite wrong when they proposed that Jesus' death on the cross was the sacrifice that atoned for our sins. Doesn't fit the Levitical theology laid down by YHWH at all; and that was, after all, Jesus' own Pharisaic theology. According to the sacrificial theology in which Jesus was swaddled atonement for our sins can't be accomplished until **after** we've made restitution. If atonement was Jesus' and YHWH's intent, then they failed to be in accord with their own sacrificial theology. First **we** must make restitution, reparation, and I don't see that requirement anywhere in our prayerbook, or in the ancient church fathers' thinking, or in the preacher's sermonizing, or in our Christian practices *(we only talk of forgiving, of the God forgiving us and of our forgiving others)*. Either God made a mistake in causing Jesus' sacrifice, or the church fathers interpreted the death wrongly, **if** Levitical sacrificial theology counts at all (for Jesus it probably did, and as I read our Eucharistic language, it seems to count for us as well.)

The earliest identification of Jesus' crucifixion as "for our sins" occurs in Paul when he cites a pre-Pauline creed, " . . . that Christ died for our sins . . . " (1Cor.15:3). So I cannot lay that interpretation at Augustine's feet as I am wont. It occurred early, and endured. Paul, a well-trained Pharisee, certainly would have known the Levitical Law and he would have recognized this as a non-Levitical interpretation. So I assume that his choice of this creedal statement was deliberate, and that he intended to fly in the face of the Levitical Law. Some scholars are clear that Paul understood Jesus to have been over-turning, or superceding the Law in some points, so this may be one of those.

Clearly the earliest church's understanding, as evidenced by Paul, was that Jesus died for our sins. In accord with the Levitical Law in which Jesus was swaddled, and which he does not seem to overturn or reject (while he does often clarify it, point to underlying intentions and correct interpretations) that Law, but to fulfill it, to fill it out, fill it up. So that understanding would certainly have run counter to anything Jesus might have accepted. Matthew has Jesus say, "So if you are offering your gift at the altar, and there remember that your neighbor has something against you, leave your gift before the altar and go; first be reconciled to your neighbor, and then come and offer your gift" (Matt 5:23-24). Very Levitical! But why Paul chose to overturn the Levitical Law on this point is a mystery he does not explain. Jesus dying for our sins is clearly not in accord with the Levitical Law and tradition regarding atonement sacrifice. And **if** keeping the tradition was the early church's intention, they too got it all wrong.

The study reported in the ***ATR*** shows that by the time Augustine was developing original sin into his linchpin and Jerome was translating into the Latin Vulgate, the nuances and core of Levitical sacrificial theology had been lost to the Church Fathers' thinking, and they had gone a different track, making break with Jewish thought and practice. And so today, when pressed, theologians can not found our atonement theology in the Bible. 'Tain't there! Not even in the Christian part. I suppose the matter could be argued from several other directions. It could be claimed that Jesus' dying was itself an act of restitution for others' sins, and his shedding of blood the atoning sacrifice. That argument begs the questions, to whom the restitution was made, and what kind of god would require the death of his own son to make restitution to himself for third-party offenses? On the other hand, it could be argued that Jesus' death was indeed the sacrifice which supplanted the temple sacrifice, that it was the atoning act which cleansed, washed away, covered over or otherwise appeased the God, but that God was requiring no restitution: clearly an abandoning of the heart of Levitical sacrificial theology (and for my money a crucial mistake). And on still another hand, I suppose one could argue from an even more remote stance, that Jesus was, rather than the cleansing, atoning sacrifice, instead the scapegoat of the Yom Kippur liturgy, the goat upon whose head the sins of the nation had been intoned; but that scapegoat was **not** sacrificed, and instead was released live out into the Wilderness of Zsin carrying

Chapter 10: Four Other Doctrinal Matters

the nation's sins on its head to meet whatever unknown and unwitnessed natural fate might befall it. So that does not really fit Jesus' death on the cross. For myself, I find all these arguments weak, incomplete and unconvincing.

Meanwhile something deep within me seems to recognize some efficacy in the Levitical atonement theology—not that we ought to be making blood sacrifices to YHWH on the altar in Jerusalem, but rather that simply forgiving (which we Christians are encouraged to do, even by the Lord's Prayer) without some kind of restitution or reparation (which we not are required or even encouraged to make) does not really work. Both that ancient theology and my own experience and sensibilities say to me that restitution is needed both by the sinner and by the sinned-against for the healing of both, and as well for the healing of the tribal relations and harmony, to regain at-one-ment within the community as well between the individuals. Alcoholics Anonymous recognizes this need in its requirement of the alcoholic in The Twelve Steps to make **some kind** of amends to those he has offended or injured. That act works toward the salving of the offense or injury, toward the healing of the relationship between the offended and the offender, and as well toward making the offender feel that he has in some way and to some degree corrected the offense or injury (and probably experienced significant pain or discomfort in the doing of it) and is himself somewhat the better for it. While the simple act of forgiving may be more expeditious, it is also one-sided, and I consider that it does not have the same threefold salving effect as restitution; and it does leave the **offended** in a *one-down* position, leaving the relationship incompletely healed (perhaps even "heaping coals on his head.")

We, as the sinned-against, are encouraged by counselors to simply forgive. That appears to make **some** psychological sense. I understand anger to be a very corrosive emotion (both psychologically and physiologically), and such an abiding anger is often a component of an unrequited injury, along with preoccupation, harboring, and festering; significant additional damage may be done to the offended along with the original injury. For the offended it is healing, or at least less self-damaging to simply forgive, to *let it go* rather than harbor and foster resentment. But it does nothing to heal or correct the offender, and it does nothing to heal the community which is witness to the offense and is itself offended when the wrong is unrequited or unrestituted. Simply forgiving offends the community's need for fairness and justice. My sense is that simply forgiving, letting go, is not enough, it leaves too much undone, especially for the community.

I remember as a kid, folded within the Protestant portion of our predominantly Catholic neighborhood, hearing my elders comment about the Catholic practice of confession and absolution, "The Catholics have it easy: three "Hail Marys" and two "Our Fathers" and it's all forgiven. 'S'not fair!" I've learned that understanding of confession and absolution is ill-founded, both for the Catholics and the Protestants. The confessional practice arose out of an older Celtic monastic practice known as *medicine for the soul*. For minor infractions against the monastic discipline (e.g., dropping the proffered wafer during the mass, or vomiting after consuming it) the offender was assigned some light and simple penance, not as punishment or retribution for the offense, but as a reminder, a modest goad to the offender to strive not to do that offense again. The monastic, much like the arch-heretic Pelagius, thought he could better himself if he rooted out destructive habits and corrected ill-behavior patterns *(unlike Augustine of Hippo who thought himself utterly unable to better himself in even the slightest way; only God could do that)*. So the monastics sought to better themselves *(which as I see as the only reason to endure a monastic discipline)*, and this medicine for the soul was one small means of encouraging that self improvement. I will beg for now the question of how efficacious the practice might have been, and simply point out that that practice over the centuries evolved into what we have come to know as confession and absolution, which gets tied into the whole complex of theologizing around Jesus' sacrificial death for our sins and for our forgiveness. A side-track, but a somewhat illuminating one.

I recall being taught in my liturgics class that the practice in the earliest church was, as the community was gathering (no alarm clocks, so they might struggle) pre-dawn (Sunday was a workday) to celebrate the liturgy, for the elders, in addition to interpreting the Scriptures, to adjudicate any disputes, differences, offenses between members of the congregation and assure they were resolved before the liturgy began. Thus when they prayed in the Lord's Prayer, ". . . forgive us our debts, as we have *[just]* forgiven our debtors . . . " they were in fact giving voice to what had taken place immediately before the liturgy; and when they passed the peace, it was indeed a sign that the dispute was resolved and the two parties were at peace, and the community as well; the **whole** community had been witness to that. I cannot vouch for the accuracy of that teaching; but it sounds good, and paints an instructive picture. And it does indicate that the resolution of dispute was as important to the community as to the two disputing parties. Simply forgiving is one-sided and ain't enough.

I may be merely nitpicking *ad absurdum* the issue of Jesus' sacrificial death because it is so repugnant to me. The concept of Jesus' dying as in some way making sacrifice for all others' sins is so abhorrent to me, the idea that the loving God would require, or worse yet would be himself required to require his own son's death (the same God who spared Abraham's Isaac) because the others's sinfulness is so off-putting. This is not a God I want to worship. I want to be responsible for my actions, not blandly forgiven because of God's son's death. None of that theology forms a center of belief for me, but conversely may even encourage me not to believe, not to trust this God, not to be faithful to and not to want the faithfulness of this God.

To sum up: I find wisdom in the old Levitical sacrificial theology. I hope we are past the age of sacrificing animals to appease a dyspeptic God. But I think it does still make good sense to understand that sinning, that is, injuring, damaging, offending another, does have multiple effects. While it primarily causes loss to the offended, it also causes disruption within the community which needs to be attended to, healed. And in some sense it also accrues some sort of corruption to the soul, or Self, or psyché of the offender, some abiding dis-ease. We (from watching myself, and those about me, and from psychological studies) are aware that having offended once, the offender usually finds it easier to offend the second time, and then easier and easier. The ill-behavior becomes less discomforting to the offender with repetition until finally it becomes easy, and even comfortable. Some healing must happen here as well, for the offender as well as for the offended, and for the community. Elsewise we are left with an offender who is less and less discomforted by his offending, and more and more likely to offend again, and then again. And Jesus dying on the cross for the sin of the offender does not bring about that healing, but instead may deter or impede the healing.

Augustine and our forebears not only misunderstood atonement theology, but in getting it wrong did a number on themselves and on us with all this "Jesus died for my sins" stuff. Instead of throwing up our hands and begging, "Forgive me God, miserable sinner that I am," we need to take responsibility for our behavior and set about making this world a better place for God's children to live in. That's what God wants.

Prayer

I've no expertise at all when it comes to prayer. I'm aware that most of the praying we do in church during the liturgies is intercessory prayer, begging God for something. That has always seemed unseemly to me. Feels like some primitive begging the spirits to do something for him that he can't do for himself.

In seminary I was taught just this side of nothing about prayer. We covered the rudiments of the structure of weekly collects. And we were bid to "read the daily offices," but given no direction or help. Just, "read 'em!" Beyond that we were on our own. In fairness, I suspect the faculty knew no more about praying than we did. They were academicians. Not pray-ers. I recall only that one dictum: "Thou shalt read the daily office(s) daily."

The Daily Offices

I tried several times in my thirty-four years to settle into a *discipline* of reading the daily office(s) *[Morning, Noonday, and Evening Prayers, and Compline]*. My failures to install the discipline were so abysmal that the fresh attempts grew more and more infrequent. I understood it was a discipline. But nothing came out of it. Not even wool-gathering. It seemed merely a struggle and a waste of time. My attempts became less frequent through the years, but the failures continued to nag at me, telling me something was amiss *(was that in me?)* In the early 1990s I became intrigued by the vague traces of the Celtic spirituality I was tripping over, our Anglican foundations suppressed by Romanism. I began searching it out. In 1994 on a pilgrimage in Wales I was introduced by Esther de Waal to Alexander Carmichael's **Carmina Gaedilica**, a collection of personal prayers from the Western Hebrides (Scotland), which, together with Douglas Hyde's lesser collection from Ireland, comprise our only knowledge of prayer life in a Celtic tradition. They are folk piety, about the matters of daily life (e.g. *smooring[6] the fire*), poetic, usually sung under the breath, and exceedingly individual and private, nearly secret, oral and so handed down by word of mouth across the generations. Because they were so private and not intended for community (as our Prayerbook offices are), they seemed to work for me. I hermitted in the Cistercians's Caldey Abbey to compose a set of daily offices in that Celtic tradition, prefixing them with a treatise on the elements of Celtic spirituality as I had unearthed it. I shaped it all into a book which I shared with a few people, and began to use for myself. They seemed to work for me, for a while. I learned that the prayers and psalms worked better when memorized and recited orally, *sans* the book which was a visual distraction. And for several months I was able to develop some discipline. But gradually that went dead for me too. A few people with whom I shared the book found the discipline and these prayers very fulfilling, but they proved not sustaining **for me**. Another, rather valiant effort which reinforced in me (with finality) that the discipline of reading the daily office(s) was an unproductive and dreadfully discouraging spiritual exercise, for me. Not my form of spiritual work. At length I gave up altogether on the discipline of reading the daily office(s).

Intercessory Prayer

This is the kind we most use in the liturgy My issue is that it's not about what it appears to be. It can't be about cajoling God, trying to talk Her into doing whatever I want done. One guy prays for rain, the other guy prays for sunshine; does God pick between them? Two countries pray for God to be on their side of the war, and both are convinced God is. How can God make both sides win? Or, how does She choose? Praying that way does not incline me to place trust or confidence when God can so be manipulated. Do we believe God does something because somebody whines a lot? I can't think that's the way life works.

And I'd say prayer is not about trying to goose God into action, either. I've little truck with a god who needs to be urged into action, and frankly, I don't see God doing much in this world anyhow. If anything needs a God to fix things up, it's this mess we're living in. But I don't see any fixings happening.

Through the years I have gradually come to understand that intercessory prayer is really not all about the God. It's more about us. It's about us reminding ourselves

---

6. "Smooring the fire" was the last of the housewife's tasks before tumbling into bed. It was hers to so bank the fire, i.e., arrange the coals, that there would still be sufficient embers in the morning to quickly start a new fire and set the morning porridge to boil.

CHAPTER 10: FOUR OTHER DOCTRINAL MATTERS

of the things about life that we really ought to have known, and once did, but have forgotten temporarily, until we remind ourselves again. And some of the prayers are about things we have not known, can never know, things beyond our knowing, things for which we haven't even words.

And then there are all sorts of questions about the efficacy of intercessory prayer. Does the God really hear and respond and do something when we pray about it? No clear evidence. Hunches and feelings and emotions and anecdotes. But no hard evidence. Not even semi-hard, squishy evidence.

Several possibilities occur to me, and maybe it's all of them. I recall hearing years and years ago that maybe intercessory prayer is a form of auto-suggestion, or auto-hypnosis. An old charismaniacal friend thought God might want me to do something about what I was praying for. When I think about it, **that** makes some sense: that saying, or begging something out loud, especially combined with the force of saying it in unison with a whole crowd of people, is a way of suggesting to myself, or even to all of our crowd, that **we** ought to be doing something about this. If it's important enough to bother God, maybe it's important enough that we should do something about it ourselves. Or if we say it together, out loud, Sunday after Sunday, maybe eventually I or somebody will hear it differently enough that a small bell will tinkle in my head, "Buddy, YOU **need** to do something about this!" Maybe intercessory prayer is not about telling God, but about goosing myself into "oughtness." Or reminding myself one more time. Steve Williamson used to say, "Pray as though only God can do anything about it, but then act as though only **you** can do anything about it!" Maybe praying is more about us than about God.

And then there's this: when I kneel down bedside, it's really more about me telling me, "It'll be alright to go to sleep. I'll still be here in the morning," and then I can sleep a little more softly. And when I utter a few thoughtless words before shoving the sloops into my mouth, maybe it's about reminding myself to live my whole life in thankfulness, not just this ten minutes I'm chowin' down. God might hear the words too, but that's just incidental. It's mainly about me.

Prayer's a lot bigger than begging God for stuff. We grew up thinking prayer was about going to church to get God into our frame of mind. Or maybe getting us into God's frame of mind. About maybe a few prudential words at bedtime, just in case. And another few words of thanks at meals. And when some things got **really** tough, some serious pleading of your case. That raises questions of whether the god is manipulable, which doesn't make a delectable picture. And it also points to the whole question of efficacy. Does God really answer prayers? There's lots of cute answers to that, most of them pretty insipid, a few outright stupid (e.g., "God doesn't always say, 'Yes,' sometimes he says, 'No,'" and "God doesn't always give us exactly what we ask for," and "God is always there.") The efficacy question gets argued every way from Sunday with all kinds of stories, but none of it terribly convincing. Soft, mucky, emotional stuff. Inconclusive at best. No use going there.

But it does all suggest to me that intercessory prayer is NOT about begging stuff off God. That bicycle that I got for Christmas, my parents got it for me from the Meeko's garage up the street, not from God, though I'd been praying to God for a bike.

Liturgy as Prayer

Not all the praying we do in church is intercessory. We sing a lot. I enjoy the singing; I was trained as a second bass, but I can't read music; I sing by ear. Usually I can pick out the bass line and sing harmony. Church is the only time these days that I get to sing harmony. So I enjoy singing the hymns, though sometimes the words choke me when the words are mushy, or repulsive, or flat-out bad theology. If the words and theology are too bad, I have to quit to endure. The music itself is the most important part of this kind of prayer, but the words are important too. Congregational singing is important prayer, doing something together, in harmony, unified. Community. A joyful noise. Joyful to me as well as to the LORD. Music is a good kind of prayer. I enjoy singing the psalms as well, with very simple tunes, sometimes in harmony, sometimes a single line of unison. I learned the pleasure of singing the psalms while in the monastery for five weeks. We sang them seven times a day. **Always** sang them. It got to be a great pleasure. So great that on Sundays now, when we're instructed that the choir will sing the psalm, I sing along too. It's my birthright to sing the psalm, and sometimes to marvel at the words the psalmist strings together before my eyes. Singing, in the presence of the God.

And there are also prayers of thankfulness, gratitude. It is good, even beneficial, and life-giving to be reminded to live life wrapped in thankfulness. Life is richer when I live it thankfully, generously. So this is a very useful kind of prayer. Prayer that helps me get into a mind-frame of thankfulness.

And then there is the confession (and absolution). I'm not sure what to make of that these days. I'm not clear that God hears me praying the confession; and if the God does, I'm not sure s/he/it cares one whit. I hear the words in my ear. And while I'm not into any Augustinian kind of penitence, it does remind me that I'm not living out the values I think I hold dear; but it does not much move me to do my life differently. There's no real repentance, or changing of my life's directions. So I hear only a tiny condemnation through those words. And the absolution? It passes by my ear almost unnoticed. Confession is probably a useful kind of prayer, a reflection-inducing kind of prayer.

I spent my life working in the church. So these Sunday prayers we say together have been my diet all my life. I know very little about any other kinds of prayer. The silent kind of prayer maybe. I write. I am a writer these days. And writers of necessity spend much of our time in silence. Listening. Listening as the ideas go flowing past my earhole. Just listening, until a particularly attractive sounding idea goes drifting past, and my mind reaches out to catch it, play with it, start to put it on the page until it takes on a life of its own and begins to write itself through my finger, into the keyboard, onto the page. And then I listen some more. I think that too is a kind of prayer. A listening. And watching. In silence. Maybe it's the God that speaks. Maybe it's just my subconscious. Maybe it's some muse of creativity to whom I've not yet been introduced.

Conversing with God

What is prayer? As a kid I was taught that prayer was about talking with God, like everyday conversation, letting Her know what's going on in my life, where my problems are. It strikes me as funny *(not humorous, but peculiar, odd, untoward)*, that the omniscient, omnipotent God would need to be told about things like that, and by me, no less!

After I grew up I read a book. A philosopher[7] posited a scenario that you're told to get help is to talk at night to an unseen person behind a large tree who will not speak back but will offer solution for your problem. Well, I thought on that for a while, and I said, what's this prayer thing about? I'm to have a conversation with someone I can't see, or hear, or smell, or touch? That's not a conversation! That's myself mumbling in the dark.

That kind of monologue is not about God-and-me, it's only about me!

Meditation

About that same time I started musing a little about other kinds of prayer. But not too seriously. Like meditation. I knew nothing about it; none of my books told me anything useful about it; no one I knew could tell me much about it. They'd not taught me anything at all about it in seminary. I'd heard of Transcendental Meditation and I knew that while a few priests tried it and said it was good, most put it down. Meditation. That means thinking prolongedly about something, doesn't it? And since I hadn't any more clues, I left that notion floating out there on the edge of my wondering without a clue what it was about.

When at Caldey Abbey brother Gildas told me that he was told that everything he needed to know he would learn from his cell! I thought I knew what he meant; but that's not something you ask a man, "What d'ja mean by **that**?" He suggested praying just before sunrise in the old abbey ruins. And as I listened in prayer I heard the fifteenth-century Benedictines processing into the chapel. I've already told the story of that morning,[8] so I'll not repeat it. But that experience did introduce me to another kind of prayer.

---

7. See whole parable in Chapter 5 (139)
8. See Chapter 2 (7–8)

Part II: My Review of Christian Doctrines

Some years later I was in Ireland and through two sheerest accidents I found myself listening to John O'Donohue talking to our small pilgrim group, and telling us about things I'd never heard anyone talk about before: about exploring your inner landscape; and making friends with your soul that lives at the back of your inner landscape and is in constant communication with God so that it can tell you what God wants for you; and about the soul being timid, and preferring candlelit shadows to confrontational florescent lights (you can't just grab for the soul, you must quietly siddle up to it). And I thought back to Tillich's words about God being the very ground of our being. And I realized maybe **that** is what this kind of prayer is really about, finding God, not out there somewhere, but at the very center, the ground of our being, looking down so deep inside myself that I find God there. And that's what opens the doors to mediation and contemplation: not being told about God but learning God first-hand, for myself, mostly by being quiet and getting out of the way. O'Donohue was a scholar of Meister Eckhart and of mysticism. Maybe that's the route he was pushing. Prayer's not about talking God into doing what I want, but about learning God up close.

So, I go back to this whole thing about talking **with** God. Alright, like Hepburn said, it's not a proper conversation if there's no one talking back to me. But maybe there's something to this stuff O'Donohue was putting out about listening, about searching out my interior landscape and getting acquainted with my soul. It's a matter of quietly and ever so gently searching for my soul *(I wouldn't recognize a soul if I fell over one!)* way down in the dark, hidden passages inside me, and hunkering down to listen and hear what my soul has to tell me about God, and about myself, and about what we could do together. Maybe conversing with God is not a tit-for-tat conversation, but about just listening, listening very intensely, listening to the silence. And whatever comes in that silence may be coming from God, or may be bubbling up out of my subconscious. And maybe those two are the very same thing! I worked with a very Episcopal psychiatric social worker who told her clients she thought God works through our subconscious. Not such a wacky thought.

Rosary Prayers

The other kind of prayer running around in my head is the simple repetitious stuff. My mother thought it was voodoo kinda stuff, saying the rosary, repeating the same little bitty prayer over and over and over. My Protestant upbringing, where everything is forced through a sieve of rationality, pronounced that kind of prayer mindless. But that's the point, isn't it? Getting into mindlessness? The Eastern Christians are much into the "Jesus Prayer." Numbs the mind. Quiets all the constant background noise. A way to listen better to the silence. Centering Prayer does the same thing. And the Eastern yogi's with their mantras; same thing. Quiet down the mind. Listen to the silence the mindless repetition creates. The yogi's and the shrinks teach us that it coaxes the brain into an altered state where we hear and see and sense things differently. That's

Chapter 10: Four Other Doctrinal Matters

the way the serious mystics do it. Empty the mind, focus on the silence where lives the God, or the soul, or something besides my constant brain-chatter.

Buddhist Meditation

And then there's the kind of meditation the Dalai Lama uses! I can tell you nothing about it, but I am impressed with the depth of the insights he comes back with from his meditations.

Mysticism

I have one last thing to say about prayer. A few years ago when I realized the YHWH I'd been preaching for years was beginning to wriggle out of my grasp, I started to wonder about the mystics. I'd paid them no heed in all my ministry. A single book of selections from the mystics of the early church had languished on my bookshelf for many decades, now old and tired and dog-eared, but still unread. I thumbed through it and realized why I'd never read it up before. It was much like some unknown foreign language. I could make little sense of it; and the little I did, I didn't like. But still, these were the great people of the church who had encountered God for themselves, like Moses on the mountain top. They knew the God, directly and intimately while I was slowly losing my finger-hold on the fringe of the God's robe. Julian of Norwich, one of the great mystics of the Anglican Church. I tried her. Got indigestion. Still I wondered, could I experience the God for myself rather than just read others' notions about the God? After I finally got around to ploughing my way through another classic languishing on my bookshelf, Evelyn Underhill's on **Mysticism**. She implied I wasn't any mystic. But I ventured an attempt anyhow, centering prayer. Nothing. Just a lot of incessant noise inside my head. But I wondered on. Finally I searched out a collection of psychiatric appraisals of mysticism that seemed not knee-jerk anti-religious, fair, even-handed.

The paper by Julian Silverman hit the mark and convinced me that the mystical experience may not be quite what it purports to be. My conclusion after studying the paper is that the insights of mystics are no more self-authenticating or to be trusted than those of certain others.[9] Their insights should be taken seriously, but scrutinized in light of the reality in which we daily live, and outside of, not from within, such perception-altered experiences.

The great mystics of the church, a collection which includes many of our great reformers, leaders and innovators, engaged in a contemplative prayer in which, through the practice of perception-altering disciplines, they *(claim to)* enter the very presence

---

9. For discussion and detail see Chapter 2 (29–30 & footnote #5)

of the God; they sometimes return with deep and exhilarating insights, which they might attribute to having been in God's immediate presence.

I look askance, somewhat convinced that their experience is akin to the schizophrenic's and drug-tripper's, and that the insights they bring back need to be scrutinized just as closely and objectively as those of the schizophrenic and the drug-tripper. Their experiences may be wonderful and life-changing; but I suspect they are no more of God than the experiences of those certain others. Consequently, this is a kind of prayer that I no longer seek; it is not my kind of spirituality. And I have to ask in each case, is this a gift from God, or a pathological mental disorder, or hypnosis and self-suggestion, or a metabolic by-product with hallucinatory properties? Or might it be mere charlatanism?

Prayer as Catharsis

Shrinks know about catharsis, the cleansing effect of saying something out loud. Works in therapy. Why not in prayer? Confession, for example. Though the Romans probably had it right there, with private confessing to the priest who listens, and makes you do something about it. I don't know that our general confession, without the specifics, would do much cleansing. The exercise is forcing your thoughts through the linear part of the brain, forcing it into words and then saying them out loud so your ear can hear it coming back at you, and it gets processed through another part of the brain. Hearing the words is different that saying the words. It puts them into a different perspective. Maybe it triggers some reasonable problem-solving instead of the useless *mea-culpa*-ing. Prayer might work in that way too. A form of catharsis. Instead of just weeping, vocal prayer might bring on some real decision-making.

Prayer as a Healing Act

One more piece just flew into my head. Vacationing on a wee island off the coast of Maine, an old seminary buddy whom I'd lost for nearly three decades came out to spend a day with me. Bill began to tell me impossible stories about his past lives and such. The least implausible of those stories was about the healing ministry he was into, sending healing energy into other peoples' bodies. He had learned how to plant his feet firmly on the ground, and then receive energy from the earth, and then shoot it out to other people. He claimed it worked; he could feel it and others could feel it too, and they often did get better. His Apache friends had dubbed him a shaman. I choked on most of that. Bill is a little given to hyperbole, but I had the feeling there was the faintest echo of truth in some of his stuff. So I withheld judgment. But it seemed like another kind of prayer had stumbled onto me.

Chapter 11: Where I Net Out

My title might be misleading; in reality I am at a temporary resting point in my spiritual pilgrimage, and in this chapter I share what I see as I take rest. That will change as soon as I start to wander again. I've come to understand that faith is not a fixed place, it is in motion, moving, growing. I remember one parishioner saying to me that he wanted his church to be a bastion against change. I suspect he is still in that same place, I have moved on, far on.

And I will say once more to ensure clarity, for me **faith is not a set of beliefs** or dogma; faith is a verb of action, not a fixed concept. "Faithing" means being there when it counts or matters. I'm sad that a *credo* (i.e., the Creed *[I believe]*) was hung around our necks in the fourth century. It has subverted the attention and energy it takes to keep being faithful. What I believe doctrinally is not terribly important. What I believe at the edges of my knowledge will change if you hang around for a few minutes. I keep having new experiences, and new ruminations, and what I know (believe) is constantly changing, in flux, in motion; not a whole lot, but it certainly is not fixed or stable. So I don't want anyone to trust *(credo)* what I think or believe, but I do want you to trust that I will be faithful, that I will be there.

I will keep this chapter brief; it could get rambly in trying to cover the whole waterfront. Not my intention. I want not to repeat what I've already said (but in some measure will), but to give you an outline of what I am thinking at this time. Not that you should agree, but to encourage you to do that same, figure out what you can believe and feel good about that. I'll hit the high points and keep moving. I expect this will seem thin; I am living with less belief these days, but with a little more clarity.

The Doctrinal Stuff

The God

Is there a God? An obviously impossible question! I have found YHWH of the Hebrew Scriptures and Abba of the Christian Writings deficient, lacking. Those seem anthropomorphized projections of human needs, both individual and communal. The God is ultimately unknowable. A friend has suggested that just because I think the God is unknowable does not mean that the God is not influencing me, and I agree. So, I am not an atheist. Atheism is unreasonable, ignorant; there is no evidence that the God does not exist. Nor can I find reliable evidence that the God is. So I am simply unknowing; and that is evidently unsatisfying for me because I do keep searching.

PART II: MY REVIEW OF CHRISTIAN DOCTRINES

Non-interventionist

We pray to the God and expect the God to respond to that request (in a sense, even the contemplative's disciplined empty mindedness is an unuttered request for the God to reveal itself to him, to at-one with him). And we also expect (or hope) the God to take some action in our world to finally set things aright (the eschaton). But if the God is unknowable, does it intervene? How can I say? I know only that I see no reliable evidence of the God's interventions; occasionally some soft (usually squishy) evidence, but none with reliability or even high plausibility.

The Scriptures

A marvelous collection of writings. Inspired by the God? If the God is unknowable for me, then how could I possibly answer that question? And once I take the God out of the question, and start taking seriously the writings's internal contradictions and inconsistencies, as well as their discontinuities with external sources (e.g., archeology and history, the sciences, the material world in which I live), then I must place them reverently on the bookshelf alongside the other great writings. Written and edited with unexpressed overlays (e.g., fostering the patriarchy, stoking national hopes and dreams, re-inventing the God for the moment) for a specific moment in history and not for eternity, compiled and redacted with assumptions that I cannot buy into, I have to take them very seriously and but also very critically. They are my Holy Book. But they are not for me the "very words" of the God.

When my first wife died she (frustrated that her brother had inherited her mother's diamond) had just purchased a ring with a large solitaire diamond. I kept it for several weeks after her death, simply because I enjoyed flashing it in the sunlight and watching it refract the different colors of the rainbow. Marvelous. For me the exquisitely crafted stories in our Scriptures are much the same as that diamond; when I hold a well constructed story up to the light it flashes brilliant bits of insight as I turn it and ask different questions of it. But I am clear that the usefulness and veracity of those insights depends upon the aptness of my questions; without my questions and my very critical reflections on whatever insights the story flashes at me, the Scriptures are simply a lump of words. I bring as much to the effort as the authors and redactors did.

The Scriptures Are Used as a Rorschach

Having watched others cherry-pick their ways through the Scriptures, and knowing that I do much the same, I have come to understand those Scriptures to be much the same as a Rorschach test (ink-blots) into which I project myself. Whether they are the inspired Word of the God or not is a question of fluff. Whatever I get out of the Scriptures is exactly what I unwittingly (or deliberately) projected into them by the presumptions I brought and the questions I asked, unless, after I have gleaned some insights from this story or that (or even from the whole), I examine those insights critically, with all my wits and knowledge, and in the glaring sunlight of the real world in which I live. If I take the time and trouble to do that, then I may come away from the Scriptures with some useful insights to apply. But if I do not, then I surely will come away with only what I've found congenial to what I brought to the Scriptures.

Jesus

I have no reason to doubt there once was a very human itinerant rabbi named Jesus who was so popular that healings and miracles were attributed to him; but I have no reason to think he was born of the God's DNA. And I am pretty convinced that without Paul of Tarsus Jesus would have been forgotten in a few generations. It took the genius of both to make this Christianity happen.

What then do I make of this Jesus, the first of the dynamic duo? He was evidently such a charismatic person that they made him over into a god. We can say with no reliability what we think happened after his execution that made his followers experience him as resurrected (in the Greek *made to re-stand up*), alive again; but that experience was the handle by which they exalted him to a divine status. Do I know him to be divine, very God of very God, begotten, not made? I have never experienced the risen Christ, so I have to reply, "I have no reason to believe Jesus to have become the resurrected Christ, a post-resurrection divine being."

So for me Jesus was a rabbi, dedicated to reforming, returning to roots of the Jewish faith, and cleaning out the accumulated garbage. (To the extent I can lean on the Jesus Seminar's judgments) his message was not eschatological. Nor was he terribly prophetic (i.e., challenging of the social structure, as I hold the eighth-century prophets to have been); and he may have been a healer (in the likeness of healers contemporaneous to him). He was very much about how to live together in the here and now in the best ways (the Kingdom of Heaven, according to the God's will).

Jesus is, for me today, in addition to an historical figure, an exemplar of living (and dying) with integrity. I discover powerful insight in many of his stories. I find in him something pointing waveringly toward the core values of living toward the *good*, an imprecise moral compass, and a sounding board for morality. One has suggested "a transparency of the ultimate" (a lot to unpack in that, but for the moment I will pass.) And finally I find in him a very rabbinic style: reflectful, pondering, challenging but seeking, a style I find quite congenial.

Saul of Tarsus

I should say a few words about the other of this dynamic duo. I appraise Paul to have been as important to the formation and success of Christianity as was Jesus, perhaps even more so. He was a driven opportunist; initially driven to eradicate Jesus' followers, but after his mystical experience on the road to Damascus driven to prosper the followers. His genius was two fold; 1) injecting into (or reshaping) Jesus' message the overriding love theme which was far from a dominant theme in Jesus' message, and 2) an intuitive talent for forming and coaching faith communities. He had no firsthand experience of Jesus (so far as I can tell), and I conclude that his message and theology were born mostly out of that mystical experience, an insightful event that reformulated what he had already learned about Jesus (whatever it was that had set him so viciously against the followers), and which was then informed by his apprenticeship in Damascus. His message was about (but not from) Jesus, significantly amended by his own messages of love and community.

Prayer

The words for prayer in both the Greek and the Latin should be translated "to beg." In as much as I do not think the God to be an interventionist, I would deem it a fool's errand to pray in the mode of begging the God to intervene in worldly matters for my benefit or for the benefit of whomever I intercede for. So I must figure out what prayer is for me, and why I should pray at all. I'm sure there are other kinds of prayer, but I'll identify three here: intercessory, praise, and contemplative.

Intercessory prayer

When my first wife was diagnosed with cancer I was somewhat amazed that I did not pray aggressively for her healing. I rationalized that many others were praying furiously for her, and my primary focus was tending to her immediate needs. Others were praying enough (in hindsight I see that it was mere rationalization). I **could** look back and tell myself that tending to her physical and emotional needs was a **sort** of prayer, but I suspect that would be somewhat disingenuous. I cannot go back to those moments and check it out, but today I suspect that I had already unwittingly given up on intercessory prayer. So these days I turn around and ask, what is intercessory prayer? Autosuggestion? Autohypnosis? I'm not clear. But I am clear that the target for my intercessory prayers is not the God, but myself, and us, and our community. I think that intercessory prayer is not about begging of the God, but about reminding ourselves, about nudging ourselves to do something about it. Anything! A prod, a mobilizer, an encourager. Intercessory prayer is about talking to ourselves, and to each other and to the whole community, out loud, in public. About encouraging ourselves to get on with it, to do something about it (whatever the "it" is). *(The God is non-interventionist; if anything good is to happen, it's up to us to do it.)*

Chapter 11: Where I Net Out

Prayers of praise

There are many kinds of praiseful prayer. The hymns we sing: the psalms we recite (which should be in unison or antiphonal, and always sung, quietly, thoughtfully, reflectively) together; the canticles; some of the non-intercessory prayers in our Book of Common Prayer are praiseful; the music, the organist, and the choirs and the occasional instrumentalists perform for us. Quietly watching the glint of a cardinal in my back yard, luxuriating in the pure whiteness of new-fallen snow, the sheer joy of silence. All ways of yielding praise. But praise of what, or to what? To the unknowable, non-interventionist God? Well, if you want to, but that doesn't much move me. So what is the praise about? I think that praise is for me and for us, to uplift, to give voice to our positive feelings, to remind ourselves to live in thankfulness and generosity. Praiseful prayers are to remind us of the goodness of this creation and of this life. They are to reinforce us in living positively with and for others. They are to point out for us the good, the beautiful, and encourage us too to live beautifully, for others and then for self.

The praising also turns out to be a community building exercise, to help us cohere, to be really with each other, and to be for each other.

Contemplative prayer

The contemplative goes into his closet and empties his mind so as to find himself embraced by the God. *(Perhaps.)* Sometimes that contemplative returns to this reality with deeply profound insight. But from the little I've read from the writings of mystics, most often he comes back with insights he thinks profound but which appear to me to simply restate differently or more forcefully what he and we already knew, or thought we knew. The contemplator is so powerfully moved that he thinks his experience self-authenticating. But so do the schizophrenic and the psychedelic (who, as evidenced by the psychiatric data, are having similar awareness altering experiences). Recent research may be indicating the use of psychedelic drugs can be as life altering and insight yielding as the contemplative's disciplines. Contemplative prayer and various forms of meditation may be health-inducing and perhaps beneficial to the spiritual life and work, but I distrust that they are particularly "of the God." It strikes me that the meditation of Tibetan Buddhism may be just as valuable, or perhaps even more.

Sin and Salvation

I pulled the lynchpin, sin, out of Western Christianity's theological system in Chapter 4, and, for me at least, the structure did not utterly collapse. It took a different shape, but held up. And when sin was taken away, salvation flew out the window too. I have become quite clear that religion and faith (spirituality) are not at in the slightest about pie in the sky by and by. They are about living in the here and now. About living with integrity. About living toward something (and that something is not the tickling of my gizzard). About living with meaning, and living meaningfully. If there is a salvation then it is one of being led away from our lesser nature, our dark side; and it is about this life which we have in hand. And I am inclined to agree with the arch-heretic Pelagius that salvation happens through honest self-appraisal and then discipline, determined effort and persistence, and with the conviction that we **can** do better.

Non-Doctrinal matters

Since the Council of Nicea our faith has been about what I believe *(credo)*; but I have come to hold that decision was a subversion for me, and that faith is really about doing; it is a verb, an action word. And it is not necessarily about trusting in the God, or believing something in particular about the God; rather I think it is about living with integrity, behaving in ways that are consistent with the core values I have inherited, evolved and chosen. That said, I scan the horizon to pick out what is most important to help me do my spiritual work, i.e., *tilling and tending* my core values and my behavior, and what I see as I scan is . . .

What is the Church Not?

In Chapter 7 I excoriated the church, such as it is; I will not repeat that here, only summarize very briefly. In its first years the church was (among other things) a counter-culture movement; but when Constantine decriminalized the church it was co-opted into the social structure, no longer counter-culture, but now a corollary of the state, if not a servant. And it has been so ever since. Whether officially or unofficially the church of state (the religion and the state have always been intimately intertwined ever since the beginning of the state), the church has served the conventional faith[1] of the state as advocate and, to a lesser degree, sanctioner of the nation's core values. *(The church's consciously primary mission, the preaching of the Good News of Jesus the Christ, while very sincerely intended, is really only a veneer disguising the deeper mission, advocating state values.)* As a prophetic voice the church is disabled. As a servant of the state it cannot be truly counter-culture. As the voice of Jesus, it speaks in inaudible whispers. And the church cannot be an *actioning* subsystem except wherein it serves the needs and purposes of the state (e.g., food pantries, homeless shelters).

---

1. To be clear, I am referring to the third of James Fowler's six stages of faith development, "conventional faith," which has been the purview of the mainline denominations since the foundation of our country. The fundamentalist denominations hold purview over that portion of the populace with a more simplistic and literalist world-view, i.e., "mythic-literal faith".

Chapter 11: Where I Net Out

What the Church Is

I remain mildly amused and slightly surprised that, my faith having grown beyond the boundaries of conventional orthodoxy, I have still a strong loyalty to the church. Not necessarily to the diocese, nor to the Episcopal Church (though it will always be my home), but to some vague, immaterial church, which happens to be expressed in material form for me in the members and staff and building of St.Luke's in Granville. There is still a need in me, and a force pulling me there; and since it's not the doctrine, I look elsewhere.

Advocate of Values

Two sets of values. On the surface values voiced and enacted by Jesus, and behind him the Jewish faith and history; but underneath that veneer the core American values (individualism, liberalism, capitalism). **Perhaps** the tension between the two sets of values is important, useful, helpful (though the usefulness of that tension is indiscernible to me). As I stand and sit in the church listening and reciting and singing, I find my attention drawn to those values, examining them, turning them over in my fingers and inspecting them, asking myself, "Which of these makes the most sense in this world, in this reality?" And it is the same as I sit here at home pounding my keyboard, writing. The church sends me home to continue that task. Listening, turning, inspecting, asking. I think the church, in fulfilling its assigned social function, is a repository of values; not a system where they are all carefully aligned and coherently integrated, but a treasure chest, a grab bag from which I can take them out one by one *(or by the handful)* to inspect, appraise, choose. And then ruminate, "What does that now imply?" The church is a time and place to re-read the metaphors and ponder what this or that metaphor is saying today? The church speaks in metaphors, so it constantly invites me to re-read, and ask again. This facet of the church may be its most attractive, most useful for me. *(This is for me "doing spiritual work.")*

Place

I've told you how my guide in Wales shared that he thought these circles of standing stones were multi-purposed; and how I came home to understand that the church, and specifically St. Luke's, is my circle of standing stones. And for a while *(and still, occasionally)* whenever I entered the church I asked myself, "What is this circle of standing stones about today? What's going on here today? What is this circle of stones saying to me today?" First of all it gives me place. Not just the pew I tend to sit in regularly. It is a place for me to stand in the world. It surrounds me with meaning and an important part of my identity. Place. A place to be who I am. It is not the only place of my life, but it is a very important one.

I think this church is also a holy place for me. I use that word guardedly. I do not mean that the God is particularly there. Nor is it any more spirit-filled than other places: I've been in lots of *thin places* and this is not one of those, at least for me. But it is somehow set apart, a place to go to do spiritual things because they happen a little easier and less distractedly there. When I was ordained I understood that I was in some undefined sense being set apart for special sacerdotal functions; and I think in some way the church is ordained too. I go there to have conversations, not necessarily with the people (though that happens too), but with some Other that I cannot identify. Not the God, I think. Though, maybe. We talk about values and other hidden things.

And there is a social place there too. I have come to be known by a fair portion of the congregation, and to be regarded. That is an important kind of place. It used to happen in neighborhoods and villages, but doesn't any more. So the church becomes more important, for me, as a place of sociality. And in particular with a small set of people who gather once every month or so to share for a couple of hours around matters such as these. That group is a particularly important place to me.

And too, I grew up in church, became a person in church, and made my profession in church. So it is not only **in** my fibre, it **is** my fibre, at the core of who I am, so I probably could not walk away from it even if I wanted.

Why do I keep coming back to church, immersing myself in its liturgies and rituals, mumbling its words, even when I know they are intellectually incomprehensible? Probably because in some measure it is who I am. But also in some measure because it obviously feeds me in ways nothing else does.

And the Future?

The church is a creature of the present, of the *status quo*, of Walter Breuggemann's Empire and as such is not a doorway into the future. The key word is "community," and while the church offers a paltry community (the evangelical mega-churches seem to have learned how to manipulate a slightly better kind of community than the mainline churches can muster), it is not the kind of community that will open the door to the future.

Communitarianism

If Darwin was right, that survival belongs to the more adaptable (and the evidence so far confirms his analysis), then the future belongs to the more adaptable (cockroaches and select bacteria). I think some kind of communitarianism (see Chsapter 13) is one viable handhold into the future of humankind.

Chapter 11: Where I Net Out

The Compelling Argument

Our planet is an isolated island with a fixed amount of non-renewable resources, and we are busily squandering the only natural resources available to us, converting them into trash. Smart phones will not carry us into the future, nor adapt us to a resource-emptied world. My analysis is that individualism, the key to innovationalism (and its tool, capitalism), has run its course, and turned self-consuming. Mindless innovation has become a fast track to the failure of the species by despoliation. The future lies in the direction of recognizing healthy community and environment as essential to survival. To become adaptable we must learn our way into healthy community, an impossibly difficult and complicated task because the community is rapidly morphing into a global village while we are still playing within social systems and moral structures and value fields that evolved ten or fifteen millennia ago, appropriate to that era but little changed since. Without the interventionist God to rescue us from ourselves, the *extremis* point for comfortable human(e) survival lies just beyond the short-range and foreseeable future. The alternative is something of the sort depicted in the post-holocaust movies popular in the eighties and nineties, a cockroach-kind of existence of sub-moral human beings. I detest making the sounds of a prophet of doom, but I do believe that **is** what lies just ahead. If the **Population Bomb** writers were anywhere in the proximity of correct, and if I am reading the trend of current events right, that the under-developed peoples are gearing up to scramble for their fair share (preferably by violence it appears) then somehow we must figure out how to adapt to the looming reality.

Can Communitarianism Play Out?

Martin Luther King, Jr. preached, "The arc of history is long, but it bends towards justice"; Robert Wright thinks there may be a moral axis of the universe. I hope both are right, but from where I stand I think the evidence is scant, and neither hard nor conclusive. I wish I could, but I cannot quite share their optimism.

I stand here with a tiny clutch of values in my hand: the absolute equality of all persons, the need to balance the community and the individual member, and justice-mercy for all. John Rawls suggests that justice may be fairness; that is elegant and simple (the physicists's standard for good theory); I would want to amend his suggestion just slightly and opine that justice equals fairness **plus** mercy. That's about all I have in my hand. Is it playable?

I have grave doubts. Given the homeostasis of social systems, given the intransigence of human foibles (greed, lust, power-mongering, egoism: the laundry list is long), given the lack of vision and will in this culture, given the radical changes that would have to be accomplished, I doubt. I hope I am wrong. On the other hand, given President Roosevelt's Social Security, given Barack Obama's one step toward universal health care (both tiny, halting, baby-steps) we have some least-possible momentum in that direction (albeit hobbled with out-sized and irrational resistence). I am given to understand (perhaps erroneously) than the barest handful of our top politicians have consulted with some communitarian philosophers; that offers some hint of hope. But the individualists's cries of "Socialism, Communism" resound in my ears.

What is Left?

For someone like me whose belief structure has crept beyond the ragged edges of his faith community, what is left is a jumble of questions about religion that seem to me as yet unanswerable. Are all religions equal? Some students of such things seem to think they are all headed in the same general direction. But I am a child of the Christian mainline stuff, largely ignorant of the others, and really cannot comment. Can some amalgamation of the major religions be made? I am vaguely aware that there have been some few attempts of something like that (e.g. the Baha'i religion), but I am not aware that any has had significant success. I recall the late nineteenth-century failed movement to create an international language, Esperanto; I think it's still around but little used. My sense is that religion, like language, grows up naturally inside a culture and cannot be made out of thin air. So I pass on that question as well.

Part III

A Vision to Move Toward

Chapter 12: Failed Values

I COME AWAY FROM all these doctrinal discursions with only a small handful of plausible remains. I still look to our Holy Scriptures for guidance; even though I've found them primarily a man-made Rorschach, they remain my only Holy Scriptures. In the Hebrew texts the eighth-century prophets point falteringly in the rough direction of some sort of social justice-mercy, but they give scant direction and less encouragement. I turn to Jesus. Given all the scholarship that has preceded me, how am I to parse him? I grasp at the results of the most recent attempt to uncover his historicity, the Jesus Seminar. Those scholars tell me that in the whole of the five (including Thomas's) gospels they find only eleven sayings they can "unequivocally," by the most stringent tests, attribute directly to Jesus. And remarkably four of those eleven are explicitly about the Kingdom of God, and another three I could easily associate with his Kingdom of God even though he does not do so explicitly. I search amongst the hundred and thirty-one sayings the Jesus Seminar attributes to him "with reservations," and altogether fourteen are explicitly about the Kingdom of God. That causes me to struggle. Paul and the gospelers had seemed to me eschatologists, taking the Kingdom of God as a description of *after* the eschaton; but the eschaton did not come as they anticipated in only a few days after Jesus' death/resurrection, or a few weeks, or months or years or decades. So theologizers had to re-interpret: maybe the Kingdom of God Jesus pointed toward was already realized, here, deep inside each believer, a potentiality rather than a completed external reality *(an exercise in radical individuality!)* None of that has ever made much sense to this person; I tend not to deal in post-eschatons, nor radically individualized, unseen, and unrealized potentialities. I tend to deal in the here-and-now, so for the most part I have left the Kingdom of God lying relatively untouched in an unused corner of my theological thinking and preaching. Today as I skim the considered opinions of the Jesus Seminar I see Jesus not so much as a prophet, certainly not a prophet of the last days, but more as a wisdom teacher, one very focused on the here and now *(am I analyzing or merely projecting?)* of his own world. This makes sense to me. Perhaps it shows me what I, following his exemplarship, need to do, to garner and share what wisdom I can about the here and now.

Jesus' Kingdom of God is a (perhaps incomplete) vision: of how life and living could be; of how it might be to live together in true peace and harmony; of an ideal, an end-goal state of being for all; of what YHWH and Abba and perhaps the God too would be intending, urging for us. The text gives us some clues about the vision: of *ḥesed* (translate "loving kindness"); of justice-mercy (in the Hebrew Scriptures those are congruent, synonymous, or at least complementary); of ultimate fairness; of what the God had in mind when it created, and placed us in the Garden of Eden *(I speak, of course, in metaphor)*. I go back to the sources: prophetic[1] cacophony scrounged from the Hebrew Prophets

> *from Amos*, the most socially conscious: "... because they sell the righteous for silver, and the needy for a pair of shoes – they that trample the head of the poor into the dust of the earth, and turn aside the way of the afflicted; a man and his father go into the same maiden ... " (2:6b-7), "... who oppress the poor, who crush the needy, who say to their husbands, 'Bring, that we may drink!'" (4:1b), "... you who afflict the righteous, who take a bribe, and turn aside the needy in the gate" (5:12b), "Woe to those who lie upon beds of ivory, and stretch themselves upon their couches, and eat lambs from the flock, and calves from the midst of the stall; who sing idle songs to the sound of the harp ... who drink wine in bowls, and anoint themselves with the finest oils, but are not grieved over the ruin of Joseph! ..." (6:4), and "Hear this, you who trample upon the needy, and bring the poor of the land to an end, saying, 'When will the new moon be over that we may sell grain? And the sabbath, that we may offer wheat for sale, that we may make the ephah small and the shekel great, and deal with false balances, that we may buy the poor for silver and the needy for a pair of sandals, and sell the refuse of the wheat?'"(8:4-6).

> *from Micah*: "They covet fields and seize them, and houses, and take them away; they oppress a man and his house, a man and his inheritance" (2:2), "... you who hate the good and love the evil, who tear the skin from off my people, and their flesh from off their bones; who eat the flesh of my people, and flay their skin from off them, and break their bones in pieces, and chop them up like meat in a kettle, like flesh in a cauldron ... " (3:2-3), "Shall I acquit the man with wicked scales and with a bag of deceitful weights? Your rich men are full of violence; your inhabitants speak lies, and their tongue is deceitful in their mouth" (6:11-12), "Their hands are upon what is evil, to do it diligently; the prince and the judge ask for a bribe, and the great man utters the evil desire of his soul; thus they weave it together. The best of them is like a brier, the most upright of them a thorn hedge" (7:3-4a).

> *from Habakkuk*:" ... His greed is as wide as Sheol; like death he has never enough. He gathers for himself all nations, and collects as his own all peoples." Shall not all these take up their taunt against him, in scoffing derision of him,

---

1. To avoid misleading, a note of clarification: the Hebrew prophets were not future tellers. The classic prophet was an advisor to the king. The king's stable of prophets was hired in to advise him what to do next. With no crystal ball for divination, they mainly kept their eyes and ears open to the political and military and social winds and calculated the most helpful suggestions. The king listened to as many and whichever he wanted, and weighing their advice, made his own thus informed decision. A few, most often ones not lodged in the king's stable, claimed relationship with YHWH, and therefore offered some esteemable, but not very palatable advice. Not future-telling, but telling the powers which way the winds are blowing; it is truth-telling, which requires telling those powers what they r-e-a-l-l-y don't wanna hear; and it purports to speak in the name of YHWH.

and say, 'Woe to him who heaps up what is not his own – for how long? – and loads himself with pledges!' Will not your debtors suddenly arise, and those awake who will make you tremble? Then you will be booty for them. Because you have plundered many nations, all the remnant of the people shall plunder you . . . Woe to him who gets evil gain for his house, to set his nest on high, to be safe from the reach of harm! You have devised shame to your house by cutting off many people; you have forfeited your life . . . . Woe to him who builds a town with blood, and founds a city on iniquity . . ." (2:5b-12).

from Isaiah: "The Lord enters into judgment with the elders and princes of his people: 'It is you who have devoured the vineyard, the spoil of the poor is in your houses. What do you mean by crushing my people, by grinding the face of the poor?'" . . . (3:14-15), "Woe to those who join house to house, who add field to field until there is no more room and you are made to dwell alone in the midst of the land" (5:8), "Woe to those who decree iniquitous decrees, and the writer who keeps writing oppression, to turn aside the needy from justice, and rob the poor of my people of their right, that widows may be their spoil, and that they may make the fatherless their prey!" (10:1-2), "Is not this the fast that I choose: to loose the bonds of wickedness, to undo the thongs of the yoke, to let the oppressed go free, and to break every yoke? Is it not to share your bread with the hungry, and bring the homeless poor into your house; when you see the naked, to cover him, and not to hide yourself from your own flesh?" (58:6-7), and "For your hands are defiled with blood, and your fingers with iniquity; your lips have spoken lies, your tongue mutters wickedness. No one enters suit justly, no one goes to the law honestly, they rely on empty pleas, they conceive mischief and bring forth iniquity . . . . Their works are works of iniquity, and deeds of violence are in their hands. Their feet run to evil, and they make haste to shed innocent blood; their thoughts are thoughts of iniquity, desolation and destruction are in their highways. The way of peace they know not, and there is no justice in their paths; they have made their roads crooked, no one who goes in them knows peace . . ." (59:3-8).

My first reflection on this exercise of scrounging through the writings of the prophets is that I am indulging in a whole lot of very subjective judgments. What constitutes a prophetic utterance in the name of YHWH? I have not studied my own screening of passages to discern what are my criteria. I realize this is a subjective collection. I looked for utterances that would indicate some directions, some ways to go, some things that needed to be changed. And I had expected at the outset of my in-gathering to come away with a huge collection of sayings which I would have to winnow down to a manageable set clearly pointing in one direction. Didn't happen! What you have just read was my entire collection. (There's where the subjectivity came in; what did I leave out, and why?) To my great consternation I found empathy for the poor and oppressed, but only railings against the powerful, the rich, and the oppressors. No correctives to the social structure or system. There was nothing to make life better, only "Bad you!" And with the collection being much smaller than I expected, I come away from the exercise concluding that on the whole the prophets were much more concerned about international affairs and the worship of YHWH than about improving the lot of the underclasses or correcting the evils of the social structure. I had adored the eighth-century prophets all my active ministry; it appears instead of learning from them I had been projecting my own yearnings onto the prophets the whole time. I am disappointed.

And then I looked at the **Magnificat** *(Luke has the meek and mild Mary sing:)*

"My soul doth magnify the Lord. . . .

. . . he hath scattered the proud in the imagination of their hearts.

He hath put down the mighty from their seat, and hath exalted the humble and meek.

He hath filled the hungry with good things, and the rich he hath sent empty away. . . ." (Luke 1:45b-53)

On reflection this Magnificat, which Luke attributed to Mary, is touted as revolutionary, making Mary an *avant garde*, way out in front; but on scanning the song a little more closely, it strikes me as fairly bland, with no payback for the evil-doers, just a small reward for the oppressed. Nothing here to offend; no systemic change suggested to or pointed out; no correctives.

And finally I scrounged through Jesus' prophetic sayings:

from Matthew: "Blessed are the poor in spirit, for theirs is the kingdom of Heaven. Blessed are those who mourn, for they shall be comforted. Blessed are the meek, for they shall inherit the earth. Blessed are those who hunger and thirst for righteousness, for they shall be satisfied. Blessed are the merciful, for they shall obtain mercy. Blessed are the pure in heart, for they shall see God. Blessed are the peacemakers, for they shall be called sons of God.. . . ." (5:3-10), and ". . . for I was hungry and you gave me food, I was thirsty and you gave me drink, I was a stranger and you welcomed me, I was naked and you clothed me, I was sick and you visited me, I was in prison and you came to me" (from 5:31-46).

from Luke ". . .proclaim release to the captives, recovering of sight to blind, set at liberty those oppressed. . ." (4:18), ". . . blessed are you poor, for yours is the kingdom of God . . . blessed are you that hunger now , for you shall be satisfied . . ." (6:20b-21), ". . . blind receive their sight, lame walk, lepers are cleansed, the deaf hear, the dead are raised up, the poor have good news preached to them . . ." (7:22), a man asks Jesus to divide the inheritance, and Jesus tells a parable of a rich farmer hoarding his wealth who hears God, "Fool, this night

Chapter 12: Failed Values

your soul is required of you . . . " (12:13-21), and the story of the rich man and Lazarus who goes to heaven while the rich man is in Hades (16:19-31).

from Thomas "Congratulations to those who go hungry, so the stomach of the one in want may be filled." (69.2) and the story of the rich man who invests in barns, and dies that night. (63:1-3).

On to the rich stuff. I confess in reflection that after I searched out all of these sayings, again the collection is much smaller and less intense than I had anticipated. I've lived out my ministry understanding Jesus to have been prophetic, confronting the powers-that-be about their ill-treatment of the underclasses. I looked at the gospels and found almost nothing, and none confrontative to the over-class. I went back and scoured all five gospels (including Thomas) and came up with nothing additional. It would again seem that my ministry-long appraisal of Jesus' ministry was quite wrong. He was not in the least critical of the **social fabric**! While he may have been more on the side of the poor than the rich, he offered no correctives to the system at all, he did nothing to better the condition of the underclass. All the stuff about the evils of the social system and efforts to set them aright in YHWH's name was in **my** heart, and I projected them into my reading and study of the Scriptures. My socialist forebear John Slayton's DNA and Raushenbush's "social gospel" have been at work within me, projecting themselves through all my years of studying the Scriptures and what I thought YHWH's will ought to have been. My apologies to the reader. My own notions about how this world ought to go are obviously more to the fore in this writing than anything YHWH ever hoped for it.

And then there came Bowers's rant *(several months ago when writing a piece to share with the discussion group I have met with regularly, this rant unexpectedly blurted out)*.

"Your capitalism is an abomination[2] to me. I created you all of equal value to me. And you ultimately stand as equals before me. It is an abomination, an affront to me that you choose, by capitalism (or whatever other means) some to be impoverished, some to be malnourished, some to be ragged and homeless, some to be ill or imprisoned, and some even to be slaughtered, but just a few to be wealthy beyond reason, to be powerful, to be arrogant and abusive beyond measure. When Cain slew his brother Abel, his very blood cried out to me from the earth, and then, before I had yet composed for you my Law, I punished Cain for this grossest abuse of his brother. Should

---

2. "Abomination" is a technical term in the book of Leviticus, quite different than "sin." Sin is an act which transgresses the Law, i.e., the "God's Torah." The "abominations" enumerated in the "Holiness Code" [Lev17-26] are those acts or conditions which render one *(and therefore the community)* unclean, unholy, not fit to be in the presence of God. For example, temple prostitution, a ritual practice of the Canaanites involving persons of both genders in heterosexual and/or homosexual hook-ups was not acceptable in YHWH worship and was deemed, not a sin, but an "abomination" which utterly disgusted YHWH and made the practitioner "unclean," unfit to worship YHWH, or to be allowed inside the Temple. While sin could be restituted and atoned for, persons committing an abomination were usually ordered stoned to death (at least in the Scriptures, if not in real practice.)

I do less for you? Rather I would that, just as enslaved Joseph forgave and embraced and gently cared for his enslaving brothers, you should love one another and mutually do compassion upon one another. If I could. Your capitalism is an utter abomination.

"Your military-industrial complex is an abomination to me. You pour vast quantities of the limited resources of my earth into a bear-pit of military presence in all the nations of my earth *(as many as you can get away with)* to try, without accountability, to compel them all to your will without overt bidding. It is an abomination, and the grossest misuse of the resources I have entrusted to you. When did I call you to be my world's super-cop? Or when did the nations of the world elect you? Yet you keep massive standing armies strewn across my globe, armed with the most technological and expensive weaponry you can dream up, and that at the cost of oppressing your own people. Your military-industrial complex drives your economy and oppresses my people. It is an utter abomination to me.

"I hate your compulsion to knee-jerk, zero-sum competition in everything you do. I did not ordain that all your transactions be designed zero-sum *sans* synergy. Nor did I command each of you to strive in every way and at all times to better himself at the expense of every other; to lord it over the others. You rationalize that your knee-jerk, zero-sum competitiveness yields higher technology and greater advancement, but tell me, if you can, in what way any of that has bettered the condition of your brothers and sisters, at home and across my globe. Your compulsive competition and zero-sum-ness is an utter abomination to me.

"I hate, I detest your rape and abuse and wanton despoliation of my creation wherein I had put you. Five days did I labor to create the garden, and the whole earth. I placed you in that garden to enjoy and be enriched by the fruits of my labors, and I commanded you to till and tend the garden. But you knew better than I, and so you despoiled the garden, and the whole earth. And you have continued to despoil it with complete abandon, with disregard for your brothers and sisters, with disregard for even your own well-being, and to no end good for you who are the epitome of my creation. I shaped you out of the mud and breathed into you my very life, but you choose to rush mindlessly toward breathless oblivion back down into the mud. Your despoliation of my creation is an utter abomination.

"I am appalled at your suicidal rush to self-obliteration[3]. My first commandment to you was to be fruitful and multiply and fill the earth. You have so filled and overfilled my earth that my creation can no more sustain all of you. You have overdone abundantly my first commandment. So this day I release you from its obligations. And if I could, I would command you to zero population growth and to bending your minds and efforts wholeheartedly to the compassionate use of my creation in caring for your brothers and sisters with the same love which I have borne for you. I would command you to curtail your destructiveness, and to bend your minds and wills instead to the wise and thoughtful husbanding of my creation for the sustenance and benefit of all

3. See Diamond, **Collapse**, *passim*

Chapter 12: Failed Values

your brothers and sisters. But you would not heed. Your self-destructiveness is an utter abomination to me.

"I am devastated by your total absorption with yourself, your *individualism*, your abandonment of the welfare of the community, your self-servingness, your chasing after silly things, empty things, stinking things, your centering of my universe around your Self. I did not create you to titillate your Self; I made you to live in community, and to do those things essential and desirable for the sustenance and enhancement of the community, as well as every persons in it. Your self-serving individualism is an utter abomination to me.

"I am stunned and stupefied at your mindless, endless, directionless drive toward increasingly invasive, goalless, complex and dominating technologies that are glitzy, but cause no real benefit. You evolve your technologies without consideration of their impact upon people or communities, without awareness of good or evil, without concern or thought for humanizing or dehumanizing. You create robots to do the works of people, but do nothing to re-engage those displaced laborers in tasks that feed them, and instead you abuse them for their aimlessness. Your techno-drivenness is an utter abomination to me."

Again, I reflected on that. I noticed that this all came out very much in the words and imagery of our Scriptures. I am not surprised. While I consider that we use the Scriptures more as a Rorschach than a source of guidance, they are still the metaphor most known to me and comfortable and expressive. And my very notions themselves arise out of the promptings in those Scriptures, though I validate them not out of Scriptures, but rather out of the growing body of scientific knowledge. So I use this language and metaphor naturally. It requires a little demythologizing, but not a whole lot. I hope my rant will speak for itself. And I think this ranting does reflect my thinking, my understanding, and in a negative way my vision.

Christian Values: now I step back from this collection of cacophonic prophesy and begin to sort through to see what values I can discern. I am searching for a values set which would create a world both fair and realistic (i.e., as congruent as possible with world as we understand it through our scientifically biased eyes.) This search through our Scriptures for values was not a straight forward exercise. Jesus nor the eighth-century prophets spoke in values language; that is a twentieth-century invention. I have to look through these sayings and try to discern the values that lie behind them and prompt them.

So I look, and the first observation is that they are mostly negative.[4] I pointed out in my discussion of sin that the Levitical code recognized two sorts of commandments, the injunctive (i.e., *aseh*, "Thou shalt") and the prohibitive (i.e., *ta-aseh*, "Thou

---

4. To be sure, there are positives, particularly in several of the prophets's summaries of the Law. To wit, Micah," . . . and what doth the LORD require of thee, but to do justly, and to love mercy, and to walk humbly with thy God?" (6:8b), and Hosea, "For I desired mercy, and not sacrifice; and the knowledge of God more than burnt offerings" (6:6), and Amos, "But let judgment run down as waters, and righteousness as a mighty stream" (5:24).

shalt not"). As I watch this collection of eighth-century prophets troop by, they are all pointing at behaviors and saying, "No, no!" but they seldom point at other behaviors and say, "Yes, yes!") The clearest positive I find in the Hebrew text is *ḥesed*, which might be translated "loving-kindness" or "justice-mercy" and is most clearly defined by Matthew (5:39-42) as turning the other cheek, going the second mile, and giving when asked; and Luke (6:29-30). The Deuteronomic Law commands care for (but not relief of) the poor, the orphan and widow, and the oppressed. But in all of this I find no defining direction, no correction of the social structure.

As I pivot to the Jesus collection I am similarly dismayed. I had always considered Jesus a social prophet; now as I study him I find a wisdom teacher embodying compassion for the sick, the disabled, and the bereaved. He seems bent on loosening the Pharisaic strictures (though in Matthew he is depicted as tightening them considerably), and acting out compassion, but shows no inclination to make the social system any better or more fair. I perceive him to be teaching better interpersonal relations, and minimally some positive adjustments of the social fabric,[5] but no correctives to the social structure. So I find it difficult, perhaps merely specious, to tease out any clear values. As one seeking to make our world more fair and humane, I do not find that whatever values I might draw out of Jesus' teachings have failed; they simply don't lead anywhere. They give no attention or corrective to the social structure, which is where I see change needed. Jesus the wisdom-teacher gives us some guides for living a little more healthily within our current social system, but offers no correctives, and points only waveringly in the general direction of a more fair and humane system.

I am searching for a few core values that will give not only sufficient direction to live by, but to shape a healthy structure to support our social fabric. I am disappointed, though not surprised that I did not find such a set in the Judeo-Christian Scriptures. In my assessment of the institutional church I concluded that our Christian church is very much a church of state (albeit unofficially), as has been the religious establishment down through all ages and cultures; political power and religion go hand-in-hand, and have always been twins. It is no surprise at all that our church covertly promulgates the core American values whilst seeming to preach Christian stuff. Having not found the guidance I am searching for in the Holy Scriptures, I need to take a hard look at their step-sister, the American core values which I think the church covertly promulgates.

I perceive that our country was founded primarily on individualism, a value imbedded in our Constitution. I have some notion of why our founding fathers thought that the most important value in establishing their independence from the despotic

---

5. Likewise Jesus does give us a "Golden Rule" (our title, not his) in Matthew, "So whatever you wish that men would do to you, do so to them..." (7:12a), and in Luke, "And as you wish that men would do to you, do so to them" (6:31) *[not unique to Jesus]*; and the "Great Commandment" in Matthew, "You shall love the Lord your God with all your heart, and with all your soul, and with all your mind... You shall love your neighbor as yourself" (22:37, 39), and again in Luke 10:27 *{both cobbled together from Deut 6:4 and Lev 19:18b]*.

Chapter 12: Failed Values

George III. In the 1800s we adopted the emerging, congruent value of *capitalism*, the economic system which had been slowly emerging in Europe since the 1600s, and was then accelerated into dominance by the industrial revolution. But I also perceive that the simplistic individualism of Maine's "Don't Tread on Me" has steadily evolved toward the libertarianism of an Ayn Rand, and the unfettered individualism of the *unorganized militias*; individualism has become all-consuming and mindless, a boundless and directionless me-first-ness. And capitalism has morphed into a hard-driving, thoughtless consumerism. Our now untethered founding values are rushing us into choosing to become a failed society[6].

I've been rebelling for some years against the unfettered (and these days, rampant) individualism, deeply imbedded in this American culture. It is argued that individualism has wrought for us some wonders, but it's not at all clear to me that those wonders have been very beneficial to us. Marvelously wondrous technological geegaws and doodads and doohickies. But beneficial? Really? The mindless technologies we are currently devising seem to be luring our social fabric away from social and mental healthiness, and toward feeding on the vulnerable edges of individuals and of our social fabric. There are some deep, dark and destructive down-sides to individualism.

My well-read friend Susan suggests to me that individualism is relatively new stuff. I find it not easy to research (is it an intentional blind spot in our vision?), but the notion seems to have grown out of the New Enlightenment of 1600-1700s thinking and the collapse of autocratic despotism. The resultant freedom seems a natural phenomenon of social evolution. But it appears to me that the pendulum of individualism has swung far past some healthy midpoint and onward toward a destructive extreme. Individualism has over flourished by virtue of the diminishing maintenance of the social fabric. Individuals grow more demanding of rights and privileges, less accountable to each other and to community maintenance, and more inattentive to the needs of the community.

Since this section begins as a rant against individualism, I suppose I ought to be clear with you what I understand "individualism" to be. In these paragraphs I am educating myself more than you. To that end:

> **Individualism**: (***Random House Dictionary of the English Language*** 1987)
> 1. advocating the liberty, rights, or independent action of the individual. 3. the pursuit of individual rather than common interests; egoism. 6. *Philos.* a. the doctrine that only individual things are real. b. the doctrine of belief that all actions are determined by, or at least take place for, the benefit of the individual, not of society as a whole.

The principles of individualism are:

---

6. Diamond op. cit.

Part III: A Vision to Move Toward

1. that we are free-standing agents,
2. that we are free, maybe even responsible, to form our own concept of **the good** *vis-a-vis* any community concept,
3. that we have the right to pursue a life (guided by reasonable deliberations and decisions) in our own self-interest, and
4. that we are bearers of inalienable rights, entitlements, with no inherent duties or obligations

I understand how individualism emerged as reaction to the decay and collapse of authoritarian despotism. Individualism assumes that the individual is a free-standing agent; I deem that a specious and unfounded assumption, in plain words simply a bare-faced lie. In this reality individuals are far from free-standing: we are born into community, shaped by our several communities (*mores*, standards, expectations, etc.), and continuously supported by community; and none of us can survive at his own hand without the supporting fabric of the community. Without community we become feral, governed by the demands of self-survival.

That we are free *(even responsible)* to form individual concepts of *the good* is tantamount to a license to do whatever I please, often regardless of the consequence to others and to the community. In the absence of community, the individual has no means of conceiving of **the good** for himself, no touchstone, no protective hedges and no correctives.

That we might be guided by reasonable deliberations and rational decisions seems reasonable at first glance, but experience and Trumpmania teach me that almost nothing in the social fabric, in interpersonal dynamics, or in individual psychology is very rational or reasonable. Choices are driven by myriad forces and factors, most of which are unseen, some even unknowable. I see no evidence that logic is a driver anywhere in our societal, social or private decision-making, and rationality is a fairly rare commodity.

It also has been observed that without community there are no rights or privileges; and conversely, community *de facto* does necessitate some duty and obligation.

While individualism may have served to maximize creativity, competition and entrepreneurship, the rampant individualism of today has become self-centeredness, a me-first-ism feeding the decay of our moral structure. The pendulum has swung, me thinks too far. The rush toward individualism has turned destructive of the community which we need to survive and thrive. We need to reappraise our fundamental values. Individualism has brought us wonders *(though I am dubious of the ultimate value of most of those* wonders*)*. But I believe it has turned sour, into morbid self-centeredness and moral decay. Somehow, some where the well-being of the community must be factored in; but individualism resists that factoring.

Chapter 12: Failed Values

Individualism and classic liberalism go so hand in hand in this culture so that in speaking of one I must also speak of the other, so herewith a few words. Classic liberalism is founded on the individualism with which it shares some principles (i.e., individuality, inalienable rights), and adds three more (equality, private property rights, and limited government). And while liberalism professes belief in the equality of all persons, it has no means or structure to bring that equality about; instead the individualism out of which liberalism grows militates against fundamental equality by emphasizing the differences and inequalities as measured by productivity, aggressiveness, and ruthlessness. Can there be equality in a system of "every man for himself" (which appeals to our baser instincts)? I judge the real core of liberalism is property rights (extended to the appropriation of any unclaimed resources and *stuff*); upon those property rights and the concomitant aversion to government the whole system of capitalism is built. Classic liberalism is really a moot point in the current scene, and the dominating principles are individualism and capitalism, with a smidgeon of libertarianism.[7]

Classic liberalism (different than contemporary "liberalism" or "progressivism") grew up along with individualism in the New Enlightenment, as part of the undoing of over-bearing governments (authoritarian, autocratic, and totalitarian, along with religious fundamentalism), coupled with the rise of industrialism and science. The principles of liberalism are:

1. the equality of all men
2. the individuality of persons,

---

7. Libertarianism appears to me liberalism run amok. I don't know whether it was the birth child of the novelist Ayn Rand, or whether she merely gave voice to what was already brewing within the American culture. The principles of libertarianism are:
   1. the primacy *(sovereignty)* of individual liberty, of *full self-ownership,*
   2. a *(rampant, perhaps rabid)* anti-authoritarianism which causes skepticism of all government (intensity runs from as little government as possible to no government at all),
   3. the right to acquire private property and to appropriate to one's own use and benefit any unclaimed resources and *stuff,*
   4. capitalism in all forms but tending toward *laissez-faire*
   5. voluntary association,
   6. moral protection against forcible interference including government interference, and
   7. morally enforceable duties *(though not by force).*

I am again reminded of Maine's, "Don't Tread on Me." And I recall the *unorganized militia* training camp near Cambridge, Ohio while I ministered there. These people *(I include Rand Paul)* seem to me dangerous *wing-nuts* dedicated to protecting and enhancing their absolute liberty, licence, and freedom to do whatever they damned well please at whatever costs to others, and even to themselves. They fantasize that we could get along with no government at all, and therefore any government, no matter how little or how weak, is too much. On my part, in the increasingly globalizing structure we live in, it's not just unfeasible and impossible, but out of touch with reality. As we globalize, governance becomes increasingly important.

3. the right to private property,

4. inalienable individual rights, and

5. limited government.

In all these "liberty" and "ownership" are the **operative** words.
In reflection, I have always considered myself a liberal and am usually considered by others to be a flaming liberal. However after searching out this definition, I am not so sure. While I can whole-heartedly ascribe to the equality of all persons, I am decreasingly committed to any of the other four principles of liberalism, and find myself wandering somewhere out in regions far to the left of socialism. The liberalism (or progressivism) we have evolved today seems functionally ignorant of the equality of all persons, and pretty thoroughly uncommited to three of the other principles. Property rights and the right to appropriate to one's own use and benefit any unclaimed resources and *stuff* seems to be fundamental to capitalism and therefore to our current brand of liberalism.

Capitalism is a system of economics based on the private ownership (by individuals or corporations) of capital and production inputs, and on the production of goods and services for profit. The production of goods and services is based on supply and demand in the general market (i.e., market economy), rather than through central planning, and is generally characterized by competition between producers.

The tenets of capitalism: trade, industry, and the means of production are largely or entirely privately owned, and are operated for profit. The essence of capitalism is the investment of money to make a profit. Its tenets are:

a. privately owned property (including capital)

b. capital accumulation

c. competitive markets, and

d. wage labor (i.e., purchased labor)

There are possible variations:

e. the degree to which government does or does not control markets, and

f. importance of property rights.

It contrasts with socialism (social ownership of the means of production, and cooperative management of the economy.)

(Note: democracy became widespread at the same time as capitalism, suggesting a causal relationship between them.)

The advocates of Capitalism claim that the world's GDP per capita has shown exponential growth since the beginning of the Industrial Revolution. From 1000 to 1800 world economy grew faster than the population yielding a 50 percent increase in individual wealth. From 1820 to 1998 the economy of the developed world grew fifty-fold, yielding a nine-fold increase of individual wealth, in Japan a thirty-one-fold increase, and in the Third World a five-fold increase. Proponents maintain that increasing GDP brings improved standards of living (greater availability of food, housing, clothing, and health care), decreased work-week, fewer children and aged in the workforce. Milton Friedman *(and Ronald Reagan!)* promoted the theory that the market mechanism is the only way of deciding what to produce, and how to distribute without coercion. Capitalism is vital for freedom to survive and thrive.

The critics of Capitalism claim that capitalism is associated with social inequality, unfair distribution of wealth and power, the tendency toward monopoly, oligopoly (a few buyers unduly influence the markets) and oligarchy (power is drawn into the hands of a few), imperialism, counter-revolutionary wars, economic and cultural exploitation, materialism, repression of workers, social alienation, economic inequality, unemployment, economic instability. Capitalism is irrational (i.e., unplanned), capitalist economies prioritize profits and capital accumulation over social needs of communities. Immanuel Wallerstein claims institutional racism has been a most significant pillar of the capitalist system. Environmentalists claim capitalism requires continual economic growth, inevitably depleting finite natural resources, destroying traditional ways of life, exacerbating inequality, and increasing global poverty. Christians criticize its materialistic aspects and inability to account for the well-being of all people. Catholic scholars criticize its disenfranchisement of the poor. Pope Francis describes unfettered capitalism as a *new tyranny*.

I would say that capitalism has become the very bedrock of our American system, and has become the economic structure of this country. It has **learned** to be the first principle and driver of our political structure, and is the very fabric of our social structure. Probably for most people it stands in as a **system of morality**. It increasingly dominates all, to the exclusion of other values and factors. And it has grown extreme, unfettered, lightly regulated, and so undirected (or misdirected) as to become destructive of our culture. And it is the ultimate *Sacred*. If one were to seriously challenge capitalism (as I am about to), he would be immediately dubbed blasphemous and a communist, or worse.

I frame this part of the conversation by asking, "Is incessantly and compulsively increasing prosperity really what life is ultimately about? Is over-abundance really the highest good for humankind? Or is that a false path? Or even a self-destructive path?" Within the context of that clump of questions then, a few words about capitalism.

As I superficially skim its history, capitalism appears not so much the rationally developed economic system it poses to be as a system that evolved without much thought or direction; like Topsy, it just growed, but without planning or systemic intention or rationality. While the roots of consumerism reach further back, our American capitalism careened rampantly (economic policies placing emphasis on consumption) after the Second World War as products once designed to last a lifetime were redesigned into consumables, products specifically intended to endure only a short while, or to be literally consumed, eaten up, worn out. I discern only the objective of making profits for the capitalist. It has further evolved, both politically and legally, to more greatly enrich those already rich at the expense of the middle and lower classes, effectively creating a new aristocracy of capital holders, plutocrats who exert oversized influence on the political system largely through lobbying and campaign funding.

Capitalism has some inherent down sides. Where profit taking is the primary goal, there can be only a superficial concern for the non-capitalists (i.e., the wage-laborers), but rarely deeper than a concern lest such concern might overwhelm the profit taking. Profit making then becomes the central pillar or principle of the moral system, ushering us into moral decay, most visible within the industry of advertizing[8]; that moral decay, by virtue of its permission giving, then bleeds into the rest of the social and political structure. Poverty, racism, and oppression become concerns only as they cause sufficient rancor to require amelioration, but no more[9]. There is no striving toward equality. Nor is there concern for the welfare and well-being of the people or the community, unless their lack of well-being reduces the possibility of profit taking.

Capitalism is basically an operating system without moral concern, without direction or correctives to protect the non-capitalists. Further, as capitalism has evolved in the United States, the legal and social structures have evolved congruently to support and protect it, so that capitalism becomes a thoroughly entrenched system, and functions as **the** primary moral structure as well as a governing and legal structure.

And finally, while the advocates assert that capitalism is vital for freedom to survive, I would counter that only if we define "freedom" radically, as in libertarianism, is captialism essential. "Freedom" is quite relative, and is a sensibility defined by the particular culture; what is "freedom" to us in the western world is deemed anarchy in the Far East.

My overview: As I ponder the American *triune* of individualism, libertarianism and liberalism, my growing sense is that the driving force behind them is economic. Without private property, individualism, and the right to appropriate unclaimed *stuff* to one's own purposes, there can be no capitalism. If I were better tutored, I might allow that in theory capitalism could be a neutral force, but I still conclude that, coupled

---

8. I recall a teen friend in the 1950s just starting his college work in advertising telling me with great excitement that Folger's Coffee had just discovered that when they promoted their coffee as having a "winey flavor" sales increased. No one had any notion how a "winey" coffee might taste, nor any suggestion that Folgers actually had a "winey flavor." But when the word "winey" was used in the advertising copy, it sold better. No matter that it was a deliberate deception, it sold. At the same time Ruth Lyons on radio in Cincinnati, and Arthur Godfrey on national radio could sell anything to all the housewives in America because they were trusted as "always telling the truth," never wavering. I look at advertising today, a major driving force in our consumerist economy, and it's all a pack of lies. If not immoral, then completely amoral. It doesn't need to have one iota of truth in it, so long as it sells. So much for morality.

9. I have a vague suspicion, but neither proof nor plausible argument that the operation of a capitalist economy in some inexplicable way requires maintaining an underclass. No rationality to this supposition, but lots of observation and hunching.

Chapter 12: Failed Values

with atomistic individualism, capitalism has grown into an ill-distributive and self-destructive system. Equality and fairness are its primary victims. Mindless rape of the natural resources and destruction of the ecology are the collateral victims which will ultimately determine survivability.

I see further destructive forces at work in our excessive individualism. Our atomization is producing an *anomie* coupled with a rising urge for freedom from interference to the degree that taxation and other governmental intrusions (e.g., gun control) are seen as unacceptable meddling; the tide of libertarianism would seem to want no government at all, or as close to nothing as can be obtained. As a people we are getting more insistent that the rights and privileges of ownership be unrestricted as to what we choose to do with whatever we own, and to be unaccountable for our use of the earth's resources. The growing sense is, "I am more important than those around me," and we are edging toward the sense that "I have the right to do as I please, regardless of how it impinges on those around me," and that "morality is an individual choice."

I know that I have for myself arrived at a simple, very fundamental understanding: I am not, could never be a free-standing, completely independent being. I have arrived at this late point of my life shaped by a multitude of forces: my DNA, my physiology, my psychology, my family, my near-community, my greater-communities, my religion, (and on and on). After eighty years I still cannot stand absolutely alone. I am imbedded in (several) communities *(however vague and ill-defined some of those are)*, and require their constant support and nurture; without them I would be wandering in an uncharted wilderness, lost and starving to death (quite literally). I know too that I am a unique unit within those communities, with a unique set of skills and talents *(such as writing this kind of stuff)* to offer back to the community. I am clear that I am both like and unlike every other human being, and so an *individual*; but also clear that none of us has ever, or could ever, stand completely alone. We emerged out of the forest and onto the savannah in hunter-gatherer groupings of interdependent beasts and we have existed in community ever since; it has never been otherwise. That much is growing clearer to me. The human brain is hard-wired to make us social animals, so community has been the basic, irreducible living entity from the very beginning.

From another overlook, our social structure, with its foundations in individualism and liberalism and its operating structure of capitalism is what engineers would call "a self-accelerating go-to-hell system." Set in motion there seems to be no effective way to direct, correct or adjust it; it just runs on, ever faster, wherever it might, with no regard for the people housed within it. In the 1960s we hailed the rush to put a man on the moon; that exquisitely engineered feat yielded us multiple technological break-throughs which are still evolving, still running their courses with no run-out in sight. What astounds me is that since that lunar accomplishment, technologies have continued to evolve out of those initial developments with utter mindlessness, with no plan whatsoever except to make greater opportunistic profits out of unending strings of derivative discoveries and technological advancements all the while gobbling up rare and critical resources at an ever-accelerating pace, and with utter disregard for benefits and destructiveness. *[One exception: the military does some planning as well as opportunistic grabbing.]* And nearly all of it is a distraction from more pragmatic and urgent concerns. No one is asking, "Is this new product good for us, beneficial, or disastrously destructive? Will it do more good than harm? Is it worth doing? What ought we to be studying, creating rather than this?" No one is empowered to even raise such questions (with the exception of a few castrated and closely hobbled federal agencies, e.g., the FDA and the EPA). Most of the government is effectively deterred from raising such questions. This Individualist-Capitalist system runs, seemingly self-propelled, willy-nilly, helter-skelter, until we know not when, or where. We seem to be reaching for, what? Flashiness? Titillation? Luxury? Endlessly increasing wealth? I've no idea what we are finally reaching for, but I am very clear it has nothing to do with the *good* of life. At the same time our planet has finite resources. Is the Smart Phone worth it? It's a cute-new-fancy toy. But does the Smart Phone give humankind sufficient betterment, welfare, *good* to be worth its cost in the consumption of valuable, limited resources and energies? Is its real effect more beneficial than disruptive or destructive? How might we even try to measure those dimensions? Was Steve Jobs a saint? A brilliant innovator? A gift from the gods? Or another paving stone in the road to the failure of our society? A side-path to nowhere? The structure is utterly blind to cost-benefits, to downsides, to caustic effects, to running itself right into the ground.

And does that make any final sense? In the mad rush *forward (I question whether it is really forward)* we have completely lost any sense of an end-goal.

Out of my negativity in this critique of individualism and capitalism I gain some little energy, but it's not enough to motivate some serious searching. And all of it points not towards, but away from, and so yields no clear directions. I need more energy than this. And I find that energy out of two deep fears. I've long known that anger and fear are both sources of valuable energy, if it can be harnessed into useful directions. So I'll go one step farther and share with you two of my great fears.

First, I'm haunted by a book from the 1960s titled *The Population Bomb,* a collection of scenerios divined by futurists about the various ways the burgeoning population of the world will wreak havoc. These days as I watch and read the news I'm seeing pieces of those scenerios working out in our present world.

One of the scenerios reported a computer simulation to estimate sustainability, i.e., how many human beings this planet can support indefinitely. The result was an estimate that this earth can sustain without exhausting the earth's resources, something like five hundred million human beings. We have now exceeded that figure by a factor of fourteen. That simulation was run half a century ago when computers were still quite primitive, programming was hardly sophisticated, and simulation was still a plaything of very limited strength. But the question remains: what might be a population sustainable on this planet indefinitely? Since the 1960s we've learned a lot. Using the latest and most sophisticated programs and equipment and brainpower and knowledge and presumptions estimates now range from less that one billion to as high as a thousand billion people (the current population is about 7.3 billion); most of the estimates are between four to sixteen billion, with a median of about ten billion. That's only half a generation away. Other analysts project that the United States itself can sustain indefinitely a **maximum** of only 200 million; in 2006 we had already exceeded that by 40 percent. We are advancing speedily toward overpopulation.

The other scenerios in *The Population Bomb* described predictions of what turns the world might take as the population grows **beyond** sustainability. None is working out exactly as written, but pieces of all those predictions are beginning to play out in our world today:

- the fragility and incompetence of governance in many underdeveloped countries, e.g., most of Africa, the Middle East, and other parts of the world;
- the unrest and rebellion of oppressed underclasses, particularly visible in the "Arab Spring" uprisings;
- re-fired sectarianism;
- the open resentment against the first-world powers amongst the lesser-developed countries and regions struggling to get their share of this world's goodies.

If the world today seems more agitated than it used to feel when we gray-hairs were kids, that feeling may be accurate; and that international, world-wide agitation will likely continue to increase along with growing social disorganization as overpopulation increases. Our progeny may be forced to live in an increasingly disrupted, violent and impoverished world.

Another haunting memory which accelerates my concerns about population reaches way back to my undergraduate days. A research paper from a collection required for an *Abnormal Psychology* course was a study of the behavioral changes observed in a colony of rats forced to live in over-crowded quarters. A variety of *social disorganizations* emerged. I can no longer recall the details, only that the social structures which managed the colony's life broke down: aggression throughout the colony increased and the rats began to bite each other, fight, kill, abandon infants, and do other such self-destructive things. I am haunted by what that research might suggest for us, and for our grandchildren as our planet becomes more and more overpopulated.

We may very well *(I would unfoundedly say, "Absolutely!")* have crossed over into overpopulation of this globe (or at least in some circumscribable areas of it) which is driving the social-disorganization beyond the manageable limits. Our overpopulation is not only over-straining the limited natural resources of this orb, but it is also forcing human-beings to live more densely together than our psycho-social systems equip us. I believe I am watching the kinds of dire predictions the futurists made happening now and with increasing frequency and intensity (daesh, terrorism, African and Middle Eastern upheavals are manifestations of that.)

PART III: A VISION TO MOVE TOWARD

I conclude the world's population should be stabilized *(and perhaps even reduced some to achieve sustainability)*. At the moment we have no means for nudging the population from continued growth to stability (China has discontinued its experiment in population stabilization). Instead the forces are arrayed to encourage continued population growth. And the other required change is to shift from a world-wide stance of competition to collaboration. We keep our world locked into zero-sum game plans. I would maintain that non-zero-sum game plans for social systems are achievable. To get there will require different modes of interacting personally, systemically, and internationally: valuing all human beings, and moving life style toward greater simplicity. We must leave off plundering the earth and determine to husband.

The very first of YHWH's commands was "be fruitful and multiply and fill the earth . . . " (Gen 1:28). The era of that commandment is completed. We've fulfilled, perhaps over-fulfilled that commandment. It's time to turn to the now pressing task of learning how to manage in ways which are healthy and life-giving for the population we have now obtained. And if we choose not to, that problem may do us in, **all** or many of us.

My second fear is fueled by the first, and by Jared Diamond's book, ***Collapse: How Societies Choose to Fail or Succeed***. Diamond examined the collapse of thirteen different societies and deduced from their stories five factors that went into their collapse, and several steps in the process of collapse. The factors he found were:

1. Society undermines itself by damaging its environment (i.e., deforestation and habitat destruction, soil depletion, water management failure, over-hunting and over-fishing, the adverse effects of introduced species on native species, human population growth, increased per capita impact, human-caused climate change, build-up of toxic chemicals, energy shortage, and exceeding the full use of earth's photosynthetic capacity),
2. natural climate change,
3. hostile neighbors,
4. decreased support by friendly trade partners, and
5. society's response to environmental problems.

The process of failing which Diamond deduced follows a pattern that varies somewhat from one failure to another but generally follows this course: population growth leads to intensified agricultural production, which leads to expansion of farming into marginal land, which leads to unsustainable practices, which causes environmental damages, which lead to abandonment of marginal lands, which leads to food shortages, starvation, wars, overthrow of governing elites by disillusioned masses, which leads to population decrease through starvation, war, disease, which leads to loss of political, economic, cultural complexity. Collapse in the modern world might not be as sudden and apocalyptic as in those ancient societies, and instead we might see

Chapter 12: Failed Values

significantly lower living standards, chronically higher risks, undermining of key values, and collapse precipitated through world-wide diseases, wars triggered by scarcity of resources, or some other global issue(s).

Diamond is clear that the society does **choose** to fail or succeed. That **choice** is not rational or deliberate, but the *choice points* are fairly obvious:

1. The failure to anticipate a problem
2. The failure to perceive the problem
3. The failure to attempt to solve the perceived problem, and
4. The solution to the problem may be beyond present capacities (too expensive, too late, attempts backfire, lacking ecological knowledge, resisting the solution).

It is my judgment that we are on track. In multiple ways we are degrading our environment (exhaustion of soil nutrients, overuse of artificial soil enrichers with runoff damaging surrounding environs, deforestation [forests are essential in several ways, but ours are being exhausted faster that they can reproduce, and forests worldwide are being despoiled], coal-mining [particularly long-wall and mountaintop removal], gas and oil [fracking is leading to earthquakes and probably the destruction of potable water sources], over-mining of rare resources [e.g., rare earth metals], accumulation of toxic tippings, and collateral damage caused by energy mining is unmeasured and unattended). The list can go on; we are despoiling our environment faster than it can recover, and faster than we can innovate substitutes for essentials. Meanwhile the world's population is exploding exponentially and may soon exceed the sustainable maximum; this country's population may have already surpassed the sustainability point, but continues to grow through increasing life-spans and immigration. This country has long exceeded its available energy sources; other economies worldwide are increasing their energy demands. Habitat degradation: my personal habitat is wonderfully comfortable in every way, but less than ten percent of the world's population can make that claim, and conversely less than half the world's population has the simplest and most basic need, a safe water source. Potable water supply has become critical in our Southwest, yet we continue to squander water with wasteful irrigation methods, green lawns, and unplanned city growth. Ages ago we over hunted and over fished this country, then relying upon domesticated animals as the primary proteins for our diets. We are proximate the point at which domesticated animals will be too expensive in grain consumption to be affordable as a dietary staple. Through over hunting, environment destruction, and encroachment we have lost many species and loss of species is occurring at an increasing rate; many of those species are not essential to human survival, but all losses contribute to despoliation of the environment and impoverishment of the ecology. We are searching for places and ways to dispose of radioactive wastes, burying toxic chemicals and metals in landfills where they eventually leach into the water supply; we have no estimate of the toxic elements we are hoarding within our environments. The per capita environmental impact of every person in this country, and around the world grows unabated, and uncalculated. We don't want to know. All the while we, as a country, as a culture, refuse to seriously confront our environmental problems (their solutions would cost too much in short-term profits and most aren't very desirable anyhow). We argue whether climate change is man-caused or natural and cyclical, which is immaterial because it's here and having very real effects, while we choose not to react to these changes, mainly just hoping it will all go away. And meanwhile the third world grows more hostile and restive toward us and our attempts to hold onto our gains at their expense (i.e., attempting to keep control over their hostilities by our worldwide military hegemony, acting as the world's supercop) and raping their natural resources.

My closing reflection: Poetically we refer to "**This fragile earth, our island home.**" I take that seriously. We are isolated to this planet; in no foreseeable future will we transplant the population of this planet to some other planet with an untapped pool of resources in some other solar system and galaxy elsewhere in this universe. It behooves mankind to take care of this island home. Any argument with that?

Yes, one! It is not in the self-interests of short-term profit-takers to take care of this planet. We are faced with a choice for the long-term: the self-interests of the profit-takers, or the wise husbanding of the habitat of humankind.

At the present rate of population growth we should reach the point of maximum sustainability within a generation or so; I will not see it, but my grandchildren certainly shall, and my children might. Since I am now eighty I shouldn't give a hoot. But I do.

In general I consider that we have over done the zero-sum-game paradigm. However, in one respect zero-sum-game rules are mandatory: we have at our disposal only one planet with a fixed amount of resources, and it is a closed system. If we fail to husband those resources we doom our economic and social systems to failure, and ourselves to extinction. This is a Hobson's choice. In his studies of failed societies Jared Diamond concludes that exhaustion of resources and despoliation of habitat are the earliest and most devastating of the causes of the failure of societies, and deforestation is right at the top of the list. How're we doin'? And as long as we agree that whatever the individual "owns" is his to do with whatever he damned well pleases *(you finish the sentence)*.

We are not autonomous individuals and we do not live in isolation. There is only one game, we are all in it together; everything I do affects you, and our future, and our childrens-children's futures.

All this has the ring of a prophet of doom. I could hope my projections are quite wrong. But the prospect does not look good. We may be half a generation from being overwhelmed, or it may be several generations before it all overtakes us. And we are right now in the act of choosing. As a country and as a culture we have failed to anticipate the problems, following willy-nilly and mindlessly the whims of our aimless

Chapter 12: Failed Values

capitalism and individualism. We treat this planet's resources as if they were limitless, inexhaustible. And in these days of governance failure we are largely failing to perceive the basic social problems, or have not the will and so are failing to attempt the solutions. Our "manifest destiny" and "exceptionalism" keep us blind to these realities.

As I ruminate all of this chapter I realize that what I am reaching for in order to replace the anarchic and inane directionlessness of individualism and capitalism, is some kind of managed society which is guided by a set of values that 1) make sense, 2) are clear and coherent, and 3) maximize species survivability.

As I study what I have written here I discern out of my Christian beliefs coupled with my own experience and thinking **three core values** that I know with all my being:

First, I do believe, I do hold as the central-most value, that we are all created equal. And I do not need YHWHism to tell me that; it is brutally apparent. That notion is imbedded in our Constitution, though we have never lived it out, racially, economically or in any other ways. We pay the *equality* lip service, and nothing more. I admit I can think of absolutely no measurable way in which we **are** equal; we are all quite unique, quite different, quite individual, in virtually every way. But I hold it to be absolutely fundamental, that we are all equal.

Second, I have become convinced that really there is no such thing as a freestanding individual. There are various sorts of animals and plants that seem to stand alone, that seem to be self-sufficient, that seem to survive without benefit of any kind of embracing ecology. But I submit that is an illusion, a fiction, a fantasy, a lie that we project upon some parts of our world in order to justify our eagerness to be freestanding, completely independent (non-dependent and completely self-governing and self-owning) individuals. But in reality there is no such independence, no such individualness. We are, all of us, every living entity (and even the non-living) in relationship, in community, in ecology, in company. We live, and die, in relationship with virtually everything around us. Alfred Whitehead suggested that we do not end at the surface of our skin; and I take that to mean that we, as human beings, are in such intimate relationship with the world around us that our skin does not define the outer limit of our person, that we are permeable, that we and the reality surrounding us are at-one, inseparable, that I reach beyond the surface of my skin and that the world around me permeates into my depths.

My conclusion borne of this is that for us human beings the fundamental human unit is not the individual but the community. The *tioš paye* survived on the Great Plains, not as an agglomeration of individuals, but as a living unit which prized and thrived every being within its bounds. And I suggest that the health and the survivability of that living community most thrives when the uniqueness of each of its beings is prized and enfolded into its communal life. Simply put, the community and its member individuals **must** live in balance of need and opportunity. Put another way, the reality is that we are all in this together; that is inescapable. So it behooves us to live as equals within community.

I hold up one more value which I acquire from Jesus, from the Dalai Lama, from virtually every wholesome religion, that living with compassion for all is the heart of living well, of living healthily, of living in wholeness. While volumes can be said about that principle, I will leave it to speak for itself: **compassion**. It is abundantly clear that we are all in this together, and that being the case, the healthiest way to live is in compassion for all.

With those three values in hand I turn and scan the horizon, not of Jesus' world, nor of YHWH's world, but of the real world in which I live every day, searching for some vision that could embody those. I find nothing; glimpses but no embodiments. So I scan farther. And what I discover out there just beyond the horizon is a bare possibility. Today it is being called "communitarianism." I might be able to take that possibility in hand, and knead and mold into something that begins to embody both those values and Jesus' Kingdom of God, and which might offer this benighted world some hope. It may not be workable right now, but it is the best I have to offer; and it is incumbent upon me, having dismantled almost everything known to me, to offer something to build upon anew.

So I offer the following thoughts on **my** version of communitarianism. It is a challenging vision. It is not likely to find wide favor. But I believe it is worth giving voice.

My Sources for Individualism, Liberalism, Libertarianism and Capitalism:

Baumer, Frankin L. "Individualism," ***Modern European Thought***, New York: MacMillan 1977 (271-78)

"Captialism", Wikipedia 17 June 2016 https://en.wikipedia.org/wiki/Capitalism

Etzioni, Amitai. "Individualism within History," ***The Hedgehog Review Vol. 4***, No. 1 49-56 http://papers.ssrn.com/sol3/papers.cfm?abstract_id=2157075

Heath, Joseph. "Methodological Individualism," in Stanford Encyclopedia of Philosophy. Nov.16, 2010 http://plato.stanford.edu/entries/methodological-individualism/

"Hegelianism," Wikipedia 20 May 2016 https://en.wikipedia.org/wiki/Hegelianism

"Kantianism," Wikipedia 3 January 2016 https://en.wikipedia.org/wiki/Kantianism

"Liberalism," Wikipedia 23 June 2016 https://en.wikipedia.org/wiki/Liberalism

"Libertarianism," Wikipedia 12 June 2016 https://en.wikipedia.org/wiki/Liberalism

Vallentyne, Peter and van der Vossen, Bas, "Libertarianism," Stanford Encyclopedia of Philosophy Jul 20, 2010 http://plato.stanford.edu/entries/libertarianism/

Chapter 13: Communitarianism

Readers of the early drafts of this book challenged me, "Why this presentation on Communitarianism in a book of doctrinal arguments by a retired priest whose beliefs are wondering?" A fair question; and the answer may not be obvious.

In Jeremiah's call (1:10) he is sent "to root out, and to pull down, and to destroy, and to thrown down, to build, and to plant." I am no Jeremiah, but I have done my best to jerk out the linchpin of the Western Christian theological system, "sin"; I have plumbed depths and heights seeking the God and have concluded only that the God is unknowable; I have searched out this Jesus fellow and found him to be a human whom we have dubbed "god" without knowing what we are saying; I have scanned and parsed the institutional church and found it simply a human creature of the state. In homiletic class, after I'd delivered a scathing rant about the institutional church, the instructor commented, "Jack, it's the easiest thing in the world to criticize the church; it's much harder to come up with some positive suggestions." He was right. All this dismantling has been the easy, no-brainer part. It's now come time to build and to plant.

As I sat down to write this chapter I was mindful of the monsters of daesh in Syria and Iraq frantically beheading journalists, capturing and kidnaping women and young girls to sell as wives and sex-slaves, and massacring by the dozens and hundreds, *in the name of Allah no less*; and, in Africa, of Boco Haram killing and kidnaping following daesh's lead; at the same time Assad slaughtering his own people by the hundreds of thousands with gas and bombs and bullets and tanks and artillery, making fugitives of millions more of his own countrymen; and meanwhile the ranks of the hungry in our own country are swelling while the rich are obscenely increasing their wealth. I am aware that in some sense Augustine was right, we and our world are pretty screwed up. But my impulse is not to wallow in that, as he did, but to try to set it aright, as Pelagius did; and not just right for me, but for us, for all of us. And so I hold onto a vision of a better world. And I know that if we have no vision before our eyes, then we are doomed to live mired in the feculence and horror we have brought into being and to think it's alright, it's the best we can get. I hold onto my vision and dream that someday it might become reality. If only we dream it so vigorously that we work at making it a reality, then perhaps.

Then this new word tumbled into my vocabulary, unexpectedly. In my ear it reverberates as somewhat ugly, a cobbled word. That's because I'm old enough that it resounds in my ear with the same timbre as "communism," referring to the tsarist Stalin's regime which was waggled threateningly in our faces for thirty years after the

Part III: A Vision to Move Toward

Second World War. But that's neither my referent nor the communitarianists's. This notion was born in the 1980s so it's relatively new, though I hear fore-echoes of it in Jack Kennedy's line, "Ask not what your country can do for you, ask what you can do for your country," with a more recent voicing in Hillary Clinton's comment that "It takes a village to raise a child," and Obama's insistence that "The entrepreneur did not do this all on his own." My great-grandfather, John Slayton was one of the pioneers of the socialist movement (1903-1924) in this country, so that set of values is likely imbedded in my DNA, and while communitarianism shares some fundamental assumptions with socialism, the two probably turn out to be quite different beasts, communitarianism having taken a turn that opens up some possibilities of first steps toward real change.

> *I need to caution you about the next pages. This chapter is quite different than all the preceding, and that makes it difficult. A friend pointed out reading a previous draft that this chapter seemed to be struggling between my two ways of thinking. My opening page of Chapter 5 was a brief report of the results of an exercise I devised to discover how Jack Bowers thinks his way through complicated issues. It turns out I think in two different ways. I begin my studies with an associative process, scouring the countryside to gather everything that is pertinent (i.e., has associative links) to the issue, and after I think I've got all I need I begin sorting it all out into common piles. Somewhere in the midst of that task my mind shifts gears and moves into an analytic mode of thought, searching for patterns, asking hard-nosed critical questions, evaluating, and trying to arrive at valid conclusions. What you have seen in the preceding chapters is the very last of that analytic process, a very linear argument from the data to the conclusion. This chapter comes out of very early in the associative process, still in the data-gathering stages, wandering this way and that, trying to locate and gather all that applies. Communitarianism is new stuff, not yet matured. So this chapter can not be analytic. Here I am simply dumping in your lap the few piles of stuff I've gathered so far. It's not a complete set, and it's not yet ready for any serious analytical work. I'm just sharing an intuitive vision, what notions I have to see if it makes the sense for you that it does for me. No conclusions, no clear proposals; just food for thought.*

Since our Revolutionary War the pendulum has swung from the oppression and dehumanizing of autocracy through midpoint and onward to the oppression and destructiveness of excessive individualism; we may have simply traded one oppression for another, replacing the warrior with the Self. I observe in my own life, having grown out of a neighborhood which looked after **all** its children into this neighborhood of my late life in which I know one next-door neighbor and one across the street but no others, a world in which I know and am known by fewer and fewer people,[1] i.e., the

---

1. As a child I grew up in Oakley, a suburb of Cincinnati which felt and behaved as though it were a small town, a village where neighboring mothers watched over me as I made my way up Taylor

steep decline of communal bonds. Robert Putnam documents the deterioration of community institutions in his ***Bowling Alone: The Collapse and Revival of American Community***. With that diminuation of acculturating community, we easily lose our social moorings, our respect for traditions, our *social capital* (i.e., the inclinations that arise from communal bonds to do things for each other). Sociologist have long warned us that excessive individualism leads to *anomie*, a state of normlessness, and a breakdown of the moral fabric. I think we are witnessing these today.

We pride ourselves that we are each free-standing, choosing individuals; but in the reality in which I live that is an absolute and dangerous falsehood. We are all social creatures, political animals. While we may have some indeterminate modicum of free choice, we have all been molded and shaped by our own idiosyncratic mix of DNA, family dynamics, several communities, environment, and micro- and macro-cultures, a shaping of which we are largely ignorant, mostly blinded. Vast areas of our lives are lived by means of unchosen habits and routines which we have acquired, learned, fabricated, and rehearsed though the years. Deliberate choosing is more the exception than the rule, and rational choosing is even more rare. *(One computerist, Rana el Kaliouby, studying the facial expressions of emotions suggests that rational thinking is an absolute fiction, that emotionality and rationality are inseparable, and further that thought without emotionality [if possible] would be as irrational as it is with too much emotionality.*[2]*)* We should ask, while it may be a *feel-good* and is certainly the heart of individualism, whether *free-choice* really is intrinsically valuable? Is a rational choice to do some act of good any better, more valuable than the spontaneous, culture-driven act of a Mother Theresa? Our social attachments are mostly involuntary, picked up along the way of living, neither rational nor conscious choices. Does that make them inherently less?

And finally I conclude that we are none of us truly self-sufficient and independent. It is obvious and irrefutable to me that we are all interdependent and dependent to some degree. Our culture was shaped in the crucible of a pioneer and frontiersman era when the closer to self-sufficiency a person and a family could be, the more likely their survival. That culture, fueled by the Enlightenment and the Industrial Revolution, has fed us the fiction that we are and should be entirely self-sufficient and free. The reality I see is that we are social creatures, quite unable to be totally free, self-determining and self-directing. The witness of these days proclaims that independence and so-called rationality are ultimately destructive of the social fabric. Far Eastern cultures appraise our excessive individualism to be anarchy. There is useful feedback in their observations.

Avenue hill, one foot in the gutter and the other on the curb, imitating a Second World War fighter plane with my hand. They amusedly reported my odd behavior to my mother. Today a neighbor who doesn't know me would conclude "He's nutty," and either write me off or call family services about this crazy kid.

2. Raffi Khatchadourian, "We Know How You Feel," ***New Yorker***, January 15, 2015 p.52.

Part III: A Vision to Move Toward

Two decades ago I spent a weekend at the feet of the **Rev. Dr. Martin Brokenleg**, an Episcopal priest of the Lakota Nation, whom our clergy association had invited to tell us about Native American spirituality. I was in those days beginning my minor love affair with Celtic Christian spirituality and was struck with the commonality of what Martin Brokenleg was telling us and what I was reading and discerning about the ancient Celtic Church. What tied the two together for me was that both were tribal spiritualities. *(Brokenleg never used the word "tribe," I had to interpolate that, but he told us a number of things that helped me verify it.)* He was at that time on the staff of a school far from his home and people on Rosebud Reservation, and he shared that his monthly telephone bill always ran between $400 and $800 (that was an astounding telephone bill in the mid 1980s). He shared that as an illustration of how important it was in his spirituality to build and maintain intimate relationships with **all** the others of his *tioš paye* (what an Anglo would call a *"tribe"*). Relationships were at the very center of his spirituality.

A *tioš paye*, he told us, consisted of two hundred to two hundred and fifty or so human beings (curiously, sociologists tell us that 250 is about the maximum number of people an individual can hold in relationship). If the *tioš paye* got much bigger it became unsustainable; maintaining the necessary quality of relationships would be overwhelming. So younger members would be sent out to find other living groups. And if the *tioš paye* got much smaller than the 200 minimum, there were not enough to share the labors and provide the skills necessary to sustain the living group.

From my readings in Celtica I deduced that the *tioš paye* was not just the aggregation of people; it was also the land they belonged to. The people and the land were one, bound together. Such a hunter-gatherer living group needed a certain land area to support their nutritional and material needs; they had to preserve that area and protect it. And to maintain the integrity of the *tioš paye* the members were bonded to the land; the body of persons and the requisite land area became one. It was essential for the people of the *tioš paye* to live harmoniously with each other and with the land. It is reported that in the late 1800s President McKinley inquired of Chief Seattle about buying tribal lands from his nation for American settlers to occupy. Chief Seattle responded:

> *"How can you buy or sell the sky? The land? If we do not own the freshness of the air and the sparkles of the water, how can you buy them? Every part of this earth is sacred to my people. Every shining pine needle, every sandy shore, every mist in the dark woods, every meadow, every humming insect. All are holy in the memory and instinct of my people. We know the sap which courses through the trees, as we know the blood which courses through our veins. We are part of the earth as the earth is part of us. The perfumed flowers are our sisters. The bear, the deer, the great eagle, these are our brothers. The rocky crests, the juices in the meadows, the body heat of a pony and man all belong to the same family."*

Chapter 13: Communitarianism

In another vein Brokenleg told us that the child, growing up in a *tioš paye* never had to worry about what he or she might want to be or do when grown up, that was never a question. The child was well known daily by virtually everyone within the *tioš paye*, and they all watched him/her mature; and gradually a consensus emerged about how this child would uniquely fit into the life of the *tioš paye*, what skills s/he should be taught, what rare talents this child would offer, how the *tioš paye* would be enriched by this child. No worry about "who I might be" or "what I might become." Or about the Anglo issue, "Who am I." Each person knew exactly how s/he fit into the life and labor of the *tioš paye*, and what his/her place in the world was.

Martin Brokenleg pointed my gaze toward two movies then current, **Dances With Wolves** and the earlier **Thunderball**, as both moderately accurate portrayals of Native American, i.e., Plains Indian, tribal life (both movies had been coached by Lakotan teams). The first, Brokenleg told us, set in the late 1800s and telling the story of a cavalry officer isolated during the Indian Wars who became a member of a *tioš paye*, was a fairly accurate portrayal of life in the *tioš paye*, austere but ample, with much attractiveness. I watched as the elder *(whom we might call a chief, but he had no vested authority, only his accrued wisdom and his consensus building skills)* gathered some into his tepee to develop a consensus about how the *tioš paye* would respond to the invasion of the white cavalry. And in another scene, as they topped a rise while tracking a run of bison, I shared their devastating dismay looking out as far as you could see at hundreds of naked carcasses of their brother buffalo whom the white hunters had slaughtered for their hides, leaving the carcasses to rot in the sun. The whole of the movie gave me some sense of what living was like for these Native Americans as the settlers and army moved in to wrest away the land to which they were bonded.

The second movie (based on fact) was set in the 1950s and tells of a young, half-blood Native American FBI agent as he learns his FBI boss is a conspirator attempting to dupe the *tioš paye* out of its mineral rights to the uranium ore deposits on their Rosebud Reservation. Brokenleg told us that movie too was a fairly accurate depiction Lakotan reservation life, quite different than it had been in the freedom of the plains. The living which had once been austere but attractive was now grossly impoverished, and yet it still embodied the same basic values of equality, of dedication to the *tioš paye*, of the prizing of each individual. Through the eyes of both movies I could discern a set of core values so radically different from ours that we are unable even to recognize them as values, or to comprehend; we are destined to misinterpret it.

In the early 1990s I had stumbled onto the roots of our Anglicanism, the **Celtic culture** (Europe north of the Rome-imposed social paradigms of the Mediterranean basin) which preceded Christianity and onto which the Christian gospel had been grafted. The Celts were a tribal culture, as opposed to the industrialized, urban culture of the Mediterranean basin, i.e., the Greco-Roman world, where Western Christianity was shaped. As I read about that tribal culture, as shown in Celtic (both pre-Christian and Christian) stuff, and discerned some of the values underlying it, I could begin to see outlines that indicate the *faith* we have received from the church of Rome, filtered through the Protestant Reformation, is only one shape that the gospel can take. Grafted[3] onto a set of cultural values different from those espoused in the Roman world, Christianity would take a quite different shape. And as I snooped around the values I was discerning in those Celtic roots, I began to regret much of the Roman tradition we have received and to search around for some values that seem to me more like the Gospel I thought I was hearing with my inner ear. Elaine Pagels was interpreting to us the *Nag Hammadi* manuscripts which showed us how differently Christianity had begun to evolve in other places before Rome stomped on the brakes and trashed all but its own version, a version which I think was peculiarly warped to fit Augustine's and the emperor's and the Western Mediterranean basin's needs.

I assume that what I saw portrayed in **Dances With Wolves** was probably a somewhat romanticized version of tribal life which may therefore be somewhat unrealistic. I do understand that the tribalism we are watching today among the forces driving the horrors of the current African and Arab Spring struggles is at least as much the reality of tribalism as that movie. And yet that movie and my readings in Celtica point my visioning in the direction of ***"could be."*** So what I was learning about Celtic culture and about Native American tribalism, in counter-point to our American *individualism*, began to suggest to me a vague ideal image, and some moral direction for our world. But I must hastily add that the image evolving in my mind may be no more realistic than that the romanticized tribalism of that movie. The variation on that romanticized tribalism which appears so attractive to me as an image I suspect to be out of our pre-history, a social system which we outgrew (or trashed) ages ago, and which failed to evolve at the pace of our growth (i.e., population and technology and productivity) and success. And I further suspect that in the global village into which we are now evolving that pre-historic system of living and of justice will be even more inadequate than it is today, in our current world(s). So the ideal welling up within me is at the moment a still unworkable ideal; it would have to be kneaded and reshaped into a social system capable of managing a world even more complex than our present world.

I watched the chief, the elder, the informal leader in the movie **Dances with Wolves** conduct the consensus-building meetings in his tepee with concern both for the whole of the *tioš paye* and for each and every individual member, searching through the lens of his own accumulated wisdom about what must be done for the survival of the *tioš paye*. And it appeared to me that his effort was aimed at holding in balance the welfares both of the *tioš paye* and of each and every individual. At that point in history of the *tioš paye* its moral structure was still intact and working. But

---

3. The Rev. Dr. Martin Brokenleg had suggested to our group that he believed God does not expect him to reject his Native Americanism and attempt to live out an ancient Hebrew culture, but instead wants him to graft the Gospel of Jesus Christ onto the Native American culture into which he was born and matured, and to live out the Gospel in that way. Made supreme sense to me!

when I turn my head to watch emerging from the murk of pre-history the social and moral structures we of the Western European world have inherited, it appears to me that, even at our first glimpses of recorded history, the size and complexity of social units had already exceeded the inherited tribal social and moral structures; chiefs *(we had already grown from tribal structures into chiefdoms)* ruled autocratically, less for the welfare of whole of the community and all its individuals, and more for the opulence and power of the chief and his family and crony aristocrats. Oppression, slavery, impoverishment had become standard features. Greed, power-mongering, inequality and cronyism were becoming the mode. The balance of the good of the individual and of the living unit had evaporated *(or been trampled into the dust.)* We inherited an already corrupt and dysfunctional social structure.

As I attempt to boil down and parse out the core values of those tribalisms which point my gaze toward the ideal I am searching for, I come up with a notion as simple as this: the individual, whose uniqueness is essential, is not more important than the community which shaped her/him and enables his/her survival and thrivity; but rather the individual is a unique part of the whole (i.e., the community), and the needs of both community and individual must be held in balance.

I'll offer a **definition of communitarianism** as I comprehend it. Communitarianism is a social and political philosophy that maintains that autonomous selves do not exist in isolation, but are shaped by the values and culture of communities and emphasizes the need to balance individual rights and interests with that of the community as a whole, and argues that individual people (or citizens) are shaped by the cultures and values of their communities. Unless we begin to redress the balance toward the pole of community our society will continue to become normless, self-centered, and driven by special interests and power seeking.

Communitarianism arose in critique of contemporary liberalism (which seeks to protect and enhance personal autonomy and individual rights) and libertarianism ("classical liberalism" which aims to protect individual rights to liberty and property through limits on government.)

While the term "communitarian" was coined only in the mid-nineteenth century, ideas that are communitarian in nature appear much earlier. They are found in the Hebrew Scriptures and the early Christian Writings and more recently in socialist doctrine (e.g., writings about early communes and about workers's solidarity), and in ideas such as *subsidiarity* (the principle that the lowest level of authority capable of addressing an issue is the one best able to handle it).

Communitarianism has been traced back to early monasticism. In the twentieth century early communitarianism began to be formulated as a philosophy by Dorothy Day and the Catholic Worker movement, and it is also related to the personalist philosophy of Emmanuel Mounier.

Two authors (Ferdinand Tönnies, Emile Durkheim) voiced concerns about the integrating role of social values and the relations between the individual and society, and warned of the dangers of *anomie* (normlessness) and alienation in modern societies composed of atomized individuals who had gained their liberty but lost their social moorings. Modern sociologists saw the rise of a mass society and the decline of communal bonds and respect for traditional values and authority in the United States as of the 1960s (e.g., Robert Nisbet ***Twilight of Authority***, Robert Bellah ***Habits of the Heart***, and Alan Ehrenhalt ***The Lost City: The Forgotten Virtues Of Community In America***). In his book ***Bowling Alone*** Robert Putnam documented the decline of ***social capital*** and stressed the importance of *bridging social capital*, in which bonds of connectedness are formed across diverse social groups.

Amitai Etzioni, a spokesman for Responsive Communitarianism, suggests that liberalism and individualism have served new, emerging classes very well, rolling back fundamentalism and restrictive governments in the decline of the old regimes, and aiding the rise of merchant and industrial classes. He observes that amongst oppressive structures it has been and continues to be a beneficial force. It has been a liberating force in the Western World, but has now become a detrimental force in American society where some better synthesis is needed between individualism and communal collectivism. *(I nod my head in agreement.)* For example, it appears to me that the trajectory of family evolution has been from larger toward small: from extended, multi-generational families to nuclear families to single (increasingly unmarried) parent families. And we have not seriously examined the multi-dimensional psychological and sociological effects of that trajectory. As we have become prone to atomization, self-centeredness is undermining the social order, all with utter disregard for the damage. Individualism leads to arrogance, preaching the delusion that if we merely put our mind to it, we can move mountains, solve unsolvable problems, and bend the world to our purpose.

Communitarianism is not a single, coherent school of philosophy, but at this stage is a conversation among several voices not always in agreement. These are **the tenets** I have deduced out of my readings; not all the voices would agree with all of this list:

a. **Community** defined: a web of affect-laden relationships among a group of individuals, relationships that often crisscross and reinforce one another, which embodies a measure of commitment to a set of shared values, norms, and meanings, and a shared history and identity, (i.e., a particular culture), and must be able to exert moral suasion and extract a measure of compliance from its members (i.e., is coercive as well as moral), using sanctions if they stray and offering certainty and stability when they don't. The community shares a culture and a set of values.

b. Communitarianism holds that the **individual** is *not* an absolutely **free-standing** entity, but rather is largely a product of the community; that liberalism and libertarianism are incoherent philosophies, misunderstanding the nature of the individual. Communitarianism understands that individual identity grows largely out of familial and social relations and interactions, and not solely from within the individual. Family, culture, norms, *mores*, and social relations are all important in both shaping and sustaining the individual.

c. A good society crafts a **balance** between the common good **and** autonomy and rights of the individual; neither takes precedent; a careful balance of individual liberty and social order, of individual rights and the individual's responsibilities to the society. The balance of community and individual has two equal foci: 1) the well-being and thrivity of the community, and 2) the welfare, integration, and enhancement of the individual.

d. The individual who is **well integrated** into the social structure is better capable of reasoning, and is more able to act responsibly toward the community.

e. The community determines the *good* and sanctions individuals.

f. The individual receives **rights** from the community and in return owes the community loyalty. It notes that without the society there can be no rights; "rights" are a product of community formation.

g. There is a **shared formulation of the *good***, which is articulated by community.

h. The community fosters open participation and dialogue.

i. Decision-making should happen at lowest level, i.e., **subsidiarity** (a principle in social organization): functions which subordinate or local organizations perform effectively belong more properly to them than to a dominant central organization; decisions should always be taken at the lowest possible level closest to where they will have their effect; matters ought to be handled by the smallest, lowest or least centralized competent authority; political decisions should be taken at a local level if possible, rather than by a central authority; central authority should be subsidiarious, performing only those tasks which cannot be performed effectively at a more immediate or local level.

I think **two fundamental issues** must be resolved before any kind of communitarianism can emerge.

I have posited three core values: (1) the absolute and unconditional equality of all persons, (2) the community as the fundamental unit of living (i.e., survival and thrivivity) not the individual, and (3) we're all in it together (e.i. all life is intertwined, socially, psychologically and ecologically), and therefore the optimal standards of living are compassion, fairness, and mercy/justice for all. For me that cluster of values points in the direction of communitarianism. Your core values may well be different, and communitarianism might be the far from working out your values. The first step then is to achieve a consensus about the core values **we** want to use to shape our life and governance as a society. Until we accomplish that *we are all adrift*. Our founding fathers assumed our national core values and built them into our Constitution through a very messy process. Re-formulating our core values will be an equally messy process.

Out of that achieved consensus about our core values drops the next question. In our liberal (verging toward libertarian) mindset government is primarily about protecting property rights, and little else. The T-Party mindset appears to be fairly libertarian, so "The least government is the better government, and the best government is none at all." Government's function is to "Protect my property-rights, and otherwise, leave me alone. Oh, and maybe protect the national borders from invasion; but involve me as little as you can in that task."

But if I propose a communitarian mindset, that definition of governance simply will not do. If the community *(not the individual)* is the basic unit, then the job of governance becomes to tend to the survivability and thrivivity of the community and to strike and maintain a balance between the wants and needs of the community on the one hand and of all its members on the other hand, quite a different and much larger complicated task. Form should follow function, so the order must be first to discern what we are about (core values), and then shape a governance to achieve that. *(Please note that I am using the word* governance *and not* government. *I make absolutely **no** assumptions about the shape that governance might take. In Martin Brokenleg's tioš paye governance **appeared** to take the form of no government at all; but in reality it was a quite sophisticated governance built out of mores, i.e., "This is the way our tioš paye has always done it," a fairly directive [but gently so] and complete governance.)*

Am I sounding like a revolutionary?

Having posited that definition and those tenets, I now find in my lap a basket of considerations. They are in no priority. And not all the necessary considerations have yet found their way into my basket; there are others yet to be uncovered. This is an associative, discovery process and we still far from any serious analysis.

First of all I wonder about the role of community. I picture the bare-foot Dalai Lama, legs folded atop an overstuffed chair, patiently explaining that the search for "Who-am-I?" is fated to be fruitless. Figuring out "Who-am-I?" is trying to trap a ball of quicksilver under your thumb; as you press down it squirts out and your thumb is on nothing. The reality is that "Who-am-I?" is not a static definable entity, not a fixed concept, not a noun which can be tied down, described, and sealed safely in a box. Instead "Who-am-I?" at any given instant is the nanosecond intersection of thousands of dynamics and experiences and circumstances and conditions all thrusting in different directions; and in the very next instant "Who-am-I?" will be different as all those factors, which are themselves in motion, change, evolve, move on, transmogrify. Have I no continuity? Some. But even that node of continuity is in motion, slowly shifting, changing, evolving and being changed by what is happening around it and to it. What seems to be a node of continuity is really only a slower transition seeming to be continuity. These are not the Dalai Lama's exact words, but my understanding of what he tells us. I report this to point out that we Westerners think of the Self as a fixed entity, the noun in the sentence, the free-standing individual, the subject of the verb. But in my reality the Self is not a noun, certainly not the subject of the sentence. The Self is much more like a verb, it is in motion, we can catch it only in its instant of becoming and moving on. It is the product of DNA, and my family's values and dynamics and everything that made us a family, and my playmates and my school and my church (this list can go on quite a while), and the myriad forces and dynamics and factors that pushed and dragged me into this instant and will carry me beyond it, all that rolled into the uniqueness that I alone am bringing to this instant. And the community is the arena in which all this happens. The Lakotan thought himself brother to the bison which voluntarily gave up its life that the *tioš paye* might have food and sustenance another day; he thought himself as at one with and a part of the earth and heavens and wind. It all happens within the context of community. I suggest that in the well-integrating community, the community shows me "Who-am-I?" the community is the medium within which I happen.

I am coming to understand that the community is the primary, fundamental life unit of which I am a unique creature. I contrast this with our rampant individualism which wants to downplay, to shun or even deny the importance of community, but in that effort is destroying the social (and material) fabric which is essential to living and survival.

Now, I realize that there are difficulties in this understanding of "community." In his *tioš paye* the Lakota had a discreet, defined, delineated living unit of the ideal size for survivability and sustainability and optimization the individual. We, on the other hand, have no such a discreet, limited, identifiable community, but instead live in a complex of overlaid, multiple communities, with discordance among and between them, and often with conflicting goals and values. The Lakota learned from his culture and *tioš paye* how to live in harmony with his limited community. We have no such advantage. But it is becoming imperative that we learn how to live together more effectively—or we perish.

Second, the **core notion of communitarianism is a carefully crafted and maintained balance** between the needs, rights, privileges, health, and welfare of the individual on the one hand, and on the other hand the sustainability, health and well-being of the social fabric, the community. My **central-most value** is the equality of all persons, in every sense (including the valuing of differences) and my **fundamental understanding** is the essentiality of community, and that we are not, can never be free-standing, completely independent human beings, but require the formation, the structure, the sustenance (of every sort) which the social fabric provides. The community is so essential to the well-being and survivability of the individual that I am inclined to understand the social fabric in all its dimensions, as the fundamental entity of human life, and the individual as an element, a functioning sub-unit within the community. Balance between the individual and social fabric is essential to the well-being and survivability of both.

Part III: A Vision to Move Toward

Absolute freedom is a fiction we created in the collapse of the totalitarian social structures. Feralness exists in the forest, humanness exists only in community. Does that constrain the liberty and licence of the individual? Certainly! But the community I envision is crafted in such ways that it enhances and incorporates the uniqueness of each individual, rather than unduly fettering it. Communitarians maintain that the individual, when well-integrated into a healthful community, has greater and more fulfilling potential than in an unequal, aggressive and competition-driven community where "Dog eat dog" and "Might (of whatever sort) makes right" are the standards. It appears to me that a well-integrating community offers the greater liberation and health (socially and psychologically) than does rampant individualism.

If my communitarian vision is founded on the **equality of all** persons, on the understanding that the **community is the fundamental** unit of human life *(not the individual),* and that the community must live out an **exquisitely designed balance** of the community's needs and the needs, abilities, desires and dreams of its members, then **certain dogma** fall out of that value set.

a. The community has only two fundamental objectives: (1) to enable *the good* for its members, and (2) to assure the survivability of the community itself. Neither takes priority over the other.

b. Essential to the survivability of the community is sustainability, living in relation to the environment such that the environment sustains the community without becoming depleted or exhausted. As I watched the *tioš paye* this was not accomplished through rules or laws, but though the values, life style, and practices infused into the members. (E.g., the Lakota understood the bison, one major source of their sustenance, to be their brothers and so lived with them with respect, never abuse, never taking more than was needed, always giving thanks for what they received.) Husbanding, conserving, using wisely the environment and its resources is primary. Comfort and luxury must be secondary. Controlling the use of resources must be the function of the community, not of individuals.

c. *The good* must be divined by the community in a process that is participatory, inclusive, **subsidiarious**, and effectively incorporates the accumulated wisdom within the community. It is not clear in my mind whether subsidiarity inevitably leads to moral *particularism* (a morality specific to that community and not necessarily like elsewhere) or *universalism* (one moral structure for all humankind). My suspicion is that it will be a curious combination of particularism and universalism: as human nature is much the same universally, the core of the moral structure will likely be fairly universal; but just as *mores* vary from place to place, so the edges of the moral structure will likely be particular to that community.) This "divination" is neither sudden nor final, but gradually emerges and evolves to meet the changes of the world.

d. What is the community about? Obviously it operates first of all in such ways as to survive long-term. It accomplishes that by providing for the welfare and well-being of all its members, not in a social welfare, or socialistic way, but by husbanding its members with insight, wisdom and pragmatism in ways that both optimize their *place* and *self-satisfaction* within the community and also meet the community's needs. Just as the community wisely husbands the environmental resources, in much the same manner it also husbands its human manpower and resources so that both the members (individually) and the community are most healthily benefitted, e.g., to the self-interests, best-interests and welfare of **both**. This community is far more than an agglomeration of members; it is a social system which operates in a collaborative, cooperative, non-competitive, synergistic, people-friendly manner[4]. While it must husband limited resources, as a social system it operates as a non-zero-sum game; the welfare of the community equals the well-being of its members, and the welfare of one does not need to detract from the well-being of the other. It provides necessary community services and infrastructure. As I envision the community it is much more than a market place or a system of governance.

e. As the communitarians define the community it is a place of shared moral culture, *mores* and values. I suspect it also has a shared sense of what life is about.

But I wonder, just what is "community"? Responding to criticism that the term "community" is too vague or cannot be defined, Amitai Etzioni, pointed out that communities can be defined with reasonable precision as having two characteristics: first, a web of affect-laden relationships among a group of individuals, relationships that often crisscross and reinforce one another (as opposed to one-on-one or chain-like individual relationships); and second, a measure of commitment to a set of shared values, norms, and meanings, and a shared history and identity – in short, a particular culture. Further, author David E. Pearson argued that "to earn the appellation *community*, it seems to me, groups must be able to exert moral suasion and extract a measure of compliance from their members. That is, communities are necessarily, indeed, by definition, coercive as well as moral, threatening their members with the stick of sanctions if they stray, offering them the carrot of certainty and stability if they don't." Academic Communitarianism maintains that good societies rely on a shared moral culture.

---

4. True story: a friend finally decided that this was the summer his family would make their generation-old dream of driving up the Pan-American Highway from Washington State across Canada to Alaska. Arriving at the ferry in Alaska to take them on toward the last lap he discovered that he needed reservations for the over-night trip for both his car and his family (which he did not have) and the next available reservation was a week away. But, "Not to worry," was the clerk's comment, "we'll work something out." He found them space for the car, but the family had to sleep on deck, out under the stars. Ted came home proclaiming, "Bureaucracy can be helpful and people-friendly."

What is specifically meant by *community* in the context of communitarianism can vary greatly between authors and time periods. Historically, communities have been small and localized. However, as the reach of economic and technological forces extended, more-expansive communities became necessary in order to provide effective normative and political guidance to these forces, prompting the rise of national communities in Europe in the seventeenth century. Since the late twentieth century there has been some growing recognition that the scope of even these communities is too limited, as many challenges that people now face, such as the threat of nuclear war and of global environmental degradation and economic crises, cannot be handled on a national basis. This has led to the quest for more-encompassing communities, such as the European Union. Whether truly supra-national communities can be developed is far from clear.

More modern communities can take many different forms, but are often limited in scope and reach. For example, members of one residential community are often also members of other communities – such as work, ethnic, or religious ones. As a result, modern community members have multiple sources of attachments, and if one threatens to become overwhelming, individuals will often pull back and turn to another community for their attachments.

Some do argue that *well integrated* individuals are able to reason better, and to be more responsible members of the community. Too high a standard of conformity leads to the undermining of individuality. In the good society there is a **crafted balance** of liberty and social order, of rights and responsibilities.

I add my own concern to this conversation. I think size of community is another major difficulty. Brokenleg's *tioš paye* was ideally between 200 and 250 persons. It is hard to find a community that small anywhere today. On the other hand, while we have cities in the tens of millions we are rapidly pushing toward a global economy, and that means a global community, at least in some aspects. And today an individual person is really a participant in several, sometimes many communities, overlain but quite separate. A communitarian system, begins to look exceedingly complex.

Another question is around the use and distribution of **wealth**. "Should all property be community owned?" I approach the question (which necessarily preoccupies all individualists, liberals and capitalists) from this direction: with the welfare and survivability of the community in mind, can wealth (which comes ultimately from the earth in the form of minerals and food) really be *owned* by individuals, or does wealth necessarily belong to the whole community which in turn allows individuals to grab hold of some fair and equitable share of it for their individual needs but only in ways that are congruent with the community's needs? Or at least not contrary to the community's self-interests? The community will fail or succeed as a function of how well the community husbands the earth's resources. Can the community afford to turn over that wealth without regulation or accountability into the hands of a few who might squander it in their individual self-interests without concern for the community or its survivability? Or does the community have the responsibility to allow the individual use of community stuff only when it is used to the benefit of the community and with husbandmanship accountability?

And what is left for the individual? As I watched the *tioš paye* lived out before my eyes I came to understand that this question is a non-starter, it comes out of an *individualist* vantage. Within the values and *mores* of the community each member has everything s/he needs, everything equitably shareable: health care, and a fair share of food, shelter, transport, amenities, place, livelihood. All these (to the best of the community's ability) are present, available and shared fairly.

Several questions have occured to me which are still hanging. One is around **privacy**. This one somewhat baffles me. I have almost no notion what the cry for "privacy" is all about. Our Supreme Court has found a *right to privacy* somewhere **in between** the words of our Constitution. There is nothing written there which speaks specifically of any right to privacy, but it has become a centerpiece of current arguments and reasoning (i.e., *privacy demarcates family space where government should not go or infringe; and any infringement of privacy becomes tantamount to a breach of individuality.*) The Declaration of Independence speaks of the right to "life, liberty and the pursuit of happiness," but it says nothing about privacy. I suspect that *privacy* is really a cover argument for the protection of private property, of ownership and indirectly of capitalism. My considered opinion is that the only reason to insist on a right to privacy is to keep something hidden. That could be something about myself that I consider flawed, an embarrassment, which I want to hide from others, or something in our relationship which I don't want you to realize, or something I've done which is illegal, immoral, bad, or incredibly messy and I want not to be discovered. But if I'm living a fairly legal, moral and decent life, then Jack Bowers feels no great need of privacy *(apart from our leftover Victorian prudishness about our bodies.)* From that point of view, the primary value of privacy is to better enable you to unaccountably offend, injure, or trespass against me. Why should I want that? Privacy may be about maintaining personal boundaries which are culturally inculcated.

Another hanging question is around freedom and liberty. From an oppressed serf working the land to the benefit of the king and the lord of the manor we've come a long way. Freedom and liberty are crucially important to us. But the complicating question is what do we mean by **freedom** and **liberty**? And the answer seems obvious, but it's not, and is not forthcoming. There are a whole bunch of hidden, unexamined assumptions built into the front end of that question. We assume first of all that freedom means individualism, living as a free-standing individual who has full ownership of himself, no strings attached. Then built into our social system is the assumption that in order to be free, one must generate a certain level of prosperity: that means a certain *(how much is a variable)* amount of wealth, the right to own property, and the means to advance one's own prosperity (which may involve the right to acquire to one's own use and ownership any unclaimed *stuff*). All of this places demands on the social system: that there be free trade and commerce, i.e., some kind of capitalist system, which may in turn require a certain non-specific rate of commercial growth in order to flourish. In order to preserve and protect my freedom/liberty I need to fight off any impinging restrictions and limitations, and at the same time prompt the social system to provide me the necessary tools to protect and enhance my freedom/liberty. And the question has not yet begun to be answered, "What do I mean by *freedom*?" Let me try to answer negatively: in the example from Dr. Turner *(see pages 323–24)* is it *freedom* to ask the elders to decide for me whether to buy insurance and get a dog? From an individualist point of view that feels like a loss of freedom; I was disallowed from making for myself a decision I felt perfectly capable of making for myself without involving the elders and the community (even if my decision was uninformed by the wisdom of the community and the deliberations of the elders, which is my right as an individual, i.e., to make an uninformed decision for myself and which may impinge upon others). On the other hand, I'm quite unsure what *freedom* might mean in the context of communitarianism.

I think probably the most important thing left to the individual is **loyalty**. In the world defined by individualism, loyalty has become an infringement, an undesirable obligation against liberty *(shall I read that as "licence"?)* It limits my absolute liberty and freedom. Today loyalty from me must be earned by you. However in a world in which the community is the fundamental entity of human life, of which you and I participate as members, and in which the community is the source of all I am, of all I need, and of all I could want, loyalty is not an infringement but a given. If I am an integral part of the community, the loyalty does not need to be demanded of me; it is simply a given of my relationship to the community. It is an important feature of the ties that bind and bond me to the community. And, obviously, it must be built upon a reciprocal loyalty of the community to me.

As I sit, sorting through the basket of considerations in my lap, I become aware that there is another basket at my knee, a collection of blockages I encounter in trying to consider, much less move toward an understanding of communitarianism.

> **Our biases**: I was born and grew up in this country, in this culture. Its values, its norms and *mores*, everything that makes this America is deep in my bones. Its presumptions are my presumptions. And while I know some of them are wrong, they are deep in my bones and I cannot simply shake them off. I wear them and still know them to be wrong.
>
> **We pre-assume**: we ought to be free-standing, self-sufficient, self-reliant, independent persons; and that it is every person's right to own whatever I want limited only by affordability; and that the *stuff* I own is mine, and I am free to do with it whatever I wish; and that we not only free but responsible to decide what to do with my Self, though maybe I **ought** to do the least injury to others; but some injury is okay if I can manage to be not accountable *(and laws* **appear** *to be undeniable restrictions but when laws infringe on my rights*

Chapter 13: Communitarianism

or freedoms they become only strong suggestions), though for some unstated reason the state prefers that I do not kill my Self.

These pre-assumptions are founded on the understanding that the Self is the essential, irreducible unit of living, and that the Self is owned exclusively by the Self. But that understanding is fatally flawed. I have already concluded that the community is the essential unit of living, in which the individual participates. Standing alone, I would not survive, nor would humankind survive. While some rare individuals might be able to keep body and soul together without benefit of the community, that would not add up to the survival of humankind. And, with Darwinism in mind, survival is the ultimate issue.

I have some fairly vague notions that these flawed pre-assumptions of individualism are built upon some very deep, very pre-conscious biases out of our ancient history. And as we go along today we drag with us cultural baggage which we term our Judeo-Christian heritage. Within that heritage are several unvoiced and unacknowledged *(and maybe even unrealized)* biases.

In the second creation story **YHWH created** as the fundamental human unit one *ha'adam* (the mud-boy). The woman, *havah* (the mother of all living) was an afterthought, someone to keep the lonely mud-boy company; but YHWH's intention was *ha'adam*, with YHWH's own life-breath breathed into the mud-boy, the essential living entity, the male; the female was secondary, an ancillary creation out of the rib of *ha'adam* (no YHWH breath was breathed in). Our ancient heritage tells us *ha'adam*, the male, was the fundamental entity. I note in passing that in the first creation story Elohim (i.e., the God) created the mud-boy male-and-female, in Elohim's own image and likeness: a mini-community, a nuclear family of co-creations. But over the course of history the male-superior position dominated down through the ages to this day. As the story in the Scriptures progresses individual **males** are paid close attention: Abraham, Isaac, Jacob, Joseph, Moses. Always individual males *(rarely an individual female such as the outcasted Hagar, the barren Hannah, the national heroine Esther)*, at the head of a clan. The emphasis in our Scriptural history is on individual males with power: incipient patriarchy, individualism, and misogyny.

I note a second bias out of our ancient heritage. Much, not all, but much of the Hebrew Scriptures, and very much of the early Christian Writings bear an unburnished, and under-verbalized hostility to the natural, physical world. The Bedouin had been nomadic shepherds in a harsh environment; the world in which they scrabbled a living was dangerous and often (if not usually) perceived as hostile. That understanding is a quiet, a barely detectable undertone throughout those Hebrew Scriptures, along with that their greater distrust of urban life. *(Cain's punishment for killing Abel was exile to the land of Nod, where Cain built a city. The city was for these Bedouin a place of evil, never to be trusted. Bad things, like Cain, happen in cities.)* Some branches of early Christianity, which grew up in the urban and industrialized Roman world, thought the physical world (as opposed to the non-physical, the spiritual realm) hostile, even fundamentally evil (particularly in Gnosticism, but in many of the Early Church Fathers as well). I find that bias still quietly residing at the foundations of our Western thinking; we experience the world as something to be **mastered**, as that from which we are obliged to **take** (sometimes violently), and as that which can be **hazardous, dangerous** to us. The result is we approach the world, and life, even the act of living, as though over-against us, to be corralled, reined in, overcome, mastered, controlled. I think these two ancient biases feed much into our attraction to individualism.

Those biases (and a clutch of others, I presume, which I've not yet recognized) in our ancient roots have been quietly important in shaping how we respond to community; we experience community as an *over-against*, as that which wishes to diminish and control us. Government is a casually evil thing to be resisted, held off, kept at safe distance. Our individualism and liberalism and capitalism all actively work toward the diminuation of government. The better government is small and the best would be none. It's irrational and unrealistic, but the inane impulse, very much in the air today.

Encouragements toward communitarianism: There are some examples out there of what I am proposing, not perfect examples, but ones indicating there are other ways to live together besides individualism.

I unintentionally stumbled into a brief taste of a different kind of world during my five weeks living within the Cistercians's Caldey Abbey. The abbot housed me in the guest quarters inside the monastic enclosure, so that I took meals with the monks and had access to their cloister and chapel. As I was leaving at the end of my time Brother Gildas told me the monks thought I had fit in better than any other guest they'd hosted. I took that to mean that I had adapted to their lifestyle such that my presence created little distraction or problem for them, ergo that I did get a real taste of their living.

And how did they live? A life of complete regularity, and not of poverty but of severe austerity and simplicity, and of obedience (in that authoritarian system one does nothing without the abbot's permission, even as a guest). I had gone there for the support of such a community for my writing, so the structure did not feel oppressive for me. Caldey Abbey was an excellent setting to do that piece of writing.

My learning out of that monastic experience was that living the way we live in this culture, is not necessarily the best way to live. Living in the monastery with somewhat less freedom was not a bad or oppressive thing. Living within a community that took care of my (nearly) every need while allowing me to be productive on my own terms was helpful, supportive, productive, unstressful. There were some powerful upsides to living in that monastic community. Understand: monastic life is not for everyone; probably good for only a few. But it is one option. I would hunch that there are other, viable, even quite desirable options. And I further hunch that living as a member of a *tioš paye* would be one of the options better than living as we do now in our liberal, capitalistic, and individualistic system.

Chapter 13: Communitarianism

I take note of two interviews by Charlie Rose. One was of the current Prime Minister of **Bhutan**, a small (population 733,000), constitutional monarchy nestled in the Himalayas in which the king has decreed that the GNP (gross national product) and GNH (gross national happiness) **must** be balanced and held in balance. Their primary industry is hydro-electric power which is exported to neighboring India and yields a negative carbon impact on the larger ecology; some 70 percent of their forestation is permanently protected, and along with it much of the indigenous species. Their lifestyle, though not impoverished, is austere.

The second interview of note was with the former Prime Minister of **Singapore**, a contemporary city-state with a population of about 5.5 million which has raised itself from a third-rate economy to a first-rate economy within a single generation, and is now one of the most prosperous in Asia. The change has not been easy, but was generally acceptable to the population even though it was effected through somewhat severe impositions on the people (e.g., the city is divided into small sections and neighborhoods, each of which is **mandated** to have the same as the national mix of people with different ethnic and cultural origins, and of all financial classes; they must live together intermixed, thereby forcing racial/ethnic, cultural and financial pluralism.)

I note that both of these examples are out of non-European cultures, with quite different cultural histories and assumptions than the Western world holds. Yet both are embracing capitalist economies couched in terms amenable to their cultures which have a quite different understanding than ours of the balance between individual and the community. They are both living examples that there are other ways to do it, and that the change can be accomplished. There may be other helpful examples closer to home which ought to be explored. One that occurs to me is the Amish community in this country. I know little about it, but it might yield some useful notions in as much as it shares some of our culture.

And from the **Rev. Dr. Philip Turner** comes a story which suggests to me that it can be done, if there is the will. His story is out of an evangelistic Christian community in the bush of Uganda. In that community decisions were arbitrated by a council of elders who first questioned the entire community to hear their thoughts. In one instance, a young couple was required by his employer to move to the big city. They came before the community to ask two questions: (1) should they, as advised by his employer, purchase insurance to cover the contents of their home in case they were robbed? and (2) should they get a watchdog to patrol their walled compound to protect them from nighttime harm? The elders conducted a hearing with the whole community for several hours, then withdrew for a period to consider all they'd heard and came back with the decision that the couple should buy insurance, because Christ did not intend for them to live in want, but they should not get the watchdog which would imply they considered their lives more valuable than others's. The community nodded in agreement and a feast was laid out in celebration of the decision. Someone later asked Dr. Turner what would have happened had the couple disagreed with the elders's proclamation. His response, "It never would have occurred to them to do that." *(Note: I am concerned here not with the content of the decision, but with the community process involved, and in particular with the attitude toward that community decision-making.)*

The major difficulty for us in this example is that we have learned to do all our thinking from the vantage of *individualism*. As I write this chapter I am discovering how pervasive, complicated and insidious that vantage is. It is almost impossible for us not to think first from the vantage of *individualism*, later recognize *(maybe)* the misstep, and then *(possibly)* translate the thinking so that it comes from a *communitarian* vantage. Dr. Turner's story illustrates: (1) we would not even consider asking the community to decide for us whether to buy insurance and get a dog. Those are *my* decisions, choices and responsibilities; why would I submit them to the elders? And, (2) to submit the decisions to the elders seems like a diminuation of my personhood. I am competent. I can do that. It seems childish to ask the elders to do what I am perfectly able to do myself (even in ignorance of the communal wisdom and lore of the community). And (3), Dr. Turner says, "It never would have occurred to them to do that *[i.e., disagree]*." It would have been our prerogative, not only to second guess the tribal members and the elders, but to disagree and even act contrary to their decision (which for us is merely half-informed advice). And we have not the slightest ability to comprehend the multitude of factors that went into the decision. I could parse this example more but my illustration is made; our mind simply has not learned to recognize and seriously consider those communal faculties.

For this couple, preparing to leave for the big city, this community from which they were taking leave was who they were. Disagreeing would not be merely unthinkable, or forbidden; it would simply not occur to them. The difficult decisions were made with and by the whole community, the people of whom they are at-one. This couple may leave the tribal compound, but they will not leave the community. They and the community are one, the same, inseparable, *(like Martin Brokenieg)* no matter how far apart. So they choose and act, and will always choose and act as an integral part of the community. It would not occur to them to do any other way.

So what might a communitarian system look like? So far as I know none exists, so I cannot point and say, "Look at this." I can only imagine. And to do that is to extrapolate from fantasies such as I already laid before you, the Rev. Dr. Martin Brokenleg's *tioš paye* of the Lakotas and the two movies he called to our attention. Much of what I heard from Brokenleg and saw in those two movies was probably my fantasy which I projected into those sources. So I will weave a tapestry now which is drawn partly from those sources, and partly my own fantasies.

I envision a social structure much like a *tioš paye* which has lovingly embraced, coddled, shaped each member from his/her birth. It has imbued in them through acculturation (as in Philip Turner's story) an unlegislated set of values and practices which maintains the exquisite balance between both the individual's nurturance and freedom and the community's strength and survivability; those values and practices are the right ones for both the community and the member for one simple reason, they grew up together with the intention of richness of life. Fairness is at the heart of those values. The members are cared for by each other; there is an abundance of what Robert Putnam calls social capital, i.e., they are inclined to do for each other. That atmosphere is pervasive. Sustenance, habitat, goods and *stuff* are shared equitably and according to need. And the community knows its members well enough that each member is found the right *place* to give to the community the best and most satisfying of his/her talents and skills.

I realize that as I wrote this paragraph I was trying to describe something similar to what Jesus called "the Kingdom of God," the ideal way for us to live this life together.

My Sources for Communitarianism:

Communitarianism:

Bell, David, "Communitarianism." Stanford Encyclopedia of Philosophy Jan 25, 2012 http://plato.stanford.edu/entries/communitarianism/

"Communitarianism," Wikipedia Dec 13, 2008 https://en.wikipedia.org/wiki/Communitarianism

Glass, Gene V. and Rudd A.G. "The Struggle Between Individualism and Communitarianism," **Research in Education,** March 2012; 36 (1) http://rre.sagepub.com/content/36/1.toc

Amitai Etzioni

"Amitai Etzioni on Communitarianism, Civil Rights and Foreign Policy," Encyclopedia Britannica Blog May 16, 2011 http://blogs.britannica.com/2011/05/amitai-etzioni-communitarianism-civil-rights-foreign-policy/

"Amitai Etzioni," Wikipedia https://en.wikipedia.org/wiki/Amitai_Etzioni

Christensen, Karen and Levinson, David eds. "Communitarianism: Etzioni," Encyclopedia of Community https://www.gwu.edu/~ccps/etzioni/A308.pdf

Younkins, Edward W. "Amitai Etzioni's Responsive Community: A Flawed Paradigm," **Capitalism & Commerce**, Montreal, September 1, 2001 / No 87. http://www.quebecoislibre.org/010901-13.htm

John Rawls

Garrett, Dr. Jan. "Rawls' Mature Theory of Social Justice, an introduction for students," August 24, 2005 http://people.wku.edu/jan.garrett/ethics/matrawls.htm

"John Rawls," Wikipedia https://en.wikipedia.org/wiki/John_Rawls

"Rawls' A Theory of Justice," Wikipedia 6 May 2016 https://en.wikipedia.org/wiki/A_Theory_of_Justice

Travis, Christine. "Philosophy: Summary, Explanation of John Rawls Theory of Justice," Yahoo Contributor Network March 12, 2010

Wenar, Leif. "John Rawls," Stanford Encyclopedia of Philosophy Sep.24, 2012 http://plato.stanford.edu/entries/rawls/

Michael Sandel

"Michael J. Sandel," Wikipedia 15 June 2016 https://en.wikipedia.org/wiki/Michael_J._Sandel

Charles Taylor

Bloor, Chris. "Charles Taylor—Interview," Philosophy Now https://philosophynow.org/issues/74/Charles_Taylor

"Charles Taylor," Wikipedia 10 June 2016 https://en.wikipedia.org/wiki/Charles_Taylor_(philosopher)

"Charles Taylor," Encyclopedia Britannica 8-24-2015 http://www.britannica.com/biography/Charles-Taylor

Taylor, Charles. Review of **A Secular Age** in Wikipedia 17 December 2015 https://en.wikipedia.org/wiki/A_Secular_Age

A Morality for Communitarianism

It is obvious that living in a communitarian system where the community and the member are equally important and the two are held in balance requires a different way of living together than we have evolved in this culture. A very certain lifestyle drops out of the very definition of communitarianism. I'll attempt a start at describing that way of living.

I need to first **clarify** aloud just what I mean by the words, "a morality for communitarianism." I have never been clear about the difference between morality and ethics. My introduction to "ethics" was a single classroom conversation about Joe Fletcher's newly published book **Situation Ethics: The New Morality**. What I did not grasp at the time was that Fletcher was attempting a reform of morality. I've worked my understandings of *ethics* out of that conversation for fifty years now. T'is time to make corrections. So to begin this part of the conversation I need to back up to a starting-point and re-educate myself about morality.

As a classics major I compulsively start with the ancient roots. The word "morality" was rooted in the Latin **mos (moris)** which translates *custom, usage, traditional line of conduct, the way of the ancestors,* and also *a quality, manner, rule, law*. And from that root comes **morali**, an adjective meaning *moral, ethical*. From the Greek **ethos** meaning *an accustomed place,* hence *a seat, a haunt, an abode,* and after that *a custom, usage, habit*. From that root comes ***ethikos*** an adjective meaning *moral, ethical, as **opposed to intellectual**(!)* Taking all that together, I understand it to mean something like "The way we've always done it," and "The way our forebears always did it." Contemporary authorities seem to make little distinction between morality and ethics, noting that the words are often used interchangeably, but also that there is some slight, if unclear difference between them. Diffen (on-line grammarian) draws a comparison between "morality" and "ethics" fixed around the principle that ethics are rules of conduct for a **particular set** of actions or for a **particular group** (such as doctors or CEO's), whereas morals are principles or habits with respect to right or wrong, good or bad, a "personal compass of right and wrong." That grammarian seems to think ethics refers primarily to professional groups, and morality to the individual or society in general. The Stanford Encyclopedia of Philosophy points out that "morality" can be used *descriptively* referring to a code of conduct put forth by a society, a group, a religion; or *normatively*, referring to a code of conduct put forward for all *rational* human beings;

After that I will now simply throw out **sound bites**: the most frequent key understanding is "a code of conduct for governing behavior." May be distinguished from etiquette, law, and religion. Concerns "living together in peace." Morality sometimes requires "accepting the traditions and customs." Two phrases that recur are "minimizing harms," and "greatest good." Bentham and Mill take "avoiding and preventing harm" to be most important. Also noted, minimizing (avoiding and preventing) harm, accepting authority and emphasizing loyalty. Most non-religious philosophers limit morality to "behavior that, directly or indirectly, **affects others**." Most universal guides prohibit such actions as killing, causing pain, deceiving, and breaking promises. Hobbes: morality is concerned with promoting people living together in peace and harmony: i.e., peaceable, sociable, comfortable. Some contemporary consequentialists require "the best overall consequences." Normative (universal) moralists would define morality as "an informal *(i.e., has no authoritative judges and no decision procedure)* and public *(i.e., everyone knows what actions are prohibited, required, discouraged, encouraged and allowed)* system applying to all rational persons, governing behavior that affects others, and has the lessening of evil or harm as its goal."

As the above words and phrases floated before my eyes I realized that what I envision does not quite fit within those words and ideas, is not really within the realm of *a morality*. It is clear to me that morality as we conceive it grows out of an era of individualism and is focused on the individual's behavior. And it seems a **least common denominator**; I hunch that as individualism, liberalism and capitalism reacted to the breakdown of authoritarianism, they resisted to the max anything that might on infringe the liberty of the three -isms; so morality also seems to take the **least infringing** way, to do no harm or the least harm. I am not seeking such a least common denominator, nor the least amount of infringement. I am seeking a way for members of a community to live harmoniously within that community, with fairly and carefully managed differences and conflicts, and harmoniously with the earth as well. And that implies to me a *positive outreach*, more than a prohibition. *(I am not prepared here to worry about law (i.e., a way of resolving disputes about harm, injury, damage or infringement, and which, when in consort with individualism, seems to veer off in the direction of litigiousness in the protection of rights and privileges)*, or about religion *(used as a tool for lending authority for the imposition of a moral structure.)* I seem more interested in *(to be colloquial and folksy)* "doing things the way we've always done them"; I am approaching the issue from the direction of community rather than individual, searching for the **how to live together** so that the community survives, is sustainable, thrives, and incorporates its members in such ways that their lives are optimized, both for themselves and for the benefit to the community. And I m not prepared at this juncture to tackle determination of *the good*. Those questions **must** be tackled eventually, but for the moment I am only interested in a community-member relationship such that the healthfulness (in all dimensions) of both is optimized, and that the accrued *social capital* causes satisfaction, even pleasure, in doing for each other. I am interested in "here's the good way to live together."

As an aside I share my untutored understanding that it is possible to **build a morality**, a moral structure or system, around almost any single principle or any very small set of principles.

- I assume that when we first left the forest and crept cautiously out onto the savannah in small clusters of hunter-gatherers, we either brought with us, or very quickly adopted a morality of "Might makes right." At least my non-historian reading of history suggests that principle goes back that far. And for many folk that single principle is still the foundation of their morality; the gun-slingers, the fist swingers, and the brutalizers all know that if they can whip their opponent, whether friend or foe, they are themselves made the better person, both better than the loser, and better within themselves for the doing of it. Over the course of time they became our warrior-bosses, the despots, the tyrants, and now the CEO's *(e.g., Donald Trump)* and such.

- Many think we live in a *Christian* nation. I fail to see what is the least bit Christian about it. As a nation we (our forefathers were deists attending Christian churches) began by embedding individualism as the core principle in our Constitution, and we swaddled ourselves in an unfettered capitalism as an operating medium. Capitalism has evolved into the core principle of our morality (i.e., if it makes a profit, it's gotta be good, even if wasteful, squanderous, destructive, non-beneficial, dys-associating, harmful, life-endangering.) Profit-taking is the primary criterion in societal decision-making and choosing.

- As Christians we claim to build our morality on a handful of Judeo-Christian principles: love (not the warm, squishy love of romance, but another "love" which is never quite defined), the Great Commandment, and the Golden Rule. And while there are a few Mother Thersa's who actually live all that stuff out, I think most of us live some concatenation of a very light Christian morality, coupled with an *Americanism* morality, but mostly capitalism. The result: "I know what I ought to do, but there's no great push to really do it; and I'd be an odd ball in this culture if I did."

It is my sense that we do need a clearer, accepted, consistent morality, one with greater integrity and transparency, one larger than me, and with authority, attractiveness and reasonableness. "Do your own thing" is not a course to survival or to harmoniously living together. But when I look through the lens of community, there simply is no moral system that fits. The best approximation I can make of the whole moral need is to posit the community as the fundamental living entity which survives and thrives by holding a balance between the community's needs and wants and the member's needs and wants; and then I ask, "How might we live together to accomplish what is best for both the community and the member?" Not so much a code of behavior as a milieu, a "This is the way it's done among us" understanding. I go back to my classicist's beginnings: the customs, the usage, the traditional line of conduct.

How about a basketful of attitudes? I am inclined to think, as I try to describe this way of living together which befits communitarian living, of a cluster of attitudes *("attitudes" is not the right word here, but I can find no better; perhaps a coterie of words will convey my notion, so pile these all together: predisposition, posture, temperament of mind, bent, leaning, inclination, propensity, heart)*. E.g., an attitude such as *parch*, a Welsh word which might be translated *respect*; when a people have lived together, labored together, suffered and rejoiced together over generations they come to have *parch*, a respect for each other that transcends differences and conflicts, a kind of social capital which inclines them to do for each other and to preserve their ties.

- Congeniality: *(synonyms: concord, symphony, understanding, good will, cordiality)* a positive expectation at the outset of encounter.

- Equality: a pervading sense that we come together as equals, in brotherhood and fairness, and that we are all in this together

- Wisdom: A pervading sense that, even though I might be brilliant, still we, if we pool together our wits and our experience and our accumulated history and wisdom, probably know and understand better than I can alone.

- Subsidiarity: the principle that matters ought to be handled by the smallest, lowest or least centralized competent authority rather than by a central authority.

One reader has suggested that what I am searching out is tantamount to the **greatest empathy for all** as the center of a communitarian morality. That's not bad. The Dalai Lama says that Tibetan Buddhists strive to live with compassion for all, all persons, all animals, all the created world. I might paraphrase, "live with thoughtfulness first for the other and for the whole" and if I can live that way, I will probably live for the good of my Self. It is not a *selflessness*, but the Self in the context of the whole.

I reflect back to Martin Brokenleg's *tioš paye* and to Dr, Turner's story. And as I watch those events unfold I see people acting out of a sense of "This is who **we** are," and a mindfulness of the welfare, the good, the benefit of the community, of the whole as well as of my own Self. I am not less than, but neither am I greater than, and so I act and choose and live as *one of us*, with as much concern for the others as for myself. And my guide is not rules and regulations and laws, but a deeply experienced sense of how we ought to be together, and how things have always been done. Life in the *tioš paye* is lived out of "The ways that have been in my bones since before I was birthed." Rules and laws are not needed. And it would not occur to me to disagree, or to ask "Why?"

I'll add some thoughts about communitarian ethics lifted from an on-line article, "Ethics at a Glance" from Regis University, Rueckert-Hartman School for Health Professionals:

> ". . . the **common good as an ideal** . . . downplays the values of individuality, autonomy, and personal rights, so prevalent in other ethical theories, in favor of a **focus on the virtues and actions that support** the interests of society as a whole. While this does include respect for human life and dignity, allowing for all persons to achieve a **meaningful potential**, the common good also calls for concern for **longterm sustainability**, intergenerational justice, an emphasis on active and informed citizenship, and a **balance between individual and communal interests**. At times, the common good may require all citizens to consider the needs of the broader community above the needs of any one individual, group, or organization. Communitarian thought clearly contributes to the ethical dialogue in the health care context. This is particularly true with respect to issues such as the best use of limited health care resources, health care as a right, and the concept of healthy communities versus an emphasis on individual health.
>
> Strengths of the communitarian perspective include the emphasis on strong connections between people, encouragement of collaboration, diminished emphasis on self-serving individualism, and **sacrifice for the greater good** as a measure of character. . . ."

I lay before you some cautions. While I have leaned heavily on Dr. Brokenleg's depiction of the Latoka *tioš paye*, I realize that was a closed system. They roamed a specific area which they did not share with other groupings; this was **their** *tioš paye* and no one else's. They knew their neighbors, e.g., the Kiowa, and interacted with them. But their customs were somewhat different; they knew and understood those differences, knew they were not Kiowa. And they would protect their *tioš paye* from the Kiowa if need be. They kept to themselves. A closed system. That is a luxury no longer available to us. Boundaries have become almost infinitely permeable; communities abut, overlap, and overlay each other, and a person is member of several communities with differing foci, force and impact. And we will have to take that into consideration when we look at them and try to devise a communitarian morality (way of living together). But for the moment and for this piece I am considering only a single *tioš paye* and how they are able to live together thrivingly.

The Lakota *tioš paye* lived in simplicity. Their living was not as deliberately austere as that of the Cistercians on Caldey Island, but was born of the availability and limits of resources. They were nomadic, moving with the seasons, and the bison herds, and so as not to overstress the land. Nomads can accumulate only as much as they and their animals can carry, so simplicity. Not possible today. We live in a consumer culture, the more you consume the more alive you are, the better you are, the more impressive and important you are. Consume! And that means accumulate! Whether you need it or not, whether it benefits, whether it impedes, whether it diminishes, estranges, enlarges, grows your soul or enslaves you. Accumulate. We likely can never return to a *tioš paye* kind of simplicity of living (that is, until we have so despoiled our environment that in turn it impoverishes us; then we will live simply again. And we will hate it.) We live in complexity, and while we might, reasonably and deliberately choose to simplify, we will still live in relative complexity.

As I sit here at my keyboard, in my armchair, I am unable to come up with the specifics of a communitarian way of living. Vague generalities slosh through my head: the Buddhists talk of living in compassion, and, when one errs through ignorance, of others compassionately, gently drawing him back into the mindset of compassion. I think that a marvelous generality, but it's hard to get specific without living it. We need to draw a much clearer vision before we can begin to test its reasonableness. I've laid out as best I can the general, over-riding principles of a communitarian morality, but if I dare go farther I will be well out of my depth. So I suspect that the next steps must be some casuistry, studying and theorizing **specific cases** and questions, necessarily in dialog or conversation. I can here offer only a couple unsophisticated thoughts.

How does the community exercise sanctions? It goes without arguing that our current justice system is broken (ill-conceived in the first place), so we should not work from it, but ditch it and start anew. For me the issue is not crime and punishment, it is **social control**: how does the community protect the community and its members from malefactors? The ancient Celts used exile. Tibetan Buddhism does not talk about sin, understands malefaction as ignorance, as a failure to comprehend how it all works together with compassion; and instead of punishment, a drawing the malefactor back into compassion. Jane Goodall, in studying the behavior of chimpanzees *(after all, we are another primate)*, discovers another direction, distraction. A chimpanzee mother, when the child is doing or is about to do something injurious or undesirable, simply distracts the child, shifts his attention.

If we can accept John Rawl's notion of justice as fairness *(a simple and elegantly stated notion)*, then the issues of social control can be as simply stated as setting standards, setting aright what was made amiss, and protecting the community from a compulsive malefactor.

The communitarians are pretty clear that the community must exert some moral force upon its members, and I expect the fundamental place where social control happens is through the moral structure which the family and neighborhood and community imbue in its members.

Working alone, my mind boggles at this point. To go further will require the ingenuity and brilliance of a community, to imagine and discern, to experiment, to polish and implement. What I have tried to do here is to demonstrate that there is potentially a morality, a way of living that fits a communitarian model. Nothing more. I began with an enlightening, manageable system to learn and fantasize from, the *tioš paye*. That yielded me some bits of useful bits, but far from a finished or usable result. And at the same time I have some cautions running around inside my head, at the peripheries of the task.

My mind dredges up Pasternak's novel of post-revolutionary Russia, **Doctor Zhivago**. I presume that those communists started out with the best of intentions. But I derive mental pictures of human nature, of incompetences, of ignorances getting in the way, distorting, perverting, debasing, and of neighborhood communities trying to dispense equity and fairness through a maze of greed, and power-mongering, homeostatic bureaucracy, and egoistic individualism, and of farming communes trying to set quotas based on ignorance and sloth. These are not nice pictures in my head, because I fear such will curtail any communitarian effort before it gets started.

My Sources for Morality, Ethics, Casuistry, Communitarian Ethics

"Casuistry," Wikipedia 11 June 2016 https://en.wikipedia.org/wiki/Casuistry

"Communitarian Ethics," Regis University, Rueckert-Hartman School for Health Professionals http://rhchp.regis.edu/hce/ethicsataglance/CommunitarianEthics/CommunitarianEthics_01.html

"Ethics," Wikipedia 15 June 2016 https://en.wikipedia.org/wiki/Ethics

"Ethics vs. Morals," Diffen. http://www.diffen.com/difference/Ethics_vs_Morals

Gert, Bernard. "Morality," Stanford Encyclopedia of Philosophy Feb 8, 2016 http://plato.stanford.edu/entries/morality-definition/

Meaning in Life

I have occasionally throughout my eighty years given some thought to the meaning of life and come to no earth-shaking conclusions. I've never approached that search for meaning in any emburdened way, just idle curiosity. But I have, in the course of that

Chapter 13: Communitarianism

process, become clear about a few things. And across my decades I've garnered a few notions about what is **not** the meaning of life.

Our Holy Scriptures reveal that YHWH (or Abba) has been very inexplicit about the meaning of life. YHWH ordered us to be fruitful, multiply and fill the earth. And while that is the assigned task, it hardly seems to me any meaning in life. YHWH seems to tell us some things about **how** to live, but I have not caught him saying anything about the **why**. His other task assignments were tilling and tending the garden; but we've not been very good about that task. Done lots of tilling, but been pretty slack in the tending department; and there again, those are tasks, not meaning.

Biblical scholars and theologians play with some notions about the why. Some suggest our purpose/meaning in life is to relate to the God. That's not much help for this guy who after six decades of trying has tentatively concluded that the God is both unknowable and *incommunicado*.

I have toyed with the notion that, man being the last act in the God's creating, I was created to enjoy the God's handiwork, this creation. Fun for a little while, but for breadwinners and laborers, not an enduring meaning; I can enjoy the brilliant color of a cardinal for a minute or so, but eventually I gotta get back to work.

Another has suggested that our purpose/meaning is to enjoy life to the fullest. One Christian theosophiser suggested that eternity, like the cross, has two directions: the horizontal arm reaching out to embrace the whole of humankind and all of creation, and the vertical pointing Godward and downward toward the depth of this very moment, the fullness of the here and now. I found that notion interesting, worth experimenting with, but concluded that, like meditating, I could only do it for a short while and then I had to come back to this life with all its plains and cliffs and crannies and dead falls; there are no plausible definitions of what "fullest" might mean; or maybe there are as many definitions as there are individuals.

One waggish scholar suggested, that since the God was all alone with no one to give him feedback, and without a physical being so that he could not look in the mirror to see himself, the God made us in his likeness and image so that he could watch us and learn who he is and what he is like, get to know himself through us. That is cute, fanciful, playful, very rabbinical, but not useful or satisfying.

I concluded they know nothing more about the meaning of life than I.

Jim Holt's book ***Why does the world Exist?*** converses across the ages with philosophers, physicists, mathematicians, and theologians, searching for some clues, some insights into the purpose of the world's existence; and integral to that search is the meaning of life. He shares some fascinating stuff, but comes up empty-handed: no clues, no hints, no insights about purpose or meaning. The brute fact is, we are here! But nothing about the why. We can trace the universe back to nanoseconds before the Big Bang, but can discover no causation and no purpose. Just the history of this evolving universe and the brute fact, we are here!

I'm definitely a Luddite, have very little interest or aptitude for these modern technological thingies. So I'm quite clear that the meaning of life is **not tied up with tweeting or texting** or such things. I'm very clear that the meaning of life is not tied up in all these wondrous technological doodads we're accumulating which are sopping up more and more of our time and energy and attention and resources, and which *(I'm fairly certain)* are of no real benefit to us, and seem to be quietly shredding our relationships and cultures, all the while gobbling up irreplaceable resources. No life-giving meaning here.

It seems to me that many around me are committed to their *individualism* as if in some way that gives meaning to their lives.

- Our Declaration of Independence claims for us the right to the **pursuit of happiness**. People search for that happiness. It appears to me that happiness is a fleeting thing, difficult to grasp and even harder to plan, but which easily, swiftly moves on, leaving us in the same-o world. No suggestion that happiness gives meaning to life, and, by my count, a lot to suggest it is a false lure, seducing us away from life-giving meaningfulness.

- Some others seek happiness/meaning in the accumulation of **wealth**, even fantastic wealth, but the reports back to me indicate that the accumulation of wealth does not necessarily bring happiness, and for some might even dampen happiness *(I note that those reports often come from those who have failed to accumulate great wealth.)*

- **Power**? Those with great power seem mostly stressed out, anxious, overworked. Not very happy. Obsessed! And not much blessed with a sense of meaning in life. The getting and the holding onto power seems to be an obsession *(and I note, not necessarily the exercising of power, much less exercising it in others's interests)*.

All this suggests to me that meaning in life is not to be found through the exercise of individualism or the operation of capitalism or the grasping of power. At the heart of those activities, individualism, i.e., showing the world the unique person I am, proving to the world and to myself how compelling my individualism is, how important it is. *(Jack Bowers is himself a fairly quirky individual, and while I get some slender taste of self-satisfaction in the acting out of my quirkiness, I cannot sense that it lends me any meaning in life.*

I've accidently stumbled across a few notions of **where I might search for meaning**. The closing article in the February 22, 2013 issue of the news magazine *The Week* (the article was originally published in *The Atlantic Magazine*) by Emily Isfahan Smith came into my hand. She opened the article talking about Viktor Frankl, the Viennese psychiatrist who was incarcerated in a Nazi concentration camp. He survived, gleaning from the experience profound learnings, particularly that the people who best survived the concentration camp were those who had a sense of meaning in their lives. Those were persons who became conscious of the responsibility they bore toward other human beings. Responsibility to something greater than oneself. Ms Smith goes on to report some research done around happiness and meaning. "Happy people get a lot of joy from receiving benefits from others, while people leading meaningful lives get a lot of joy from giving to others." Participants in the study reported deriving meaning from giving a part of themselves away to others and making a sacrifice on behalf of the overall group. The study concludes, in part, that happiness is a taking, while meaning is a giving away. " . . . What we do as human beings is to take care of others and contribute to others." Happiness occurs in the present moment, meaning is about transcending the self, but also about transcending the moment. " . . . Negative events happening to you . . . increases the amount of meaning you have in life." Before his incarceration Frankl had obtained a visa and was about to leave Vienna for America with his young family, but was aware his parents were inescapably soon to be incarcerated. To flee safely with his family, or to stay with his parents in their incarceration? Prodded by a *hint from heaven* he decided to stay. The wisdom he experienced and accumulated there has fed the world. "Being human always points, and is directed, to something or someone other than oneself . . . " "By . . . serving someone or something larger than ourselves, by devoting our lives to giving rather than taking, we are not only expressing our fundamental humanity, but are also acknowledging that there is more to the good life than the pursuit of simple happiness."

It seems to me that while "individualism" has been a boonful step away from an oppressive authoritarian world, it has also been a seduction away from meaningfulness in life. I hope that individualism has now run its course; it has become a blind alley, reaching the limits of tolerability. I deem we have been looking in the wrong places for meaning in life. When we live as discreet and separate and independent individuals, I think we lose the meaningfulness in living. Meaning comes not from within ourselves, searching out whatever may be most unique about ourselves; meaning in living comes from beyond ourselves, from something larger than our Selves. It comes from giving of ourselves to that which transcends. And for me, beginning to espouse communitarianism, I think meaning most likely comes from being a **well-integrated and self-giving member of community**.

I close by musing about meaning in living. It appears to me that communitarianism does offer us some places for finding meaning in living, a "larger than Self" to which we can give ourselves. As I conceive it, the community provides us the essentials of living, material and spiritual (relational), and, as can be afforded, some goodies beyond the essentials, some extras, some luxuries, some play toys. And it gives us the most promising assurances of human survival. It gives us *place*, and it does so with equity. And it is the one place where we can experience meaning in living. What is life about? It is about us, not me. It is about the member being well-integrated into the community, being an integral part, contributing to the community's life and wellbeing, giving of her/himself to others and to the whole community, and receiving back. The community, the fundamental entity of human life, is the arena in which the members experience and live out meaning; I think individuals search in vain for the meaning of **my** unique life (as opposed to, different than, **your** meaning)

> *You might have noted that I made a slightest grammatical shift. I began by talking about the "meaning **of** life." That's the phrase we all use. That phrase may be a red herring, luring us away from reality, as though "meaning" were a concept, an abstract, some handle out there (or inside ourselves) which we could grab hold of to get a sure ride. If Viktor Frankl was headed in the useful direction, if my hunch about meaning in relation to communitarianism is helpful, then it is not "the meaning **of** life," but the "meaning **in** life." "Meaning" is an action rather than a concept; meaning is a verb, a doing. And meaning happens in the doing, i.e., giving, in relating to others rather than self.*

Afterthoughts

After thinking about communitarianism the question remains "How do we get from here to there? A roadmap, please." I have none. I've a few paltry thoughts to share. It's brutally hard to conceive of living in a community with true equality and mutuality; but it's even harder to figure out how to get there.

The history of communes: The commune is the first model that comes to mind *(though I'm not much interested in communes that withdraw from society; I'm fixated on systemic change, on making the system work better.)* Perhaps following the lead of the Essenes, Christian communes began in Acts 2:44-46, when they sold and shared everything. But their context was that they expected the world to end in a matter of days. Not clear that was a commune as we envision one, but this often has been cited as a first effort at communism, everything held in common and shared. No evidence in the Scriptures or other Christian writings that such an effort persisted or survived. Could have been a fiction in the first place. The monastic movement certainly became a specialized kind of communality. It grew out of the Egyptian Desert Fathers who were themselves solitaries, hermits who attracted encircling encampments of admiring followers. Martin of Tours carried their example into Europe and Benedict regularized it. Communes of various sorts have sprung up through the ages, some quite exemplary, others, like Jim Jones' and Charles Manson's, notoriously evil. I have watched several come and go, and was even asked to serve as pastor-advisor to one tiny, incipient attempt which failed to materialize. The history of communes is quite mixed, but marked mostly with failures. I have no delusions about what I am proposing. Communitarianism is at the very best, highly unlikely. And it is fraught with problems. A commune may be one way to begin, but I award that method only the most meager chance of developing.

On the other hand, I lived for five weeks among the **Cistercian monks** on Caldey Island. Now I realize this is a very special, unusual example. But it is real. Those fifteen men committed themselves for the rest of their lives to live together in this way. They gave themselves no escape; to seek relief would require beseeching the pope himself to vacate their vows. This is real commitment. They gave themselves to Christ in a life of simplicity (read "austerity, near impoverishment, really bare bones"), chastity (not just "no sex," but purity of every ilk), and contemplation (not silence but no unnecessary conversation). It takes a very special (or peculiar, i.e., particular, odd) kind of person to live that life; it is not for everyman. But they have screened themselves into it, and live it successfully. Given the right people and the right circumstances, it is possible. I found myself comfortable among them, so I know it's possible, even for me. One of their number was rarely seen except at Sunday mass when he always arrived suddenly, just as the monks were going to the altar to receive communion, and disappeared immediately afterward, just as suddenly. I was told he had *troubles* and lived alone on the other side of the monastic enclosure. But he was one of the community, and they and he found the way to accommodate his needs and frailties. They live out compassion for each other. Their example suggests to me that communitarianism is a possibility, if we would want it.

Two other examples come to mind. The **Amish** in this country operate as a sort of community which meets some of the criteria of the communitarians's *community*: theirs is a web of relationships that crisscross and reinforce; it has values; it does exert moral suasion and extracts a measure of compliance; it uses sanctions when necessary; it has considerable social capital. I know almost nothing about the Amish, but they might have something to teach us in this effort. I also note that I have heard scant reports that the Amish community may be starting to fray, some hints of social disorganization, and some soft evidence that the allure of individualism and capitalism is luring some of the young away from the community. It merits some cautious study.

The other which occurs to me is the **Aboriginal culture** in Australia. I barely brushed up against it as a tourist in Australia nearly three decades ago. It was a culture quite distinct from the dominant white society, quite misunderstood, and with remarkably different values. I'm not sure it would qualify as a community. There certainly were shared values and *mores*, but the network of relationships was considerably looser and more temporary than the communitarians would want. They did live apart and kept their own ways and customs. Their culture was evidently perceived as a rank threat by the dominant Caucasian culture. And there is some doubt that the Aboriginal culture will survive the allure of the Australian individualism and capitalism; the Aborigines are more being absorbed and acculturated into the dominant white culture (where they are clearly second-class and usually despised citizens) than keeping to their own ways. They may have some things to teach us, though survival is not among them.

Getting from here to there: I am talking about a radical change of core values, and an attending radical change in nearly all living standards, customs and ways. The road from here to there is completely uncharted. Haven't even sent a scout out to survey the landscape yet. First, there would have to be some determination that the change is desired, and then some careful and thoughtful planning of how to enact the change.

I suspect that the most likely way the change might happen will be what I can only call the "the **worst case scenario**." In the previous chapter I shared my two great fears, that the population explosion will overwhelm us and the resources of this planet, and that we will fail to choose to succeed. Watching the debate over global warming, I come to suspect that the population explosion will overwhelm us and that we will choose to fail. And in the collapse of our social system and fabric we may be forced to turn to some form of communitarianism in order to survive.

There is built into us this **fatal flaw, i.e., human nature**. We crept out of the forest and onto the savannah not merely to survive; we could have survived in the forest with less thrivity. In addition to the impulse to survive was aggression. We seem horribly beset by our own tendencies: the lust for power, for control, for self-centeredness with the attendant greed and sexual lust (all of which may be Darwined into our DNA). These comprise **the** hazard to a communitarian life-style which requires compassion, cooperation, collaboration, self-giving, equality, and mutuality. How then do we build a community that will faithfully serve its members and gather them into healthy survivability without the greed and power lusts of its leaders? *(I sound like the fatalistic pessimist Augustine instead of the hopeful heretic, Pelagius.)* That answer I do not pretend to know. And I don't know whether we have sufficient time left to figure out how to get there.

Here endeth my visioning.

Bibliography

Anderson, Megory and Culbertson, Philip, "The Inadequacy of the Christian Doctrine of Atonement in Light of Levitical Sin Offering" ATR LXVIII:4 303-28

Armstrong, Karen, *A History of God: The 4,000 Year Quest of Judaism, Christianity and Islam*, New York: Ballantine 1993, ISBN 0-345-38456-3

Arndt, William F. And Gingrich, F. Wilbur, *A Greek-English Lexicon of the New Testament and other Christian Literature*, a translation and adaptation of Walter Bauer's, University of Chicago 1957 ISBN 0-226-03932-2

Baumer, Franklin L. *Modern European Thought*, New York: Macmillan 1977, ISBN 0-02-306450-1

Black, Matthew, gen'l and NT ed., Rowley, H.H., OT ed. *Peake's Commentary on the Bible*, New York: Nelson and Sons, 1962

The Book of Common Prayer (Protestant Episcopal Church), New York: Church Pension Fund 1928

Brown, Francis, Driver, S. R., Briggs, Charles A., *A Hebrew and English Lexicon of the Old Testament*, Oxford University Press 1959

Cross, F. L., *The Oxford Dictionary of the Christian Church*, London: Oxford University Press, 1961

The Dalai Lama, *Beyond Religion: Ethics for a Whole World*, New York: Houghton Mifflin Harcourt, 2011 ISBN 978-0-547-63635-1

———, *How to See Yourself as You Really Are*, New York: Atri Books, 2006 ISBN 978-0-7432-9046-3

Diamond, Jared, *Collapse: How Societies Choose to Fail or Succeed*, Penquin 2011 ISBN 978-0-14-311700-1

Dumsday, Travis, "C. S. Lewis on the Problem of Divine Hiddenness" ATR Winter 2015 Volume 97 Number 1 33-51

Eagleman, David, *The Brain: the story of you*, New York: Pantheon 2015 ISBN 978-1-101-87053-2

Ehrman, Bart D., *How Jesus became GOD; the Exaltation of a Jewish Preacher from Galilee*, New York: Harper One, 2014, ISBN 978-0-06-177818-6

Ehrlich, Paul R., *The Population Bomb*, Buccaneer 1968, BL 99003979

Fowler, James, *Stages of Faith: the Psychology of Human Development and the Quest for Meaning*, HarperOne 1995 ISBN: 9780060628666

Funk, Robert W., Roy W. Hoover, and the Jesus Seminar, *The Five Gospels: What Did Jesus Really Say, The Search for the Authentic Words of Jesus*, New York: Harper One 1993, ISBN 978-0-06-063040-9

Holladay, William A., ed. *A Concise Hebrew and Aramaic Lexicon of the Old Testament*, Eerdmans 1985

Holt, Jim, *Why Does the World Exist? an existential detective story*, New York: Liveright 2012 ISBN 978-0-87140-409-1

Bibliography

James, William, *The Varieties of Religious Experience*, Kessinger reprint, orig. Harvard, ISBN 1-4191-8661-2

Kittel, Rud. ed. *Biblica Hebraica*, Württembergishe Bibelanstalt Stuttgart 1961

Knitter, Paul F. *Without Buddha I Could not be a Christian*, Oxford England: Oneworld 2009 ISBN 978–1-85168-673-5

Kunzel, Harold S., *When Bad Things Happen to Good People*, Anchor 2004, ISBN 978-1400034728

Liddell & Scott, *Greek-English Lexicon*, Chicago: Follett 1951

McFague, Sallie, *Metaphotrical Theology: Models of God in Religious Language*, Fortress 1982, ISBN 978-0800616878

Miles, Jack, *GOD: a Biography*, New York: Vintage (Random House) 1995, ISBN 0-679-74368-5

Nestle, Erwin and Nestle, Eberhard, *Novem Testamentum Graece*, Bibilanstalt, Stuttgart

O'Donohue, John, *Anamchara*, audio book (also in print New York: HarperCollins, 1997 ISBN 0-06-018279-2)

Phillips, J.B., *Your God IsToo Small*, Simon and Schuster 2004, ISBN 9780743255097

Rees, B. R., *Pelagius: Life and Letters*, Rochester NY: Boydell 1998, ISBN 0 85115 714 9

Rolheiser, Ronald, *The Holy Longing*, Doubleday, New York 1999 ISBN 0-385-49418-1

Schriven, Charles, "Conflict and Persuasion after Foundationalism: Toward a Philosophy of Witness," *ATR* summer 2014, Volume 96 Number 3 527-34

Silverman, Julian. "On the Sensory Bases of Transcendental States of Consciousness" in *Psychiatry & Mysticism*, edited by Stanley R. Dean MD, 365-398. Chicago: Nelson-Hall 1975 ISBN 0-88229-657-4

Spong, John Shelby, *The Fourth Gospel: Tales of a Jewish Mystic,* Harper One 2013, ISBN 978-0-06-201130-5

———, *Jesus for the Non Religious*, SanFrancisco: Harper 2007 ISBN 978-0-06-076207-0

———, *Why Christianity Must Change or Die: A Bishop Speaks to Believers in Exile*. New York: HarperOne 1998 ISBN 978-0-06-067536-3

Underhill, Evelyn, *MYSTICSM, A Study in the Nature and Development of Man's Spiritual Consciousness*, New York: E. F. Dutton & Co.1981

Wright, Robert, *The Evolution of God,* New York: Little, Brown & Co. 2009, ISBN 978-0-316-73491-2

www.ingramcontent.com/pod-product-compliance
Lightning Source LLC
Chambersburg PA
CBHW060507300426
44112CB00017B/2573